Historical Archives and the Historians' Commission to Investigate the Armenian Events of 1915

Yücel Güçlü

University Press of America,® Inc.
Lanham • Boulder • New York • Toronto • Plymouth, UK

4501 Forbes Boulevard, Suite 200, Lanham, Maryland 20706
UPA Acquisitions Department (301) 459-3366

Unit A, Whitacre Mews, 26-34 Stannary Street,
London SE11 4AB, United Kingdom

Printed in the United States of America
British Library Cataloguing in Publication Information Available

Library of Congress Control Number: 2015931910
ISBN: 978-0-7618-6566-7 (pbk : alk. paper)—ISBN: 978-0-7618-6567-4 (electronic)

∞™ The paper used in this publication meets the minimum requirements of American National Standard for Information Sciences Permanence of Paper for Printed Library Materials, ANSI/NISO Z39.48-1992.

Contents

Preface and Acknowledgments

The idea for this book was born on 10 October 2009 with the signing of two protocols of cooperation between Turkey and Armenia at the Swiss city of Zurich. At that time I had been in Washington DC for more than four years, engaged in research on topics of early twentieth-century Ottoman Armenian history. The stirring events beginning on October 10 quickly provoked a new research interest.

Works on the history of the modern Middle East abound. There is the enormous body of writings on the traditional Eastern Question since 1878. The reader has available a rich diversity of broad interpretative accounts presented by different historians in this century and the previous century. Scores of monographs and articles produced over the past several decades clarify many of the fine points. There is more scholarly writing on modern Middle Eastern history than many realize. The best is of the highest quality. Many older works that may now appear to be somewhat off target in their general approach remain excellent contributions, not only in their careful documentation, but in their scope and methodology. Even what these books omit, offers clues to those who would explore the always-changing styles and outlooks of historical writings.

Writing this book has proved to be both challenging and stimulating. In the course of drafting the text, I have incurred many personal and intellectual debts. Not the least of them is to the Vice President and Publisher of University Press of America, Julie Kirsch, who has been as supportive as she has been patient. I would also like to thank Abby Grossblatt and Stella Donovan, also at University Press of America, for their advice and guidance in steering me through the publication process.

Historians spend a lot of time in solitary study in archives and libraries, or deep in thought in all manner of places, but none of them truly works in isolation; they all rely on the efforts and the help of others.

Historical Archives and the Historians' Commission to Investigate the Armenian Events of 1915 was crafted with the help of many colleagues and friends who read sections—often sizeable—in areas of their expertise and offered many suggestions at different stages on rather controversial and complicated matters, most of which I heeded. Their high standards and critical judgment helped make it a better work. My gratitude to them is immense. Other debts are no less happily acknowledged.

I owe a great deal to Maxime Gauin, who was kind enough to read the final draft of the work and offer a detailed criticism which helped me greatly in getting the manuscript ready for publication. For his detailed critique, especially of the French segment of the study, and for his encouraging remarks about the work itself, I am in his debt.

Without the archivists, who over the years have made records available or offered valuable guidance, my task could not have been accomplished. I hope they will accept the bare mention of their names as a token of my gratitude.

Associate Professor Mustafa Budak, Deputy Director General of the Turkish State Archives, gave to the author freely and abundantly of his unrivaled knowledge of Ottoman records of the First World War, as he has done for other researchers beyond number. The staff of the Turkish General Staff Military History and Strategic Studies Directorate provided not only quantities of documents—usually with exemplary speed—but friendship as well. Ahmet Tetik, Suat Akgül, and Himmet Gündüz were quick to put their resources at my disposal. To have proceeded without such help would have been impossible.

The staff of the Turkish Ministry of Foreign Affairs Archive made my life as a researcher much easier than it might otherwise have been. I wish to acknowledge each of them: Anıl Gökalp, Nevin Yılmaz, and Ebru Dikmen. I am grateful to Yasemin Sağlayan of the library of the Turkish Ministry of Foreign Affairs for locating, and allowing me to keep for weeks, books and periodicals I needed to consult and quote.

This book is the result of work that began at the National Library in Ankara. The reference staff of the National Library, who labored with my numerous requests, offered as always, extremely friendly and efficient help. They were most gracious in providing extensive logistical support in accessing and photocoping publications. The enthusiastic help given by the able and conscientious staff of the National Library went far beyond the strict limits of their duties and I am very grateful to them, especially to Mehmet Emin Fidan, the Deputy Director, and to Sinan Öztürk, the Chief of Microfilms Section. Not only have they been generous with advice and knowledge, they have also encouraged me to consult the numerous experts and enthusiasts with whom their offices abound.

Without the resources of the Turkish Historical Society Archive and Library, this book would be a great deal poorer. And without the friendliness of its reading room, where I worked, I would be much the poorer. The staff of the Turkish Historical Society Library have been most cooperative. I must especially note Mustafa Sönmez, who so often went far beyond the call of duty, making my work both possible and easier. I owe an enormous debt to his extraordinary efforts and effective work in tracking down and obtaining materials I would otherwise have missed. His unstinting willingness to help kept alive my sometimes flickering ideal of what a librarian should be.

The assistance of archivists and librarians in College Park, Maryland and Washington DC has been both rewarding and full of friendship. Over the years experts at the United States National Archives and Records Administration and the Library of Congress have borne with my requests and queries with exemplary patience. Also the many archivists at the National Archives in Kew, London at various times helped me to get through the maze of British materials. My mainstays in the British capital were the British Library and the library of the School of Oriental and African Studies, London University.

Over the past years, I have enjoyed a number of personal conversations with scholars about the issues mentioned in this study. These include: Professor Yusuf Halaçoğlu, formerly chairman of the Turkish Historical Society; Professor Kemal Çiçek, dean of the Faculty of Humanities and Social Sciences of İpek University in Ankara; Professor Yusuf Sarınay, dean of the Faculty of Natural Sciences and Humanities of TOBB University in Ankara; Professor Ömer Turan, head of History Department of the Middle East Technical University in Ankara; Professor Metin Hülagü of Erciyes University in Kayseri and Associate Professor Feridun Ata of Selçuk University in Konya, whose comments have been very valuable to me.

My thanks and praise are due to Professor Şükrü Hanioğlu and Associate Professor Michael Reynolds, both of Princeton University, for the opportunity to discuss and develop my ideas. I might not always share their views, but my work has been immeasurably enriched by the insights provided by their publications on many of the different aspects of the subject studied here.

Some individuals merit special attention. Professor Edward Erickson of the United States Marine Corps University in Quantico, Virginia has been a source of sage advice, unwavering friendship, and tremendous personal support since the very beginning of this project. I expect that people will still be reading and debating his corpus of work for decades to come. Professor Hikmet Özdemir also has been extremely generous with his time, advice, and friendship for many years and provided sound insights on the Armenian question. I have benefited from discussions on early twentieth-century Ottoman history with Professor Gökhan Çetinsaya, formerly chairman of the Higher Education Board of Turkey, who brought to my attention many crucial points of detail. He has opened my mind to new possibilities. Professor Behçet Yeşilbursa of Uludağ University in Bursa was a source of common sense, who has given me unstinting assistance over many years and whose advice has been invaluable to me. Ayten Eler, Yiğit Canay and Sadık Serhat Akkoç have kindly responded to my questions. They have enlightened me by discussion and by providing specific information. They also went to great lengths to send me documents that were not easy for me to access. Polat Safi kindly allowed me to consult his unpublished doctoral dissertation.

By listing all these names, I am not for one moment suggesting that they endorse the arguments of this book, let alone that they bear any responsibility for its shortcomings and for the interpretations contained therein. That responsibility is mine alone.

Vital computer support with much good humor and efficiency came from Kamil Dalyan. His efforts were ably complemented at various times by Hakan Kılıç.

I thank Ethem Coşkun, the celebrated antiquarian bookseller, whose premises in Ankara serve as a meeting place for historians in the Turkish capital. I benefited from his rare ability to find out-of-print books.

I would also like to gratefully acknowledge *Journal of South Asian and Middle Eastern Studies* and *The Middle East Quarterly* for allowing me to use material I have published in "Current Political Implications of the Armenian Question," Vol. 31, No. 4 (Summer 2008), pp. 1–10 and in "Will Untapped Ottoman Archives Reshape the Armenian Debate?" Vol. 16, No. 2 (Spring 2009), pp. 35–42 respectively.

It is my hope that readers will take the trouble to call errors to my attention so that they might be corrected in any future edition.

Introduction

WHY THE PRESENT STUDY?

The Caucasus has been a disturbed region, to put it no stronger, throughout the twentieth century, and it looks as though that reputation will continue into the twenty-first.[1] In fact, its disturbance as a major international concern began in the nineteenth century, when Russia seized a portion of Caucasia under the Treaties of Peace and Commerce of Türkmençay of 10–22 February 1828, that were notable because they included the ecclesiastical center of the Armenian Catholicos at Echmiadzin.[2] Victory in the war of 1826–1828 with Iran enabled Russia to annex the coveted provinces of Yerevan and Nahçıvan under Article 4.

This book is intended to demonstrate the vital importance of Ottoman and other relevant archives in Turkey for the study of the Armenian question. It also seeks to explore the importance of Turkey's proposal to establish an international historians' commission to investigate the Armenian events of 1915. Historians, assisted by newly discovered or recently published materials, must continually reassess past events. The events of 1915 are certainly no exception. The study attempts to encourage further engagement between the policy-making and the scholarly communities by demonstrating the continued importance of past records and documents for today's pressing debates. One of the purposes of the inquiry is to identify and acknowledge the life-long specialists in the field of Ottoman studies.

Hitherto not much has been written in English about the extent and particular features of the Ottoman archival documentation. Here, among bound volumes and files of loose papers of all government departments, is contained the vital evidence which reveals the making of the First World War. This survey aims to draw attention to the richness and depth of the Turkish archival holdings for the examination of Ottoman-Armenian history and to serve as a reflective methodological clarification on the subject.

SUBJECT MATTER

As an introduction to the Ottoman archival repositories in Turkey and to the opportunities for research there, each of the several archival institutions will be discussed briefly and the growing body of literature that describes the collections in detail will be cited. Since principal Ottoman archives are in Turkey, this book will indicate what their Turkish custodians and authorities have done—and should continue to do—to encourage and facilitate their full and proper use. The history of archival reorganization is recounted only insofar as it might be of interest for the historian who wishes to trace a collection from some former archive to its present home. Considerable space will be devoted to the history and technique of registry of archival materials and the important role of archives in modern documentation.

In order to give a fuller picture, this survey also looks at some major relevant archival sources outside Turkey. The state of archives of the First Republic of Armenia and that of the Dashnak Party (Dashnaksutiun, known in English as the Armenian Revolutionary Federation [ARF]) is one of these. The National Archives of Armenia (NAA) in Yerevan and its working order will be considered. The inquiry further seeks to shed light on some of the British records relating to the First World War and its immediate aftermath, that remain locked at the National Archives (NA) in Kew, London. It is almost certain that in this new collection there will be substantial new sources. Anyone interested in fully exploring the minutiae of any operation or any other aspect of the story must now do so by examining the original documents. The 1914–1918 war continues to attract serious scholarly attention and the British intelligence documents of the period are long overdue for declassification. The special relevance of repositories in Moscow and St. Petersburg in understanding the Turkish-Armenian conflict is referred to. One benefit for historians from the end of the Cold War has been the opening of Russian archives. Mainly with the policy of openness or *glasnost* under President Mikhail Gorbachev did czarist foreign policy archives relating to the Ottoman Empire begin to open to non-communists following the late 1980s. Since the collapse of the Soviet Union in 1991, scholars of all nationalities have devoted increasing attention to conducting research in Russian archives. Access to the repositories has been particularly sensitive to the winds of political change. Progress has been uneven, and much top level material remains closed.

Also, the importance of Turkey's proposal to establish an international historians' commission to investigate the Armenian events of 1915 will be assessed and the meaning and implications of the protocols of cooperation signed between Turkey and Armenia on 10 October 2009 are reviewed at length. Much attention has been given to discovering the precise chronology, meaning, and development of the continuing negotiations between Turkey and Armenia. There have been until now neither books, nor scholarly articles on this specific subject. The pages that follow attempt to fill the gap.

Apart from the introduction, the book is divided into twenty chapters, followed by a conclusion and eight appendices. Chapters discuss: "The First Origins and Structures of the Ottoman Archives," "The Emergence of Modern Turkey's Archive System," "Developments in the Turkish Archives Since 1989," "The Archives and Historical Controversy," "Turkish Archives and Foreign Scholars," "The Directorate General of State Archives," "Military Archives," "The Turkish Historical Society's Archive and the National Library," "Muslim Court Records and Others," "The Armenian Archives," "The British Archives," "The Russian Archives," "Whither the Turkish-Armenian Debate?" "The First World War and Its Archival Records," "From Historical Controversy to Political Campaigning," "The Quest for the Facts," "What Next?" "Attempting to Overcome History: The Signing of the Protocols," "The Collapse of the Protocols," and "The International Debate and the Archives."

The approach will be basically chronological although, since the discussion will involve the complexities of international events, a strict progression in time will not always be the most convenient way. It will also be necessary on occasion to broaden the focus from the basic Turkish subject of attention to other parts of the world, and back to Turkey especially.

SOURCES AND METHODOLOGY

The book is based upon a range of primary and secondary sources. The primary sources used are found for the most part in the Prime Minister's Office Ottoman Archive[3] (BOA), İstanbul; the Turkish General Staff Military History and Strategic Studies Directorate's Archive (ATASE), Ankara; the British NA; and the United States Congressional Records, Washington, DC. Various secondary sources have also been used to provide a comprehensive background of the subject matter. Much information is culled from the media. This material includes wire-service reports by local and international news agencies; numerous articles from local newspapers, periodicals, and newsletters; numerous articles from newspapers, periodicals, and newsletters of the Turkish and Armenian communities in the West; numerous articles from newspapers, periodicals, newsletters, and academic journals in the United States, Europe, Turkey, Armenia, etc.; transcripts of broadcasts by the electronic media; and large quantities of original source material retrieved through the Internet.

This book utilizes many previously unavailable sources, but it is also a synthetic study bringing together many arguments and findings from a number of scholars who have worked on the Turkish-Armenian conflict. It relies most on the groundbreaking scholarship of Bernard Lewis, Stanford Shaw, Halil İnalcık and İlber Ortaylı, whose relevant books and articles are listed in the bibliography. Their works are an invaluable resource that no one can afford to ignore.

Because of the highly controversial nature of the subject, I have tried to substantiate every important point in my exposition with a large number of carefully selected sources—quoted directly in the body of the text—as well as an even larger number of endnote citations. These should be helpful to scholars and students in furthering their own research on the Armenian events of 1915.

The endnotes in this study incorporate references to primary materials designed to familiarize the reader with the evidentiary basis from which a particular argument has been launched and conclusions reached. The endnote is the source of reference; it records the origin of, or the authority for, a statement in the text. It will help other researchers find archives and documents where they may obtain additional details and pursue other subjects. And it will allow others to check the accuracy of information put forward here. But, most important, endnotes will give some sense of the quality of the sources on which the information contained in this book is based. Readers need as much information as possible to find their way through the difficulties of comprehension and the competing interpretations of the Turkish-Armenian conflict.

Whenever a document from an archive is cited in the text, the reference given has deliberately been made sufficiently specific to enable anyone, either desirous of checking the interpretation, or wishing to pursue further research, to locate the original. The British documents cited in this book are referred to by the designation used at the NA, including the class and file number which identifies the file in which the original is to be found. In the case of Foreign Office documents, the archive designation originally applied to the item in the Foreign Office is given.

Although the emphasis here is on books and articles in English, there are subjects on which the most important literature is in other languages, primarily Turkish, so that some of these are included.

All books and articles referred to in the endnotes have been provided with full citations at their first mention. The full name of the author, the full title of the work, the name of the publisher, and the place and date of publication are given. Where the practice would not produce confusion, short titles have been substituted for longer ones after the first mention of a study. The titles of Turkish books and articles are given in English translation. Whenever the publisher of the Turkish volume or journal has provided an English title, I have generally preferred to use it. The date of publication is that of the edition consulted, not necessarily the date of first publication.

In the discussion which follows, only those sources which were of most importance in the preparation of this book have been cited. The inclusion or absence of a particular source is not intended to reflect on its overall value to students of Ottoman and Turkish history but only its relevance to the present understanding.

The Sources section of this book is far from comprehensive. It offers, however, a list of primary and secondary sources from which the present author has gained important insights. It contains a small number of titles from the hundreds available. Mainly titles which have been explicitly cited or quoted in the text are listed. These few are considered particularly useful in pursuing further the analysis in the text, either as expansion of subject matter or as criticism of the present treatment. They will open the way to numerous other works of special interest. The place of publication of each newspaper cited in the text or endnotes is given in Sources.

The index gives alphabetically arranged, detailed reference to all important matters discussed in the work, such as names of persons and places, events, titles of books, definitions, and vital statements. It consists of main entries or headings, subentries, and cross references.

In a few instances, because of the frequency of references, abbreviated citations have been used throughout the book. Crown copyright material in the custody of the NA is reproduced by kind permission of the Keeper of Public Records.

For Turkish terms the standard modern Turkish orthography has been used, i.e., all transliterations follow modern Turkish spelling and vowel harmony rules. Thus dotting the capital İ as in *İstanbul* is employed. Ottoman terms that have become part of the English language, and are included in English dictionaries, are given with their English rather than their Turkish spellings, thus Pasha rather than Paşa and kadi for kadı. In quotations, original grammar, spelling, punctuation, capitalization, and abbreviations are maintained within the quotation marks. Words that have been added or deleted in order to clarify meaning are noted respectively with brackets or ellipses. Although extracts used are reproduced as originally written, it is occasionally necessary to add a comma or some other form of punctuation in order to make the sense more easily understood. For Ottoman dates, whether expressed in lunar Hijri or solar Rumi calendars, Gregorian equivalents have been used.

Certain assumptions are made in the writing of this book. One is that the majority of readers will not know Turkish. Apart from certain transcribed terms, quotations from Turkish sources are given in translation, in most cases my own, although reliable published translations are used from the sources cited in the endnotes, where available, to allow readers to access to the whole.

NOTES

1. *The Caucasus* is a geographical term which includes the modern states of Armenia, Azerbaijan, and Georgia, together with parts of the Russian Federation and Turkey.

2. The text of the Treaties of Peace and Commerce of Türkmençay of 10–22 February 1828 between Russia and Iran is contained in J. C. Hurewitz, *Diplomacy in the Near and Middle East A Documentary Record: 1535–1914*, Vol. 1, (Princeton, NJ: D. Van Nostrand Company, Inc., 1956), pp. 96–102.

3. The term *archives* usually appears only in the plural in English, but the singular form in translation from the Turkish has been retained here, where appropriate, since the distinction between singular and plural as in Turkish usage is important, particularly with reference to a single repository or the records of a single agency.

Chapter One

Earliest Origins and Structures of the Ottoman Archives

For most archivists and archival historians, an archive is a place where historical documents are kept or an institution providing such places. This concept has also long been a basic principle of archivists' training. The American T. R. Schellenberg, an archivist with the National Archives and Records Administration, in the 1968 edition of his manual entitled *Modern Archives: Principles and Techniques* published in Chicago, aptly defines the term *archives* as follows: "Those records of any public or private institution which are adjudged worthy of permanent preservation for reference and research purposes and which have been deposited or have been selected for deposit in an archival institution."[1] The essential characteristics of archives, then, relate to the reasons why records came into being and to the reasons why they were preserved. It is accepted that to be archives, records must have been produced or accumulated to accomplish a specific purpose and must have values for purposes other than those for which they were produced or accumulated. Public archives, then, have two types of values: the primary values to the originating agency and the secondary values for other agencies and for non-government users.

ORIGINS OF THE OTTOMAN ARCHIVES

The formation of the Ottoman archives begins with the rise of the Ottoman state, but the present collection dates only from the Turkish conquest of İstanbul in 1453. Earlier collections of documents were left in the previous capitals in Bursa and Edirne. A number of documents are still to be found in Bursa. An important collection was in existence in Edirne until the Balkan

War of 1912 when it was destroyed by Bulgarian artillery fire. Even in the İstanbul collection there are a number of individual documents dating from before the conquest. The archives become really full in the sixteenth century, and continue to the end of the empire.[2]

The existence of state papers almost from the beginning of the Ottoman Empire in 1299 attests to bureaucratic ability and thoroughness of spirit which has protected a great portion of materials or their duplicates sent from the capital to the various provinces. The number of documents up to the year 1453 is small enough to permit simple classification, but after the conquest of İstanbul, and particularly since the time of Sultan Süleyman I (1520–1566) (the Magnificent or the Lawgiver), the papers have proliferated in almost geometrical progression. Some of the documents are bound, such as the directives and orders of the grand viziers. Likewise, many of the Treasury receipt books (*Maliye Defterleri*) are in volumes. On the other hand, tens of thousands of separate papers, tied in packages, lie at the disposal of those who are masters in the study of Ottoman institutions: Pious Foundation grants, or *vakfiye*, or firmans describing the acquisition of property by some important man, in brilliantly colored gold, blue, green, purple and black, with the signature of the sultan (*tuğra*).[3]

OTTOMAN PALEOGRAPHY AND DIPLOMATICS

The language of the archives is Ottoman Turkish, which was used during the many centuries of the Ottoman Empire. It has a basically Turkish structure with an immense vocabulary of loan words from Arabic and Persian, as much as, and rather similar to, the vocabulary of Latin, Greek and Norman French words in English. Ottoman Turkish was written in the Arabic script with some additional letters to indicate Turkish sounds that do not exist in Arabic.[4]

Almost all of the materials in the Ottoman archives are handwritten, and there are several different types of handwriting that can be found. The most important script from the standpoint of research in Ottoman Turkish diplomatics is the *divani* with its different variations. This script differs somewhat from the widely accepted and better known *neshi* script. *Rıka* was the most commonly used handwriting style, and the one used throughout late Ottoman civil officialdom. *Siyakat* script is undoubtedly the most difficult to read. It was used in tax registers, conscription lists, lists of impositions, trade registers, census lists, minutes of meetings, etc., until about 1880. Deciphering these documents presents a considerable challenge for the modern scholar. Not much advantage has yet been taken of the vast bulk of Ottoman materials, due to the difficulties involved in using the special scripts and the administrative language in which they are written.[5]

In 1979, Tayyip Gökbilgin, professor of history at the Faculty of Letters in İstanbul University, documented his life-long concern with Ottoman archival material by the publication of his *Osmanlı Paleografya ve Diplomatik İlmi*. Basing himself on an enormous mass of original documentation, an area where he had proven expertise and experience that few Ottomanists could match, Gökbilgin gave judicious verdicts on a vast range of subjects and in almost every instance he carried conviction. After briefly discussing his predecessors in the field, the author gave a short account of papers, scripts, seals, and the structure of documents. He followed the Hungarian scholar, Lajos Fekete, in division of his material into the categories of lay and religious. Special emphasis was placed on the titles used for both Ottoman dignitaries and foreign rulers. An additional division was devoted to documents produced by viziers and other dignitaries. The documents connected in one way or another with religious affairs were given space; judicial records, documents establishing pious foundations and legal opinions were all accorded places.[6]

In 1994, readers wishing to familiarize themselves with the state of the art of Ottoman paleography and diplomatics turned first and foremost to the new volume on *Osmanlı Belgelerinin Dili (Diplomatik)* by Mübahat Kütükoğlu, professor of history at the Faculty of Letters in İstanbul University. This volume is notable for the care with which the secondary literature of the last decades has been incorporated. For example, the two-page section dealing with paper in Fekete's book[7] has been developed into a major chapter. This includes imported papers from both east and west, Ottoman attempts at paper manufacture, watermarks and the types of paper preferred by different official bodies. In the same fashion, the treatment of seals, which Fekete had relegated to a single page, in Kütükoğlu's hands has blossomed into an important area of study. Here we find an introduction to the seals used by the sultans, as well as those employed by officeholders in the course of their official functions. Separate sections are devoted to the seals imprinted on foundation documents and those used by private individuals. We even find a discussion of the rules of precedence when a number of people were called upon to add their seals to a single document, and the author also discusses the use of seals containing only a word of authentication. In similar fashion, the section on sultanic documents has been greatly amplified. Apart from the conventional discussion of their formal structure, the author explains why sultanic commands were published in the first place. She also makes clear why documents issued by previous rulers needed confirmation—and how they were often confirmed—whenever a new sultan ascended the throne. There is a section concerning the privileges granted to foreign rulers, often on behalf of their merchants. They were known as *ahidname* in Ottoman and as capitulations in European sources; Kütükoğlu's analysis is based on original documentation from the BOA.[8]

It is gratifying that Suraiya Faroqhi deems Kütükoğlu's remarkable accomplishment worthy of recognition and praise. She regards the attention consistently paid to the nineteenth century as the major innovation of Kütükoğlu's book; the detailed treatment of the *muahede* (treaty) constitutes just one example among many. According to Faroqhi, this attention was very timely, because the great work of cataloging, which has been carried out in the BOA since 1985, has made available enormous quantities of nineteenth-century archival sources. Yet as far as previous work on Ottoman diplomatics was concerned, these recent documents have gone practically unstudied. Faroqhi considered Kütükoğlu's work the first attempt at systematizing this vast body of material, that ranked as a pioneering effort in the history of Ottoman paleography and diplomatics.[9] Faroqhi is an eminent historian of the economic and social history of the Ottoman Empire. An enthusiastic practitioner of the *Annales* paradigm, she has written extensively on, among other topics, property ownership in Anatolian towns. She has exploited the richness of the Ottoman archives, the manuscript and printed sources in Turkish.

CONSERVATION AND CLASSIFICATION IN THE BOA

In the BOA every effort is made to preserve even the most unimportant-appearing paper. A new start was made in 1985, and since then excellent work has been done in housing, cleaning, and cataloging the records.[10]

The conservation and classification processes work as follows. In a room where experts are seated at tables, the process begins. Taking a jumble of documents, and carefully disentangling the covers with deft strokes, the expert opens the packet with a minimum of tearing. He passes the single paper to the next in line who brushes and analyzes it for damage. The third refines this process and the fourth and fifth make appropriate backing and reparation papers to fit the original. When as much is assembled as possible, it is carefully glued to a special backing paper and then placed in a box to be sent to the next room. Here classification begins. The men who read these documents are truly experts in this field. They classify the greater proportion of documents according to subject, recipient, sometimes place and date of transmission and author. These experts easily recognize such things as the handwriting and literary style of important authors, sultans, or grand viziers. When the document has been determined to be of a certain subject, date, or location, it is placed in a suitable container to be sent to the boxing room. Here the papers are tied together, put in easy-to-handle boxes, and placed in the storage spaces in various depositories around the complex of the Archives.[11]

INTRODUCTIONS AND GUIDES TO THE BOA

Since sources fill whole archives, the availability of tools to guide research is of vital importance for the historian as well as the interested layperson. The first published catalog of Ottoman archival holdings authored by Midhat Sertoğlu, director of the Prime Minister's Office Archive and a noted specialist in the area, appeared in 1955 and consisted of ninety pages of archival inventory and commentary. This slim volume is a masterful introduction to the archives, with a general description and classification of the papers and registers. The summary guide introduces the reader to the holdings of the BOA, its acquisition policy, the scope of its holdings, how the whole collection came about, inventories of creating agencies and series titles and date ranges. It also discusses how to use the records and what finding aids exist. It illustrates not only the creating agencies but also connections between them and the record series attached to each. Connections between series are shown. Sertoğlu's book also covers other materials technically belonging to the BOA but deposited in various places in İstanbul.[12]

A far more complete catalog by first-rank scholar-archivist, Attila Çetin, followed in 1979, comprising 171 pages of catalog entries and other archival data. It describes the holdings of the BOA and explains developments there since 1955. The introduction tells briefly the history of the BOA and the strenuous efforts over the years to catalog its holdings. Then the author proceeds to depict the collection. In Chapters 1 to 4, Çetin analyzes the various classifications of documents in the BOA and provides lists of the documents contained therein. In these chapters one finds many improvements over the work of Sertoğlu. In numerous cases Çetin has given more detailed descriptions of the holdings, often citing numbers of individual files and cartons, as well as supplying more comprehensive dating of the material. In addition, he is able to add information on documents which were processed in the last quarter of the twentieth century. This authoritative work was translated into Italian in 1985. The Italian translation is more fully documented than the Turkish edition, incorporating more recent archival finds. Many sections have been rewritten to accommodate the Italian reader. But otherwise, the book remains the same.[13]

As classifying and organizing of the archives continued, the catalog grew accordingly and reached 634 pages in the 1992 edition prepared by Yusuf İhsan Genç et al. The authors have marshaled and listed an extraordinary number of document holdings according to department, series and piece numbers, and, in order to make sense of all this, have divided the book into a number of relevant chapters. After a preface, the book is composed of an introduction, six chapters and three appendices describing the years of reign of Ottoman sultans and grand viziers as well as official calendars. The introduction sets the stage in time and in space, examining the Ottoman state organization, archives administration, Ottoman archives and classifications. It also stresses the significance of advance preparation for archival research and the importance of analyzing both the outward aspects and the textological features of archival documents. The chapters cover: the classifications of registers and documents; other materials found in the Ottoman archives; activities of the Directorate General of State Archives (DGSA); catalogs; and Ottoman archival terminology and forms of correspondence. Within these chapters, there are also subheadings. Then, within these subheadings, there are further divisions, as the book gathers departmental records into categories.[14]

The *Başbakanlık Osmanlı Arşivi Rehberi* is vital to scholars and students in a range of disciplines such as history, political science, sociology, literature, and linguistics, who intend to carry out research in Turkish archives. "This guide is an indispensable tool for historians," states Professor Nesimi Yazıcı; that is a true assessment of the value of this work for anyone interested in the Ottoman past.[15]

The expanded and updated *Başbakanlık Osmanlı Arşivi Katalogları Rehberi* by Mustafa Küçük and others makes it possible for the researchers to find their way through a jungle of historical material. For a measure of the increase in documentation available for research in the BOA, one can compare the contents of this volume with that of the Genç's edition. Historians reviewing the *Başbakanlık Osmanlı Arşivi Katalogları Rehberi* praised its comprehensiveness, organization, and depth of analysis. The work was seen as an improvement over previously published guides. American historian James Meyer said, "This guide book is very useful and anyone planning on conducting research in the BOA should make a point of studying it prior to arriving in İstanbul."[16]

Although Küçük's catalog is far from complete, sufficient material is already listed and accessible to occupy generations of researchers and to enable the rewriting of most of what has already been written on Ottoman history. Revised editions are forthcoming, from time to time, as more detailed descriptions become available for the various *fonds* or individual record groups. In the BOA practice, a *fond* designates an integral group of records or a collection from a single office or source, or papers of an individual or family. An annotated English translation of the *Başbakanlık Osmanlı Arşivi Katalogları Rehberi* is something much to be desired.[17]

Studies are made and dictionaries are prepared of the administrative terms peculiar to the official materials and of the various symbols and marks applied to documents by different departments and officials. Atilla Çetin has provided a handy glossary of Turkish archival terminology. Such resources have made access to primary materials much easier for scholars and have changed the nature of archival research.[18]

NOTES

1. T. R. Schellenberg, *Modern Archives: Principles and Techniques* (Chicago: University of Chicago Press, reprinted, 1968), p. 16. For other definitions of archives, see Tülin Aren, *Arşiv Problemleri ve Arşivcilik* (Problems of Archives and Archival Administration), (Ankara: Başbakanlık Basımevi, 1976) and Bekir Kemal Ataman, *Arşivcilik Terimleri Sözlüğü* (Dictionary of Archival Administration Terms), (İstanbul: Librairie Péra, 1995).

2. Yusuf Halaçoğlu, "Osmanlı Devletinde Arşivcilik" (Archival Administration in the Ottoman State), in *XIII. Türk Tarih Kongresi, Ankara 4–8 Ekim 1999. Kongreye Sunulan Bildiriler* (Thirteenth Turkish Historical Congress, Ankara 4–8 October 1999. Communications Presented to the Congress), Vol. 2, (Ankara: Türk Tarih Kurumu Basımevi, 2002), pp. 87–88; Ali Akyıldız, "Hazine-i Evrak'ın Kurulması ve İlk Tasnif Usulleri (1846–1856)" (The Establishment of the Treasury of Documentation and the First Declassification Methods [1846–1856]), in Mustafa Çetin Varlık, İnci Enginün, Mücteba İlgürel, İsmail Erünsal, Zikri Altun and Mustafa Berkem, eds., *Prof. Dr. Hakkı Dursun Yıldız'a Armağan* (Dedication to Prof. Dr. Hakkı Dursun Yıldız), (İstanbul: Marmara Üniversitesi Fen-Edebiyat Fakültesi Yayınları, 1995), p. 69.

3. William Griswold, "The National Archives in Turkey," *The Muslim World*, Vol. 64, No. 1 (January 1974), pp. 40–41.

4. Bernard Lewis, *Notes on a Century: Reflections of a Middle East Historian* (London: Weidenfeld and Nicolson, 2012), pp. 90–91.

5. Tayyib Gökbilgin, *Osmanlı Paleografya ve Diplomatik İlmi* (Ottoman Paleography and Diplomatics), (İstanbul: Enderun Kitabevi, reprinted, 1992), pp. 34–46; Mübahat Kütükoğlu, *Osmanlı Belgelerinin Dili (Diplomatik)* (Language of the Ottoman Documents [Diplomatics]), (İstanbul: Kubbealtı Neşriyatı, 1994), pp. 55–68; Said Öztürk, *Osmanlı Belgelerinde Siyakat Yazısı* (The Siyakat Script in Ottoman Documents), (Ankara: Başbakanlık Basımevi, 1994); Yılmaz Kurt and Mehmed Ceyhan, *Osmanlı Paleografyası ve Osmanlı Diplomatikası* (Ottoman Paleography and Diplomatics), (Ankara: Akçağ Yayınları, 2012). On the difficulties of Ottoman paleography, see also Dündar Günday, *Arşiv Belgelerinde Siyakat Yazısı Özellikleri ve Divan Rakamları* (Characteristics of the Siyakat Script and Divan Numbers in Archival Documents), (Ankara: Türk Tarih Kurumu Basımevi, 1974); Lajos Fekete, *Die Siyaqat-Schrift in der Türkischen Finanzverwaltung* (Budapest: Akadémiai Kiadó, 1955) and Stanford Shaw, "Cairo's Archives and the History of Ottoman Egypt," *Report on Current Research on the Middle East, 1956* (Washington, D.C.: The Middle East Institute, 1956), pp. 59–72.

6. Suraiya Faroqhi, *Approaching Ottoman History: An Introduction to the Sources* (Cambridge: Cambridge University Press, 1999), pp. 73–74.

7. Lajos Fekete, *Einführung in die osmanisch-türkische Diplomatik der türkischen Botmäþigkeit zu Ungarn* (Budapest: Royal Hungarian State Archive, 1926).

8. Faroqhi, *Approaching Ottoman History*, pp. 74–75. On Mübahat Kütükoğlu's scholarship, see Zeynep Tarım Ertuğ, "Prof. Dr. Mübahat Kütükoğlu Hayatı ve Eserleri" (Prof. Dr. Mübahat Kütükoğlu Her Life and Works), in Zeynep Tarım Ertuğ, ed., *Prof. Dr. Mübahat Kütükoğlu'na Armağan* (Dedication to Prof. Dr. Mübahat Kütükoğlu), (İstanbul: İstanbul Üniversitesi Edebiyat Fakültesi Yayınları, 2006), pp. 1–16.

9. Faroqhi, *Approaching Ottoman History*, p. 75. See also appraisal of Mübahat Kütükoğlu's book by Mücteba İlgürel in *Belleten*, Vol. 59, No. 224–226 (1996), pp. 242–244. It seems that it would be of great importance and assistance to Ottoman studies if an English translation of Kütükoğlu's tome could be made and published.

10. Mehmet Ali Beyhan, "Zengin Bir Kültür Kaynağımız Olarak Osmanlı Arşivleri" (Ottoman Archives as One of Our Rich Cultural Sources), *Milli Kültür*, No. 68 (January 1990), pp. 56–58.

11. Griswold, "The National Archives in Turkey," p. 41.

12. Midhat Sertoğlu, *Muhteva Bakımından Başvekalet Arşivi* (Contents of the Prime Minister's Office Archive), (Ankara: Türk Tarih Kurumu Basımevi, 1955).

13. Attila Çetin, *Başbakanlık Arşivi Kılavuzu* (Guide to the Prime Minister's Office Archive), (İstanbul: Enderun Kitabevi, 1979). For assessments of the book, see Mark Epstein, "Review of Atilla Çetin's Başbakanlık Arşivi Kılavuzu," *Middle East Studies Association*

Bulletin, Vol. 14, No. 1 (July 1980), pp. 61–63 and Mahmut Şakiroğlu, "Başbakanlık Arşivi Kılavuzu" (Guide to the Prime Minister's Office Archive), *Belleten*, Vol. 46, No. 181 (January 1982), pp. 883–885. For comparisons of Sertoğlu's and Çetin's books, see Yaşar Duru, "Atilla Çetin'in Başbakanlık Arşivi Kılavuzu" (Atilla Çetin's Başbakanlık Arşivi Kılavuzu), *Türk Dünyası Araştırmaları Dergisi*, Vol. 1, No. 5 (April 1980), pp. 204–206 and Roderic Davison, "Review of Atilla Çetin's Başbakanlık Arşivi Kılavuzu," *The Turkish Studies Association Bulletin*, Vol. 4, No. 2 (September 1980), pp. 27–28.

14. Yusuf İhsan Genç et al., *Başbakanlık Osmanlı Arşivi Rehberi* (Guide to the Prime Minister's Office Ottoman Archive), (Ankara: Başbakanlık Basımevi, 1992). Second and third revised editions of the guide appeared in 2000 and 2010.

15. Nesimi Yazıcı, "Başbakanlık Osmanlı Arşivi Rehberi" (Guide to the Prime Minister's Office Ottoman Archive), *Belleten*, Vol. 57, No. 220 (December 1993), p. 884.

16. James Meyer, "For the Russianist in Istanbul and the Ottomanist in Russia: A Guide to the Archives of Eurasia," *Ab Imperio*, Vol. 4 (2008), p. 289.

17. Mustafa Küçük et al., *Başbakanlık Osmanlı Arşivi Katalogları Rehberi* (Guide to the Catalogs of the Prime Minister's Office Ottoman Archive), (Ankara: Başbakanlık Basımevi, 1995); İlber Ortaylı, "Başbakanlık Arşivinin 1995 Yılı Yayınları Üzerine: Verimli Bir Yılın Değerlendirilmesi" (On the Publications of the Prime Minister's Office Archive in 1995: Assessment of a Productive Year), *Türkiye Günlüğü*, No. 38 (January–February 1996), pp. 217–221.

18. Atilla Çetin, "Arşiv Terimleri ve Deyimleri" (Archival Terms and Expressions), *Vakıflar Dergisi*, No. 12 (1978), pp. 351–394.

Chapter Two

Emergence of Modern Turkey's Archive System

THE FIRST MODERN ARCHIVES

Modern archives developed as a by-product of the French Revolution. On 29 July 1789, France established the first of the modern national archives in order to document newly won freedoms and to protect the rights of citizens. France also was the first nation to pass a law guaranteeing citizens the right of access to archival records.[1] In 1838, forty-nine years after the French Revolution, Britain established its first central archives, the Public Record Office. In contrast to the situation in France, the Public Record Office was a separate department, not part of a larger ministry.[2] This independence of the archival function was later to become a key part of archival development in the Ottoman Empire. On 8 November 1846, a central archival authority was established in İstanbul by Grand Vizier Mustafa Reşit Pasha, who had earlier served as ambassador in Paris and London, knew French well, and was quite familiar with European politics. This was the *Hazine-i Evrak Dairesi* (Department of Treasury of Documentation), the forerunner of the BOA in the Republican period.[3] On 20 February 1847, by an imperial decision the name of the institution was changed to the Ministry of Treasury of Documentation.[4]

ARCHIVAL AND LIBRARY RESOURCES IN İSTANBUL

İstanbul is one of the richest cities in the world in its archival and library resources, rivaling the known treasures of Rome. These archives and libraries unquestionably have the most precious sources in the world in Turkish, Arabic, and Islamic manuscripts.[5] Many historians express their feelings of indebtedness to the directors and staffs of the archives and libraries in İstanbul for the patient assistance and professional guidance provided to them during their studies. A few illustrative references are given here. The American historian, Christine Isom-Verhaaren, indicates that she used extensively the BOA, Topkapı Palace Museum Archive[6] and Library, Archaelogy Museum Library, and the Süleymaniye Library in crafting her book *Allies with the Infidel.*[7] Another American historian, Alan Mikhail, tells that the amazingly rich archival and manuscript collections in İstanbul provided some of the most fantastic, humbling research of his life.[8] Most importantly Bernard Lewis, Cleveland Dodge Professor Emeritus of Near Eastern Studies at Princeton University, and one of the greatest living authorities on the Middle East, points out that the unique richness of libraries and archives in İstanbul offers special attractions to the historian of the Middle East.[9]

The BOA is the closest equivalent to a National Archives for Turkey, since it includes the archives of several government departments and is under the direct control of the Prime Minister's Office.[10] The fully opening of the BOA at the five-story building located on Ticarethane Sokağı behind the Yerebatan Cistern Museum, opposite the majestic Sultan Ahmet and Ayasofya mosques, in İstanbul less than twenty-six years ago provided historians with masses of abundant material relevant to the study of the Armenian question including its political, economic, and sociocultural attributes and enabled many of the uncertainties of the past to be rendered more intelligible.[11]

The Ottoman archival material was originally housed in the grounds of the Sublime Porte.[12] In 1754 it was transferred to a store house near the prison of the *Mehterhane* (former barracks of the grand vizier's military band). In 1846 the reforming Grand Vizier, Mustafa Reşit Pasha, provided for the archives a special building called the *Hazine-i Evrak* (Treasury of Documentation). Here the archival materials were partially sorted according to departmental categories. This collection contained some 63,312 documents dating from 1730 to 1839. During the grand vizierate of Ali Pasha the collection was expanded by the transfer of the financial records, which had previously been kept in the *Mehterhane*. Copies of outgoing documents recorded in registers were arranged according to subject matter. Separate documents (firmans and incoming letters) were kept in boxes. By 1910 the total number of documents in the archives in question amounted to 350,000 items.[13]

What one may call the discovery of the Ottoman archives begins after the Young Turk revolution of 23 July 1908. In 1911 the Ottoman Historical Society was formed; its first president was Abdurrahman Şeref, who was also the imperial historiographer. The first issue of the journal published by the

Society contains a statement of its aims, the first of which was the classification, study, and publication of archive documents.[14]

In the years that followed, Turkish scholars in the archives began to sort and classify the documents, and also published many individual documents of the highest importance. A Hungarian Turcologist, Imre Karácson, was brought in to advise. In the period 1918–1921 the first serious attempts were made at a systematic cataloging of the papers. A committee under the direction of the famous Ottoman historian Ali Emiri sorted 180,316 documents. Approximately one-fifth of this collection was removed in later years for insertion into later classifications and one-fifth are small receipts (*tezkires*) which are of relatively minor use. This committee arranged the documents and registers which it found chronologically by sultan, but with no further classification by year or by subject within the period of each sultan. This collection contains the oldest items in the archives, a few papers attributed to the reign of the founder of the Ottoman dynasty, Osman I (1299–1326), and its catalogs are indexed for the sultans through Sultan İbrahim (1640–1648). However, by far the bulk of the documents comes from the two centuries between the reign of his son Mehmed IV (1648–1687) and Mahmud II (1808–1839); and there are also a few scattered documents from the time of his son Abdülmecid (1839–1861).[15]

In 1921 a second committee, under the well-known historian İbnülemin Mahmut Kemal (İnal),[16] sorted 46,467 documents from the fifteenth to the nineteenth centuries into twenty-three subject groups with a rough chronological sequence in each group. It includes both documents and registers, many of which were removed from the Ali Emiri collection. Its catalogs are arranged according to the following general subjects: *Adliye* (justice), *Askeri* (military affairs), *Bahriye* (naval affairs), *Dahiliye* (internal affairs), *Darbhane ve meskukat* (the Mint and coinage), *Defatir-i atika* (miscellaneous old registers), *Müstediyat* (petitions), *Muhallefat* (estates and inheritance), *Muharrerat-ı hususiye* (private papers), *Muafiyat ve imtiyazat* (exemptions and privileges), *Saray* (palace), *Ensab* (genealogies), *Hariciye* (foreign affairs), *Hatt-ı Hümayun* (imperial rescripts), *Hilat* (honorific dress), *Maadin* (mines), *Maliye* (financial matters), *Sıhhiye* (health), *Şükr-ü şikayet* (thanks and complaints), *Tevcihat* (appointments), *Timar ve zeamet* (fiefs), *Vakıf* (foundations), *Umur-u Nafia* (public works). The work was interrupted by the Turkish War of Independence.[17]

A new start was made in 1932 and a third team, under Muallim Cevdet, worked from 1932 to 1937 on much the same lines as İnal, and sorted 184,256 documents into sixteen subject categories. This classification contains a much larger proportion of orders and papers not duplicated in the registers, chiefly reports coming from the provinces and from foreign countries, and it has far fewer of the relatively useless receipts which are prevalent in the other classifications. Also its geographic scope is much wider, and it has a far greater number of documents concerning the Arab countries under Ottoman rule, including North Africa. However, while it has some documents from the seventeenth century, the bulk of the collection comes from the late eighteenth and first half of the nineteenth centuries. And it is especially important for its information concerning the administrative and military reforms instituted in the Ottoman Empire under Selim III (1789–1807) and Mahmud II. Like the İnal collection, its catalogs are classified by general subject, but their number was reduced: *Adliye* (justice), *Askeri* (military affairs), *Bahriye* (naval affairs), *Belediye* (municipal), *Dahiliye* (internal affairs), *Darphane* (mint), *Evkaf* (foundations), *İktisat* (economics), *Maliyye* (finance), *Hariciye* (foreign affairs), *Sıhhiye* (health), *Nafia* (public works), *Saray* (palace), *Timar* (fiefs), *Zaptiye* (police), *Eyalet-i mümtaze* (Eflak, Boğdan, Egypt and others), and *Maarif* (education). Most of the documents have been exhaustively summarized in the catalogs, and many of them are copied in full.[18]

In 1936–1937 another Hungarian, Lajos Fekete, was invited to advise on the methods to be adopted in preparing the catalog. Upon his advice, a systematic chronological classification was inaugurated, divided into three main sections corresponding to the Imperial Council, the Grand Vizier's Office, and miscellaneous others.[19]

This was carried as far as the late-seventeenth century, and was being accompanied by an index of personal and geographical names. A working classification of registers, especially those of the finance departments, was introduced by Kamil Kepeci, of the archives staff. In addition, a whole series of other catalogs, both of registers and of documents, was prepared or started by the staff. These included catalogs of imperial writings (*hatt-ı hümayun*), of decrees (*irade*), of wakf documents, and, most interesting to the modern historian, of the personal papers and records of Sultan Abdülhamid II (1876–1909), which were transferred to the archives from the Yıldız Palace. These papers are of considerable interest for every aspect of the internal and external policies of the Sultan, and cover the whole period of his reign. The task was an enormous one, and only a beginning was made. But already, work of great value had been done by the archives staff and also by Turkish scholars who had published a growing number of documents.[20]

THE PRIME MINISTER'S OFFICE OTTOMAN ARCHIVE

The central state archives of the Ottoman Empire originally consisted of two main groups of documents: the records of the Imperial Council (*Divan-ı Hümayun*) and of the Grand Vizier's Office (*Bab-ı Asafi*). To this core other collections were from time to time added, notably the records of the finance departments and the cadastral survey office. These hold a wealth of data unavailable elsewhere. The government registers of important (i.e., public) affairs (*Mühimme Defterleri*) are the best known and most widely used and publicized of the available Ottoman archival material. They cover (with gaps) the period from 1553 to 1905 comprising international agreements (*ahitnames*); firmans and other documents issued in the name of the sultan (*berats and menşur*); imperial writings (*hatt-ı hümayuns*); and personal letters or annotations of the sultans relating to their correspondence with army and navy commanders and provincial governors. They concern questions of law and order, state revenues, military arrangements, foreign relations, administrative assignments, and any other matter that was submitted for sultan's consideration.[21]

This collection, consisting of 263 volumes, is of widely varying measurements, script, and scope of content. It is one of the most important sources for affairs concerning the non-Muslims and their organizations in the Ottoman Empire. The documents there deal with all aspects of the relations of non-Muslims individually or collectively with the Ottoman government. They also show the Sublime Porte's concern for matters affecting its non-Muslim subjects, especially in relation to taxation, security, and peace among them.[22]

THE STRUCTURE OF OTTOMAN GOVERNMENT ORDERS

Each *mühimme* register contains copies of hundreds, and sometimes thousands, of orders issued by the central government to provincial governors, judicial authorities, administrative functionaries of various kinds, or private individuals. In many cases, if not most, these orders were issued in response to petitions, complaints, or reports sent from the provinces concerning public or private matters. Orders dealing with complaints of a purely personal nature against state officials or other private individuals came to be preserved in a special "Register of Complaints," starting in 1649. A typical order would begin by explaining the nature of the petition, complaint, or report received. This introductory part of the order is especially important as historical source material because it gives detailed information about local situations, developments, events or irregularities in the province, administrative region, or administrative district from which the petition, complaint, or report originated. What follows is the official reaction to the information the central government, as personified by the sultan, received, written in the first person to express approval, disapproval or condemnation of what has been reported. In the former case, the central government applauds the local administrative action taken; in the latter, it instructs the responsible local official or officials to take the necessary corrective or punitive measures, or commands further inquiry where the rights and wrongs of a given case remain questionable or unclear. In this section of the order, the rationale behind the reaction is normally elaborated, often with reference to Islamic law, statute, established custom, or Ottoman state interests. Next follows the specific order, which sums up the case once more, reiterating the official reaction to it and the rationale behind this reaction, and gives instructions regarding the measures to be taken.[23]

Due to their nature, the significance of the *Mühimme* registers as historical source material is obvious. On the one hand, they provide historical information, much of which is usually lacking or, at best, mentioned only in passing in contemporary local sources—to the extent that these sources exist. This information sheds light on a wide variety of local administrative, fiscal, financial, military and judicial matters, as well as on problems faced by local functionaries, private individuals, or groups, or by the general run of the local civilian population. Thus, in many instances, the *Mühimme* registers can be invaluably helpful in explaining events or developments that are left unexplained in the local sources—one would suspect deliberately and for understandable reasons, not least of which was the local political motive, more often than not a strong variance with central government policy. The registers also help to establish historical facts that these same local sources obscure, or about which they maintain a suspicious silence. What they further provide is basic information on Ottoman policy regarding the provinces—provincial and regional regulations, official appointments and changes of personnel, and a variety of other matters—which the contemporary local literature ignores, or of which it makes no more than cursory mention. The information yielded by these registers is eminently useful for filling certain gaps in the historical knowledge of Ottoman affairs, providing answers to a number of questions which cannot be answered from other sources.[24]

FORMAT

The format of the *Mühimme* registers, apart from the orders themselves, makes them useful for historical analysis in a number of ways. The introductory sections are a reflection of the events taking place in the Ottoman provinces. The subsidiary instructions often included in the registers indicate the chains of command set up by the central government. The side and end notes appended to the body of the registers give an indication of the Sublime Porte's response to changing circumstances in the provinces. Summaries and indexes are available for the volumes of this collection.[25]

TAX REGISTERS

Tax registers (*Tahrir Defterleri*) of rural and urban populations and their production, more than 2,000 in number, running from the sixteenth through the nineteenth centuries, are preserved mostly at the BOA. Tax registers of individual administrative districts numbering 1,925, and cadastral records, some of them dealing with later periods, were transferred to Ankara in 1930. They are now kept in the Directorate General of Land Deed Registration in Ankara and are still in use for governmental and legal reference. These are consulted in the adjudication of land cases both in Turkey and in the successor states. They must be regarded as the most important source for the study of Ottoman administrative and military organization, for they provide in a much more detailed, organized, and authoritative way the administrative and financial details from which the information contained in the decrees and orders was extracted. The importance of this *fonds* was first demonstrated in studies carried out by the late Professor Ömer Lûtfı Barkan. Since the 1940s they have formed the subject of active publication both within Turkey and internationally. Barkan's acute understanding of Ottoman Empire's socioeconomic history rivaled that of any international scholar. Tax registers convey figures and other factual information required and collected for various administrative purposes. They bear significance for statistical data on the non-Muslims in the areas of demography, economic conditions, and taxation. Frequently the contents of important diplomas granting exemptions or appointments, as well as laws and regulations, are entered in these registers along with the persons or groups to whom they apply.[26]

The tax registers series is one of the best-known series of the Ottoman archives, which can be subdivided into detailed registers, summarizing registers and pious foundations registers. They were mainly designed to keep track of that part of Ottoman state revenue which did not reach the central treasury, but was assigned locally, to *tımar*[27] holders, garrison soldiers, pious foundation administrators, or even owners of private property. The most elaborate form of tax registers is the detailed register, which provides extensive information on the urban and rural population and administrative organization in most of the provinces of the Ottoman Empire, especially for the sixteenth and seventeenth centuries, and to a lesser degree for the centuries thereafter. They contain an enumeration of taxpayers, organized in administrative divisions, towns, and villages. Furthermore, the figures for taxes such as the tithes, farm taxes, and, where applicable, the *cizye* (non-Muslim tax) due from many of the towns and villages, were appended to the list of taxpayers, along with the expected yield in each case. Summarizing registers include periodic financial summaries of the revenues and expenditures of the central Imperial Treasury and of the various provincial treasuries from the sixteenth through the nineteenth centuries. They gave only the names of the settlements concerned, with the number of taxpayers registered and the value of the taxes officially expected from each place. Finally we have separate listings of the pious foundations established in almost every province, along with the revenue-producing institutions assigned to mosques, schools, dervish convents, and hospices.[28]

REGISTERS OF OTTOMAN NON-MUSLIMS

In addition, there are specific registers dealing with the non-Muslim peoples of the Ottoman Empire, namely: (1) Registers of the Muslim poll tax, which go back to the fifteenth century. (2) Registers of appointment of bishops. These contain diplomas and decrees on appointments, changes, and other matters concerning the title and jurisdiction of the metropolitans and bishops in the country. They are essential for the study of church organization throughout the empire and its relations with the Ottoman government. (3) Registers of non-Muslim communities, altogether eighteen volumes of notebooks containing copies of papers on all matters of affairs concerning the non-Muslim subjects from the year 1837 on. (4) The church registers, which start in 1837, and include permissions for construction and repair of churches, schools, and other buildings, as well as cemeteries run by the non-Muslim communities or foreigners. These registers of varying length contain most of the administrative orders issued concerning the different *millets* and churches during the First World War.[29]

YILDIZ PALACE ARCHIVE

An event of major importance for scholars wishing to undertake research on the history of the Middle East and Southeastern Europe in the late nineteenth and early twentieth centuries was the opening in 1970 of the famous collection of documents gathered by Sultan Abdülhamid II, the Yıldız Palace archive collection, in İstanbul. Its materials are classified into nine main sections: the Constitution and Parliament of 1876; administrative organization and development of the central government; education and cultural affairs; justice and legal organization; papers of important Ottoman political figures; important political events; miscellaneous political activities; restoration of the Ottoman Constitution and Parliament in 1908; and Ottoman provincial organization and problems. While Sultans' archives long have been available at the Topkapı Palace to supplement the regular administrative archives for previous reigns, none in any way approaches the value of Yıldız collection, because no Ottoman regime ever concentrated the important policies and actions of government around the person of the Sultan and his associates so completely as was done during the reign of Abdülhamid II.[30]

Named after the palace which Sultan Abdülhamid II built for himself on a hill overlooking the quarter of Beşiktaş, and from which he conducted government business, the Yıldız section contains records such as the minutes of the Council of Ministers, which one would not ordinarily expect in a palace archive. These papers, collated as registers, summarize discussions about issues brought to the attention of the Council of Ministers. Each entry includes a brief summary of the problem under consideration and of the Council's recommendation for action. The Yıldız Palace Archive includes essential documents which shed considerable light on most of the important events which occurred during Sultan Abdülhamid II's long reign—events involving not only strictly palace affairs and political matters in İstanbul, but also relations with the Great Powers of Europe, problems created by the rise of nationalism and terrorism on the part of the subject peoples of the Empire, and other developments in the provinces which remained in the far-flung empire of the Sultan. An especially rich series (15,679 registers) comprises the Yıldız Petition Registers. Here we find the requests submitted to Sultan Abdülhamid II throughout his long reign, which in 1992, had been cataloged down to the year 1904. Another important section is known as Yıldız Basic Papers, which contains documentation on affairs with which the ruler occupied himself without necessarily involving a government office. Another set of series specific to this period, also found in the Yıldız collection, emanates from the so-called inspectorate of Rumelia instituted from 1902 onward upon Austrian and Russian pressure. In addition, the collection includes important documents surviving from the reigns of the earlier nineteenth-century Ottoman sultans, as well as of their administrators who undertook the gigantic tasks of reform consummated and manifested in the legislative movement known as the *Tanzimat* (Reorganization) (1839–1876). This material is indispensable for researchers concerning themselves with the wars, uprisings and negotiations which accompanied the last decades of the Ottoman Empire.[31]

It should be remembered that the papers cited above are only a sample of the materials available in Turkey concerning the reign of Sultan Abdülhamid II. A more detailed cataloging of the Yıldız Archive itself as prepared by the staff of the BOA, and many more papers, were uncovered in the process. In addition, many papers from the Yıldız Palace were retained as part of its library collection, and may be found at the İstanbul University Library. Finally, even more detailed materials concerning most of the subjects which came to the Sultan's attention are available in the collections of the various administrative departments of government, now found in the BOA, and the Topkapı Palace Archive.[32]

THE STATE OF OTTOMAN RECORDS AND PAPERS

Government offices in the Ottoman Empire recorded the minutest detail of their operations and preserved copies and registers of outgoing acts and collected incoming documents. The Ottomans were obsessive about paper and bureaucratic filing. In fact, almost nothing happened in the highly centralized and "top-down" Ottoman bureaucracy without written and stamped official directives and orders. In the process a rich historical archive was created.[33]

Wherever the historian of the Ottoman Empire turns, he is confronted not only by highly complex events but also by staggering documentation. There are at least 150 million ancient documents and 366,000 registers of inestimable value that span every period and region of the realm in the stacks and vaults of the BOA. They fill more than seventy-five kilometers of shelves. How to attack this mountain of material is one of the historian's major problems. The great mass of documents is in Turkish, although some of the documents are in Latin, Greek, and European languages, as well as in Persian and Arabic. The last named is used for religious endowment documents and some others dealing with religious matters. Each day new collections are opened and made readily accessible to researchers.[34]

During the First World War, not one of İstanbul's archives, libraries and museums was destroyed by shelling or fires. Losses caused by accidental fire are very minor. On 15 December 1972, one of the two remaining portions of the nineteenth-century Sublime Porte in İstanbul, more recently used by the Ministry of Finance and the Ottoman Ministry of Foreign Affairs Archive, burned to the ground. The reading rooms of the latter were destroyed, but the invaluable catalogs of the collection were saved by being thrown out of the window before the archives staff escaped. Fortunately, the fire was extinguished before it reached the wing of the building that housed the millions of documents that comprise the Ottoman Ministry of Foreign Affairs Archive itself, and before it could spread to the adjacent buildings of the principal BOA. The Ottoman Ministry of Foreign Affairs Archive reopened to researchers in a new location, adjacent to the old, and continued to provide all those working on Ottoman diplomatic history with an indispensable source for their research.[35]

The BOA also has a collection of books and papers in Greek, Latin, French, Armenian, Hebrew and other non-Islamic languages. These have been cataloged and are available for study.

A fair proportion of the documents from Middle Eastern, Balkan and Danubian repositories dealing with the Ottoman Empire are to be found on microfilm or microfilm prints in the BOA. The microfilms of a large part of those documents that had been sold to Bulgaria in 1931 have been brought back. All these extensive and priceless records are well preserved and carefully organized. Photographs are kept in separate files or boxes but generally kept with manuscript collections or records of which they are a part. The photograph collections have inventories that describe each individual image. The images are generally arranged alphabetically by people, places, and subjects.[36] These archives are a precious, indeed an indispensable source for the history of all the lands that had ever formed part of the Ottoman Empire and even, to a lesser degree, those that had had relations with the empire.[37]

NOTES

1. Faruk Bildirici, "Fransız ve Türk Arşivlerinin Karşılaştırılmalı Denemesi: Tarih ve Teşkilat" (A Comparative Trial of French and Turkish Archives: History and Organization), in Hamza Kandur, ed., *Arşivcilik Konferansları I* (Conferences on Archival Administration I), (İstanbul: Librairie de Péra, 1995), p. 83; Ahmet Kavas, "Fransız Arşivleri" (French Archives), *Arşiv Dünyası*, No. 4 (August–September 2004), pp. 24–27.

2. Gregory Hunter, *Developing and Maintaining Practical Archives* (New York and London: Neal-Schuman Publishers, 1997), pp. 11–12.

3. Başbakanlık Osmanlı Arşivi (Prime Minister's Office Ottoman Archive), İstanbul (henceforth referred to as BOA), Mesail-i Mühimme Tasnifi (Declassification of Important Matters), No. 658; Selahattin Elker, "Mustafa Reşit Paşa ve Türk Arşivciliği" (Mustafa Reşit Pasha and Turkish Archival Administration), in *IV. Türk Tarih Kongresi, Ankara 10–14 Kasım 1948. Kongreye Sunulan Tebliğler* (Fourth Turkish Historical Congress, Ankara 10–14 November 1948. Communications Presented to the Congress), (Ankara:Türk Tarih Kurumu Basımevi, 1952), pp. 183–184; Küçük, *Başbakanlık Osmanlı Arşivi Katalogları Rehberi*, p. viii; Akyıldız, "Hazine-i Evrakın Kurulması ve İlk Tasnif Usulleri (1846–1856)," p. 71; Necati Aktaş, "Osmanlı Dönemi Arşivciliğimiz ve Tasnif Çalışmaları" (Our Ottoman Period Archival Administration and the Declassification Activities), in Alâaddin Aköz, Bayram Ürekli and Ruhi Özcan, eds., *Uluslararası Kuruluşunun 700. Yıl Dönümünde Bütün Yönleriyle Osmanlı Devleti Kongresi, Konya 7–9 Nisan 1999. Bildiriler* (International Congress on the Ottoman Empire with All Its Aspects on the 700th Anniversary of Its Foundation, Konya 7–9 April 1999. Communications), (Konya: Selçuk Üniversitesi Basımevi, 2000), p. 380.

4. BOA, İrade Tasnifi, Dahiliye (Declassification of Imperial Decisions, Ministry of the Interior), No. 7066.

5. Harry Howard, "Preliminary Materials for a Survey of the Libraries and Archives of Istanbul," *Journal of the American Oriental Society*, Vol. 59, No. 2 (June 1939), p. 227; Chantal Lemercier-Quelquejay, "Les Bibliothèques et les archives de Turquie en tant que sources de documents sur l'histoire de Russie," *Cahiers du Monde russe et soviétique*, Vol. 5, No. 1 (janvier–mars 1964), pp. 105–140.

6. These are the archives of the court and treasury of the Sultan and his family, located in the famous Grand Seraglio, which was the principal residence of the Ottoman sultans from the conquest of İstanbul until the middle of the nineteenth century when the Yıldız palace was built. For details on the subject, see Ülkü Altındağ, *Topkapı Sarayı Müzesi Osmanlı Saray Arşivi Kataloğu (Hükümler-Beratlar)* (Ottoman Palace Archive Catalog of the Topkapı Palace Museum [Rulings-Berats]), 2 Vols., (Ankara: Türk Tarih Kurumu Basımevi, 1988). This properly constructed descriptive catalog is compiled in the form of an index to the principal subjects mentioned in the registers and documents. It is not only a mine of historical data, but in itself a kind of historical monograph, in which the description of each item, technical and cryptic as it may be, is a miniature essay in cultural history.

7. Christine Isom-Verhaaren, *Allies with the Infidel: The Ottoman and French Alliance in the Sixteenth Century* (London and New York: I. B. Tauris, 2011), p. x.

8. Alan Mikhail, *Nature and Empire in Ottoman Egypt: An Environmental History* (New York: Cambridge University Press, 2011), pp. xxii–xxiii.

9. Lewis, *Notes on a Century*, p. 89.

10. Oktay Özel, "Arşiv Meselemiz" (Our Archive Question), *Toplumsal Tarih*, No. 217 (January 2012), p. 26.

11. The BOA was earlier situated on Divanyolu Street in the Defterdarlık section of İstanbul.

12. The actual Departments of State, that in their aggregate are known officially as the Sublime Porte, comprise the Grand Vizier's Office, the Ministries of Foreign Affairs, the Interior, Finance, Justice, Public Instruction, Marine, War, Commerce and Public Works, Pious Foundations, Mines and Forests, and Police. See Nermi Haskan and Çelik Gülersoy, *Hükümet Kapısı Bab-ı Ali Kuruluşundan Cumhuriyete Kadar* (Gate of Government Sublime Porte: From Its Foundation to the Republic), (İstanbul: Çelik Gülersoy Vakfı, 2000).

13. Jan Reychman and Ananiasz Zajaczkowski, trans. Andrew Ehrenkreutz, *Handbook of Ottoman-Turkish Diplomatics* (Mouton: J. J. Augustin, rev. and expanded, 1968), p. 25.

14. Paul Wittek, "Les Archives de Turquie," *Byzantion*, Vol. 13 (1938), pp. 691–699.

15. Sertoğlu, *Muhteva Bakımından Başvekalet Arşivi*, pp. 68–69; Stanford Shaw, "Archival Sources for Ottoman History: The Archives of Turkey," *Journal of the American Oriental Society*, Vol. 80, No. 1 (January–March 1960), p. 4.

16. According to the law of 2 July 1934, all Turks assumed a family name. İbnülemin Mahmut Kemal adopted the name İnal. When appropriate, new family names will be given in parentheses on the first appearance of the particular person.

17. Sertoğlu, *Muhteva Bakımından Başvekalet Arşivi*, p. 70; Shaw, "Archival Sources for Ottoman History," p. 5.

18. Sertoğlu, *Muhteva Bakımından Başvekalet Arşivi*, p. 71; Shaw, "Archival Sources for Ottoman History," p. 5.

19. Lajos Fekete, "Über Archivalien und Archivwesen in der Türkei," *Acta Orientalia*, Vol. 3 (1953), pp.179–206.

20. Bernard Lewis, "Ottoman Archives: A Source for European History," *Archives*, Vol. 4, No. 24 (Michaelmas 1969), pp. 226–228.

21. Yusuf Sarınay, "Türk Arşivleri ve Ermeni Meselesi" (Turkish Archives and the Armenian Question), *Belleten*, Vol. 70, No. 257 (April 2006), pp. 291–293; Atilla Çetin, "Osmanlı Devleti Arşivinin Kuruluşu ve Tasnif Çalışmaları" (Founding of the Ottoman State Archive and Declassification Activities), *Türk Dünyası Araştırmaları Dergisi*, Vol. 14, No. 21 (December 1982), pp. 96–98; Cevdet Türkay, "Osmanlı İmparatorluğunda Arşiv"(Archive in the Ottoman Empire), *Belgelerle Türk Tarih Dergisi*, Vol. 2, No. 7 (1968), pp. 44–48.

22. Halil İnalcık, " Ottoman Archival Materials on *Millets*," in Benjamin Braude and Bernard Lewis, eds., *Christians and Jews in the Ottoman Empire: The Functioning of a Plural Society*, Vol. 1: *The Central Lands*, (New York and London: Holmes and Meier Publishers, 1982), p. 468. The two-volume book contains revised versions of a series of lectures given at a Princeton University symposium on the *millet* system in 1978, held at the instance of Professor Bernard Lewis. This is the best work now available on the subject, but there is still considerable room for historians to reexamine this topic in the future. Also Nezihi Aykut, İdris Bostan, Feridun Emecen, Yusuf Halaçoğlu, Mehmet İpşirli, İsmet Miroğlu, Abdülkadir Özcan and İlhan Şahin, eds., *Mühimme Defteri 90* (Important Affairs Register 90), (İstanbul: Türk Dünyası Araştırmaları Vakfı, 1993), pp. ii–iv; Mübahat Kütükoğlu, "Mühimme Defterlerindeki Muamele Kayıdları Üzerine" (On the Transaction Notes in the Important Affairs Registers), in *Tarih Boyunca Paleografya ve Diplomatik Semineri 30 Nisan–2 Mayıs 1986 Bildiriler* (Seminar on Paleography and Diplomatics 30 April–2 May 1986 Communications), (İstanbul: Edebiyat Fakültesi Basımevi, 1988), pp. 95–112; Chantal Lemercier-Quelquejay, "Une source inédite pour l'histoire de la Russie au XVIe siècle: Les registres des "Mühimme Defterleri" des Archives du Baş-vekâlet," *Cahiers du Monde russe et soviétique*, Vol. 8, No. 2 (avril–juin 1967), p. 335.

23. Abdul-Rahim Abu-Husayn, *The View from Istanbul: Lebanon and the Druze Emirate in the Ottoman Chancery Documents, 1546–1711* (London and New York: I. B. Tauris, 2004), p. 3.

24. Ibid., pp. 4–5.

25. Yılmaz Öztuna, "Mühimme Defteri" (Important Affairs Register), *Türkiye*, 10 October 1993, p. 8; Palmira Brummett, "Mühimme 959: A Source for Ottoman Central Government

Interaction with the Eastern Beys," *The Turkish Studies Association Bulletin*, Vol. 10, No. 1 (March 1986), p. 22.

26. The bibliography on this subject is extensive. Only the most informative items will be cited: Sarınay, "Türk Arşivleri ve Ermeni Meselesi," p. 293; Yılmaz Kurt, "Tapu Tahrir Defterleri ve Bunların Yayınlanması Hakkında" (On Land Deed Registers and Their Publication), in Rahim Erişti, Hacı Osman Yıldırım, Vahdettin Atik and Yusuf Yay, eds., *Birinci Milli Arşiv Şurası (Tebliğler-Tartışmalar) 20–21 Nisan 1998* (First National Archives Congress [Communications-Discussions] 20–21 April 1998), (Ankara: Başbakanlık Basımevi, 1998), pp. 175–186; Metin Coşgel, "Ottoman Tax Registers (Tahrir Defterleri)," *Historical Methods*, Vol. 37, No. 2 (Spring 2004), pp. 87–100; Erhan Afyoncu, "Türkiye'de Tahrir Defterlerine Dayalı Olarak Hazırlanmış Çalışmalar Hakkında Bazı Görüşler" (Some Reflections on the Studies Based Upon Tax Registers in Turkey), *Türkiye Araştırmaları Literatür Dergisi*, No. 1 (2003), pp. 267–286; İnalcık, "Ottoman Archival Materials on *Millets*," p. 439. On the Archive of the Directorate General of Land Deed Registration in Ankara see Adnan Darendeliler and İhsan Dede, *Arşivin Bugünkü Durumu Hukuk ve İlim Açısından Arşiv İdaresi* (The Current Condition of the Turkish Archives: Archival Administration from a Legal and Scholarly Point of View), (Ankara: Gürsoy Basımevi, 1968), pp. 27–28; İsmail Özçelik, *Tarih Araştırmalarında Yöntem ve Teknikler* (Method and Techniques in Historical Studies), (Ankara: Gündüz Eğitim ve Yayıncılık, 2001), pp. 90–91; Atilla Çetin, "Türkiye'de Önemli Arşivler ve Özellikleri" (Important Archives in Turkey and Their Features), *Türk Dünyası Araştırmaları Dergisi*, Vol. 1, No. 5 (April 1980), pp. 84–85 and Özel, "Arşiv Meselemiz," p. 30.

27. Fief. A grant of land revenue collection rights assigned to a military commander in lieu of a salary.

28. In the past few decades a growing number of articles based on primary sources have been published on the subject, mostly in journals in Turkey and the United States. See, among others, Zeki Arıkan, "Tahrir Defterlerinde Geçen Deyimler" (Expressions Used in the Tax Registers), *Osmanlı Araştırmaları*, No. 16 (1996), pp. 1–5; Hasan Bahar, "Osmanlı Tahrir Defterleri Çalışmalarındaki Gelişmeler Üzerine Gözlemler" (Observations on Developments Regarding the Studies About the Ottoman Tax Registers), *Osmanlı Araştırmaları*, No. 16 (1996), pp. 61–66; Kemal Çiçek, "Osmanlı Tahrir Defterlerinin Kullanımında Görülen Bazı Problemler ve Metod Arayışları" (Some Problems and Quests for Method Seen in the Use of Ottoman Tax Registers), *Türk Dünyası Araştırmaları Dergisi*, No. 97 (1995), pp. 93–112; Mehmet Ali Ünal, "Tahrir Defterlerindeki Bilgilerin Güvenilirliği" (Reliability of the Data in the Tax Registers), *Süleyman Demirel Üniversitesi Sosyal Bilimler Dergisi*, No. 1 (1995), pp. 295–300; Suraiya Faroqhi, "Taxation and Urban Activities in Sixteenth-Century Anatolia," *International Journal of Turkish Studies*, Vol. 1 (1979–1980), p. 23.

29. Sarınay, "Türk Arşivleri ve Ermeni Meselesi," pp. 294–295; İnalcık, "Ottoman Archival Materials on *Millets*," p. 439; Ali Güler, "Osmanlı Devletinde Gayrımüslimlerin Din-İbadet, Eğitim-Öğretim Hürriyetleri ve Bu Bakımdan Kilise Defterlerinin Kaynak Olarak Önemi" (The Religion-Worship, Education-Instruction Liberties of Non-Muslims in the Ottoman State and the Importance of Church Registers as Sources in This Regard), *Ankara Üniversitesi Osmanlı Tarihi Araştırma ve Uygulama Merkezi Dergisi*, No. 9 (1998), pp. 155–175.

30. Atilla Çetin, "Yıldız Arşivine Dair" (On the Yıldız Archive), *İstanbul Üniversitesi Edebiyat Fakültesi Tarih Dergisi*, No. 32 (1979), pp. 563–586; Turgut Işıksal, "Arşivlerimizin Durumu ve Problemleri" (The Condition of Our Archives and Their Problems), *Türk Kültürü*, Vol. 10, No. 119 (September 1972), p. 1200; Stanford Shaw, "The Yıldız Palace Archives of Abdülhamid II," *Archivum Ottomanicum*, Vol. 3 (1971), p. 211; Ertuğrul Zekai Ökte, ed., *Osmanlı Arşivi, Yıldız Tasnifi, Ermeni Meselesi* (Ottoman Archives, Yıldız Collection, The Armenian Question), 3 Vols., (İstanbul: Tarihi Araştırmalar ve Dokümantasyon Merkezleri Kurma ve Geliştirme Vakfı, 1989).

31. Shaw, "The Yıldız Palace Archives of Abdülhamid II," p. 211; Tahsin Öz, "Yıldız Maruzat Dairesi Arşivi" (Yıldız Petition Registers), in *IV. Türk Tarih Kongresi Ankara, 10–14 Kasım 1948. Kongreye Sunulan Tebliğler*, pp. 451–463; Küçük, *Başbakanlık Osmanlı Arşivi Katalogları Rehberi*, pp. 256–261 and 212–216; Faroqhi, *Approaching Ottoman History*, pp. 52–53.

32. Shaw, "The Yıldız Palace Archives of Abdülhamid II," pp. 236–237.

33. Akyıldız, "Hazine-i Evrak'ın Kurulması ve İlk Tasnif Usulleri (1846–1856)," p. 69; Edward Erickson, *Ottomans and Armenians: A Study in Counterinsurgency* (New York: Palgrave Macmillan, 2013), p. 227.

34. İsa Özkul, *Türk Arşivleri Bugünü ve Geleceği* (Turkish Archives Present and Future), (Ankara: Başbakanlık Basımevi, 2000), pp. 4, 30–36 and 45–48; Halil İnalcık and Bülent Arı, "Klasik Dönem Osmanlı Tarihçiliği" (Classical Period Ottoman Historianship), in Vahdettin Engin and Ahmet Şimşek, eds., *Türkiye'de Tarihyazımı* (Historiography in Turkey), (İstanbul: Yeditepe Yayınevi, 2011), p. 108.

35. Stanford Shaw, "The Editor's Desk," *International Journal of Middle East Studies*, Vol. 4, No. 1–2 (1973), p. 128.

36. Özcan Ünlü, "Yurtdışındaki Osmanlı Belgeleri" (Ottoman Documents Abroad), *Türkiye*, 22 December 1993, p. 8; Orhan Sakin, *Makedonya'daki Osmanlı Evrakı* (Ottoman Documents in Macedonia), (Ankara: Başbakanlık Basımevi, 1996); Atilla Çetin, "Yabancı Ülkelerde Bulunan Osmanlı Arşiv Malzemeleri, Yayınları ve Önemi" (Ottoman Archival Materials and Publications Abroad and Their Importance), *Türk Dünyası Araştırmaları Dergisi*, Vol. 2, No. 7 (August 1980), pp. 184–199; Aktaş, "Osmanlı Dönemi Arşivciliğimiz ve Tasnif Çalışmaları," p. 386; Işıksal, "Arşivlerimizin Durumu ve Problemleri," p. 1203; Evangelia Balta, "Ottoman Archives in Greece," in *Balkanlar ve İtalya'da Şehir ve Manastır Arşivlerindeki Türkçe Belgeler Semineri (16–17 Kasım 2000)* (Seminar on Turkish Documents in the Archives of Balkan Countries and Italian Cities and Monastries [16–17 November 2000]), (Ankara: Türk Tarih Kurumu Basımevi, 2003), pp. 15–24; G. Bayerle, "Ottoman Records in the Hungarian Archives," *Archivum Ottomanicum*, Vol. 4 (1972), pp. 5–22; Elöd Vass, "The Ottoman Documents in the Archives of Hungary From the XVIth to the XVIIth Century," in Jean-Louis Bacqué-Grammont and Emeri van Donzel, eds., *Comité International D'Etudes Pré-Ottomanes et Ottomanes VIth Symposium Cambridge, 1rst–4th July 1984* (Istanbul, Paris and Leiden: The Divit Press, 1987), pp. 203–207.

37. Lewis, *Notes on a Century*, p. 90.

Chapter Three

Developments in the Turkish Archives since 1989

The Turkish government announced on 2 January 1989 plans to throw open the vast Ottoman archives in an attempt to shed light on the Armenian question. Disclosing the plans in an interview on state-run television, the Minister of Foreign Affairs, Mesut Yılmaz, said opening all the archives, which date back to the fourteenth century and before, would take years. But he said those relating to the Armenian question could be made available in four months. "This will make sure the allegations of an Armenian massacre shall be no more of political abuse. The issue of Armenian claims must no longer be a subject of political exploitation. This is not a matter for politicians to solve but for historians and we want to contribute to this effort," Yılmaz stated. He stressed that the Turkish government, which rejects that genocide took place, had not changed its position. "The allegations of a genocide are a slander against the Turkish nation," he said. "Everybody knows that the Turkish nation is extremely sensitive on this subject. Now we are going to contribute to the process of shedding light on the matter." Other Turkish officials were also unequivocal in expressing their opinion on the subject. "Historians will see that most of the prejudices used by Armenians all over the world against Turkey are unrealistic and misplaced," the Minister of National Defense Ercan Vuralhan said in an interview.[1]

İnal Batu, spokesman of the Turkish Ministry of Foreign Affairs, confirmed on 3 January 1989 that researchers had already sifted through Armenian-related material covering the period from 1691 to 1895, and everything from then until 1923 should be sorted by the month of May. Turkey hoped in this way to defuse critics abroad, and in particular, to improve relations with the United States and Western European countries, where strong Armenian lobbies exist. The spokesman added:

> We certainly hope that after the archives open Turkey will have the means to refute in the eyes of the world Armenian claims of genocide. Turkey has always said this was a matter for historians, who can only reach a verdict by studying documents. Up to now, irresponsible people have made judgments and assessments.[2]

İsmet Miroğlu, Director General of State Archives, also declared on 3 January 1989:

> No restrictions to anybody are in question. The archives will be open to everyone who applies in the proper procedure. We are also making some preparations to ease the bureaucracy for foreign researchers. The move followed the arrival of a new team of archivists at the BOA. They had the task of cataloging more than 80 million documents and 240,000 registers.[3]

On 23 June 1989, the Council of Ministers of the Republic of Turkey signed into law the "Regulations Governing Individuals and Institutions of Turkish and Foreign Citizenships Wishing to Conduct Research in the State Archives." This law No.89/14269, greatly simplified the procedures whereby foreign and Turkish scholars may obtain permission to conduct research in the State Archives. As a result, whereas the application procedures once took an average of six to ten months, scholars could now apply for permission one day and begin their studies the following day. Article 2 of the newly instituted regulations stated that all "archival materials which have been declassified and which are at least fifty years old" were available to would-be researchers. Prior to 23 June 1989 all archival materials since May 1915 had been closed to scholars. In other words, all cataloged materials through 1939 became open and available. This encompasses up to 100 million records from Ottoman administrators collected over a period of 500 years. Study of these records should give historians a better understanding of life from the fifteenth to the early twentieth century.[4]

Between 1984 and 1989, the Turkish government allocated well over 20 million dollars to a massive program to declassify and catalog all documents covering the period from 1691 to 1894, and made these documents available to the international scholarly community from which the real history of the Ottoman Armenians will ultimately be written. Fifteen microfilm copies of these documents were presented to major libraries around the world, including the United States Library of Congress. This gesture enabled scholars and researchers to have access to these documents even if they were unable to travel to Turkey. Work on the remaining documents covering the years 1895 to 1923 continued, and materials of this period were added to those already available as soon as their processing was completed.[5]

During the first half of 1989, literally tens of thousands of documents pertaining to the Ottoman Armenian history were opened for scholarly study.

Many documents already cataloged and made available had direct relevance to the dispute over what happened in eastern Anatolia. Registers specifically devoted to the non-Muslim peoples of the Ottoman Empire containing a great deal of information on Turkish-Armenian relations were among the new material. Some of the most important releases were the 224 bound and cataloged volumes of the deliberations and decisions of the Ottoman Council of Ministers. These records covered the years from 1885 to 1922. In the past, many scholars had used these registers to study events that occurred prior to May 1914. For the first time, all the deliberations and actions of the Council of Ministers during the First World War were now available to the scholars. These records obviously include many decisions relating to the relocation of the Ottoman Armenians during the war.[6]

Dozens of other categories of records in the BOA, containing thousands of documents from the period of the First World War, were automatically opened to scholars with the implementation of the new law. It is no exaggeration to suggest that attempts to describe Turkish-Armenian relations in any way whatsoever without utilizing the original sources of the ruling Ottoman state are comparable to trying to write the history of the American Civil War on the basis of Confederate memoirs alone, with no reference to the contents of the United States National Archives.

TURGUT ÖZAL AND THE ARCHIVES

Heath Lowry, the editor and cofounder of the *Journal of Ottoman Studies* and director of the Institute of Turkish Studies, Washington, DC,[7] in an open letter signed on behalf of sixty-eight American experts on Turkey, addressed the following on 18 May 1985 to Prime Minister Turgut Özal[8]:

> For the overwhelming majority of US lawmakers who support the Armenian genocide resolution, it is ignorance of Ottoman history rather than intentional malice which accounts for their action. The same is true for the educated American public at large which has been subjected to sixty years of exposure to only the Armenian version of history. For this ignorance of history, Turkey must bear a large share of responsibility, as its failure to date to facilitate scholarly inquiry into the events of World War I, especially by not opening the relevant historical archives to international scholars, has allowed Armenian spokesmen to propagate at will their own version of history of the Ottoman Empire.

Prime Minister Özal indicated that the opening of the Ottoman archives was a matter of high priority and imminent action for him and his government. His reply of 14 June 1985 to Lowry was as follows:

> As you stressed in your message, the opening of documents and information inherited by us from the past to the scrutiny of scholars, is a matter of great importance in understanding the real history of the past. Likewise, those who possess such documents are held for the sake of humanity to great responsibility. For this reason, we have undertaken the necessary steps in our country to ensure the rapid declassification of great numbers of documents which have been preserved from our long and rich history, as well as steps which will facilitate the access of scholars to these materials. It gives me great personal pleasure to use this opportunity to announce that within the past few days the Turkish Grand National Assembly has enacted special legislation to provide the necessary financial means for this endeavor. This means that the scope of ongoing work in the Archives will be expanded and expedited. Already, those documents whose declassification has been completed are open to researchers. As their declassification procedures are completed new documents are being added for the scrutiny of scholars.[9]

Prime Minister Özal was thus committed to making the Ottoman archives accessible to researchers as quickly as possible.

"We will accept whatever reality emerges from the Ottoman archives," Prime Minister Özal told a news conference on 4 January 1989.[10] He was a man of great vision, imagination, and above all, energy. Özal, who managed to move the Turkish economy several decades forward in less than four years, had similar success with the Ottoman archives. He would bring the archives to the Western European and American standards of the 1980s. The steps taken by the Turkish government both to increase the number of qualified personnel engaged in cataloging the relevant documents, and the appropriations made to upgrade the physical plant of the archives facilities, were major innovations.[11]

Perhaps the most conspicuous display of Prime Minister Özal's interest in the matter was the visit he made on 16 January 1989 to the BOA building. In the Division of Repair and Preservation, he showed a lively interest in the methods of fumigating, cleaning, flattening, and laminating documents, about which he fired a perfect barrage of questions at the staff members present. Next came the Division of Photographic Reproduction. Here his chief interest was in microfilming. He lingered long, inspecting equipment and asking searching questions about processes, and the possibilities of microfilming as a means of conserving storage space and of reproducing documentary material at low cost.[12]

United States Congressman James Hansen had announced on the floor of the House of Representatives as early as 9 July 1985 that Turgut Özal, the Turkish Prime Minister, committed his government to opening the Ottoman archives to assist in determining the truth regarding the Armenian events of 1915. According to Hansen, this was a step in the right direction and indicated that the Turkish government was not attempting to conceal the facts.[13]

On 26 May 1987, United States Senator Larry Pressler, a ranking member of the Senate Foreign Relations Subcommittee on European Affairs, wrote that Turgut Özal's personal expressions of commitment to seeing that the Ottoman archives were opened to scholars under reasonable conditions had been gratifying and had raised expectations in the American scholarly community. Pressler said he knew that he did not have to tell the Turkish Prime Minister of the importance of making progress on this issue. The Senator was also aware of Özal's expressions of confidence that opening of the archives to scholars would serve to refute many of the charges currently being made against Ottoman authorities. He also added that the priceless quality and value of the work of Turkish archivists were deservedly recognized and praised by scholars throughout the world.[14]

Larry Pressler said on the floor of the Senate on 13 May 1988 that several years earlier he had written Prime Minister Turgut Özal to encourage the opening of the Ottoman archives to history scholars from around the world. Since that time, some progress had been made in making some of these records available to foreign researchers. Unfortunately, according to Pressler, much more needed to be done to give interested scholars the opportunity to examine the Ottoman archives. The week before, he had spoken with President Kenan Evren and Prime Minister Özal in Ankara regarding the opening of the archives. They assured him that the Ottoman records increasingly would be made available to foreign researchers. He made the point that it would be in the best interest of the Republic of Turkey to open the archives of the Ottoman Empire. Pressler applauded the Turkish leaders' support for a further opening of the Ottoman archives, and he hoped this process would go both accurately and quickly.[15]

United States Senator Robert Byrd indicated in his speech on the floor of the Senate on 20 February 1990 that "in the last year the Government of the Republic of Turkey has opened the Ottoman Archives spanning the World War I era." And he added: "So there is new information freely available which could help historians make a determination about this [Armenian] matter."[16] Senator Timothy Wirth expressed his views on the subject the following day:

> The relevant documents in the Ottoman archives are being made accessible to researchers. That commitment has been made by the Turkish Government. The Turkish Government has responded to calls for these documents and has invested significant resources into cataloging 4 centuries of archives relating to the Armenians. All documents are available for review by scholars, although only documents through 1895 have so far been catalogued. This process is ongoing. I think the Turkish Government has certainly been forthcoming on this front.[17]

From now on scholars could pose sharper questions and dig deeper into newly available information to offer a discerning audience realistic pictures of the Ottoman heritage.[18] The emerging archival sources relating to the late Ottoman period were of sufficient quality and quantity to allow numerous topics in Armenian history to be explored. By inviting all scholars to peruse its archives, Turkey hoped to disarm its critics.[19]

NOTES

1. Anatolian News Agency, 2 January 1989; İsmail Cem, "Batı, Erivan, Ankara..." (West, Yerevan, Ankara...), Olayların İzinde (Tracing the Events), *Güneş*, 7 January 1989, p. 3; Ufuk Güldemir, "Ermeni Tasarısı İçin Bekleyiş" (Waiting for the Armenian Resolution), *Cumhuriyet*, 7 January 1989, p. 3; "Government Says It Will Open Archives on Armenian Killings," *The Washington Post*, 4 January 1989, p. A12; "Turkey Will Open Files on Genocide," *Chicago Sun Times*, 4 January 1989, p. A16; Clyde Haberman, "Turkey Says It Will Open Ottoman Archives on Armenians," *The New York Times*, 7 January 1989, p. A4; "Turkey to Reopen Mass Armenian Death Files," *Houston Chronicle*, 8 January 1989, p. 27A; Jane Howard, "Turkey to Open Ottoman Records," *The Guardian*, 4 January 1989, p. 9; Tim Kelsey, "Ottoman Files May Help Settle Genocide Issue," *The Independent*, 4 January 1989, p. 7; "Armenian Bill Haunts US-Turkey Ties," *Arab Times*, 4 January 1990, p. 3; "Les archives couvrant l'année 1915 seraient prochainement ouvertes," *Le Monde*, 4 January 1989, p. 3; "Génocide arménien: Ankara ouvre ses dossiers," *Le Quotidien de Paris*, 4 January 1989, p. 3.

2. Anatolian News Agency, 3 January 1989; Raşit Gürdilek, "Turkey Opens Archives to Counter Armenian Claims," *The Times*, 4 January 1989, p. 6; John Owen-Davies, "Genocide Charges Haunt Turkish-US Relations," *Arab News*, 4 January 1990, p. 3.

3. Anatolian News Agency, 3 January 1989.

4. Şinasi Orel, Başbakanlık Arşiv Araştırma Kurulu Faaliyetleri (Activities of the Prime Minister's Office Archival Research Council), 1 May 1990, Unpublished paper, pp. 11–12.

5. Sedat Ergin, "Ermeni Belgelerine Ermeni Çamuru" (Armenian Mud to Armenian Documents), *Hürriyet*, 29 June 1989, pp. 1 and 17; "ABD'de Bir Öneri Türkiye'ye Yardımı Kıs, Arşivleri İncele!" (A Proposal in the United States of America: Cut Down the Assistance to Turkey, Examine the Archives), *Cumhuriyet*, 29 June 1989, p. 1; Ufuk Güldemir, "Ermeni Tasarısı 1990'a Kaldı" (The Armenian Resolution Is Deferred to 1990), *Cumhuriyet*, 21 November 1989, p. 1; Nermin Ahmad, "Stirring Sensitivities in Turkey," *The Washington Times*, 7 November 1989, p. 11.

6. Küçük, *Başbakanlık Osmanlı Arşivi Katalogları Rehberi*, p. 352.

7. The Washington-based Institute of Turkish Studies is a registered nonprofit educational foundation, more than 95 percent of whose income derives from a trust administered by the institute. The board consists of leading United States scholars in the field of Turkish studies (Bernard Lewis was one), former United States ambassadors and business executives.

8. Turgut Özal was Deputy Prime Minister, Prime Minister, and President of Turkey between 1980 and 1993. For a most recent biography of Özal, see Hikmet Özdemir, *Turgut Özal: Biyografi* (Turgut Özal: Biography), (İstanbul: Doğan Kitapçılık, 2014). Also Osman Özsoy, *Özal'ın Misyonu* (The Mission of Özal), (İstanbul: Türdav Yayınları, 1998).

9. The full text of the Prime Minister Turgut Özal's reply to Heath Lowry is in *Armenian Allegations: Myth and Reality. A Handbook of Facts and Documents* (Washington, D. C.: The Assembly of Turkish American Associations, 1987), p. 107.

10. Anatolian News Agency, 4 January 1989.

11. Oktay Özel and Gökhan Çetinsaya, "Türkiye'de Osmanlı Tarihçiliğinin Son Çeyrek Yüzyılı: Bir Bilanço Denemesi" (The Last Quarter Century of Ottoman Historianship in Turkey: A Trial Balance Sheet), *Toplum ve Bilim*, No. 91 (2001–2002), p. 14.

12. "Osmanlı Katipleri Çok Kültürlüymüş" (The Ottoman Scribers Had Been Very Cultivated), *Türkiye*, 17 January 1989, pp. 1 and 9.

13. Congressional Record-House of Representatives, Proceedings and Debates of the 99th Congress 1st Session, Report 99–193, 9 July 1985.

14. Letter from Larry Pressler, United States Senator for South Dakota, to Turgut Özal, Prime Minister of Turkey, 26 May 1987.

15. Congressional Record-Senate, Proceedings and Debates of the 100th Congress 2nd Session, Vol.134, No.67, 13 May 1988, S 5801.

16. Congressional Record-Senate, Proceedings and Debates of the 101th Congress 2nd Session, Vol.136, No.14, 20 February 1990, S 1216.

17. Ibid., 21 February 1990, S 1321.

18. Ayşe Yazıcıoğlu, "Suraiya Farooqhi ile Mülakat" (Interview with Suraiya Farooqhi), *Toplumsal Tarih*, No. 222 (June 2012), p. 49; Ergun Göze, "Arşivden Düşünceler" (Reflections on the Archives), Köşebaşı (At the Corner), *Türkiye*, 22 May 1989, p. 3.

19. Mustafa Balbay, "Arşivleri Kim Değerlendirecek? İnalcık: Ermeni Tarihini Bizler Yazmalıyız" (Who Will Evaluate the Archives? İnalcık: It Is We Who Must Write the Armenian History), *Cumhuriyet*, 13 June 1989, pp. 13–14.

Chapter Four

The Archives and Historical Controversy

For scholars seeking to understand the early modern history of the Ottoman Empire and its successor Balkan and Middle Eastern states, information preserved in the Ottoman archives is crucially important.[1] Many of them, of course, bring different perspectives to bear which means that there will be varying view points and controversies. If this is conducted at a scholarly level it is healthy and can lead all sides to a fuller understanding of the past. But when particular views of history are used as weapons against other countries or peoples, a different and less pleasant sort of controversy arises, one with sharp political and national overtones. But this is wrong. The story of the Armenian controversy is told here to show how important it is to anchor history securely in archival documents and definite historical facts.

As will already be evident, there is an enormous amount of disagreement between present-day Turks and Armenians over the historical facts and interpretations of their recent past. The two sides disagree vehemently on many of the precise details about this controversial period. Many Turks and Armenians hold diametrically opposed views on what happened during those years. The members of foreign legislatures are to be asked then: Should your Parliament be inserting itself into such a controversial issue without hearing from independent scholars and historians? That is not the way one in those Parliaments dealt with even the least controversial of bills from other places. Should your Parliament be inserting itself into an issue between two other countries, both of which had themselves an obligation to open their archives to independent researchers to try to settle this matter? Foreign legislatures should not be taking a stand on this issue until historians, unbiased researchers and scholars have had full access to any archives that may hold documents about that time.

As a sign of the importance which Turkish scholars attached to the study of the Armenian issue, the Turkish Historical Society (THS) placed on the agenda of its quintennial congress, scheduled for 5–9 September 1990, a special panel devoted to the topic. Further, the THS invited specialists (including a number of European and American Armenian scholars) to participate as their guests in this congress. Levon Marashlian, professor of history at Glendale Community College in California, where he has been teaching courses in Armenian, Middle Eastern, Russian/Soviet, and American history and politics since 1980, was the sole Armenian scholar to accept the invitation of the THS and to appear in Ankara. His paper, "Economic and Moral Influences on US Policies toward Turkey and the Armenians, 1919–1923," was published among the congress' proceedings.[2]

Marashlian defended the views of his compatriots and the resulting Turkish-Armenian dialogue represented the first time in history that a more or less dispassionate discussion between the two major protagonists ensued. Turkish historians hoped that this would be simply the first step towards a new dialogue and debate.

DEVELOPMENTS SINCE OPENING THE ARCHIVES

In the first year of the new Archival regulations over fifty scholars applied for permission and not one was turned down. The steps Turkish government took in regard to modernizing and upgrading the archives, in conjunction with an improvement in the climate for research, served to ensure the continuation of a nucleus of foreign scholars ready and willing to engage in solid research on Ottoman-Armenian history when the relevant documents were cataloged and opened to the scholarly community. The Turkish government was doing everything it could to facilitate true scholarly research of the period around the First World War, and of the Armenian relocation specifically.[3]

Ottoman documents were like magnets, attracting increasing numbers of researchers over the years. Serious historians came to review what had been released.[4] Selim Deringil of Lebanese American University in Beirut likens the BOA to an African water hole where the most unlikely creatures come to imbibe side by side, out of sheer necessity. The BOA reading room, he says, must be the only place in the world where an American graduate student and a Japanese graduate student speak Turkish as their only common language.[5]

Deringil has published widely on aspects of Turkish and Ottoman history. He is first and foremost a man of the archives. His career began just as the Ottoman archives were fully opened to the researchers, and he is a pioneer in exploiting their riches while also supplementing them with documentation from the archives of other countries. He not only extracts factual information from these archival sources but also pays attention to the words they use and to the subtleties of diplomatics—an essential concern that enables him to enrich his analysis and avoid misinterpretations.

A certain amount of work had been done by Westerners studying the Ottoman Empire and some of their work was very good, although based on Western archives and sources. The only Ottoman evidence available to them consisted of chronicles and other literary works. The opening of the archives brought a major change in the study and understanding of Ottoman, and, more broadly, European history.[6]

Ottoman history is certainly one of the richest areas of research open to modern historians. The Ottomans, and their successors in the Republic of Turkey, carefully preserved a wealth of manuscript and archival material and a sophisticated historiographical tradition, that renders the history of the Empire, in those diverse facets of its political, economic, and cultural life accessible to scholars from many disciplines. Since the opening of the BOA to research, a small but growing number of Ottoman specialists have mined an incalculable wealth of raw data offered by innumerable official registers and have, quite understandably, focused their attention on the political and economic institutions and the demographic issues illuminated by these materials.[7]

Contrary to claims by some Armenian scholars, fresh Ottoman sources and evidence have been discovered that permit better analysis of historical issues. Many of these scholars do not bother to learn Ottoman Turkish—an extinct language that is difficult to master—to decipher Ottoman documents and understand other relevant material. Certainly opening the Ottoman archives has afforded further opportunities to distinguish propaganda from fact, myth from history.[8]

As for the oft-repeated charge by some United States senators during the debate on Senate Joint Resolution 212 on 20–22 February 1990 that "even if the Archives are opened, how are we to know that all relevant materials have been included in the cataloged sections?" The answer is simple. As noted above, most of the relevant documents are contained in bound, consecutively paginated registers. For example, each decision taken by the Council of Ministers was recorded daily in such registers. Were even a single document to be missing, a simple perusal of the page numbers would reveal that fact. In short, this allegation was nothing but a "smoke screen" advanced by the resolution's proponents.[9]

As Taner Akçam, who holds the Kaloosdian/Mugar Chair for the Study of Modern Armenian History and Armenian Genocide at Clark University, rightly points out:

> A complete purge of all potentially "damaging" archival materials [in the BOA] is virtually inconceivable [...] For a vast, multibranched, and [...] com-

> plex organization like the Ottoman Interior Ministry, with its constant, voluminous correspondence among the myriad divisions and departments of its central apparatus, as well as between the center and its dozens of provincial and subprovincial representatives, such a task would be well-nigh impossible. The redundancy inherent in bureaucratic government ensures a vast amount of duplication, copies, and returned and attached correspondence, all of which greatly decrease the likelihood that the simple removal of specific papers and documents from a single branch would solve the problem.[10]

On 16 November 1989 United States Senator Brock Adams indicated that the historical interpretation of the events in the Ottoman Empire during the early twentieth century remained the subject of considerable debate, and that the circumstances surrounding the collapse of the Ottoman Empire during the larger, more critical events of the First World War were complex. Many of the foremost experts on this period of history stated that outstanding questions must be answered before a definite response to these events should be considered. Senator Adams was of the opinion that the recent decision of Turkey to open the Ottoman archives provided an excellent opportunity for historians to conduct extensive research into this issue.[11]

While the opening of the Ottoman archives was an extremely important development, the historical debate raged on. Rapid evolution of regimes in Eastern Europe and the increasing openness of the Soviet Union encouraged further research into events of the First World War. Relevant documents from the Ottoman Empire surely existed in Bulgaria, the Soviet Union, and Syria, and other countries as well. Those governments partly followed the lead of Turkey and granted scholars the freedom they needed to resolve these important historical questions. One awaits further analyses and explorations of these valuable materials.

The massive amounts of documents already accessible force one to remain open to different interpretations. They also challenge one to put Ottoman history into its international context, so that it does not suffer as an enclave outside the more comprehensive study of international history. The archival opening, along with memoirs, the contemporary press, and other sources, have made possible the appearance of a new scholarly literature on Ottoman history.

Over the past two decades, a number of research studies have unearthed new information about important personalities, movements or fateful decisions of the past, while others offered critical new perspectives for rethinking the origins and development of the Turkish-Armenian dispute. Archive-based studies of the Ottoman past are being produced by a new generation of scholars, often contributing to revised interpretations of the development of the historical clash between Turks and Armenians.[12] Hans-Lukas Kieser, professor of modern history at the University of Zurich and president of the Research Foundation Switzerland-Turkey in Basel, notes that serious research has been done since the 1990s when Ottoman archives became increasingly accessible, and has restructured the framework of debate.[13]

Yusuf Halaçoğlu, an Ottomanist and one of the former chairmen of the THS, and Kemal Çiçek, professor of history and a specialist on Armenian affairs, have devoted considerable energy to discrediting the "new historians," while other scholars, such as Feridun Ata of Selçuk University in Konya and Bülent Bakar of Marmara University in İstanbul, have methodically incorporated the new historical challenges into their own, more nuanced interpretations of the respective Turkish and Armenian roles in perpetuating their century-old controversy. Following their original archival research and penetrating interpretations of selected episodes in the history of Turkish-Armenian relations, they have produced hefty volumes which aim to recover and present a picture of wider conflict. In the spirit of healthy historical research, the new material these publications bring to light and the new interpretations their authors offer should be duly evaluated and integrated into the corpus of ongoing archival and other research on this ever-challenging subject.[14]

The school of Turkish historiography on the question of Turkish-Armenian relations is a positive development, if the opportunities it presents are grasped by the Armenian scholarly community. However, the attitudes espoused by Richard Hovannisian, emeritus chair of modern Armenian history at the University of California at Los Angeles (UCLA), in branding any and all such attempts as "revisionism" and "genocide denial," represent a stumbling block of some magnitude. For dispassionate dialogue on this issue will not begin on a premise which states: "Certainly there can be discussion. First you accept and acknowledge the historical reality of the Armenian genocide and then we can begin to discuss why you perpetrated it." At the very least there must be a willingness to distinguish between primary and propagandistic sources for the history of the events in question, coupled with an Armenian willingness to discard the propaganda (which actually has no relevance to their case aside from its appeal in shaping non-scholarly public opinion).

The ongoing debate in Turkey has spilled out beyond the academy and into public life. Scholarly books on the subject reach wide markets; there is scarcely an issue of the weekend newspapers that does not review some Armenian-related study or other. Unfortunately, only a small fraction appears in English. Current legal controversies—the Armenian cases for compensation regarding the immovable property against Turkish Central Bank and Agricultural Bank in California and the appeal of Doğu Perinçek to the European Court of Human Rights (ECHR) in Strasbourg over his condemnation by a Swiss court because of his "denialist" statements—only add to the public debate.[15]

THE MILESTONE CASE OF PERİNÇEK V. SWITZERLAND

On 17 December 2013, the ECHR reversed the criminal conviction by the Police Court of the District of Lausanne (*Tribunal de Police de l'Arrondissement de Lausanne*) of Perinçek, who publicly challenged that Armenians were subject to genocide in the final years of the Ottoman Empire nearly a hundred years ago. The decision was by way of majority, two of the seven judges dissenting. The ECHR was set up in Strasbourg by the Council of Europe member states in 1959 to deal with alleged violations of the 1950 European Convention on Human Rights and Fundamental Freedoms. It is an international court whose decisions are binding in forty-seven countries, including all of the European Union (EU) and every North Atlantic Treaty Organization member state except the United States and Iceland. Some 800 million people are subject to its jurisdiction. It has rendered judgment in more than 10,000 cases since its founding in 1959.

Perinçek had claimed in conferences on 7 May 2005 in Lausanne, on 22 July 2005 in Opfikon, and on 18 September 2005 in Köniz that the use of the genocide label to describe the fate of the Ottoman Armenians during the First World War was incorrect. Massacres had occurred, he acknowledged, but large numbers of Turks as well as Armenians had lost their lives. The Armenians had been killed during a relocation made necessary because of their treasonous conduct in support of the Russian invaders. A criminal complaint was then filed against him by an ethnic advocacy group called "Switzerland-Armenia" in July 2005. He was questioned by the police, and the prosecutor of the district of Lausanne subsequently charged him with genocide denial in violation of Article 261bis (4) (2) of the Swiss Criminal Court.[16]

On 9 March 2007, the Police Court of the District of Lausanne found Perinçek guilty as charged. In its opinion the court noted that important legal and historical works of scholarship accepted the reality of the Armenian genocide. Various governments (including that of the Canton Vaud located in Lausanne) and international bodies such as the European Parliament also had recognized the Armenian genocide. This sufficed to show that the Armenian genocide was an established historical fact according to the Swiss public. Moreover, the court concluded, Perinçek had acted out of "racist and nationalistic motives." He had alleged an imperialist plot against Turkey and had charged the Armenians with being the aggressors against the Turkish people. Thus Perinçek's statements had fulfilled both the subjective and objective elements of the offense of genocide denial. In assessing the penalty, the court found no mitigating circumstances. On the contrary, Perinçek was an arrogant agitator who had come to Switzerland to provoke. The words "international lie" were especially violent. Judge Pierre-Henri Winzap therefore imposed a suspended jail term of ninety days and a fine of 3,000 Swiss Francs, in line with the prosecutor's request. Perinçek also was held responsible for court costs and ordered to pay a "symbolic compensation" of 1,000 Swiss Francs to the Switzerland-Armenia Association for "moral injury."[17]

Sarkis Shahinian, president of the Switzerland-Armenia Association welcomed the decision: "This verdict is very important, as it sets a legal precedent in Switzerland and also sends a signal internationally." The Turkish Ministry of Foreign Affairs reacted swiftly to the decision, saying in a statement that it was saddened by the Swiss court's ruling to punish Perinçek, and to ignore "his freedom of expression." It called into question the legitimacy of the Swiss law and said the case was "inappropriate, baseless and debatable." Ferai Tinç, a foreign affairs columnist with the Turkish newspaper *Hürriyet*, told the Swiss news agency Swisinfo that the Perinçek case had been widely followed in his country because it was the first time that a Turkish citizen had been tried and punished abroad for stating his opinions. "Whether we agree or not with Perinçek," Tinç added, "we find these types of [penal] articles against freedom of opinion dangerous because we are struggling in our country to achieve freedom of thought." Swiss Minister of Justice Christoph Blocher declined to comment on the case but expressed the view that the conviction would not lead to a serious deterioration in Swiss-Turkish relations.[18]

The holding was upheld, first, by the Criminal Cassation Division of the Vaud Cantonal Court (*Cour de cassation pénale du Tribunal cantonal du canton de Vaud*) on 13 June 2007 and, finally, by the Federal Tribunal (*Bundesgericht*), the highest court in Switzerland, on 12 December 2007. It was not the task of judges, the high court ruled, to undertake historical research. The courts could take note of the "consensus of scholarly opinion" that the events of 1915 constituted genocide. A consensus was not the same as unanimity, but it was sufficient for courts to accept the historical reality of the Armenian genocide. Perinçek, the court found, had acted out of nationalistic as well as racist motives. It therefore was unnecessary to enter the doctrinal debate as to whether a racist motive was required for a conviction under Article 261 bis (4) (2). His coming to Switzerland had been a provocative act. Perinçek's conviction contributed to the protection of the human dignity of the members of the Armenian community who define themselves by the memory of the genocide of 1915.[19]

The American political scientist and historian Guenter Lewy says the way Swiss courts have handled the matter of the racist motive in the Perinçek case is unsatisfactory. The judges have ruled that anyone who regards the relocation of the Armenian population into the interior of the country as a justified wartime security measure thereby accepts the proposition that it is acceptable to organize death marches and pursue the partial extermination of an ethnic group. Those who explain the occurrence of the relocation as a security measure therefore are considered guilty of justifying genocide, which consists precisely in seeking such partial extermination. Lewy maintains that for this linking to be valid, however, would require evidence that the Ottoman government indeed launched the relocation in order to achieve the "partial extermination" of the Ottoman-Armenian community. The existence of conclusive evidence for such an intent remains one of the key bones of contention in this historical dispute. The American scholar is convinced that only by assuming that the destructive intent of the Ottoman government is fully established can the judges in the Perinçek case rule that any defense of the relocation amounts to accepting the inherent inferiority of the Armenians—a belief that is racially discriminating and unlawful under the Swiss genocidal denial law.[20]

Georg Kreis, the president of the official Swiss Commission against Racism (*Eidgenössische Kommission gegen Rassismus*), has similarly expressed doubt that denial of the Armenian genocide is racist in character and therefore in need of legal action. Article 261bis, Kreis argues, was enacted to prevent racist defamation. An obvious example of such defamation is anti-Semitism. Yet unlike the denial of the Holocaust that nourishes anti-Semitism, denial of the Armenian genocide is not part of a racist anti-Armenian ideology. Kreis therefore questions the need to apply Article 261bis (4) (2) against denial of events that happened a hundred years ago.[21]

Perinçek eventually brought his case—*Perinçek v. Switzerland (application no. 27510/08, filed 10 June 2008)*—to the ECHR. The Turkish government exercised its right to intervene as a third party in accordance with Article 36 Subclause 1 of the European Convention on Human Rights and Fundamental Freedoms Convention, and presented its opinion to the ECHR on 15 September 2011.

The ECHR found that Perinçek had not committed an abuse of his rights within the meaning of Article 17 of the European Convention on Human Rights and Fundamental Freedoms.[22] The court took notice of the judgments of the Spanish Constitutional Court in November 2007 and of the French Constitutional Council in February 2012, both of which had rejected the imposition of criminal sanctions on persons who questioned the official recognition of genocide. The court also noted the view of the United Nations (UN) Human Rights Committee expressed in 2011 that "[l]aws that penalize[d] the expression of opinions about historical facts [were] incompatible with the obligations that the Covenant [on Civil and Political Rights] impose[d] on state parties…" and that the "Covenant [did] not permit general prohibition of expressions of an erroneous opinion or an incorrect interpretation of past events." The essential ground for Perinçek's conviction by the Police Court of the District of Lausanne was the supposed existence of a consensus—particularly within academic circles—concerning the characterization of the Armenian case as one of genocide. However, even the Swiss Federal Tribunal itself admitted that there was no unanimity in the academic community concerning the matter. The ECHR's analysis demonstrated exactly the same.[23]

The ECHR referred to the complexity of the legal debates about the definition of *genocide*. The court called genocide "a very narrow legal concept" quite "difficult to substantiate." The court added, "Mr. Perinçek had engaged in speech of a historical, legal and political nature which was part of a heated debate." It disagreed with the Lausanne district court that there was a "general consensus" on this as far as the Armenian "genocide" was concerned. It said:

> It is doubtful that there can be a 'general census,' especially scientific, on events such as those at issue here, since historical research is controversial and debatable definition does not lend itself to definitive conclusions or objective truths and absolute.[24]

In conjunction with this, the ECHR also clearly distinguished the Armenian case from the Holocaust. In cases alleging Holocaust denial, the court noted, the applicants had denied concrete historical facts, crimes perpetrated by the Nazi regime that were easily proscribed in clear legal terms, and acts that had been clearly established by an international court. The court diligently contradicted claims by Armenian groups that so-called genocide recognition was globally widespread, indicating that in reality, of the 190 countries of the world only about twenty had taken this step, and even then these often were in the form of parliamentary resolutions or the simple vote of a single chamber.

The ECHR thus upheld that freedom of expression protected minority viewpoints capable of contributing to debate on issues that were not fully settled. The court also underlined that the free exercise of the right to openly discuss questions of a sensitive and controversial nature such as the Ottoman-Armenian tragedy, was one of the fundamental aspects of freedom of expression that distinguished a tolerant and pluralistic democratic society from a totalitarian or a dictatorial regime.[25]

This is important for the United States. First, the ECHR applied a statute, the European Convention on Human Rights and Fundamental Freedoms, whose key provisions mirror the First Amendment to the United States Constitution. Second, the ECHR proved the folly of United States legislators stating with absolute certainty that they know the historical facts and legal conclusion of the ongoing, hotly debated controversy concerning the Ottoman Armenians. Third, by emphasizing the fundamental right to openly discuss and debate historical controversies, the court took a stand against what is often seen in the United States—threats, intimidation and boycotting of any scholar who may research this controversy from any viewpoint other than that acceptable to Armenian pressure groups.[26]

The verdict will also affect France, where a government-sponsored bill proposing to ban denial of the Armenian "genocide" was rejected two years ago. The judges cited a 2012 ruling by France's Nicolas Sarkozy government as "an unconstitutional violation of the right to freedom of speech and communication." According to French media, the present government is planning to resubmit the bill, in an attempt to outlaw denial of the Armenian "genocide."[27]

On 2 June 2014 the Swiss Federal Office of Justice and Police announced that Switzerland requested the ECHR have the case of Perinçek referred to the Grand Chamber for review. The question arises, were the five concurring judges right in their reasoning or is there scope to adopt the views of the two dissenting judges who voice a very different take on the interpretation conferred by the European Convention on Human Rights and Fundamental Freedoms? If the two dissenting are right then it poses this question—would imposing the Swiss sanctions constitute censorship and cause the public to refrain from criticism in debates of general interest? This is a fascinating case by any stretch of imagination. Does the judgment continue to maintain the integrity of the right to freedom of speech in a democratic society where thoughts can be debated without fear of prosecution? The issues are fundamental to the modern world and the decisions to be made by the Grand Chamber will have pivotal effects on all non-totalitarian, pluralistic, democratic societies.

THE IMPORTANCE OF STUDYING OTTOMAN DOCUMENTS

A major drawback of much that is published in the field of Ottoman history in the Western countries is that comparatively few Turkish-language sources have been used. As a result there is a natural but unfortunate tendency to absorb uncritically the assumptions about the world held at the time by British, French, German, and American officials. Not surprisingly all too many of the resulting books and theses do little more than replicate Foreign Office, Quai d'Orsay, Auswärtigen Amtes, or State Department views of the international situation at any given time.

The trouble in Ottoman studies comes from historians of non-Turkish subject peoples, including the Armenians, who fail to use Turkish sources in studying those people under Ottoman rule, resulting in serious distortions and prejudice. There are, moreover, all too many diplomatic historians who, while commendably studying all relevant documents in European and American archives regarding European diplomacy concerning the late Ottoman Empire, entirely ignore the voluminous Ottoman diplomatic documents found in the BOA. They, instead content themselves with accepting what

European diplomats assumed Ottoman attitudes, positions, and policies to have been.[28]

Only by using primary sources from Turkey can one hope to counteract this inevitable bias. So anyone interested in the Ottoman Empire's involvement in the First World War should refer to the BOA and to the ATASE.

Ottoman archival documentation constitutes an unequaled treasure trove of reliable information about how people lived from the fifteenth through the early twentieth centuries in a territory now taken up by thirty-nine nations. They offer an immense and unexplored source for the study of the political, economic, and social organization and development of those areas which were under the dominion of the Ottoman Empire during all or part of the four centuries.[29]

The Ottoman Empire, founded in 1299, played a formative role in the shaping of the Mediterranean and European cultures, civilization and political landscape; it was one of the major European powers. The Republic of Turkey was one of the states that came into being from the ashes of this liquidated empire. There were, however, significant differences between the Republic of Turkey and the other states that were created. The transition from the Ottoman Empire to the Republic of Turkey was a transition from one state to another. This occurred on the land that formerly belonged to the empire, Ottoman Anatolia and what was left of Ottoman Europe—Eastern Thrace and İstanbul.

Professor İlber Ortaylı, of Galatasaray University and former director of the Topkapı Palace Museum in İstanbul—one of the most prolific and perspicacious historians of the nineteenth-century Ottoman Empire—explains superbly how authentic sources are essential to a full understanding of Ottoman and Turkish history and the role of the Ottomans and Turks in world affairs. Ortaylı himself has played a pivotal role in accessing new source materials and suggesting ways of interpreting them. This Turkish scholar is rightly adamant that the history of the Ottoman Empire should not be written without Ottoman sources. It is difficult to imagine how a study that deals with the effects of governmental decisions on the society can avoid reference to records or publications of the government in question.[30] He is not alone on this point. His position has reinforced those of many specialists in the study of the Ottoman state and society.

Salo Baron, in his monumental *A Social and Religious History of the Jews* encompassing Jewish history from ancient to modern times, remarked in 1983:

> The Ottoman archives, both central and regional, have become an inexhaustible resource for Turkish and foreign scholars. . . . Decades of intensive research will be required to publish the more important documents and to analyze them in connection with other sources.[31]

Professor Albert Hourani, eminent British scholar of Middle Eastern affairs, wrote in 1976 and 1982 that in the last two generations, the vast store of Ottoman documents had gradually been opened to scholars, and when fully used would throw light not only on the central institutions of the empire but on all the provinces it ruled, and on all the countries with which the Ottoman sultan had dealings: eastern and central Europe, Russia, the Caucasus, and Iran. They contain information not only about the period of Ottoman rule, but about earlier periods as well.[32] When asked, during an interview with Nancy Gallagher conducted in 1988, for his advice to students considering a specialization in Middle East history, Hourani recommended: "At least some of them should learn Ottoman Turkish well and learn also how to use Ottoman documents, since the exploitation of Ottoman archives, located in Istanbul and in smaller cities and towns, is perhaps the most important task of the next generation."[33] It should be recalled that Paul Wittek and Bernard Lewis of the University of London, Franz Babinger of the University of Munich, Jean Deny of the University of Paris, and Walter Livingston Wright and his successor at Princeton, Lewis Thomas, had earlier led the way in insisting that students learn Ottoman Turkish and modern Turkish, and provided the means for this to be accomplished.[34]

In 1991 Hourani reiterated that perhaps the greatest task for that generation of Middle Eastern historians was to explore the Ottoman world. It had become possible because of the opening and exploitation of multiple relevant sources, not only the vast archives of the Ottoman central government in İstanbul, but those in provincial cities. The latter were of equal—and for some subjects even greater—importance. They are to be found wherever direct Ottoman rule existed, from Bosnia to Algiers. They include not only administrative papers, but records of the kadi (Muslim judge) courts. The kadi was not only a judge in the narrow sense, but also played an essential part in Ottoman administration and urban life. Kadi records contain not only judicial decisions, but also orders sent from the Ottoman sultan, contracts of marriage and of property sales, as well as registers of the property of deceased persons: it was a kadi's duty to make sure property was divided among heirs according to the prescriptions of Islamic law.[35]

Stanford Shaw, professor of Turkish and Judeo-Turkish history at UCLA and professor of Turkish history at Bilkent University in Ankara, said in 1989 that the essays in Braude and Lewis's *Christians and Jews in the Ottoman Empire* show very clearly that it was no longer possible to study any aspect of Ottoman society, including the different non-Muslim communities, without reference to Ottoman sources, many of which were indicated in Halil İnalcık's useful survey of "Ottoman Archival Materials on *Millets*."[36] Professor Shaw pioneered the use of the Ottoman archives in İstanbul while writing numerous books and articles on Ottoman and Turkish history and society.[37]

Daniel Goffman, professor of history at Ball State University, asserted in 2002 that the writing of Ottoman history had changed dramatically for the better in the past few decades. According to Goffman, in part, a widening access to Ottoman source materials in İstanbul, Ankara, Jerusalem, Cairo, and elsewhere, has supplemented—and in some cases supplanted—the Ottoman chronicles and western European correspondence and observations that previously had constituted the documentary backbone of our knowledge of the empire. Increasing reliance upon the views of the Ottomans about themselves in place of often hostile observers has allowed us to better imagine an Ottoman world from the inside. In addition, a growing appreciation for non-European societies and civilizations and the generation of new historical and literary analytical techniques have helped us take advantage of this plethora of documentation, while enlivening and making more sophisticated the historiography of the Ottoman world.[38]

Donald Quataert, professor of history at Binghamton State University of New York, maintained in 2006 that little of the writing about the Armenian events of 1915 had utilized Ottoman-language materials. Yet, he argued, Ottomanists had a responsibility to research these occurrences and their origins to promote a more complete understanding of them. Providing explanations of the measures taken against Armenians should be the task of historians able to read the documentary record of the Ottoman state.[39] Quataert defined Ottoman studies as the examination of the Ottoman historical record through the use of a multitude of sources, always including a significant body of Ottoman-language materials.[40]

Abraham Krikorian and Eugene Taylor aptly point out that reports or findings based on Ottoman records are sure to be important for they will, or should, give a perspective that is frequently unavailable to those who cannot read Ottoman script. According to them, serious scholars everywhere are expected to examine archival records with great care and to seek always to ferret out diverse documents which complement each other.[41] Recent scholarship has revealed more clearly than ever that "archival access and skill in reading Ottoman, elevated writing about the tragic events of the late Ottoman Empire to new levels of professional authority."[42] It is, however, curious that most of those political scholars who have been so sure and so vociferous about their propaganda have not cared to look into the Ottoman archives, not even to look for material favorable to their preconceived understanding and interpretation of the events.[43]

Garabet Moumdjian, Middle East security consultant and independent historian in Los Angeles, says that given the wealth of detail one gathers from Ottoman documents, research in the BOA, as well as in the ATASE, is truly important. He hopes that a generation of Armenian scholars with knowledge of the Ottoman language will rise to the occasion, to accomplish this task and to fully preserve the Armenian nation's memory.[44]

Şükrü Hanioğlu of Princeton University, Garrett Professor in Foreign Affairs and Professor of Near Eastern Studies, stresses that post-Ottoman developments cannot be fully understood without a solid knowledge of late Ottoman history and the use of Ottoman sources.[45] Few historians of the Ottoman Empire are as prolific in their output as Professor Hanioğlu. It is equally true that few can match his meticulous scholarship. He invariably produces books that combine sound and balanced analysis with mastery of an extensive range of primary and secondary sources.[46]

Professor Hanioğlu is a leading world authority on the period of Second Constitutionalism (1908–1918) in the Ottoman Empire. He is the recipient of several international honors and awards. He has appeared widely on television and radio. Translations of his books have been published throughout the globe.

While Western historiography still has not made much use of Turkish primary sources on the study of the Armenian question, Turkish historians have translated and utilized hundreds of Western sources in the field. In addition, a number of previously published Turkish memoirs, diaries, and compilations on the Armenian issue have been reprinted.[47]

The Ottoman Ministry of the Interior was the most important government department directing and supervising the relocation and resettlement of Armenian populations. The collection of the ministry documents covers the period from 1866 to 1922 and consists of 4,598 registers or notebooks. It is organized into twenty-one sub-collections, each according to its office of origin.[48] Among the bureaus attached to the Ministry of the Interior, the Cipher Office functioned as a separate unit. In the communications between the central administration and its various officials, telegraphic communication—and its introduction in particular of the Cipher Office—gained ever-increasing importance. The Cipher Office was generally the means by which communications between the Ministry of the Interior, its affiliated departments and offices, and the various provinces and districts, were effected. In addition to these functions, the office also acted as an intermediary bureau through which other ministries and government departments would occasionally encode their urgent or confidential communications. There are 20,640 documents that comprise the papers of the Cipher Office. In general these contain the original encoded telegrams that were sent to and by the Ministry of the Interior. At present, a 10-volume catalog of the Cipher Office documents has been prepared and made available to researchers.[49]

NOTES

1. Yusuf Sarınay, "Arap Ülkelerinin Tarihi Kaynakları Bakımından Türk Arşivlerinin Önemi" (The Importance of the Turkish Archives As Regards the Historical Sources of the Arab Countries), *Belleten*, Vol. 74, No. 4 (December 2010), pp. 673–696.

2. For more on the subject, see *XI. Türk Tarih Kongresi, Ankara 5–9 Eylül 1990. Kongreye Sunulan Bildiriler* (Eleventh Turkish Historical Congress, Ankara 5–9 September 1990. Communications Presented to the Congress), Vol. 5, (Ankara: Türk Tarih Kurumu Basımevi, 1994), pp. 1755–2139 and Yusuf Halaçoğlu, *Tarih Gelecektir* (History Is the Future), (İstanbul: Babıali Kültür Yayıncılığı, reprinted, 2011), p. 99. Papers contributed to the massive fifth volume of the Eleventh Turkish Historical Congress represented a considerable effort to bring the work of both established and young scholars to the attention of the wider academic community. The first such congress was held in Ankara in 1932, and thereafter at four-year intervals. Turkish Historical Congresses remain vibrant places where research is shared and issues are debated. Their published proceedings provide a treasure trove of invaluable information gathered from various Turkish and foreign archives.

3. Alan Fisher, "Research Access in Turkey," *The Turkish Studies Association Bulletin*, Vol. 14, No. 2 (September 1990), pp. 148–149.

4. İsa Özkul, "Osmanlı Arşivlerinin Osmanlı Coğrafyası ve Dünya Tarih Araştırmaları Bakımından Önemi" (The Importance of the Ottoman Archives Regarding Ottoman Geography and World Historical Studies), in Aköz, Ürekli and Özcan, *Uluslarası Kuruluşunun 700. Yıl Dönümünde Bütün Yönleriyle Osmanlı Devleti Kongresi, 7–9 Nisan 1999. Bildiriler*, pp. 3–4.

5. Selim Deringil, *The Ottomans, the Turks, and World Power Politics* (Istanbul: The Isis Press, 2000), p. 8.

6. Lewis, *Notes on a Century*, p. 90.

7. Cornell Fleischer, *Bureaucrat and Intellectual in the Ottoman Empire: The Historian Mustafa Ali (1541–1600)* (Princeton, NJ: Princeton University Press, 1986), p. 3.

8. For Armenian claims in this regard, see Vahakn Dadrian, "Documents of the World War I: Armenian Massacres in the Proceedings of the Turkish Military Tribunal," *International Journal of Middle East Studies*, Vol. 23, No. 4 (November 1991), pp. 549–551; idem, "Ottoman Archives and Denial of the Armenian Genocide," in Richard Hovannisian, ed., *The Armenian Genocide: History, Politics, Ethics* (New York: St. Martin's Press, 1992), p. 303; Raymond Kévorkian, *The Armenian Genocide: A Complete History* (London and New York: I. B. Tauris, 2011; French origin, 2006), p. 3; Moorad Mooradian, "Turkey's Offensive of Denial," *The Armenian Observer*, 27 April 2005, pp. 3 and 12.

9. Congressional Record-Senate, Proceedings and Debates of the 101th Congress 2nd Session, Vol. 136, No. 14, 20–22 February 1990, passim.

10. Taner Akçam, *The Young Turks' Crime Against Humanity: The Armenian Genocide and Ethnic Cleansing in the Ottoman Empire* (Princeton, NJ: Princeton University Press, 2012), p. 26. This monograph is a revised version of the Turkish-language edition that appeared in 2008.

11. Letter from Brock Adams, United States Senator, to Lawrence Stone, president of Scafco Corporation in Spokane/Washington, 16 November 1989.

12. Oktay Özel, "Bir Tarih Okuma ve Yazma Pratiği Olarak Türkiye'de Osmanlı Tarihçiliği" (Ottoman Historianship in Turkey as a Practice of Historical Reading and Writing) in Oktay Özel, ed., *Dün Sancısı Türkiye'de Geçmiş Algısı ve Akademik Tarihçilik* (Pain of Yesterday: Perception of the Past and the Academic Historianship in Turkey), (İstanbul: Tarih Vakfı Yurt Yayınları, reprinted, 2012), p. 7.

13. Margaret Lavinia Anderson, Michael Reynolds, Hans-Lukas Kieser, Peter Balakian, A. Dirk Moses and Taner Akçam, "Taner Akçam, The Young Turks' Crime Against Humanity: the Armenian Genocide and Ethnic Cleansing in the Ottoman Empire (Princeton, NJ: Princeton University Press, 2012)," *Journal of Genocide Research*, Vol. 15, No. 4 (December 2013), p. 480.

14. See Yusuf Halaçoğlu, *Ermeni Tehciri* (Armenian Relocations), (İstanbul: Babıali Kültür Yayıncılığı, 2005). The book has also appeared in English, German, and Arabic. Idem, *Sürgünden Soykırıma: Ermeni İddiaları* (From Exile to Genocide: Armenian Claims), (İstanbul: Babıali Kültür Yayıncılığı, 2006); idem, *Tarih Gelecektir*; Kemal Çiçek, *Ermenilerin Zorunlu Göçü, 1915–1917* (Relocation of the Armenians, 1915–1917), (Ankara: Türk Tarih Kurumu Basımevi, 2005). An English translation exists. Feridun Ata, *İşgal İstanbul'unda Tehcir Yargılamaları* (Trials for Relocations in Occupied İstanbul), (Ankara: Türk Tarih Kurumu Basımevi, 2005). An English translation of it will appear shortly. Idem, *Süleymaniyeli Nemrut Mustafa Paşa (Bir İşbirlikçinin Portresi)* (Nemrut Mustafa Pasha of Süleymaniye: The

Portrait of a Collaborator), (Konya: Palet Yayınları, reprinted, 2010); Bülent Bakar, *Ermeni Tehciri* (Armenian Relocations), (Ankara: Atatürk Araştırma Merkezi, 2009).

15. On the appeal of Doğu Perinçek to the ECHR, see *Perinçek-İsviçre Davası "Ermeni Soykırımı Yalanı" AİHM'de* (Perinçek-Switzerland Case: "Armenian Genocide Lie" Is in the ECHR), (İstanbul: Kaynak Yayınları, 2012).

16. Article 261bis (4) (2) of the Swiss Penal Code reads: "Any person who publicly incites hatred or discrimination against a person or a group of persons on the grounds of their race, ethnic origin or religion, any person who publicly disseminates ideologies that have as their object the systematic denigration or defamation of the members of a race, ethnic group or religion, any person who with the same objective organizes, encourages or participates in propaganda campaigns, any person who publicly denigrates or discriminates against another or a group of persons on the grounds of their race, ethnic origin or religion in a manner that violates human dignity, whether verbally, in writing or pictorially, by using gestures, through acts of aggression or by other means, or any person who on any of these grounds denies, trivializes or seeks justification for genocide or other crimes against humanity, any person who refuses to provide a service to another on the grounds of that person's race, ethnic origin or religion when that service is intended to be provided to the general public, is liable to a custodial sentence not exceeding three years or to a monetary penalty."

17. Guenter Lewy, *Outlawing Genocide Denial: The Dilemmas of Official Historical Truth* (Salt Lake City, UT: University of Utah Press, 2014), p. 84; "Swiss Convict Turkish Politician for Denying Armenian Genocide," The Associated Press, 9 March 2007.

18. Lewy, *Outlawing Genocide Denial*, pp. 84–85.

19. Ibid., p. 85.

20. Ibid., p. 88.

21. Ibid., pp. 88–89.

22. Article 17 of the European Convention on Human Rights and Fundamental Freedoms reads as: " Nothing in this Convention may be interpreted as implying for any State, group or persons any right to engage in any activity or perform any act aimed at the destruction of any of the rights and freedoms set forth herein or at their limitation to a greater extent than is provided for in the Convention." For the full text see http://conventions.coe.int/treaty/en/ treaties.html.

23. "Criminal Conviction for Denial that the Atrocities Perpetrated Against the Armenian People in 1915 and Years After Constituted Genocide Was Unjustified," Press Release Issued by the Registrar of the European Court of Human Rights. ECHR 370 (2013), 17 December 2013, p. 1. Full text of the Press Release is in Appendix 1.

24. Case of Perinçek v. Switzerland in http://hudoc.echr.coe.int//sites/eng/pages/search.aspx?i=001-139724

25. Paolo Lobba, "A European Halt to Laws Against Genocide Denial?" *European Criminal Law Review*, Vol. 4, No. 1 (2014), pp. 59–77.

26. "Major International Court Finds the Ottoman Armenian Controversy Not Settled History and Not Like the Holocaust," 17 December 2013, http://www.tc-america.org/issues-information/tca-issue.

27. Reuters, 17 December 2013; Ofert Aderet, "European Court: Denying Armenian 'Genocide' Is No Crime," *Haaretz*, 18 December 2013, p. 1; "Nier le génocide arménien n'est pas un délit, le CEDH," Reuters, 18 December 2013; Karl-Otto Sattler, "Strassbourg überrascht Freund und Feind: Menschenrechtsgerichtshof tadelt die Schweiz," *Neue Zürcher Zeitung*, 18 December 2013, pp. 1 and 9.

28. Stanford Shaw, "To the Editor," Communications, *The American Historical Review*, Vol. 90, No. 4 (October 1985), p. 1061.

29. Halil İnalcık, "Son Yıllarda Türkiye'de Kaynak Çalışmaları" (Recent Source Studies in Turkey), in *Communications Presented to the IXth International Congress of Economic and Social History of Turkey, Dubrovnik 20–23 August 2002* (Ankara: Atatürk Supreme Council for Culture, Language and History Publications of the Turkish Historical Society, 2005), p. 1.

30. İlber Ortaylı, *Osmanlı Barışı* (Pax Ottomana), (İstanbul: Timaş Yayınları, 2007), pp. 217–229; idem, *Osmanlıyı Yeniden Keşfetmek* (Rediscovering the Ottoman), (İstanbul: Timaş Yayınları, 2006), p. 184; idem, *Son İmparatorluk Osmanlı* (The Last Empire Ottoman), (İstanbul: Timaş Yayınları, 2006). On İlber Ortaylı as historian see Gökhan Çetinsaya, "İlber Ortaylı

ve Türk Modernleşmesi" (İlber Ortaylı and the Turkish Modernization), in Erol Özvar, ed., *Türk Tarihçiliğinde Dört Sima: Halil İnalcık, Halil Sahillioğlu, Mehmet Genç, İlber Ortaylı* (Four Faces in Turkish Historianship: Halil İnalcık, Halil Sahillioğlu, Mehmet Genç, İlber Ortaylı), (İstanbul: Timaş Yayınları, 2013), pp. 257–261; Yılmaz Öztuna, "Türk Tarihçiliği ve İlber Ortaylı" (Turkish Historianship and İlber Ortaylı), in Ahmet Nezihi Turan, ed., *Gezgin ve Bilgin İlber Ortaylı'yı Tanımak* (To Know the Traveler and Scholar İlber Ortaylı), (İstanbul: Paradigma Yayıncılık, 2009), pp. 3–33; Taha Akyol, "İlber Ortaylı Tarihçiliği" (The İlber Ortaylı Historianship), in Taha Akyol and İlber Ortaylı, *Osmanlı Mirası* (The Ottoman Heritage), (İstanbul: Timaş Yayınları, 2010), pp. 7–14.

31. Salo Baron, *A Social and Religious History of the Jews*, Vol. 18, (New York: Columbia University Press, 2nd rev.ed., 1983), p. 48. Salo Baron is usually considered the leading Jewish historian of the twentieth century, and, together with Heinrich Graetz and Simon Dubnow, one of the three most important Jewish historians of the modern period.

32. Albert Hourani's review of Carter Findley's *Bureucratic Reform in the Ottoman Empire: The Sublime Porte, 1789–1922* in *The Journal of Modern History*, Vol. 54, No. 1 (March 1982), p. 194; Leonard Binder, ed., *The Study of the Middle East: Research and Scholarship in the Humanities and the Social Sciences* (New York: John Wiley and Sons, Inc., 1976), p. 102.

33. Nancy Gallagher, ed., *Approaches to the History of the Middle East: Interviews with Leading Middle East Historians* (Reading: Ithaca Press, 1994), p. 43. Professor Nancy Gallagher's publication of her interviews with eight prominent Middle Eastern historians is a real service to scholarship. *Approaches to the History of the Middle East* makes an excellent companion volume to Thomas Naff, ed. and comp., *Paths to the Middle East: Ten Scholars Look Back* (Albany, New York: State University of New York Press, 1993).

34. Stanford Shaw, "Ottoman and Turkish Studies in the United States," in Kemal Karpat, ed., *The Ottoman State and Its Place in World History* (Leiden: E. J. Brill, 1974), p. 122.

35. Albert Hourani, "How Should We Write the History of the Middle East?" *International Journal of Middle East Studies*, Vol. 23, No. 2 (May 1991), pp. 129–130. Also Abdulaziz Al-Sudairi, *A Vision of the Middle East: An Intellectual Biography of Albert Hourani* (London: I. B. Tauris, 1999), p. 49. For the relevance and importance of Muslim court records see chapter nine. More about kadi see İlber Ortaylı, "Osmanlı Kadısı (Tarihi Temeli ve Yargı Görevi)" (Ottoman Kadi [Its Historical Basis and Judicial Duty]), *Ankara Üniversitesi Siyasal Bilgiler Fakültesi Dergisi*, Vol. 30, No. 1–4 (1977), pp. 117–128 and idem, *Osmanlı'yı Yeniden Keşfetmek*, pp. 127–134.

36. Stanford Shaw's review of Braude and Lewis's *Christians and Jews in the Ottoman Empire* in *The American Historical Review*, Vol. 94, No. 4 (October 1989), p. 1143.

37. Stanford Shaw's scholarship will be discussed more fully in the next chapter.

38. Daniel Goffman, *The Ottoman Empire and Early Modern Europe* (Cambridge: Cambridge University Press, 2002), p. xii.

39. Donald Quataert, "The Massacres of Ottoman Armenians and the Writing of Ottoman History," *The Journal of Interdisciplinary History*, Vol. 37, No. 2 (Autumn 2006), pp. 249–259. On Ottoman history writing, see also idem, "Ottoman History Writing at a Crossroads," in Donald Quataert and Sabri Sayarı, eds., *Turkish Studies in the United States* (Bloomington, IN: Indiana University Ottoman and Modern Turkish Studies Publications, 2003), pp. 15–30 and idem, "Recent Writings in Late Ottoman History," *International Journal of Middle East Studies*, Vol. 35, No. 1 (February 2003), p. 138.

40. Quataert, "The Massacres of Ottoman Armenians and the Writing of Ottoman History," p. 249n1.

41. Abraham Krikorian and Eugene Taylor, "Massacres Averted in Mammouret ul Aziz (Kharpert) in April 1909," Armenian News Network/Groong, 16 December 2009, p. 2.

42. Ronald Grigor Suny, "Writing Genocide:The Fate of the Ottoman Armenians," in Ronald Grigor Suny, Fatma Müge Göçek, and Norman Naimark, eds., *A Question of Genocide: Armenians and Turks at the End of the Ottoman Empire* (New York: Oxford University Press, 2011), p. 35.

43. To this effect see, for example, Vahakn Dadrian, *The History of the Armenian Genocide: Ethnic Conflict from the Balkans to Anatolia to the Caucasus* (Providence, RI: Berghahn Books, 1995); Richard Hovannisian, *The Republic of Armenia: From Versailles to London,*

1919–1920, 3 Vols., (Berkeley and Los Angeles, CA: University of California Press, 1971–1982); Kévorkian, *The Armenian Genocide*; Yves Ternon, *Enquête sur la négation d'un génocide* (Paris: Parenthèses, 1989); Patrice Bastiera, "Génocide Arménien: L'insupportable négation," *Le Méridional*, 18 March 1989, p. 3.

44. Garabet Moumdjian, "Tracing Ottoman Documents: A Letter Delivered 95 Years Late," *Journal of the Society for Armenian Studies*, Vol. 18, No. 2 (December 2009), p. 157.

45. Şükrü Hanioğlu, "Review of Sarah Shields's *Fezzes in the River: Identity Politics and European Diplomacy in the Middle East on the Eve of World War II*," in *The American Historical Review*, Vol. 117, No. 5 (December 2012), p. 1335.

46. See his latest *Atatürk: An Intellectual Biography* (Princeton, NJ: Princeton University Press, 2011). This masterful study amply merits republication in paperback. On Şükrü Hanioğlu's scholarship consult Özel and Çetinsaya, "Türkiye'de Osmanlı Tarihçiliğinin Son Çeyrek Yüzyılı: Bir Bilanço Denemesi," pp. 17–18.

47. On the last point see, for instance, Abdülgani Girici, *1920 Adana Ermeni Mezalimi Hatıraları* (Recollections of the 1920 Adana Armenian Atrocities), (Ankara: Türk Tarih Kurumu Basımevi, 2011).

48. Genç, *Başbakanlık Osmanlı Arşivi Rehberi*, p. 384.

49. Ibid., p. 375.

Chapter Five

Turkish Archives and Foreign Scholars

THE TURKISH MINISTRY OF FOREIGN AFFAIRS ARCHIVE FROM THE TWENTIETH CENTURY

The Turkish Ministry of Foreign Affairs Archive contains extensive day-to-day records of Turkey's foreign relations from 1919 until the present. In the Turkish diplomatic records there exists an extraordinary wealth of dispatches, both embassy and consular, which are highly informative and politically perceptive. These are stored in the new annex Ministry building in the Karakusunlar section of Ankara. The materials are put into folders, labeled, and placed into archival storage boxes, and a folder-level finding aid is created. Some of the recent files are held in the main building of the Ministry. The work for declassification, cataloging and digitizing the archival materials is being done in the new facility in line with the requirements of modern document management. With the progress in digitization and declassification of the records, it is expected that these materials will be completed in the next few years. The declassification review of records is going forward in accordance with the Statutes of Regulations on State Archives of 29 September 1988 and 1 February 2000. It is to be fervently hoped that these archives, which are so vital for the study of Turkish foreign policy in the twentieth century, will soon be available for scholarly inquiry.[1]

Turkey could follow the Western example and also publish volumes of selected documents on its foreign relations. Access to Turkish diplomatic documents will provide researchers with a more accurate picture of Turkey's relations with the outside world than the one they obtain from foreign sources. And that will provide them with a better perspective on the motivations and thoughts of policy makers in Ankara.

THE OTTOMAN MINISTRY OF FOREIGN AFFAIRS ARCHIVE

The archive of the Ottoman Ministry of Foreign Affairs was kept independently of the BOA and administered by the Turkish Ministry of Foreign Affairs. In 1990, it was incorporated into that of the BOA. Of the correspondence between the Ottoman Ministry of Foreign Affairs and the missions abroad and the foreign embassies in İstanbul, 95 percent is in French. For scholars who have had no Ottoman-script training, therefore, there are possibilities for benefiting from the French-language records here.[2]

These deposits date from 1835, with a smattering of items reaching back to the eighteenth century, and consist of the following main sections: political and administrative affairs, Chamber of Consultation, Correspondence Office, Translation Bureau (legal-political-miscellaneous), Balkan Wars, Great War, legal affairs, laws and regulations, mixed population exchange and miscellaneous items. Documents in the Office of Legal Advisors relate to matters pertaining to international law, while those in the Political Division contain reports written by Ottoman diplomatic officials stationed abroad and correspondence between the Ottoman Ministry of Foreign Affairs officials and foreign diplomats based in the Ottoman Empire. These confirm all other evidence that the Ottoman government kept a very watchful eye on Armenian affairs after 1878. Documents in the Division of Miscellaneous Matters contain an assortment of materials including correspondence between Ottoman and foreign officials, the awarding of ranks and awards, the appointment of Ottoman officials to positions in the Ministry of Foreign Affairs, and the arrival of foreign ambassadors to the Ottoman Empire. Few Embassy and Consulate archives were destroyed during the Balkan Wars and the First World War. It is estimated that the total number of documents, registers, books, press clippings and maps in the archive of the Ottoman Ministry of Foreign Affairs exceeds ten million. They include telegrams, letters, orders, minutes of conversations, communications, speeches, announcements, notes, conventions, agreements and treaties. Alongside original documents are drafts, random notes, envelopes, and copies. Within this huge archive lies material of great value, shedding light on the history of late period Ottoman diplomacy.[3]

RECORDS OF THE SUBLIME PORTE

Substantial documentation—including the copious correspondence between the grand vizier and the ministries, as well as the central government and the provinces beginning in 1892—is also found in the Records Office of the Sublime Porte. These are arranged in 354,000 dossiers, arranged only by ministry and date and whether they were part of incoming or outgoing correspondence, but not by subject, in some 1,000 catalogs, which must be carefully and exhaustively examined to find all relevant documents. Files often include copies of relevant correspondence, and the numbers of previous related files are usually noted on the front cover of individual drafts. Although the correspondence coming from the grand vizier was not systematically saved, the contents of messages were summarized in catalogs covering each province or ministry with the numbers of related draft files noted. Some of the documentation of the Ministries of the Interior and War are duplicated in the records of the Sublime Porte. Even to the uninitiated, the importance of these materials to determine the validity or lack thereof of the genocide charge should be apparent.[4]

Here are some of the documents in the Records Office of the Sublime Porte collection. The list in chronological order will give an idea of what there is: (1) Report from Talat Pasha proposing transportation of Armenians, their protection during journey, providing new homes, jobs, tools, etc. for them (No.326758, 26 May 1915), (2) Order from the Grand Vizier providing transportation of Armenians on the basis proposed by Talat Pasha (No. 326758, 31 May 1915), (3) Report from Talat Pasha asking appointment of investigation committees to look into allegations of mistreatment of some Armenians during the transportation (No. 328299, 28 September 1915), (4) Order from the Grand Vizier for conducting investigation in different parts of eastern Anatolia. Names of members of each committee (No. 328299, 30 September 1915), (5) Order from the Grand Vizier establishing a commission to take possession of property of transported Armenians deposit proceeds from sales in bank accounts for them (No. 328197, 28 September 1915), (6) Order from the Grand Vizier to facilitate the return of transported Armenians. Payment to them of sums of money deposited in bank accounts in their behalf (No. 340662, 2 December 1918), (7) Order from the Grand Vizier establishing court martials to investigate and try all found to have committed crimes during the war (No. 341346, 29 January 1919), (8) Formation of a committee to investigate revolutionary activities that took place during the transportation and prompted transportation of Armenians (No. 341529, 11 February 1919), (9) Payment to the Armenian patriarchate of full compensation for all church properties sold during the war, from funds deposited to its account, by law of 26 September 1915, and compensation for properties of Armenians transported to other places during the war.

Documents produced by various Ottoman authorities provide answers to many open and contentious questions, as well as confirm or trigger a reassessment of past notions regarding the Armenian issue. They provide an effective response to those who would obfuscate the truth of the events of 1915. Not much can be known about Armenians in Asia Minor in 1915 without reference to the Ottoman records, and no valid historical conclusions can be reached without consulting these. Consequently, historians must withhold judgment on the Armenian question until these are fully examined.[5] As the Australian scholar Jeremy Salt, who has done extensive research work on Ottoman Armenians, put it in 2003:

> The Ottoman archives remain largely unconsulted. When so much is missing from the fundamental source material, no historical narrative can be called complete and no conclusions can be deemed balanced. If the Ottoman sources are properly utilized, the way in which the Armenian question is understood is bound to change.[6]

Salt's opinion seems entirely sound.

ARCHIVES NOT CONSULTED BECAUSE UNAVAILABLE TO SCHOLARS

The British journalist Chris Morris wrote on 25 January 2001 that Turkey had proposed that a commission of historians should be appointed to examine all the claims over the Armenian case but added it was questionable whether that would resolve the issue. He asserted that many researchers said they had not been allowed full access to the Ottoman archives to make a proper assessment of the facts.[7]

Dorian Jones, of *The Times Higher Education Supplement*, reported on 27 April 2001 from İstanbul that academic access to Turkey's Ottoman archives, which could shed light on Armenian claims of genocide, was manipulated by the authorities. He wrote that the Turkish authorities said there were no restrictions on access to the archives and researchers could have access but statistics for access to the archives during the past decade have been disputed. Turkish associate professor Halil Berktay, of Sabancı University, said: "Those controlling the archives approach access on the basis of extremely short-sighted national interest—what is good for Turkey. They give access to those people who they see as being friends of Turkey and refuse those who they see as hostile. We know that some archives relating to the period are completely sealed off." International academics have also accused the Turkish authorities of hindering research into the dispute over the alleged genocide. Rubyn Safrasayan, director of Turkish studies at Armenia's Yerevan University, said: "Researchers have been blocked from carrying out research even after being granted permission. We have scandalous cases where authorities physically prevented and tampered with foreign researchers' findings."[8]

However scholars with a stronger background in Ottoman history have generally rejected these claims. Stanford Shaw was very puzzled by Halil Berktay's criticism of the Ottoman Archives. Perhaps Berktay had not visited them for some time. The BOA in İstanbul was in fact fully open. Since moving to its new location at Sultan Ahmet Square it has been thronged with researchers. Usually several hundred scholars, young and old, Turkish and foreign (including scholars from Armenia and Greece) were studying there at all times. To say that these were a few persons selected by the Turkish government was absurd. The only persons Shaw knew to have been excluded from the archives were a few persons who had abused the employees or who have attempted to steal documents.[9] When Shaw first came to these archives in 1961, only a few elderly gentlemen who could read the old script were employed and their cataloging went very slowly. The archives later had a large staff of catalogers, and it had made available an amazing variety of all sorts of important documents, including the files of the Ministry of the Interior and the complete archives of Sultan Abdülhamid II's Yıldız Palace, as well as large amounts of secret correspondence stemming from the Young Turk period. There might be documents that had not been made available. Shaw did not know. But he has been able to see every document he has asked for in some forty years of doing research in these archives, and most others he knew have had the same experience. On the other hand, when he studied in the archives of the French Ministry of Foreign Affairs at the Quai d'Orsay in Paris, almost all the materials he wished to examine concerning French and Nazi persecution of Jews in Nazi-occupied France were "not available." When Shaw sought to study the archives of the British occupation of İstanbul following the First World War, he was told that these also were "not available," and the Official Secrets Act of 1967 prevented all researchers from examining the records of the British intelligence services in the Ottoman Empire during and after the First World War.[10] Why, moreover, have we not heard more about the availability of the archives of the Republic of Armenia in Yerevan and of the Armenian nationalist Dashnak archives held at the Zoryan Institute in Boston which are still closed to researchers?[11]

Ervand Abrahamian of City University of New York claimed in December 2002 that any topic related to Armenians remains taboo for the guardians of the Ottoman files.[12] It is somewhat amazing that the eminent Swiss historian Christian Gerlach, in one of his books also refers to the "inaccessibility of Ottoman files" and asserts that "permissions given [for access to Turkish archives] are erratic, far from all records are available to researchers, and some scholars may be allowed to see more than others."[13] More recently Artyom Tonoyan of East View Information Services contends that for the past several decades countless foreign scholars were either barred from working with the Ottoman archives or obstructed in the process.[14]

This is certainly not the case. Any scholar is indisputably allowed to study unfettered in the BOA.[15] Britain and almost all western governments keep some national archives permanently closed. Despite considerable practical constraints, Turkey has done its best to open its archives to researchers from all countries, including to the British Armenian Ara Sarafian, whom it knew to be opposed to it. As early as April 1979 Alan Fisher of Michigan State University offered a factual correction to Richard Dekmejian's review of Dickran Boyajian's *Armenia: The Case for a Forgotten Genocide*, which appeared in Vol. 81, No. 4 (October 1976), pp. 916–917 of *The American Historical Review*. The "relevant sections of the Ottoman Archives of Istanbul" were not closed for foreign scholars who were able to read the language of the documents, Ottoman Turkish, nor had they ever been closed to qualified scholars since the administrative changes in the archives after 1961. Indeed, Fisher added, one American scholar had recently received permission to use these very sources about Ottoman Armenia.[16]

Between 1921 and December 2000, 3,040 researchers from 78 countries consulted the BOA. And between 1995 and 2000, about 180 foreign researchers used the BOA each year. Ever since the late 1980s, when virtually all the Ottoman state papers housed in the BOA became readily available to Turks and foreigners alike, historians, who deal with Ottoman-related topics, no longer can claim inaccessibility as a legitimate reason for failing to use these repositories.

APPLICATION FORMALITIES AND WORKING CONDITIONS GREATLY EASED

Previous generations of foreign researchers had to request their own Embassy to submit for them an application to the Turkish Ministry of Foreign Affairs in Ankara, stating the applicant's credentials and qualifications, the exact subject of research, and, if desired, a request for permission to photograph archival materials pertaining to the research subject.[17] This long and cumbersome procedure of the past years to secure permission to enter the archives has been replaced with a new and simple formality. Foreign scholars do not need to apply through embassies months ahead of time in order to obtain permission. The application is submitted directly to the DGSA in İstanbul and permission is usually granted within a few hours. The usual admission formalities take place at the entrance. All documents open for inspection may be reproduced.[18]

Laptop computers and dictionaries are permitted in the reading room. The BOA provides extensive logistical support in accessing and photocopying documents. Self-service photocopying, usually using a prepaid card or ticket system, is available. The price per photocopy is approximately ten United States cents per page. The photocopying of older material may not be permitted or may be done only by the staff in a photographic or document delivery department. Copies of some types of documents are also available for purchase on CD-ROM. On 2 June 2013 the BOA moved to its new facilities in the Kağıthane area of İstanbul, providing visitors a much larger public research room with more researcher stations that accommodate laptops, scanners, and other equipment.[19]

No additional fees beyond those for copying are required, even for publication of rights, because all government documents are considered legally in the public domain and hence freely accessible by all with copyright restrictions. The BOA also has no limits on the percentage of a *fond* or file that may be copied. There are no charges for readers' passes in archives in Turkey.

RECRUITMENT AND TRAINING OF NEW ARCHIVISTS

The declassification and cataloging of the old Ottoman documents has been greatly accelerated thanks to the recruitment and training of an army of archivists since 1985 under the direction of İsmet Miroğlu. After being made Director General of State Archives, Miroğlu assembled a team of over 100 archivists to analyze and catalog the boxes, bags, and stacks of ledgers, decrees, and surveys. Turkish universities have even created courses to train historians and other specialists to assist with this monumental task. The Turkish government began to spend large amounts of money on hiring staff and buying equipment to make four centuries' worth of documents accessible to researchers. At the end 1989 there were approximately 350 trained archivists—as compared to 18 or 20 before 1985—sorting and declassifying the vast array of documents that had lain in various warehouses untouched for centuries.[20]

Former Minister of National Education and historian Şinasi Orel mentions that while the archival staff in the BOA was confined to 54 in 1980, this number reached 507 after a decade.[21] It should be noted parenthetically that Hasan Celal Güzel, former Under Secretary of the Prime Minister's Office, State Minister and the Minister of National Education under Turgut Özal in mid-1980s, remembers that there were only six or seven archivists working in the BOA in 1984.[22]

By 1999 the cataloging of the BOA advanced rapidly, and various instructive library catalogs have appeared, both in Turkey and abroad. Archivists have accelerated declassifying materials and making previously closed collections available to domestic and foreign scholars. Within a relatively short time, researchers gained access to enormous resources. As a result of the availability of new archival materials, the nature of scholarship on the Balkan and Middle Eastern countries has undergone dramatic changes. On the basis of this source material it has become possible to question, thoroughly revise, and at times totally abandon, the conventional images of Ottoman history which populated the secondary literature as little as thirty years ago.[23]

Archivists in the BOA are trained partly through absorbing the necessary skills of reading and understanding historical documents, principles of archive administration and the history of the public records, and partly through brief practical detachments to the various curatorial and administrative sections of the office. What they do is vitally important to historians, not to mention genealogists, government researchers, and others.[24]

Scores of experts pore through sheaves of centuries-old documents of the imperial Ottoman state. As more records were opened to public scrutiny, and more historians made use of them, the BOA was forced to expand, and the principle of provenance and the maintenance of original order were overwhelmingly accepted as the foundational principles of the Turkish archival profession.[25]

PROVENANCE AND MAINTENANCE OF ORDER

Reliance on provenance assumes that records result from organized purposeful activity and that they were created organically and have a relationship to one another. It further assumes that important information can be derived from examining the records in the context of their creation and their relationship. It keeps related groups of records intact, enabling a review of them in their totality. The second principle, the maintenance of original order, is basically an elaboration of the first one. In addition to considering their origin, it touches on the general order of records and holds that records should be kept in the order in which they were first created or that which was imposed on them by the person, organization, or institution that created them. It posits that all individual records are part of a larger series. Undoubtedly, this is the only order that might allow historians to retrieve the original context of an action. Thus the BOA, corresponding with these two principles, facilitates the appreciation of a document in the most comprehensive way, enabling a researcher to know exactly where it was created, in the framework of what process, to what end, for whom, as well as when and how it came to the archivists' hands.[26]

Documents are categorized and filed by the government agency—Prime Minister's Office DGSA Department of Ottoman Records—that originally created them, forcing researchers to divine decades-old record-keeping systems. Dozens of specialists a day make relentless demands for documents, often the same documents at the same time. At the peak summer period the floor staff at Kağıthane take out and put back around 1,000 documents a day, trundling along those vast corridors anything from precious medieval charters to the census returns of the nineteenth century. Amid these mountains of files within which historic reality is buried, the archivists function as guides to the information researchers need.

The post-Second World War period saw a cascade of scholarly research in the Ottoman archives, mostly by Turkish scholars, including the multivolume *Osmanlı Tarihi* (1941–1983) written by İsmail Hakkı Uzunçarşılı and Enver Ziya Karal. An important resource available to the researcher was the expertise of staff in the BOA. They all were knowledgeable about the holdings of the office and about the systems. They could not undertake research on behalf of others but they could advise on possible sources for a research topic. In the BOA, the archivists were often established authorities in their own right and could provide specialist subject advice to other researchers.

By the 1950s some foreign scholars were admitted to do research in the Ottoman archives. Albertine Jwaideh worked in the Ottoman archives, and some parts of his findings on Iraqi land were published in a series of studies.[27] Uriel Heyd was allowed to study in and order photographs from the Prime Minister's Office Archive. He grasped the thread that would thereafter guide students of Jewish history through the maze of Ottoman diplomatics. He drew attention to the *Cizye Defterleri*, which, as their name indicates, deal primarily with the poll tax paid by non-Muslims, but they also shed light on other forms of taxation, as well as on wider demographic and economic issues. Heyd expressed his sincere gratitude to the director and staff of the institution for their friendly cooperation, and especially Midhat Sertoğlu for his kind help in deciphering difficult passages in the documents.[28] Roderic Davison was able to do so on a number of occasions.[29] The studies of Amnon Cohen and Haim Gerber are based on Ottoman government documents such as edicts and instructions, writs of appointment, replies to petitions, writs granting rights, land registrations, censuses, and tax registers.[30]

Philip Stoddard labored in the Ottoman archives in the 1950s to lay bare Enver Pasha's Special Organization. Carter Findley deeply enriched Ottoman studies with his subsequently published Harvard doctoral dissertation on the Ottoman bureaucracy in 1969, based on extensive research in the Ottoman archives. In 1973 Barbara Jelavich of Indiana University thanked the Turkish Ministry of Foreign Affairs for permission to use the Ottoman archives and to Turgut Işıksal and Kamil Ayhan for their assistance with this material.[31] In 1979 Rhoads Murphey of the University of Chicago expressed his thanks to the BOA for permission to carry out his research in Turkey, and for courtesy shown to him during his various visits to the successive directors of the BOA, Midhat Sertoğlu and Feyyaz Gürkan as well as to all the staff of the reading room. Without their help, he said, completion of his doctoral thesis would have been impossible. Heath Lowry, Herbert Bodman, Timothy Childs, Mark Epstein, Ronald Carlton Jennings Jr., Vincent Illardi, Robert Olson, Donald Quartaert, Rudi Linder, James Maccaferri, Raymond Neilly, David Thomas, Carl Petry, J. C. Hurewitz, Tibor Halasi Kun, Howard Crane and David Cox all put the archives in good use.[32]

BERNARD LEWIS'S WORK IN THE OTTOMAN ARCHIVES

Bernard Lewis was one of the first Western scholars to use the Ottoman archives. "Feeling rather like a child turned loose in a toy shop or like an intruder in Ali Baba's cave, I hardly knew where to turn first," he said.[33] Lewis began to work in them as early as 1949 and after two years was able to provide the most detailed and accurate survey of these archives and their contents having himself made the best possible use of them. He systematically examined part of the Prime Minister's Office Archive with the specific aim of reaching general conclusions based on a wide perusal of the documents. He thereby also provided other scholars with guidelines for further research.[34] The Ottoman Archives were a congenial place in which to work, and scholars were fortunate that at that time Midhat Sertoğlu, director of the Prime Minister's Office Archive, acted as a presiding genius and help to researchers. Many historians were in his debt, not least for the way in which he was able to catalog into a manageable form the vast complexities of the Ottoman archives, upon which many books were based.[35] Lewis wrote in 1954:

> It is my pleasant duty to record my thanks to the office of the Turkish Prime Minister for giving me access to the state archives in Istanbul; to the Director and staff of the archives, and especially Midhat Sertoğlu of the General Directorate, for their unfailing courtesy and co-operation and to Professor Tayyib Okiç of the Faculty of Divinity of the University of Ankara, who first initiated me into the mysteries of Siyaqat and was always ready at hand with assistance and advice during my work in the archives.[36]

Lewis belonged to the first generation of Ottoman historians in Britain who regularly traveled across the Continent to conduct archival research in İstanbul. Born in 1916, he has a long career behind him as an expert on Turkish language and history. Lewis was educated in the Ecole nationale des langues orientales in Paris, where he earned his bachelor's in linguistics and history. He has published several general works on history, religion, and philosophy and a host of more specialized studies on Turkish etymology and grammar. Almost all of his books are translated into Turkish, and he is one of the few historians of the Ottoman Empire working in the United States whose influence on the Turkish scholarly world is commensurate with his influence in the United States. He remembers when he first worked in the BOA, the archival staff, though small, was remarkably good. To paraphrase him,

> they were dedicated professionals, with, a real commitment to history and the search for truth, and a real understanding of what scholarship was about and

> what scholars were trying to accomplish. Researchers who came to the archives, from Turkey and abroad, were welcomed as colleagues, and often became friends.[37]

Lewis says Ottoman archivists at İstanbul are ready at hand with assistance and advice and gives credit to them by noting that:

> the Ottoman archives are in the care of a competent and devoted staff who are always willing to place their time and knowledge at the disposal of the visiting scholar, with a personal helpfulness and courtesy that will surprise those with purely Western experience. They are open to all who can read them.[38]

Other sources supply supporting evidence.

The American historian William Griswold agreed with Lewis that working in the Ottoman archives is comfortable and convenient and that the archivists are friendly, helpful and anxious to serve. Griswold elaborates:

> As one works with the civil servants in charge of the Reading Room, and meets the likeable old men who labor in the inner areas of the archives, he begins to sense a spirit of devotion to a calling, a true vocation. They work with love and respect for the papers which pass through their hands. . . . How delighted they are to pass on their knowledge to anyone interested, be he foreigner or native Turk.[39]

During the year of his sabbatical leave in Turkey (1966–1967), Carl Max Kortepeter had pursued research in the Archives of the Prime Ministry which were then under the direction of Midhat Sertoğlu and his able assistants, Rauf Tunçay and Turgut Işıksal.[40] Their distinguished careers as archivists spanned four decades and involved administration, research, and teaching. In the 1970s Suraiya Faroqhi felt obliged to Rauf Tunçay and Fazıl Işıközlü for their help in deciphering the old script.[41] İlber Ortaylı recounts that in the BOA in 1972 Rauf Beygu and Turgut Işıksal, the two very knowledgeable archivists, served the readers ably by providing expert guidance.[42] In 1973–1974, Hayri Mutluçağ initiated Engin Deniz Akarlı into the labyrinth of nineteenth-century Ottoman documents. A senior archivist at the BOA, Mutluçağ worked as a cataloger of the records and as a research advisor for many years. Akarlı owed him a special debt of gratitude.[43] Cemal Kafadar concurred with them.[44]

STANFORD SHAW'S WORK IN THE OTTOMAN ARCHIVES

Referring to the Turkish archival staff in İstanbul, Stanford Shaw wrote that their genuine interest in easing the task of the researcher greatly facilitates the work of the serious scholar, and there are few, indeed, who return from their inquiry without tremendous gratitude for the efforts of the Turkish archivists.[45] Shaw further contended that the main problem remaining to researchers on Ottoman history now was to go through and consult the immense volume of materials being made available to them. In Shaw's view, there could no longer be any excuse for a scholar investigating any subject pertaining to the Ottoman Empire—even involving relations between it and the Great Powers or matters concerning the various nationalist revolts that inflamed the empire during its last century—not taking the time required to examine the sources accessible in the Ottoman archives in İstanbul.[46]

Shaw was an indefatigable searcher of archives. His research benefited from extensive use of documents available at the BOA since 1956. *The Financial and Administrative Organization and Development of Ottoman Egypt, 1517–1798* was the first effort to use the records in İstanbul concerning an individual Ottoman province, organize them in logical form and place them at the disposal of the historian. This was a pioneering work based on all the available records in the Ottoman archives in İstanbul and Cairo, in public libraries in Turkey, Egypt, Britain, and France, and on published materials on Ottoman Egypt in several languages, all of which made up an impressive bibliography.[47] Following the completion of his degree at Princeton, Shaw joined the Near Eastern Languages (and later the History) department at Harvard in 1958, where he began offering regular courses in Ottoman History and Ottoman and Modern Turkish. During his tenure at Harvard, he, in addition to his own teaching and research, devoted a great deal of time to building up the university library holdings in Ottoman and Turkish studies. It was largely through his efforts, that Harvard's collection achieved the eminence that it still enjoys today. American historians who worked with Shaw at the UCLA, such as Heath Lowry and Justin McCarthy, greatly appreciated his skills in reading and understanding the Ottoman source material and seem to have learned much from him.[48]

International Journal of Middle East Studies, published by Cambridge University Press on behalf of the Middle East Studies Association of North America and the British Society for Middle East Studies, which Shaw edited from its inception in 1970 until the end of 1979, provided a vehicle for the publication of new research into Ottoman, Turkish, and other Middle Eastern archives and sources as well as suitable reviews of new books relating to the area. In short, Shaw's numerous contributions to scholarship, to the scholarly community, and to furthering Ottoman studies counted much.

It must be noted that no arrests were made in 1977 firebombing of the home of Shaw in Los Angeles. Shaw, his wife and daughter were sleeping in their suburban home in Los Angeles at 4 am, 3 October 1977, when a bomb blew up the front of the house. Arriving several hours later at his seminar on Turkish history at the UCLA, he learned that a release in Paris from an

Armenian terrorist group had announced his assassination. Very much to his surprise, he had become the first American to be targeted by an obscure but deadly campaign of international terror—a crusade to avenge the killings of Armenians in the Ottoman Empire during the First World War. Shaw stopped teaching and left town with his Turkish wife, Ezel Kural Shaw, who taught history at California State University, Northridge, shortly after campus police were warned that a "Turkish professor" might become a target.[49]

A longstanding dispute between Shaw and Richard Hovannisian of the UCLA, a historian of Armenian extraction, over the events of 1915 distilled the academic controversy over the incident. In his *History of the Ottoman Empire and Modern Turkey*, which he wrote with his wife, Shaw argued that the Ottoman government orders for the 1915 relocation called for a humane evacuation of the Armenians rather than the wholesale deaths that actually occurred. He said the usual Armenian estimate of more than one million Armenians killed in the massacre is inflated because the Ottoman census showed only 1.3 million Armenians in the whole country and only half of them living in areas affected by the relocations. Estimating that about 700,000 fled the country, the Shaws suggested that about 300,000 died. But they added that their search of Ottoman records revealed no evidence of a planned policy of genocide.[50]

In 2000 Shaw's particular appreciation went to the archivists and librarians who assisted his research in Turkey over the years: in İstanbul at the BOA, directors Midhat Sertoğlu and Yusuf Halaçoğlu; among the BOA staff members Ziya Eşrefoğlu, who, with great patience, taught him how to read the various Ottoman scripts, as well as Turgut Işıksal and Rauf Tunçay; at the Topkapı Palace Archive, directors Haluk Şehsuvaroğlu, Hayrullah Örs and Ahmet Menteş and the Turkish historian İsmail Hakkı Uzunçarşılı, who made available to him the new catalog he was compiling of the materials in the Palace archive; the director of the İstanbul University Library for many years, Nurettin Kalkandelen, son of Sultan Abdülhamid II's librarian, who came to İstanbul University with the Yıldız Palace Library and lived in the library building until his death; Fehmi Ethem Karatay, who compiled the principal catalogs of the Yıldız Palace Library's printed and manuscript collections; and the librarians and staff of the Atatürk Municipal Library, who made available to him its rich collection of Ottoman and Turkish newspapers. In Ankara Shaw expressed his gratitude to the Director General of State Archives from 1987 to 1997, İsmet Binark,[51] who brought the level of Turkish archival work to a high standard of professionalism at the Republican Archive (RA); also the directors and staff of the ATASE, in particular Hüseyin Görür, Cemalettin Taşkıran and Hamit Pehlivanlı; the Institute for the Study of the History of the Turkish Revolution; successive Secretaries General of the THS, Uluğ İğdemir and Yaşar Yücel and the director Yusuf Halaçoğlu, who made available to him the manuscript and photograph materials in the THS's archive and library; and the founder of the National Library (NL), Adnan Ötüken, who was his first guide to studying in Turkish libraries.[52]

SOME DISTINGUISHED TURKISH HISTORIANS

On 17 May 1985, a symposium was held at the Faculty of Letters of the İstanbul University on Ottoman archives and research. Its wide audience included the Prime Minister Turgut Özal, the State Ministers Mesut Yılmaz and Kazım Oksay, and the Under Secretary of the Prime Minister's Office Hasan Celal Güzel. In his opening remarks, Özal stressed the significance of the Ottoman archives, both to the government and to scholars, pointed out some of its problems that required immediate attention, and assured the participants that they could rely on his continued interest in its development. A collection of the papers presented was subsequently published, which emphasized the importance of archival holdings and the importance of the Ottoman archives for historical research.[53] On that instance, together with Halil İnalcık, Kemal Karpat, İhsan Doğramacı and İlber Ortaylı, Stanford Shaw encouraged the Turkish government to expand access to the archives by hiring additional staff to catalog the massive collection of documents.[54] İnalcık said:

> For years I have been emphasizing the importance of the Turkish archives, their scholarly declassification, their full openness to research, to scholars. I have called for opening all archives dealing with the Armenian issue also. Let the truth come forward, no one can oppose the documents.[55]

İnalcık, the generally acknowledged dean of Turkish historians—who has had a profound impact on Ottoman historiography, both in Turkey and the West, with a series of path-breaking studies, exploratory articles, and penetrating reviews—assessed the BOA in 1993:

> At the present time the Ottoman archives in Istanbul are on the way to becoming an international center for scholarly research on a par with the London and Paris archives. Hundreds of cataloguing personnel are now working to classify the millions of documents preserved at the archives, and for the first time a trained cadre of archivists is now in place in Turkey. If we recollect that from the ruins of the Ottoman Empire there emerged more than twenty independent nations, the need for historians from these countries to turn to the Ottoman archives for the illumination of their own historical past is obvious.[56]

In an interview with Madeline Zilfi, editor of *The Turkish Studies Association Bulletin*, in the fall of 1993 in Chicago, İnalcık stated:

> Serious historical study requires first the expertise to interpret the historical sources. It is a healthy development that more and more historians of the young generation are now choosing research in the Ottoman archives. . . . It has to be said that Ottoman studies in the West have been the object of growing interest in the last two decades, thanks to the use of the Ottoman archives in İstanbul. . . .To abstract and exaggerate just one aspect of social-historical reality can only provide a distorted picture of the past. I believe it is time for history to go back to honest interpretation and hermeneutical methods. This is particularly crucial in our field of Ottoman studies, where there are such rich stores of source material still untouched. When you work in the Ottoman archives you are surprised to find so many fascinating aspects of Ottoman reality which enable you to interpret and understand the Ottoman past in a much more convincing way than theoretical sociological models.[57]

Like most Ottomanists, Zilfi owed a special debt to Professor İnalcık, whose path-breaking research on Ottoman society led her to undertake her study *The Politics of Piety*.[58] The American historian James Reid said: "Professor Inalcik is a moderate whose historical approach to Ottoman history must be hailed as a breakthrough. He gives an excellent and impartial account of this practice."[59] In fact, the rigorous studies of İnalcık and some of his Turkish contemporaries laid the foundations for modern Ottoman studies. İnalcık has made ongoing contributions to the thinking of many either personally or in his scholarly writings. His scholarly works and personal insights have inspired a whole generation of students in the field of Ottoman history.

Through his publications, his presentations at international conferences, and his teaching, which won him disciples not only in Turkey but elsewhere in the world, İnalcık established himself as one of the world's top experts in Ottoman history and, in Turkey, as the leader of this field.

VIEWS OF INTERNATIONAL SCHOLARS ON THE OTTOMAN ARCHIVAL SERVICES TODAY

Turkish archivists continue to provide assistance and information to researchers who have traveled to İstanbul to consult documents available nowhere else in the world. Daniel Goffman, a historian specializing in the eighteenth-century Ottoman Empire and author of two major books on the subject, pointed out in 1998: "In Istanbul the personnel of Başbakanlık Osmanlı Arşivi [Prime Minister's Office Ottoman Archive], in which are housed most documents generated by the Ottoman bureaucracy, courteously responded to my many requests and helped me through that facility's tortuous catalogs."[60] After four years the American scholar added that one of the principal repositories he had made use of in his research projects was the Ottoman archives and that the staff of this facility was knowledgeable and exceptionally gracious. They had his profound thanks. For his books, he dug deeply into the rich troves of Ottoman records.[61]

Knowledge of Ottoman Turkish gives Goffman first-hand access to the historical sources. The evidence he musters to test his contentions is derived mainly from Ottoman archival sources. Like everyone who has worked with the BOA, Goffman is finding his task larger than he anticipated.

Bruce Masters, professor of history at Wesleyan University and a specialist responding to fresh evidence from Ottoman archives, gives credit where it is due. He noted in 2001 that one of the places where the research for his *Christians and Jews in the Ottoman Arab World: The Roots of Sectarianism* was primarily conducted was the BOA and he thanked the staff of this institution for their help.[62] Masters had also thanked in 1992 "the staff of the Başbakanlık Arşivi in Istanbul for their help and assistance." He used Ottoman archival documents to explain Ottoman views and actions.[63]

Hayashi Kayoko of Tokyo University of Foreign Studies expressed in 2004 his gratitude to the director and staff of the BOA in İstanbul for giving him full facilities for research.[64] The collection of essays in *The Ottoman State and Societies in Change: A Study of the Nineteenth Century Temettuat Registers* represents the outcome of several years of patient archival excavation of a whole range of largely untouched—if not unknown—documentary sources.

The Ottoman archives proved to be an invaluable source for the studies of George Gawrych, associate professor of history at Baylor University. In his balanced and original picture of Ottoman rule and the Albanians during a critical period of Balkan and Middle East history, *The Crescent and the Eagle*, he mentioned in 2006 that the officials at the BOA, the NL in Ankara, the Atatürk Library in İstanbul, and the Library of the Turkish Grand National Assembly (TGNA) in Ankara were professional and most helpful in facilitating his research in Turkey.[65] Gawrych's book is indeed a contribution in that he has gathered and assessed an enormous volume of source material which, while often assumed, had not hitherto been historically evaluated.

In point of fact, Taner Akçam conceded in 2006 that working conditions in the BOA have improved enormously in the past few years. Akçam thanks the staff, and especially Deputy Director General of State Archives, Associate Professor Mustafa Budak, for their generous help and openness during his last visit. He comments that this is a very hopeful development, and all scholars interested in the period should use this new opportunity to examine these materials.[66] Together with Vahakn Dadrian he acknowledged in 2011 what he said earlier: "Several recent, very positive changes in the procedures of this archive have met with appreciation from local as well as foreign researchers."[67] Again he wrote in 2012: "During my 2006 visit, I experienced nothing but courtesy and an effort to facilitate my work, and I would like to express my debt of gratitude to the entire archival staff and, in particular, to Mustafa Budak."[68]

Ryan Gingeras, assistant professor of history at Long Island University, who delves deep into Turkish history on the basis of the Ottoman archives, remarks:

> Yes, archivists, scholars, and staff I met in Istanbul and Ankara were indeed helpful, courteous, and, at times, a real pleasure to be around. The sheer mention of my interest in Muslim immigrants in Anatolia was greeted with sincere enthusiasm and support by the archivists who helped make my research possible . . . . I have nothing but thanks and kind words for the staff of the Ottoman and Republican archives in Istanbul and Ankara.[69]

Roberto Mazza, assistant professor of history in Western Illinois University, felt the need to thank staff of the Ottoman archives who helped him to find what he was looking for and who always offered him their hospitality. Mazza also conveyed his gratitude to the personnel of the libraries in İstanbul. *Jerusalem: From the Ottomans to the British* is partly based on documents in the BOA, many of which have not been previously published. This extra material allows one to see the development of Ottoman policy at closer hand though there is still much that remains unexplored.[70]

As German historian Hilmar Kaiser—a frequent visitor to Turkey—spoke tellingly in the spring of 2009: "In recent years Ottoman archives are world class in terms of service and are open to all interested experts." Kaiser also mentioned the full and unhindered cooperation of the BOA staff. He credits numerous archivists and colleagues with aiding his investigations.[71] Kaiser's knowledge of many languages has been instrumental in his research and has allowed him to perform extensive work in historical archives from various countries.

Like many other researchers in the complex and voluminous records of the Ottoman Empire, Orlando Figes, professor of history at Birkbeck College of University of London, has benefited immensely from the knowledge and experience of archivists at the BOA. He was helped by Murat Siviloğlu and Melek Maksudoğlu in the research for his book on the Crimean War of 1853–1856, in 2010 in the BOA.[72]

During his time in the field as a research fellow in İstanbul, Giancarlo Casale, Assistant Professor of the Islamic World and the 2009–2011 McKnight Land Grant Professor at the University of Minnesota, was fortunate to benefit from the guidance of many selfless archivists and librarians, particularly Ahmet Kılıç of the BOA, Gülendam Nakipoğlu and Zeynep Çelik of Topkapı Palace Library, Ülkü Altındağ of the Topkapı Palace Archive, and Havva Koç at the İstanbul Archaeology Museum, as well as the entire staff of Süleymaniye Library. Casale emphasized that the Ottoman archival documents were very rich for the second half of the sixteenth century, and in his *The Ottoman Age of Exploration*, he made particularly heavy use of the *Mühimme Defterleri* collection in the BOA. He pointed out that these "Registers of Important Affairs" were essentially day-to-day, verbatim records of the sultan's outgoing correspondence with their own provincial officials, as well as with visiting dignitaries from abroad and with foreign heads of state. Most remained unpublished, he continued, but they were well cataloged and relatively complete from the mid-1560s, and even from this date, they survived in fragmentary form. When available, the American historian also made generous use of the sultan's incoming correspondence. Of the documents still extant, some were housed in the archive of the Topkapı Palace Museum; others, especially the sultan's epistolary exchanges with foreign leaders, were preserved in bound volumes of hand-copied letters known as *münşeatnames*, today scattered in a number of different manuscript collections.[73]

Illustrative quotations could be multiplied. The experiences of all these scholars may serve as instructive examples of benefits that researchers receive when gaining access to the BOA. The Turkish archivists make clear the current commitment to a modern archive, in which ease of access (using the latest technical finding aids) and open entry to all files can be guaranteed.

It is clear that research opportunities in the BOA are as good and as varied those in most archives around the world. The massive documentation that is available between 1453 and 1922 is a challenge as well as an opportunity for historians that cannot be ignored. To meet the challenge and take advantage of the opportunity will require a good knowledge of resources, a great deal of persistence, and a lot of imagination—but that it will be worth it, there can be no doubt.

MUSTAFA BUDAK

At present, the BOA is directed by Associate Professor Mustafa Budak, while the daily work of supervision and research assistance is carried out by his specialists. Anyone who has had cause to work in the BOA is likely to owe a debt of gratitude to Budak, the genial figure who for years has presided over those archives. He is the man to consult for scholarly advice, for the most effective ways to move bureaucratic mountains or for another delightful anecdote about this or that figure in the Turkish establishment. An archivist and highly productive academic historian, Budak has known them all. His training in İstanbul perhaps encouraged him to be a very open person in a world too often closed by a narrow definition of *raison d'état*. He has been particularly active in building up scholarly contacts outside Turkey, with Britain, France, Germany and the Russian Federation, and even with Libya and Australia. Budak's published output is vast and has addressed, over the decades, a variety of subjects.[74]

Western scholarship is today at work "rediscovering" the Ottoman archives. Scholars have in the past two decades converged on İstanbul in ever growing numbers to mine the archival treasures hidden away there. Many historians from former Ottoman possessions in southeastern Europe, Asia, and North Africa are working there. Contemporary affairs in the Middle East continue to heighten the significance of Ottoman studies. Bernard Lewis wrote in the summer of 1990: "One can only hope that others will follow the Turkish example."[75]

NOTES

1. *Türkiye Cumhuriyeti Dışişleri Bakanlığı Arşivlerimiz Hakkında Bilgi Aralık 2011* (Republic of Turkey Ministry of Foreign Affairs Information on Our Archives December 2011), (Ankara: Dışişleri Bakanlığı Matbaası, 2011), pp. 2–15.

2. Orel, Başbakanlık Arşiv Araştırma Kurulu Faaliyetleri, p. 2; İlber Ortaylı, *Türkiye'nin Yakın Tarihi* (The Recent History of Turkey), (İstanbul: Timaş Yayınları, 2010), p. 197.

3. Küçük, *Başbakanlık Osmanlı Arşivi Katalogları Rehberi*, pp. 136–137; Gökbilgin, *Osmanlı Paleografya ve Diplomatik İlmi*, p. 69; Çetin, "Türkiye'de Önemli Arşivler ve Özellikleri," pp. 88–90; Nejat Ertüzün, Ermeni Meselesi İle İlgili Çalışmalar (Studies on the Armenian Question), 16 May 2005, Unpublished paper, pp. 1–2; Celadet Kiyasi, Başbakanlık Arşiv Araştırma Kurulu Birinci Grup Faaliyetleri (Activities of the Prime Minister's Office Archival Research Council's First Group), 5 August 1988, Unpublished paper, pp. 1–4; İlhant Akant, Osmanlı Arşivlerinde Reform ve Yeniden Düzenleme (Reform and Reorganization in the Ottoman Archives), Text of the Speech in Turkish on Research Opportunities in the Ottoman Archives, Columbia University, 8 August 1989, pp. 1–12. On the importance of the full use of the Ottoman Ministry of Foreign Affairs archive, see Gotthard Jaeschke, trans. Cemal Köprülü, *Kurtuluş Savaşı İle İlgili İngiliz Belgeleri* (British Documents on the War of Liberation), (Ankara: Türk Tarih Kurumu Basımevi, 1991), p. 258.

4. Küçük, *Başbakanlık Osmanlı Arşivi Katalogları Rehberi*, p. 346. The same interpretation, with slight differences in emphasis, may be found in Aktaş, "Osmanlı Dönemi Arşivciliğimiz ve Tasnif Çalışmaları," pp. 382–383.

5. Zafer Toprak, "Stanford Shaw İle Mülakat" (Interview With Stanford Shaw), *Tarih ve Toplum*, Vol. 13, No. 76 (April 1990), pp. 9–10.

6. Jeremy Salt, "The Narrative Gap in Ottoman Armenian History," *Middle Eastern Studies*, Vol. 39, No. 1 (January 2003), p. 35.

7. Chris Morris, "A Question of Cause and Casualties," *The Guardian*, 25 January 2001, p. 5.

8. Dorian Jones, "Sealed Turkish Archives Could Support Genocide Claims," *The Times Higher Education Supplement*, 27 April 2001, p. 10.

9. Stanford Shaw, Reader's Letter, Turkish Forum, 3 May 2001, p. 1.

10. For more on British archives see chapter eleven.

11. Shaw, Reader's Letter, p. 1.

12. See Ervand Abrahamian's review of Houri Berberian's *Armenians and the Iranian Constitutional Revolution of 1905–1911: "The Love for Freedom Has No Fatherland"* in *The American Historical Review*, Vol. 107, No. 5 (December 2002), p. 1675.

13. Christian Gerlach, *Extremely Violent Societies: Mass Violence in the Twentieth–Century World* (New York: Cambridge University Press, 2010), p. 9.

14. Artyom Tonoyan's review of Taner Akçam's *The Young Turks' Crime Against Humanity: The Armenian Genocide and Ethnic Cleansing in the Ottoman Empire* in *Journal of Church and State*, Vol. 55, No. 4 (December 2013), p. 2.

15. Özkul, "Osmanlı Arşivlerinin Osmanlı Coğrafyası ve Dünya Tarih Araştırmaları Bakımından Önemi," p. 9.

16. Alan Fisher, "To the Editor," Communications, *The American Historical Review*, Vol. 84, No. 2 (April 1979), p. 616.

17. Shaw, "Archival Sources for Ottoman History," p. 1.

18. Heath Lowry, "The Reorganization of the Ottoman Archives," *The Turkish Studies Association Bulletin*, Vol. 13, No. 2 (Fall 1989), pp. 107–111; Fisher, "Research Access in Turkey," pp. 139–149; Kemal Karpat, "An Update on Turkish Archives," *Middle East Studies Association Bulletin*, Vol. 23, No. 2 (December 1989), p. 183; idem, "Introduction: Turks Remember Their Ottoman Ancestors," in Kemal Karpat, ed., *Ottoman Past and Today's Turkey* (Leiden: E. J. Brill, 2000), p. xiv and n11; Meyer, "For the Russianist in Istanbul and the Ottomanist in Russia," p. 289.

19. On the BOA's move to the Kağıthane area of İstanbul see the next chapter.

20. Süreyya Yuca, Başbakanlık Arşiv Araştırma Kurulu İkinci Grup Faaliyetleri (Activities of the Prime Minister's Office Archival Research Council's Second Group), 5 August 1988, Unpublished paper, pp. 1–2; Aktaş, "Osmanlı Dönemi Arşivciliğimiz ve Tasnif Çalışmaları," p. 387; Özel and Çetinsaya, "Türkiye'de Osmanlı Tarihçiliğinin Son Çeyrek Yüzyılı," p. 14; A. Faruki Çelik, "Arşivlerimiz 2000'li Yılların Kültür Hadisesi Olacak" (Our Archives Will Be the Cultural Event of the Years 2000), *Türkiye*, 12 March 1989, p. 11; Karpat, "An Update on Turkish Archives," p. 182.

21. Orel, Başbakanlık Arşiv Araştırma Kurulu Faaliyetleri, p. 3.

22. Hasan Celal Güzel, "Devlet Arşivlerinde Yeniden Yapılanmanın Yirminci Yılı 1987–2007" (The Twentieth Year of the Restructuring of the State Archives 1987–2007), *Arşiv Dünyası*, No. 9 (January 2007), p. 99.

23. Faroqhi, *Approaching Ottoman History*, p. 1.

24. Yusuf Sancak, "Başbakanlık Devlet Arşivleri Genel Müdürü İsmet Miroğlu: 1 Ayda 46 Milyon Belgeyi Günışığına Çıkardık" (Director General of State Archives İsmet Miroğlu: We Have Brought to Daylight 46 Million Documents In One Month), *Türkiye*, 18 May 1989, p. 11. Regarding the importance and training of Turkish archivists, see İlber Ortaylı, *Tarih Yazıcılık Üzerine* (On Historiography), (Ankara: Cedit Neşriyat, 2009), pp. 202–203.

25. Sertoğlu, *Muhteva Bakımından Başvekalet Arşivi*, p. 71.

26. Küçük, *Başbakanlık Osmanlı Arşivi Katalogları Rehberi*, pp. xvi–xviii; Aktaş, "Osmanlı Dönemi Arşivciliğimiz ve Tasnif Çalışmaları," p. 386; Işıksal, "Arşivlerimizin Durumu ve Problemleri," pp. 1204–1205.

27. See Albertine Jwaideh, "Midhat Pasha and the Land System of Lower Iraq," in Albert Hourani, ed., *St. Anthony's Papers: Middle Eastern Affairs*, No. 3 (London: Chatto and Windus, 1963), pp. 105–136; idem, "The Saniya Lands of Sultan Abdülhamid II in Iraq," in George Makdisi, ed., *Arabic and Islamic Studies in Honor of H.A.R. Gibb* (Leiden: Brill, 1965), pp. 326—336; idem, "Aspects of Land Tenure and Social Change in Lower Iraq During Late Ottoman Times," in Tarif Khalidi, ed., *Land Tenure and Social Transformation in the Middle East* (Beirut: American University of Beirut Press, 1984), pp. 333–356.

28. Uriel Heyd, *Ottoman Documents on Palestine 1552–1615: A Study of the Firman According the Mühimme Defteri* (London: Oxford University Press, 1960), p. v; Amnon Cohen, "Ottoman Sources for the History of Ottoman Jews: How Important?" in Avigdor Levy, ed., *The Jews of the Ottoman Empire* (Princeton, NJ: The Darwin Press, 1994), p. 691.

29. Roderic Davison, *Essays in Ottoman and Turkish History, 1774–1923: The Impact of the West* (Austin, TX: University of Texas Press, 1990), p. xvi.

30. Yaron Ben-Naeh, *Jews in the Realm of the Sultans* (Tübingen: Mohr Siebeck, 2008), p. 14.

31. Barbara Jelavich, *The Ottoman Empire, the Great Powers, and the Straits Question 1870–1887* (Bloomington and London: Indiana University Press, 1973), p. xi.

32. George Harris, "Communications," *The Middle East Journal*, Vol. 51, No. 2 (Spring 1997), p. 331.

33. Lewis, *Notes on a Century*, p. 90.

34. Cohen, "Ottoman Sources for the History of Ottoman Jews," p. 690.

35. Elker, "Mustafa Reşit Paşa ve Türk Arşivciliği," p. 82; Bernard Lewis, "The Ottoman Archives as a Source for the History of the Arab Lands," *Journal of the Royal Asiatic Society*, Nos. 3–4 (October 1951), pp. 139–155. See also idem, *Notes and Documents from the Turkish Archives: A Contribution to the History of the Jews in the Ottoman Empire* (Oriental Notes and Studies, No. 3) (Jerusalem: The Israel Oriental Society, 1952), pp. 1–52; idem, "Studies in the Ottoman Archives I," *Bulletin of the School of Oriental and African Studies*, Vol. 16 (1954), pp. 469–501 and idem, "Ottoman Archives," pp. 226–230.

36. Lewis, "Studies in the Ottoman Archives—I," p. 469n1.

37. Letter from Bernard Lewis to Metin İnegöllüoğlu, Princeton/New Jersey, 7 March 1989.

38. Bernard Lewis, *From Babel to Dragomans: Interpreting the Middle East* (Oxford and New York: Oxford University Press, 2004), pp. 418–419.

39. Griswold, "The National Archives in Turkey," pp. 41–42.

40. Carl Max Kortepeter, *Ottoman Imperialism During the Reformation: Europe and the Caucasus* (London: University of London Press Ltd, 1973), p. xi. On Rauf Tunçay and Turgut Işıksal, see Sinan Çuluk, "Heath Lowry İle Tarih Metodu, Arşiv Çalışmaları ve Türkiye Macerası Üzerine Mülakat" (Interview With Heath Lowry on the Historical Method, Archival Studies and His Experiences in Turkey), *Arşiv Dünyası*, No. 5 (January 2005), pp. 24–29 and idem, "Yaşayan En Eski Arşivcimiz Turgut Işıksal" (Our Oldest Living Archivist: Turgut Işıksal), *Arşiv Dünyası*, No. 11 (July 2008), pp. 23–28.

41. Sinan Çuluk, "Prof. Dr. Suraiya Faroqhi İle Mülakat" (Interview With Prof. Dr. Suraiya Faroqhi), *Arşiv Dünyası*, No. 7 (January 2006), pp. 46–60.

42. Nilgün Uysal, ed., *Zaman Kaybolmaz İlber Ortaylı Kitabı* (Time Is Not Lost: The İlber Ortaylı Book), (İstanbul: Türkiye İş Bankası Kültür Yayınları, 2006), p. 172.

43. Engin Deniz Akarlı, *The Long Peace: Ottoman Lebanon, 1861–1920* (Berkeley and Los Angeles, CA: University of California Press, 1993), p. xi.

44. Ayşe Yazıcıoğlu, "Cemal Kafadar İle Mülakat" (Interview With Cemal Kafadar), *Toplumsal Tarih*, No. 219 (March 2012), p. 30.

45. Shaw, "Archival Sources for Ottoman History," pp. 1–12; idem, "The Archives of Turkey: An Evaluation," *Wiener Zeitschrift für die Kunde des Morgenlandes*, No. 69 (1977), pp. 91–98; idem, *Studies in Ottoman and Turkish History* (İstanbul: The Isis Press, 2000), p. 600.

46. Stanford Shaw, "New Research Opportunities in the Ottoman Archives of Istanbul," *Belleten*, Vol. 58, No. 222 (August 1994), p. 465.

47. Stanford Shaw, *The Financial and Administrative Organization and Development of Ottoman Egypt, 1517–1798* (Princeton, NJ: Princeton University Press, 1962).

48. Stanford Shaw, "Turkish Source Material for Egyptian History," in P. M. Holt, ed., *Political and Social Change in Modern Egypt* (London: Oxford University Press, 1968), pp. 28–48; Heath Lowry, "The State of the Field: A Retrospective Overview and Assessment of Ottoman Studies in the United States of America and Canada," in *XIII. Türk Tarih Kongresi, Ankara 4–8 Ekim 1999. Kongreye Sunulan Bildiriler* (Thirteenth Turkish Historical Congress, Ankara 4–8 October 1999. Communications Presented to the Congress), Vol. 1, (Ankara: Türk Tarih Kurumu Basımevi, 2002), pp. 15–16.

49. James Ring Adams, "Armenian Terrorism: L. A.'s Mideast Connections," *The Wall Street Journal*, 9 August 1983, Part 1, p. 32.

50. See Stanford Shaw and Ezel Kural Shaw, *History of the Ottoman Empire and Modern Turkey*, Vol. 2: *The Rise of Modern Turkey*, (Cambridge: Cambridge University Press, 1977) and Richard Hovannisian and Stanford Shaw and Ezel Kural Shaw, "Forum: The Armenian Question: The Critic's View: Beyond Revisionism and the Author's Respond," *International Journal of Middle East Studies*, Vol. 9, No. 3 (August 1978), pp. 379–400.

51. On İsmet Binark see more in Chapter 6.

52. Stanford Shaw, *From Empire to Republic. The Turkish War of National Liberation 1918–1923: A Documentary Study*, Vol. 1: *The Rise and Fall of the Ottoman Empire, 1300–1918* (Ankara: Türk Tarih Kurumu Basımevi, 2000), pp. xxv–xxvi.

53. *Osmanlı Arşivleri ve Osmanlı Araştırmaları Sempozyumu 17 Mayıs 1985* (Symposium on Ottoman Archives and Ottoman Studies 17 May 1985), (İstanbul: Türk-Arap İlişkileri İncelemeleri Vakfı, 1985); "Özal: Daha Sıkı İşbirliği" (Özal: Firmer Cooperation), *Milliyet*, 18

May 1985, p. 7; "Osmanlı Belgeleri Açığa Çıkıyor" (The Ottoman Documents Are Brought Out), *Cumhuriyet*, 18 May 1985, p. 12; "Özal: Tarihimizin Saklanacak Hiçbir Yönü Yoktur" (Our History Has No Aspect to Be Hidden), *Tercüman*, 18 May 1985, p. 12; Ahmet Kabaklı, "Osmanlı ve Biz" (The Ottoman and Us), *Tercüman*, 20 May 1985, p. 2; "Osmanlı Arşivleri ve Osmanlı Araştırmaları Sempozyumunun Ardından Birçok Ülkenin Tarihi, Osmanlı Arşivlerinde Yatmaktadır" (After the Symposium on Ottoman Archives and Ottoman Studies: The Histories of Many Countries Lie in the Ottoman Archives), *Tercüman*, 22 May 1985, p. 10.

54. Güzel, "Devlet Arşivlerinde Yeniden Yapılanmanın Yirminci Yılı 1987–2007," p. 98; Özel and Çetinsaya, "Türkiye'de Osmanlı Tarihçiliğinin Son Çeyrek Yüzyılı," p. 14; Robert Zens, "Turkish Historiography in the United States," *Türkiye Araştırmaları Literatür Dergisi*, Vol. 8, No. 15 (2010), p. 150.

55. Emine Çaykara, ed., *Tarihçilerin Kutbu Halil İnalcık Kitabı* (Pole of the Historians: The Halil İnalcık Book), (İstanbul: Türkiye İş Bankası Kültür Yayınları, 2005), pp. 275–276.

56. Halil İnalcık, "The Shaykh's Story Told by Himself," in Naff, *Paths to the Middle East*, p. 130. On Halil İnalcık as historian see İlber Ortaylı, *Defterimden Portreler: Tarihten ve Günümüzden* (Portraits From My Notebook: From History and Our Day), (İstanbul: Timaş Yayıncılık, 2011), pp. 151–156; Cemal Kafadar, "Halil İnalcık'ın Osmanlı Tarihçiliği İçindeki Yeri" (The Place of Halil İnalcık in Ottoman Historianship), in Özvar, *Türk Tarihçiliğinde Dört Sima*, pp. 27–34 and Özer Ergeç, "Halil İnalcık'ın Türkiye'nin Sosyal ve Ekonomik Tarihçiliğindeki Yeri" (The Place of Halil İnalcık in the Social and Economic Historianship of Turkey), in Mehmet Öz, ed., *Cumhuriyet Döneminde Türkiye'de Tarihçilik ve Tarih Yayıncılığı Sempozyumu Bildiriler Ankara, 18–20 Mart 2010* (Symposium on Historianship and Historical Publications in Republican Turkey Communications Ankara, 18–20 March 2010), (Ankara: Türk Tarih Kurumu Basımevi, 2011), pp. 7–11. For assessment of İnalcık as man and scholar by his colleagues and former students, see Çaykara, *Tarihçilerin Kutbu Halil İnalcık Kitabı*, pp. 487–511.

57. "An Interview with Halil İnalcık by the Editor," *The Turkish Studies Association Bulletin*, Vol. 17, No. 2 (Fall 1993), pp. 141–142.

58. Madeline Zilfi, *The Politics of Piety* (Minneapolis, MN: Bibliotheca Islamica, 1988), p. 17.

59. James Reid, "The Armenian Massacres in Ottoman and Turkish Historiography," *The Armenian Review*, Vol. 37, No. 1–145 (Spring 1984), p. 23n2.

60. Daniel Goffman, *Britons in the Ottoman Empire 1642–1660* (Seattle and London: University of Washington Press, 1998), p. xii.

61. Goffman, *The Ottoman Empire and Early Modern Europe*, p. xvii.

62. Bruce Masters, *Christians and Jews in the Ottoman Arab World: The Roots of Sectarianism* (Cambridge: Cambridge University Press, 2001), p. x.

63. Bruce Masters, "The Sultan's Entrepreneurs: The *Avrupa Tüccarıs* and the *Hayriye Tüccarıs* in Syria," *International Journal of Middle East Studies*, Vol. 24, No. 4 (November 1992), p. 594.

64. Hayashi Kayoko and Mahir Aydın, eds., *The Ottoman State and Societies in Change: A Study of the Nineteenth Century Temettuat Registers* (London, New York and Bahrain: Kegan Paul Limited, 2004), pp. ix–x.

65. George Gawrych, *The Crescent and the Eagle: Ottoman Rule, Islam and the Albanians, 1874–1913* (London and New York: I. B. Tauris, 2006), p. 4.

66. Taner Akçam, "Deportation and Massacres in the Cipher Telegrams of the Interior Ministry in the Prime Ministerial Archive (Başbakanlık Arşivi)," *Genocide Studies and Prevention*, Vol. 1, No. 3 (December 2006), pp. 320–321n6 and idem, *'Ermeni Meselesi Hallolunmuştur': Osmanlı Belgelerine Göre Savaş Yıllarında Ermenilere Yönelik Politikalar* ('The Armenian Problem Is Solved': The Policies Towards Armenians During the War Years According to Ottoman Documents), (İstanbul: İletişim Yayınları, 2008), pp. 16–17.

67. Vahakn Dadrian and Taner Akçam, *Judgment at Istanbul: The Armenian Genocide Trials* (New York and Oxford: Berghahn Books, 2011), p. 4.

68. Akçam, *The Young Turks' Crime Against Humanity*, p. 4n5.

69. Ryan Gingeras, *Sorrowful Shores Violence, Ethnicity, and the End of the Ottoman Empire, 1912–1913* (Oxford and New York: Oxford University Press, 2009), pp. vii and ix.

70. Roberto Mazza, *Jerusalem: From the Ottomans to the British* (London and New York: Tauris Academic Studies, 2009), p. xvi.

71. "Scholar: Ottoman Documents Corroborate Armenian Genocide," *Armenian Reporter*, 14 March 2009, p. 2.

72. Orlando Figes, *Crimea: The Last Crusade* (London: Allen Lane, 2010), p. xv.

73. Giancarlo Casale, *The Ottoman Age of Exploration* (New York: Oxford University Press, 2010), pp. x and xvii.

74. "Mustafa Budak 25 Mayıs 2004'te Devlet Arşivleri Genel Müdür Yardımcısı Oldu" (Mustafa Budak Has Become the Deputy Director General of the State Archives on 25 May 2004), *Arşiv Dünyası*, No. 4 (August–September 2004), p. 37.

75. Bernard Lewis, "Other People's History," *The American Scholar*, Summer 1990, p. 404.

Chapter Six

The Directorate General of State Archives

THE CENTENARY OF 1915

The centenary of the 1915 relocation of Armenians spawns the inevitable crop of monographs, biographies, and collections of essays all relating to the turbulent history of the First World War and its immediate aftermath.[1] The events which led to the cataclysm of 1915 itself have been much debated, and a long line of scholars has gone into the elucidation of no less important provincial aspects of those troubles. Oddly, however, very fundamental questions remain unanswered, such as what were the real motives and the true intentions of the Ottoman government regarding the displacement of the Armenian population? It is precisely in this context that research in the BOA and the ATASE may well turn out to be the most valuable contribution of the present decade to the history of the 1910s and 1920s.

Taner Akçam admits that the BOA "has been underutilized as a basis for arguments about the events of 1915." And he goes on:

> Despite the inevitable gaps in its holdings, this repository [BOA] can be considered an extremely rich resource for illuminating the period under review—so rich, in fact, that by no means can it be said to have been fully exploited by researchers (for a variety of reasons), and its value, acknowledged as well as undiscovered, must not be underestimated.[2]

WEBSITE OF THE DIRECTORATE GENERAL OF STATE ARCHIVES

For many years, a visit to the BOA meant standing in long lines, then elbowing your way through crowds to view historic documents. Or spending hours in the BOA reading rooms sorting through boxes of old documents or scrolling through frame after frame of microfilm. Not anymore. The BOA provides leaflets to help the researcher and a useful computer reference system. Since 18 April 2002 a comprehensive list of internet sites directs scholars to the DGSA website and the related links. Descriptions of manuscript depositories include information on what documents may be available on-line.[3]

The website of the DGSA (www.devletarsivleri.gov.tr) provides information on both the BOA and the RA. The first page is written only in Turkish, but other pages on the site have both Turkish and English versions. For example, when clicked on "Katalog Tarama" (Catalog Search) on the left hand of the page, a window pops up which asks for a username and password. It will be noticed that this page can be read in both Turkish and English. One must register for the site, but registration is an uncomplicated process. The form must be simply filled out, a username and password be chosen, and within a few hours one should be able to use the site. Once one has its username and password, one will be able to search the online catalogs of the archive. It is important to keep in mind that the online catalogs represent only a tiny percentage of the BOA's actual holdings. However, new listings are frequently added to the online catalog, so its potential as a useful preparation for working in the BOA is continuously increasing. This catalog is searchable by keyword, and allows the user to search in multiple catalogs simultaneously. When James Meyer first started working in the BOA in 2004, he found around thirty documents via this catalog. Several of these documents ended up being quite helpful in his work, and several others nevertheless pointed him in the right direction with respect to the types of catalogs he needed to be working with. Indeed, when Meyer first used the BOA in 2004, his keyword search for "Akçura" turned up only seven or eight results relating to the Turkish political thinker Yusuf Akçura. Four years later, the same search resulted in twenty-five hits, and several of the new results have led him to documents of whose existence he had previously been unaware.[4]

Many thousands of digital records from the BOA are available to the public. They provide an invaluable collection of primary source material for academic researchers and students.[5]

Over the past twenty years or so, the BOA has helped scholars with its frequent publications as well as through the speed with which collections have been cataloged and made available. Notwithstanding the BOA's early and enthusiastic embrace of electronic access, it also continues with traditional forms of publication.[6]

The whole BOA series has undergone a number of changes since the mid-1990s, which represent, if not a full-scale renaissance, at least a significant enhancement of a major source for Ottomanists. Much of this was made possible by the decision of the Prime Minister's Office at that time to hire additional staff, permitting an expansion of activities and an intensification of research effort. There was an appreciation that the volume and scope of the documentation now available required a rethink of the standard publication format. Electronic versions of the print volumes would now be generated as a matter of course, and the older volumes would also be offered in this form to any visitor to the DGSA's website—all available free for use over the Internet.[7]

The website of the DGSA advertises its publications to researchers. When on the main page, "Yayınlar" (Publications) is clicked on the right-hand side of the menu bar at the top of the page, that opens a screen that lists the titles and prices of its publications. James Meyer mentions that these publications can be of great use to scholars, particularly those not proficient in Ottoman Turkish. He adds that many of these books are of first-rate quality, with excellent photo reproductions of original documents printed alongside Latin-script transliterations of their texts.[8]

PUBLICATIONS OF THE DIRECTORATE GENERAL OF STATE ARCHIVES

Armenians in Ottoman Documents, 1915–1920 provides a wealth of documentary material on Ottoman policy toward Armenians in the crucial years of the First World War and the early stage of the Turkish War of Independence.[9] In the 639 pages of documents, the first 15 deal with an overview of the Turkish-Armenian relations throughout history. The remaining pages consist of documents in Ottoman transcript with their transliteration into modern Turkish and translation to English. Admirably produced by İsmet Binark's editorial team, the volume is arranged chronologically. From the huge quantity of material that survives in the BOA, it is limited to a representative sample of fewer than 272 documents. Those familiar with the archives will appreciate both the difficulty of the editors' task and the skill with which it has been undertaken. The material presented here provides a vivid sense of the wide range of social, economic, political, and military problems that confronted Ottoman policy makers. These problems were inextricably interlinked; so much so that the job of dividing the documents into neatly demarcated thematic chapters presents huge difficulties of its own. The arrangement editors have chosen is certainly as logical as any one could imagine. An excellent *table méthodique* divides up the contents into major subjects. To an increasing extent, volumes in these series are edited to facilitate their use by scholars and students, rather than simply to publish relevant documents. The arrangement of the documents in this volume, while not imposing any particular line of interpretation, allows the reader to follow the sequence of events very clearly. The editorial principles of selection and methodology are clearly explained. The layout is improved, with such matters as numbering of documents, use of darker and lighter print and helpful lists of works published by the DGSA at the end.[10]

A series of volumes tracing the relations between the Ottoman Armenians and the Western powers publishes substantial extracts from the documentary sources at the BOA. Each volume covers documents within a given period of time. The volumes in their order represent a chronological series. One group of volumes offers a survey of Armenian-French collaboration in 1879–1922.[11] A second, third and fourth deal with Armenian collaboration efforts with Britain, Russia and the United States respectively in 1845–1922, 1841–1921 and 1839–1919.[12] A significant proportion of the archival record is available to the interested reader or scholar, who will be able the more easily to question the somewhat speculative conclusions reached thus far by historians about the Armenian relocations.

In every volume there is an analytic table of contents, in which the editors provide a summary of each document under topical headings arranged in chronological order. A reader can easily follow a theme or a bilateral relationship, stopping to consult important documents on the way. The editors supply cross-references within the collection, and short summaries of dispatches and telegrams not included in the collection but referred to in documents selected for printing. There is also a full index of names, another of places, and, in addition, several annexes with very full organigrams of the officials.

THE SUBLIME PORTE AND THE ARMENIANS IN DOCUMENTS

Any documentary project of this kind raises difficult issues. In this case, the editor-in-chief had to take account of the existing or projected publication of official records on closely related subjects. Repetition would be redundant, but as these volumes firmly recognize, the Sublime Porte's policy toward its Armenian subjects is incomprehensible unless placed in the wider context of international diplomacy, strategy and politics. A second issue is how far to be guided by the existing secondary literature: should the documents be chosen to illustrate the topics and themes already identified by historians? A third is how far to offer the reader, through elaborate footnoting, a detailed context for the documents printed, effectively incorporating them into a form of narrative. A fourth, related to this, is whether to print whole documents, arguably an extravagance, or to be content with pithy extracts. With several works of Ottoman Armenian history to his credit, Associate Professor Recep Karacakaya was well qualified to make a confident judgment on these fundamentals; and while they may quibble over the precise arrangement and internal balance of these twelve volumes, few readers will want to quarrel seriously with the strategic decisions that he and the general editors have made.

In the first place, Karacakaya rejects any idea of merely illustrating established themes. Instead he has chosen the course of sifting through vast masses of material at the BOA, being guided by the depth and fertility of the archival residue in making his selection. This has the great virtue of offering a kind of control on the existing secondary literature. To escape from the dilemma of either ignoring or reprinting material on closely related questions, volumes offer a selection of documents on "high policy" to give a sense of the policy makers' thinking on such major issues as the Armenian provincial rebellions and the events of 1915. In particular, excellent use of Cabinet records is made to demonstrate the interconnectedness of policy in the empire. The third decision, to eschew detailed footnoting in favor of long introductory sections, is more arguable. These sections do offer extremely useful surveys of relations between the Ottoman Armenians and France, Britain, Russia and the United States and go some—though not all—of the way toward providing an adequate context for the mass of documentary material. Moreover, to have added detailed footnoting to the labor of sifting and collecting would doubtless have made the recruitment of associate editors impossible. But there was perhaps a case for shorter sectional introductions directly focused on the economic, strategic, political and international material as the reader encountered it.

On the last point—the whole or partial printing of documents—the decision here is the corollary of Karacakaya's determination to offer the archival record uncorrupted by any attempt to incorporate it into a grand narrative. Within these constraints, these volumes provide a superb insight into the relations between the Ottoman Armenians and France, Britain, Russia, and the United States in the nineteenth and early twentieth centuries.

OTTOMAN MATERIALS IN ENGLISH

These are immensely useful volumes. The presentation of the Ottoman materials in English translation undoubtedly helps to broaden Anglophone scholars' perceptions of a period not rich in relevant British documents. For the historian working on contemporary politics, administration, or society, they conveniently present a wide range of important evidence. The series can be used as a guide for scholars who may wish to go on to the archives for more specialized research. In 1999, Suraiya Faroqhi noted that future researchers will appreciate the documentary series published by the DGSA which has become so much more intensive during the last few years.[13]

One should never undervalue the huge efforts of the teams of editors who bring to publication series of original Ottoman documents, nor underestimate the frustrations and delays involved in selecting and reselecting of archive materials, which presumably lie behind the otherwise incomprehensible chasms of time separating the appearance of related publications. The editors are particularly to be praised for guiding the BOA series through completion; others would be well advised to follow their example of an intelligent and comprehensive selection of materials, produced at a regular pace.

Official series of documents produced by other foreign sources in other countries always seem to end up in the prisoner's dock charged not only with having doctored the evidence—if only by selection and exclusion—but also tampering with texts. Precautions were taken to ensure that the BOA did not sin. The result is a reference work that no library that deals with Ottoman studies can afford to be without.

İSMET BİNARK

The DGSA supports a wide range of public programs designed to reach a variety of audiences. It has maintained a special relationship with the scholarly community that stretches back to its founding and the pioneering efforts of İsmet Binark and others who worked hard for its birth. To continue its dialogue with the research community, the DGSA held a number of scholarly conferences that were organized around a certain theme or major event in Turkish history.[14]

İsmet Binark, Director General of State Archives, served for 32 consecutive years, from 1965 to 1997, in the archival profession and made Ottoman and Republican repositories available for researchers. In 1992, when Binark was appointed director general, there were around 20 million documents in the BOA accessible for researchers cataloged during the previous 146 years. He raised this number to 50 million within the next five years. Moreover, he rendered another important service by organizing during his tenure as director general, the publication of 98 books within the State Archives structure. Binark, the author of 30 books and 200 articles in the field, and one of the names who helped raise the studying of archives to university level, is known for the services he has rendered to Turkish foreign policy and universities, as well as by the documents that he has made accessible through computerization. During Binark's office, the DGSA signed and implemented agreements of cooperation with many of the relevant government archival agencies from all over the world. He was also active in the International Council on Archives and participated in European-wide discussions of archival declassification and access norms.[15]

In a country where the archival profession is yet comparatively young and the field of archival theorists uncrowded, Binark's contribution stands as a significant achievement. Like their European counterparts who function as active scholars in addition to performing archival tasks, the staff of the BOA has engaged in scholarly writing. Many staff members have the academic requisites for scholarly publication.

LEGISLATION ON STATE ARCHIVES

The Turkish government has prepared a Draft Bill on State Archives, which consists of four sections and thirty-nine articles which, when enacted, will be the first law about the subject. Most of the articles are related to the organization, functions, and responsibilities of a reorganized DGSA; definitions of archival documents; and the protection, preservation, and classification of archival documents. The bill states that the DGSA will have supervisory authority over archival material in the custody of public institutions such as universities, libraries, institutes, local governments, etc. The bill, however, exempts the Presidential Office, the TGNA, the General Staff, the Ministry of Foreign Affairs, the Ministry of National Defense, and the National Intelligence Organization from direct supervision. These agencies are required to implement the principles stated in the law through their own organizational units.

The bill will also create four departments within the directorate, of which, the two most important are the Ottoman Archive Department and the Republican Archive Department. The other two departments are related to documentation and relations with foreign archive departments. Several consultative entities such as legal counsels, public relations, human sources, and strategy development units, are also enumerated in the new organization. The bill establishes principles and guidelines that regulate the sorting and destruction of archival documents at even the lowest levels of government. It also formally criminalizes the theft, willful destruction and adulteration, and trading of archival documents. The draft bill is expected to go to the TGNA for discussion and enactment into law in the near future.

BOA MOVED TO A NEW SITE

On 2 June 2013, the BOA's site was moved to a gigantic new campus located in a suburban setting past the end of the Golden Horn in the Kağıthane area. The new facility offers expanded research space and the opportunity to house the documents at an on-site depot, with climate control to protect documents from decay caused by humidity. The site also includes architectural features to protect against natural disasters such as flooding or earthquakes. The reading room is open for digital document services, providing access to the total documents available. The site is a three-story system, with the entrance on the first floor, document room on the second floor, and computer room on the third. The actual researching rooms are well lit and bright in contrast to the first level. Each level has easily two-to-three times the seating capacity of the rooms at the old facility and reading desks and computers are in abundant supply. The employees' desk in the reading room stretches across much of one wall, which relieves some of the crowding that was a familiar sight at the old location.[16]

NOTES

1. See, among many others, Michael Gunter, *Armenian History and the Question of Genocide* (New York: Palgrave Macmillan, 2011); Dadrian and Akçam, *Judgment at Istanbul*; Kévorkian, *The Armenian Genocide*; Suny, Göçek and Naimark, *A Question of Genocide*; Erickson, *Ottomans and Armenians*.
2. Akçam, *The Young Turks' Crime Against Humanity*, pp. xxxi and 4.
3. İbrahim Karaer, Rahim Erişti and Ahmet Ceylan, eds., *Dünden Bugüne Başbakanlık 1920–2004* (The Prime Minister's Office from Yesterday to the Present 1920–2004), (Ankara: Başbakanlık Basımevi, 2004), p. 120.
4. Meyer, "For the Russianist in Istanbul and the Ottomanist in Russia," p. 288.
5. Gültekin Yıldız, "Bütüncül, Karşılaştırmalı ve Felsefi Bir Askeri Tarihe Doğru: Türkiye'de Askeri Tarih Araştırması ve Öğretiminin Geleceği Üzerine" (Toward a Total, Comparative and Philosophical Military History: On the Future of the Research and Teaching of Military History in Turkey), in Cevat Şayin and Gültekin Yıldız, eds., *Osmanlı Askeri Tarihini Araştırmak: Yeni Kaynaklar: Yeni Yaklaşımlar* (Researching Ottoman Military History: New Sources New Approaches), (İstanbul: Tarih Vakfı Yurt Yayınları, 2012), p. 17.
6. Özkul, "Osmanlı Arşivlerinin Osmanlı Coğrafyası ve Dünya Tarih Araştırmaları Bakımından Önemi," pp. 7–8; Özel and Çetinsaya, "Türkiye'de Osmanlı Tarihçiliğinin Son Çeyrek Yüzyılı," p. 31.
7. Özkul, "Osmanlı Arşivlerinin Osmanlı Coğrafyası ve Dünya Tarih Araştırmaları Bakımından Önemi," p. 7; Mustafa Küçük, "Türkiye'yi Geçmişten Geleceğe Taşıyan Güç: Başbakanlık Osmanlı Arşivi" (The Force That Carries Turkey from the Past to the Future: The Prime Minister's Office Ottoman Archive), *Arşiv Dünyası*, No. 4 (August–September 2004), pp. 28–30.
8. Meyer, "For the Russianist in Istanbul and the Ottomanist in Russia," p. 289.
9. Süleyman Beyoğlu, "Ermeni Tehcirine Dair Araştırmalara Toplu Bir Bakış" (An Overview of Studies on Armenian Relocations), in Şenol Kantarcı, Kamer Kasım, İbrahim Kaya and Sedat Laçiner, eds., *Ermeni Araştırmaları 1. Türkiye Kongresi Bildirileri* (Communications Presented to the First Turkish Congress on Armenian Studies), Vol. 1, (Ankara: Avrasya Stratejik Araştırmalar Merkezi Ermeni Araştırmaları Enstitüsü Yayınları, 2003), pp. 24–25 and 27.
10. İsmet Binark, ed., *Armenians in Ottoman Documents, 1915–1920* (Ankara: Başbakanlık Basımevi, 1995).
11. Recep Karacakaya et al., eds., *Osmanlı Belgelerinde Ermeni-Fransız İlişkileri, 1879–1922* (Armenian-French Relations in Ottoman Documents, 1879–1922), Vols. 1–3, (Ankara: Başbakanlık Basımevi, 2002).

12. Recep Karacakaya et al., eds., *Osmanlı Belgelerinde Ermeni-İngiliz İlişkileri, 1845–1922* (Armenian-British Relations in Ottoman Documents, 1845–1922), Vols. 1–4, (Ankara: Başbakanlık Basımevi, 2004 and 2006); idem, *Osmanlı Belgelerinde Ermeni-Rus İlişkileri, 1841–1921* (Armenian-Russian Relations in Ottoman Documents, 1841–1921), Vols. 1–3, (Ankara: Başbakanlık Basımevi, 2006) and idem, *Osmanlı Belgelerinde Ermeni-Amerikan İlişkileri, 1839–1919* (Armenian-American Relations in Ottoman Documents, 1839–1919), Vols. 1–2, (Ankara: Başbakanlık Basımevi, 2007).

13. Faroqhi, *Approaching Ottoman History*, p. 206.

14. See, for instance, Erişti, Yıldırım, Atik and Yay, *Birinci Milli Arşiv Şurası (Tebliğler-Tartışmalar) 20–21 Nisan 1998* and *International Symposium on Turkish Archives 17–19 November 2005 (Presentations and Discussions)*, (Ankara: Başbakanlık Basımevi, 2006).

15. For more on İsmet Binark see Taha Akyol, ed., *Osmanlı Mirasından Cumhuriyet Türkiye'sine İlber Ortaylı İle Konuşmalar* (From the Ottoman Heritage to the Republican Turkey: Conversations With İlber Ortaylı)), (İstanbul: Ufuk Kitapları, 2002), p. 17; Ayça Atikoğlu, "Başarmanın Bedeli" (The Cost of Succeeding), *Milliyet*, 19 August 1997, p. 27 and "Head of Turkish Archives, Ismet Binark, Dismissed," *The Armenian Observer*, 10 September 1997, p. 14.

16. Patrick Adamiak, Jeffrey Dyer and Michael Christopher Low, The End of an Era: The Less Than Grand Opening of the New Ottoman Archives, 25 April 2013. http://www.jadaliyya.com/pages/index/11370/the-end-of-an-era_the-less-than-grand-opening-of-t.

Chapter Seven

Military Archives

THE TURKISH GENERAL STAFF MILITARY HISTORY AND STRATEGIC STUDIES DIRECTORATE'S ARCHIVE

The ATASE, located opposite the Parliament building at Ankara, provides a military perspective. Many controversial questions regarding the relocation of Armenian populations can be elucidated through fresh references found there. Since the Ottoman government was controlled almost entirely during the First World War by the martial law administration, a part of the Ministry of War, ATASE, holds far more than the BOA, of the documents concerning internal conditions in the empire at that time and on operations of the Ottoman army and the Special Organization. The Special Organization, established on 17 November 1913, was used for special military operations in the Caucasus, Egypt, and Mesopotamia. It was also employed in dealing with the cause of Arab separatism in Syria.[1]

HOLDINGS OF THE ATASE

The First World War and the Turkish War of Independence archives alone number over five and one half million documents. The former category includes the following holdings: (1) The Turkish General Staff Division Reports, Division 1 (Operations), contains military operations plans and orders, operations and situation reports, maps and overlays, general staff orders, mobilization instructions and orders, organizational orders, training and exercise instructions, combat spot reports. Division 2 (Intelligence), contains intelligence estimates and reports, orders of battle. Divisions 3 and 4 (Logistics), contain all manner of files concerning procurement, animals, munitions, transportation, rations and accounting. (2) The Ministry of War files contain the General Command's ciphered cables to military units, as well as the papers of the various departments, such as the infantry, and fortress artillery. (3) Numbered field army files and mobilization districts contain the files of various staff divisions. The files of Vehip Pasha's Third Army (Erzurum), Cemal Pasha's Fourth Army (Damascus) and Ali İhsan Pasha's Sixth Army (Baghdad) are notably large. These also include the army groups (Lightning and Caucasus). An important addition to the archives at army level and below are the daily war journals. (4) The army corps, provisional combat groups, and expeditionary forces contain files of all staff division formations. (5) Numbered infantry and cavalry divisions, provisional divisions, and numbered regiments contain the files of the various area commands, the depot regiments, some of the field gendarmerie regiments and battalions, and fortress commands.[2]

The operational documents are revealing from several respects. They include rare firsthand contemporary accounts of operations, as well as notes on the strategic thinking and decision making of Ottoman commanders. They offer an understanding of Ottoman activity in seminal episodes, such as War Minister and Acting Commander-in-Chief Enver Pasha's military offensive of 21 December 1914 on the Caucasian front. The intelligence-related files focus on discrete sources of information: ground observations, aerial reconnaissance, penetration of enemy positions, prisoners-of-war interrogations, and foreign embassy communications. Included in the archive is also a mass of day-to-day correspondence on the crucial questions of how the army was recruited, trained, fed and supplied before and during campaigns, activities that sometimes took units thousands of kilometers from their bases.[3]

In addition to the archives, the ATASE maintains a large number of unpublished staff studies on army units (divisions and regiments). These staff studies were written by Turkish army officers and were based directly on Ottoman army war diaries and records held by the archives division.[4]

The cataloging and microfilming of military archives repository up to the end of 1945 is completed. Most of the items are summarized in the catalogs, and the documents are classified according to year and subject. From sifting through thousands of files and millions of documents—now unclassified—researchers anticipate further revelations about what happened in wartime. And they expect declassified documents to shed a more intense light on the Armenian issue than in the past.[5] These documents were intended for internal use only, and as such they are more credible than Armenian publications pursuing a political agenda. Justin McCarthy, a leading demography scholar and Professor of Middle Eastern history at the University of Louisville in Kentucky, one of the Western scholars to have done systematic research in the Ottoman archives, wrote: "The reports of Ottoman soldiers and officials were not political documents or public relations exercises. They were secret internal reports in which responsible men relayed what they believed to be true to their governments."[6]

Administered by qualified military personnel and civilian workers, these archives have a less formal atmosphere than some other depositories in Turkey. The staff is pleased to aid foreign researchers and they have an extensive knowledge of the materials there. The collective knowledge of the staff of the Ottoman and Turkish military history and its records is probably unmatched anywhere in the country. They are well-trained professionals. Most of them are selflessly devoted to their work.

Generally, for the nineteenth and twentieth-century historian, the most essential collections are the Crimean War (1853–1856), the Ottoman-Serbian/Montenegrin War (1875–1877), the Ottoman-Russian War (1877–1878), the Ottoman-Greek War (1897), the Ottoman-Italian War (1911–1912), the Balkan Wars (1912–1913), the First World War (1914–1918), the War of Independence (1919–1922), Republican Period Internal Revolts (1923–1938), the Second World War (1939–1945), the Korean War (1950–1953), the Cyprus Peace Operation (1974), the Atatürk Collection (1919–1938), the Peace Activities, the Gulf War (1991) and the Maps-Albums series. Seventy-five percent of the archival documents, maps, plans and sketches are in Ottoman Turkish, the remaining in other languages. These deal with a wide range of subjects all related to the military aspects of the Ottoman Empire and Turkey. However, contained within the many thousands of dossiers, are non-military sources which give important, detailed insights into the daily situation of the country. From the many civil and military papers, the researchers can clearly identify the actions and attitudes of the Ottoman leadership toward enemy powers and the national minority groups. The huge amount of informative material concerning such events as the Armenian population displacements are easily available in the First World War collection and can be fully studied for content and emphasis. Detailed reports and dispatches from the provincial officials and local military commanders to the Ministers of War, and to the Ministers of the Interior constitute a relatively untapped source of knowledge. Besides the standard army reports, the dossiers contain many letters and notes from the various Ottoman diplomatic representatives abroad. These documents, not always found in the Ottoman archives in İstanbul, are of extensive value to the serious researcher and, of course, the marginal remarks made by such men as Enver and Cemal Pashas do not appear in the printed collections. By utilizing the First World War collection files, the scholar can open new areas of historical knowledge.[7]

Research in the ATASE will open a new stage in the historical study of the Armenian question. The ATASE contains evidence of an Armenian threat to the Ottoman Empire in 1915 and of Armenian collaboration with the Russian army in its invasion.[8]

Ottoman military and civilian officials made carbon copies of everything and carefully filed them in several different places. They recorded revealing candid statements, never suspecting that historians would be reading them later. Ottoman papers of importance were not intentionally burned, as happened in Paris in 1940 and in Moscow in 1941.

The ATASE is open to all qualified scholars.[9] All requests should include the following information: full name of the applicant, his profession, citizenship, permanent address while visiting the archive (if known), the institution sponsoring his research, the purpose of his use of the archive, and the theme of his research. But the ATASE remains comparatively unused. Talha Çiçek says the documents in this archive are not completely open to scholars. He contends that the officials employed in the ATASE survey the documents and select those they consider relevant according to the subjects specified by the researchers.[10] This may be due to the lack of a published guide to ATASE's contents, and perhaps to a certain confusion regarding conditions of access and regulations governing the availability of individual files.[11] It is also apparent that Taner Akçam is not correct when claiming that "due to the tight restrictions that have been put in place, the ATASE archives are as good as closed to most civilian or foreign researchers."[12]

SCHOLARS IN THE ATASE

The ATASE records attract a great many researchers because its vast assortment of files reveals information never before available about one of the greatest defining moments in modern history, the First World War. They offer the researcher a kind of précis of that war, providing a wealth of research material from every theater of the Ottoman war effort.

With each new stage of access, there were exciting revelations, important articles and books, revisions of earlier interpretations, and new rounds of debates among scholars. At the beginning of the 1970s, a London-based Canadian, Gwynne Dyer, became one of the first Western historians to plunge into the exploration of the Ottoman military records. Archivists in the ATASE opened their vaults for him. In the autumn of 2009 he noted that he read the archival reports on British and Russian negotiations with Armenian revolutionaries that took place in early 1915. He also read the documents in the ATASE ordering the relocation of the Armenian population from eastern Anatolia later that year. What happened, according to Dyer, was quite clear. The British and the Russians planned to knock the Ottoman Empire out of the war quickly by simultaneous invasions of eastern Anatolia—Russians from the north and British by landings on Asia Minor's south coast. So they welcomed the approaches of Armenian nationalist groups and asked them to launch uprisings behind the Ottoman lines to synchronize with the invasions.

The usual half-promises about independence were made, and the Armenian groups fell for it. The British later switched their attack to the Dardanelles in an attempt to grab İstanbul, but they never warned their Armenian allies that the south-coast was called off. The Russians did invade, but the Ottomans managed to stop them. The Armenian revolutionaries launched their uprisings as promised, and the Ottoman government ordered the Armenian population to be removed from eastern Anatolia on the grounds that their presence behind the lines posed a danger to Ottoman defenses. If genocide means a policy that aims to exterminate a particular ethnic and religious group, Dyer concludes, then it [the Armenian relocation] wasn't.[13]

A considerable number of doctoral dissertations and monographs have been published on the basis of army files. Amid the most notable ones is the path-breaking survey of the logistics of food supply and armaments to the Ottoman army fighting in eastern Anatolia and the Caucasus in 1914–1918 by Tuncay Öğün; the Ottoman Empire's entry in the First World War, by Mustafa Aksakal; and the outstanding pioneering investigations of the Ottoman army during the Balkan Wars and the First World War by Edward Erickson. These books are striking in their originality, their depth of research, and their breadth of interpretation.[14]

No scholar outside Turkey has done as much work on the Ottoman military as Erickson. His books on the Balkan Wars and the First World War are standard reference works. For the first time a Western scholar was turning his attention to these wars from the perspective of the Ottoman military command rather than the viewpoint of countries attacking the Ottoman Empire. His basic source materials are the records of the Ottoman military.[15]

Recent Turkish military historians have shown a welcome tendency to move away from the pursuit of the origins of strategic policy in official records toward their reinterpretation in a wider sociopolitical and economic context. This trend has already produced valuable analyses of the economies of the Ottoman Caucasian campaign during the First World War by Öğün. It makes a distinguished contribution to the literature, and should serve as a focus for debate for years to come.

Besides Erickson, the military archival sources at Ankara have been amply used as research vehicle by such Western historians as Stanford Shaw, Tim Travers, Harvey Broadbent, Michael Reynolds, Hilmar Kaiser, and Benjamin Fortna.[16] They were able to use the archival catalogs and to see almost all of the documents they requested. Drawing on newly available materials from the ATASE, and a sophisticated reading of these materials in the light of prior scholarship, each of the authors captures the most fundamental element of contemporary history—the enduring influence of decisions made at one moment for those living years and decades later. The past is also part of the present in the well-researched books of these scholars.

At the heart of the new evaluation of the Ottoman past must lie scrupulous and painstaking research. Delving into the military archives of the Ottoman Empire, Shaw, Travers and Broadbent have uncovered numerous documents that reveal much about the mental outlook and professional behavior of those individuals who filled senior positions in the Ottoman Ministry of War and the General Staff. However, while many different new sources have been discovered, particularly useful for the task of reconstructing the mindset of those in charge of the security apparatus of the Ottoman Empire have been the reports of the military attachés. These soldier-diplomats were sent out by the Ministry of War as expert commentators on the military affairs of their host countries, and they provided much of the intelligence information upon which army commanders at home based their threat-perception analyses. This included not only factual data on force levels and weapons developments, but also more intangible impressions, such as the ethos, temperament and levels of belligerence of the officer corps of their host nations. As this was something that the subjects of such evaluations might not always choose to record for themselves, these military attaché reports provide numerous insights into the military milieu of the period that are generally unavailable elsewhere.

These materials are of immense importance because they reflect not only affairs internal to the Ottoman diplomatic and military services but because they report on the countries where Ottoman military attachés were stationed. There is a vast amount of material on all aspects of the war which, if studied patiently, reveals much about the way in which Enver Pasha ran the Ottoman war effort.

Erickson's thanks went to the director of the archives division of the ATASE, Major Tufan Yorgancıoğlu, translator and researcher Ahmet Çalışkan, and Librarian Gülümser Mutlu for making his research easier and far more fun that it probably warranted.[17]

Travers, professor emeritus of history at Calgary University in Alberta, Canada, emphasizes that the European and American scholars have spent much time looking at the military campaigns in the Ottoman Empire during the First World War from the Allied point of view and that little has been done to evaluate Turkish intentions and expectations. He particularly stresses that the ATASE in Ankara, which contain a wide range of Ottoman documents of 1915, have been neglected.[18] He also says Ottoman army officers and men did not keep private diaries, since this was not a cultural tradition in the country. Hence the documents in the ATASE are some of the few original resources for the Ottoman military campaigns available to the researcher.[19]

The Canadian historian further notes that in Ankara, he is grateful to Lieutenant General Gökalp Yuğnak and Colonel Görür for giving him permission to work in the Turkish General Staff archives.[20] A special tribute went to Birten Çelik who gave up a month of her time to translate documents from Ottoman Turkish into English. Travers considered her contributions absolutely necessary, and cheerfully given, and he felt fortunate to have the instruction and assistance of such a scholar. Many thanks were also due to the very helpful staff at the ATASE, who worked hard to satisfy the multitude of document requests throughout the research.[21]

Broadbent wrote in 2005:

> I explored the First World War holdings of the Turkish General Staff Archives, Ankara, a rich source of information about the Turkish side. This material supplies new insight into outcomes at Gallipoli and is a special feature of the book.[22]

He owed a great deal to the archivists and librarians of the ATASE who have helped him locate the materials on which his study was based:

> My gratitude for their invaluable assistance in the archives and repositories of official records go to Majors Tufan Yorgancıoğlu, Gürdeniz Horzum and Ahmet Tetik, archivists Erbil Koparan, Sema Kiper, Nuri Bayrak and librarian Derer Çelik of the Turkish General Staff Military History Archives and Strategic Institute, Ankara.[23]

Yigal Sheffy, senior lecturer at the Program for Security Studies at Tel Aviv University, who teaches military history of the Middle East and intelligence, wrote in the summer of 2009:

> I was granted access in 2004 to the Military Archives in Ankara (ATASE) in order to examine documentation related to the Palestine Campaign during the First World War. The Archives graciously agreed to put an interpreter fluent in the Ottoman Turkish language (Osmanlıca) at my disposal.[24]

Benjamin Fortna, professor of the history of the Middle East at the School of Oriental and African Studies in the University of London, conducted research at the ATASE in 2014 and was very pleased with both access to materials and the help of the staff there. It was a very positive experience for him.[25]

There are many other examples.

PUBLICATIONS OF THE ATASE

There are several scholars working in the military archives at present, and the ATASE itself publishes volumes from its collection, including both photographs and Latin transliterations of all documents. The eight-volume *Arşiv Belgeleriyle Ermeni Faaliyetleri 1914–1918*, written in modern Turkish and translated to English, allows researchers the opportunity to further study an astounding historical record. It also contains original documents in Ottoman script. The annotations are intended both to provide greater context for understanding the documents and to identify specific individuals, groups, and geographic features. The annotations also highlight any gaps and mistakes that arise in a particular document. When the mistakes are minor and are of no substantive import (for example a spelling or grammatical mistake), they have been corrected in the translated text, and the corrections are then indicated in the annotations. The wording of the translated documents is clear and concise, with the translators doing their best to convey their meaning in English. Within translated documents editorial comments are placed in brackets, parenthetical comments from the documents themselves between slash marks, and Turkish wording included to clarify translations within parentheses. Where material is omitted from the original document, ellipses are placed between brackets. Ellipses without brackets are from the original document itself. In quotations outside actual documents, occasional omissions of text are without brackets and original parenthetical comments appear without parentheses. Serving as an invaluable record of the Armenian question in all its complexities, the eight books reveal to what extent the Ottoman government knew about the Armenian revolutionary activities during the First World War.[26]

However, as the number of documents that can be collected between hard covers is strictly limited and as minutes and various in-service position papers are often not included in these published volumes this means that the serious scholar must usually still go to the ATASE. Unfortunately, these published volumes also fail to give the preliminary help he needs to shorten his labors there because the editors do not give file numbers or any other form of reference for the documents that they have published.

Large amounts of military documents on Ottoman and Turkish history can be found in the quarterly *Askeri Tarih Belgeleri Dergisi*, published since 1952. The quality of the reproduction of the documents reprinted here reflects the quality of the original print. Considerable care has been taken to ensure that the new edition of the print is legible, and the reader should be aware that the quality of the original print was never perfect and, in fact, had deteriorated due to the passage of time. The articles that appear in this journal lead highly productive lives. They contribute to vital trends in scholarship, inspire new research, and, in many cases, find their way into influential books.[27] The American political scientist and historian, Dankwart Rustow, said in 1962:

> Historians owe a warm debt of gratitude to the War History Division of the Turkish General Staff [later to be called the ATASE] for making available an abundant series of documents on the military and political aspects of the War

of Independence in its *Harp Tarihi Vesikaları Dergisi* [later to be called *Askeri Tarih Belgeleri Dergisi*].[28]

The Armenian historian Richard Hovannisian added in 1971:

> Beginning in 1952 the Turkish General Staff began publication, in serial form, of documents relating to the Nationalist movement and the War of Independence. This valuable collection, entitled *Harb Tarihi Vesikaları Dergisi*, provides a broader perspective in evaluating Armeno-Turkish relations.[29]

A series of four special issues of the *Askeri Tarih Belgeleri Dergisi*, devoted to the publication of documents from the ATASE, appeared respectively in 1982, 1983, 1985 and 1987. These collections included facsimiles and modern Turkish transliterations of several hundred documents relating to Ottoman-Armenian history from the years 1914–1918, none of which had previously been available for scholarly scrutiny. For the use of scholars not familiar with the intricacies of Ottoman Turkish, English translations of the first three special issues were subsequently published as separate volumes. While the level of the English translations leaves something to be desired, an important corpus of primary Ottoman source material has been made available. To date, not a single work published by an Armenian scholar has utilized these documents.

One of the best—but unfortunately least used—forms of coverage of the Ottoman Empire's participation in the First World War is the volumes of official histories published by the ATASE. Written in many cases by specialists with early and almost unlimited access to the archives, these are frequently of high quality. The opportunity their authors had to consult individuals who had held key positions no doubt at times led to the smoothing over of criticisms, but it also helped illuminate issues and events which might otherwise have remained obscure.[30]

For military historians of the Middle East in particular, these represent a remarkable treasure chest. However, they are little known outside Turkey because they can be obtained only from the publishing office and are not available through the normal commercial channels. It is to be hoped that these series can be provided in electronic form for Internet use, as they are rarely cited by scholars but contain much invaluable material.

NOTES

1. More details in the ATASE, Genelkurmay Başkanlığı Harp Tarihi Dairesi Tarihçesi (A Brief History of the War History Department of the Turkish General Staff) (henceforth referred to as HTDT), 1961, Folder: 1, File: 5, No. 1–14. The study has since been rewritten, expanded, and brought up to date as the cataloging work continues. In *The Armenian Genocide*, p. 807 Raymond Kévorkian errs when he says "there are no known archival funds for" the Ottoman Special Organization and that "this constitutes a major lacuna." On documents relating to the

Special Organization found in the ATASE, see Polat Safi, "History in the Trench: The Ottoman Special Organization—*Teşkilat-ı Mahsusa* Literature," *Middle Eastern Studies*, Vol. 48, No. 1 (January 2012), pp. 94–95. On the Special Organization itself see Ahmet Tetik, *Teşkilat-ı Mahsusa (Umur-ı Şarkıyye Dairesi) Tarihi Cilt I:1914–1916* (History of the Special Organization [Department of Eastern Affairs] Vol. I: 1914–1916), (İstanbul: Türkiye İş Bankası Kültür Yayınları, 2014) and Polat Safi, The Ottoman Special Organization—*Teşkilat-ı Mahsusa*: An Inquiry Into Its Operational and Administrative Characteristics, Doctoral Dissertation, Bilkent University, 2012.

2. Author interview, Colonel Ahmet Tetik, chief of the archive division of the ATASE, 11 July 2008; ATASE, HTDT, 1961, Folder: 1, File: 7, No. 1–15. On the importance of the Ottoman military archival sources see in particular, Edward Erickson, "The Turkish Official Military Histories of the First World War: A Bibliographic Essay," *Middle Eastern Studies*, Vol. 38, No. 3. (July 2003), pp. 190–198. Talha Çiçek, in his *War and State Formation in Syria: Cemal Pasha's Governorate During World War I, 1914–1917* (London and New York: Routledge, 2014), p. 25, mentions that the ATASE contains very valuable documents covering Cemal Pasha's era as commander of the Fourth Army in Syria.

3. Ahmet Tetik, "Dünden Bugüne Genelkurmay ATASE Arşivi" (Turkish General Staff Military History and Strategic Studies Directorate Archive: From Yesterday to Present), in *International Symposium on Turkish Archives 17–19 November 2005 (Presentations and Discussions)*, pp. 106–112. At this symposium, research methodology and archival resources were among the primary topics of discussion.

4. Edward Erickson, *Ottoman Army Effectiveness in World War I: A Comparative Study* (London and New York: Routledge, 2007), pp. 5 and 185n34.

5. *Türkiye Cumhuriyeti Genelkurmay ATASE ve Denetleme Başkanlığı Yayın Kataloğu* (Publication Catalog of the Turkish General Staff Directorate of Military History and Strategic Studies and Directorate of Inspection), (Ankara: Genelkurmay Basımevi, 2005).

6. Justin McCarthy, *Conference on the Reality of the Armenian Question* (Ankara: Türkiye Büyük Millet Meclisi Basımevi, 2005), p. 57.

7. Tetik, "Dünden Bugüne Genelkurmay ATASE Arşivi," pp. 106–112; Gülsüm Budaybek, "Osmanlı Askeri Arşivleri" (Ottoman Military Archives), in *Osmanlı Arşivleri ve Osmanlı Araştırmaları Sempozyumu 17 Mayıs 1985*, pp. 85–93; Nasır Yüceer, "Genelkurmay Askeri Tarih ve Stratejik Etüt (ATASE) Başkanlığı Arşivi (Tasnif, Bakım-Onarım, Yararlanmaya Sunma, Kopyalama)" (Turkish General Staff Directorate of Military History and Strategic Studies Archive [Declassification, Maintenance-Reparation, Presenting for Utilization, Duplication]), in *Birinci Milli Arşiv Şurası (Tebliğler-Tartışmalar) 20–21 Nisan 1998*, pp. 353–361.

8. Yitzchak Kerem, "The Armenian Catastrophe," *The Jerusalem Post*, 22 February 1995, p. 3.

9. İlber Ortaylı, "Cumhuriyet Devri Tarihyazıcılığının Umumi Görünümü" (The General View of the Republican Period Historiography), in Ertuğ, *Prof. Dr. Mübahat Kütükoğlu'na Armağan*, p. 223. For a different view on access to the ATASE see Özel, "Arşivler Meselemiz," pp. 30–31.

10. Çiçek, *War and State Formation in Syria*, p. 25.

11. Author interview, Colonel Suat Akgül, chief of the archive division of the ATASE, 3 August 2011. Suat Akgül is an experienced archivist well aware of the problems faced by researchers, and scholars almost always wish to thank him for his kind attention during the time they spent in the ATASE.

12. Akçam, *The Young Turks' Crime Against Humanity*, p. 9.

13. Gwynne Dyer, "Was a Massacre Genocide? The Armenian Diaspora Won't Take No for an Answer," *Pittsburgh Post-Gazette*, 19 October 2009, p. A 11 and idem, "Armenia: The End of the Debate?" *Embassy Magazine*, 21 October 2009, p. 6. Gwynne Dyer's principal current activity remains his twice-weekly syndicated column on international affairs, which he has been writing regularly since 1973. It is published by approximately 150 papers in some thirty countries.

14. See Tuncay Öğün, *Kafkas Cephesinin Birinci Dünya Savaşındaki Lojistik Desteği* (Logistical Support of the Caucasian Front in the First World War), (Ankara: Atatürk Araştırma Merkezi, 1999); Mustafa Aksakal, *The Ottoman Road to War in 1914: The Ottoman Empire*

and the First World War (Cambridge: Cambridge University Press, 2008) and Edward Erickson, *Ordered to Die: A History of the Ottoman Army in the First World War* (Westport, CT: Greenwood Press, 2001); idem, *Defeat in Detail: The Ottoman Army in the Balkans, 1912–1913* (Westport, CT: Praeger, 2003); idem, *Ottoman Army Effectiveness in World War 1*; idem, *Ottomans and Armenians*.

15. Jeremy Salt, "The Armenian 'Relocation': The Case For 'Military Necessity'," *Review of Armenian Studies*, No. 29 (2014), p. 66.

16. Shaw, *From Empire to Republic*, 5 Vols. and idem, *The Ottoman Empire in World War I*, 2 Vols., (Ankara: Türk Tarih Kurumu Basımevi, 2006–2008); Tim Travers, *Gallipoli 1915* (Stroud, Gloucestershire: Tempus Publishing, 2001); Harvey Broadbent, *Gallipoli: The Fatal Shore* (Camberwell, Victoria: Penguin Books, 2009); Michael Reynolds, *Shattering Empires: The Clash and Collapse of the Ottoman and Russian Empires 1908–1918* (New York: Cambridge University Press, 2011); Hilmar Kaiser, "Regional Resistance to Central Government Policies: Ahmed Djemal Pasha, the Governors of Aleppo, and Armenian Deportees in the Spring and Summer of 1915," *Journal of Genocide Research*, Vol. 12, No. 3–4 (September–December 2010), pp. 173–218; idem, *The Extermination of Armenians in the Diyarbekir Region* (İstanbul: İstanbul Bilgi Üniversitesi Yayınları, 2014). A review of Michael Reynolds's book by the present author is in *Middle East Quarterly*,Vol. 19, No. 3 (Summer 2012), p. 94.

17. Erickson, *Ordered to Die*, p. xxi.

18. Tim Travers, "Liman von Sanders, the Capture of Lieutenant Palmer, and Ottoman Anticipation of the Allied Landings at Gallipoli on 25 April 1915," *The Journal of Military History*, Vol. 65, No. 4 (October 2001), p. 966.

19. Travers, *Gallipoli 1915*, p. 11.

20. Travers, "Liman von Sanders, the Capture of Lieutenant Palmer, and Ottoman Anticipation of the Allied Landings at Gallipoli on 25 April 1915," p. 966n1.

21. Travers, *Gallipoli 1915*, p. 16.

22. Broadbent, *Gallipoli*, pp. x–xi.

23. Ibid., p. 349.

24. Yigal Sheffy, "Chemical Warfare and the Palestine Campaign, 1916–1918," *The Journal of Military History*, Vol. 73, No. 3 (July 2009), pp. 804–805n6.

25. Personal Communication, 11 January 2015.

26. *Arşiv Belgeleriyle Ermeni Faaliyetleri 1914–1918* (Armenian Activities Through Archival Documents 1914–1918), 8 Vols., (Ankara: Genelkurmay Basımevi, 2005–2008).

27. Consult Hamit Pehlivanlı, *Genelkurmay Askeri Tarih ve Stratejik Etüt Başkanlığı Süreli Yayınları Makaleler Dizini I* (Periodical Publications of the Turkish General Staff Directorate of Military History and Strategic Studies: Article Series I), (Ankara: Genelkurmay Basımevi, 1992) and idem, *Genelkurmay Askeri Tarih ve Stratejik Etüt Başkanlığı Süreli Yayınları Makaleler Dizini II* (Periodical Publications of the Turkish General Staff Directorate of Military History and Strategic Studies: Article Series II), (Ankara: Genelkurmay Basımevi, 2000). *On Askeri Tarih Belgeleri Dergisi* see Jaeschke, *Kurtuluş Savaşı İle İlgili İngiliz Belgeleri*, p. 258; Hikmet Özdemir, *Ermeni İddiaları Karşısında Türkiye'nin Birikimi* (Accumulation of Turkey Regarding the Armenian Allegations), (Ankara: Türkiye Büyük Millet Meclisi Kültür, Sanat ve Yayın Kurulu Yayınları, 2008), p. 84 and Yılmaz Çetiner, "Ermenilerin Katliam Belgelerini Değerlendiremiyoruz" (We Cannot Evaluate the Documents on Massacres Committed by Armenians), Haberiniz Var mı? (Are You Well Informed?), *Milliyet*, 16 April 1987, p. 3.

28. Dankwart Rustow's review of Ali Fuat Cebesoy's *Siyasi Hatıralar* (Political Recollections) and *Siyasi Hatıralar II. Kısım* (Political Recollections: Second Part) and Kazım Karabekir's *İstiklal Harbimiz* (Our War of Independence) in *The Middle East Journal*, Vol. 16, No. 1 (Winter 1962), p. 104.

29. Richard Hovannisian, *The Republic of Armenia*, Vol. 1: *The First Year, 1918–1919*, (Berkeley and Los Angeles, CA: University of California Press, 1971), p. xiii.

30. See Fahri Belen, *Birinci Dünya Harbinde Türk Harbi 1914–1918 Yılı Hareketleri* (Turkish War in the First World War: Movements of the Years 1914–1918), 5 Vols., (Ankara: Genelkurmay Basımevi, 1965–1967); Cemal Akbay, *Birinci Dünya Harbinde Türk Harbi* (Turkish War in the First World War), 2 Vols., (Ankara: Genelkurmay Basımevi, 1991); *Birinci Dünya Harbinde Türk Harbi Kafkas Cephesi Üçüncü Ordu Harekatı* (Turkish War in

the First World War: Caucasian Front Operations of the Third Army), 2 Vols., (Ankara: Genelkurmay Basımevi, 1993).

Chapter Eight

The Turkish Historical Society's Archive and the National Library

THE TURKISH HISTORICAL SOCIETY

Since its inception on 15 April 1931, the THS in Ankara has been the country's central research institution for history. Its membership is composed of the scholars of history who are engaged in teaching, writing, and research. It appoints many and various committees to recommend, supervise, and investigate historical projects. It encourages historical research in every manner possible, administers prizes and cooperates with government and private agencies in historical projects.[1]

The THS Library and Archive carries out: acquisition, appraisal, preservation, accessioning, researcher support, and large historiographical projects. Thousands of books in Turkish, English, French, and German are published by the THS, and there are hundreds of thousands of books and articles based on its library holdings. In recent years the institution has justified its existence by publishing several doctoral dissertations which had failed to catch the eye of publishers. One meritorious beneficiary of this finely meshed safety-net is Nevzat Artuç's *Cemal Paşa*.[2]

One of the THS' challenging mandates is to stimulate scholarship on the Armenian issue. It recognizes that for scholarship to flourish, preservation of and access to the historical record is essential. In 1982 the THS began publication of a series of volumes entitled *British Documents on Ottoman Armenians*. To date, four volumes have appeared covering respectively the years 1856–1880, 1880–1890, 1891–1895, and 1895. Compiled from the collections housed in the NA in London, this work serves as a handy reference tool. To the knowledge of the present author no scholar has yet examined the collection from which these documents were collected in an effort to determine if they were in fact a comprehensive corpus, or simply a selection. While providing useful background material to the larger question of Ottoman-Armenian history in the nineteenth century, one could only wish that the compiler had reversed the order of publication by working backward from the years of the First World War, rather than forward from 1856. As currently constructed it will be another generation before the volumes with direct relevance to the "genocide" question actually appear.

THE THS JOURNALS

Each year since 1 January 1937 the THS has regularly published a quarterly journal, *Belleten*, intended to serve as an international forum for the exchange of current scholarly research in Ottoman and Turkish studies and to cultivate an interdisciplinary approach to the field. *Belleten* brings out Turkey's vital and long-standing role in the Balkans and the Middle East over the centuries and describes and evaluates various avenues of contact and cooperation as well as historical, social and cultural topics. In the task the editors are assisted by a distinguished editorial board of scholars in disciplines relevant to the field working both in Turkey and abroad. Each volume contains articles, review essays, documents, and book reviews. The principal language of publication is Turkish, although articles in English or French are accepted from time to time. Many of the issues dealt with in contemporary history are still politically controversial, and arouse strong feelings. It has been the achievement of this journal, under the wise and imaginative guidance of its editorial board, to have overcome these difficulties and to have provided space for serious, scholarly work in the field, based on rigorous research and addressing questions of wide and enduring significance.[3]

Another THS review, *Belgeler*, published its first issue on 1 January 1964 and has continued to produce work mainly on Turkish historical documents. Published biannually, *Belgeler* rapidly established itself as the leading forum for the presentation and discussion of new research in the field. It offers its readers densely printed pages of recently declassified documents, with introductions and annotations. Most of these documents are from the BOA and the ATASE. The review also contains useful information about current activities at institutions in Turkey devoted to historical research, including certain archives.[4]

THE THS ARCHIVE

The archive of the THS, with its constantly growing materials, are open for public scrutiny and research. They house important private collections relating to strategy and political matters in the twentieth century, such as the

Enver Pasha and Kazım Orbay papers. The collections may be consulted by any person engaged in serious research who presents proper identification bearing his or her photograph and current or permanent address, completes the THS' registration process, and agrees to adhere to THS' rules for the use of rare materials. Student access to the collections is generally limited to those engaged in graduate study; undergraduates with previous experience in using manuscripts who are working on a senior thesis or similar research project under the direction of a faculty member are admitted upon an introduction in person or in writing by their advisors.

ENVER PASHA COLLECTION

Enver Pasha was undoubtedly the supreme power behind the Ottoman First World War effort.[5] He had an almost entirely free hand in military affairs. In addition to his portfolio as minister of war, Enver Pasha further consolidated his hold over the army by retaining the title of acting commander-in-chief and chief of the general staff as well. Holding these three offices concurrently enabled him to establish primacy over strategic direction and policy, supervise and direct the general staff, and command the Ottoman army operationally. It was a staggering consolidation of power in the hands of a single person and no other individual in any country had similar authority. Enver Pasha's influence was far superior to the Sultan's, and his power not even the Sheikh-ul-Islam, that supreme authority of the Muslim world, cared to challenge.[6]

Enver Pasha remains the most controversial Ottoman general of the First World War. Thanks to the work of a number of historians, the standing of the Ottoman army has been refurbished in recent years. The fate of Enver Pasha's reputation has, however, been rather different. That is not because of lack of attention from writers. All the same, consensus about Enver Pasha remains elusive.

The Enver Pasha collection, donated to the THS in 1972 by Mahpeyker Ürgüb, his eldest daughter, consists of some 789 single, disparate items including handwritten notes, typescripts, scrapbooks, memoranda, reports, military records, cards and invitations, dispatches, evaluations by colleagues and opponents, photographic albums, topographic maps, charts, private correspondence, diaries, travel documents and miscellany from the period 1914–1922. Enver Pasha's major role in the Ottoman Empire's internal and external policies, as well as the broad array of issues that came under his jurisdiction, explain the wide range of documents in his archive and make it a first-rank collection. This superlative repository for scholars of Ottoman history and armed forces is represented by one series of unbound papers, mostly chronologically arranged. It contains documents in Turkish, German, and

French. A subject index lists the boxes by number and sometimes by dossiers.[7] There are no restrictions governing access to these and they are open to all scholars.[8]

The records of Enver Pasha's tenure of office at the War Ministry (1914–1918) are especially important because they document a tumultuous time in late Ottoman history—one that saw the empire's participation in the First World War, large-scale internal revolts, and Armenian population displacements. The private correspondence that Enver Pasha stored away was of extraordinary variety. It is the most precious part of this unparalleled manuscript section. This group of letters to and from the Ottoman general is a firsthand, detailed history of the Turks from 1914 to 1922. It should be noted that Enver Pasha saved, evidently, most of correspondence initiated by him and directed to him.[9]

The Enver Pasha collection constitutes a mine of information that remains to be fully investigated. Such documentation is especially valuable because in the early decades of the twentieth century, ministers and senior officials routinely retained possession of whatever papers they chose and normally made no distinction in the case of sensitive or secret material. It was quite common in those years for a minister to keep in his personal files, papers which should have gone to the archives. On leaving office a minister would carry off his personal files. Also, it was not unknown for a minister to have certain papers removed from the official record. Enver Pasha's correspondence is one of the most comprehensive surviving collections of the Ottoman Empire's participation in the First World War, drawn on by a succession of biographers of this Ottoman general, but it has not been as widely used by most historians of the period as it should have been. Additional research into the Enver Pasha collection should prove most valuable in this connection.

It is gratifying that Murat Bardakçı, an Ottomanist and one of the leading private archivists in Turkey, is about to complete a book on Enver Pasha based mostly on the latter's private letters kept in his family. In no sense has the last word been written on this Ottoman commander.

KAZIM ORBAY COLLECTION

Kazım Orbay was Enver Pasha's brother-in-law and served as his chief aide-de-camp during the whole First World War period. Being a most trusted confidential adjunct, his opinion carried considerable weight on Enver Pasha's conduct of day-to-day affairs. In 1926–1928 he served as chief of staff of Afghanistan's army and in 1944–1946 of the army of the Turkish Republic.[10]

Orbay's papers, chiefly a diverse collection of documents, reports, notes, resolutions, telegrams, manuscripts, personal letters, correspondence, maps, cuttings and photographs— mostly dating from the First World War—enable one to see which issues most engaged the supreme Ottoman commander's attention. The distinct events and politico-military personages involved in these papers make it a rich source of historical data. Orbay was frequently referred to by German staff officers and ambassadors in a number of German reports, particularly in the years 1914 through 1918. He was alluded to as "Kazim Bey," or as a "trusted source in the War Ministry." Surprisingly few have used this voluminous collection over four decades, perhaps because it has not been well publicized or because its systematic arrangement has been recent. Relevant documents, which have survived to a remarkable extent, are still awaiting discovery and exploitation.[11]

Mustafa Aksakal's *The Ottoman Road to War in 1914*, benefiting from the archival sources at the Turkish Historical Society, does its work creditably and with considerable originality of interpretation, since this young Turkish scholar has not hesitated to challenge long-accepted opinions about Enver Pasha. The author has invited comparison of his evidence—elaborately fortified with footnotes and appendices—with his conclusions. The net product is a book with which historians of the Ottoman Empire and the First World War must reckon. Here Aksakal is staking a real claim to pioneer scholarship. It is surprising that more research has not been done along these lines.[12]

THE NATIONAL LIBRARY

Libraries are the gateways to the sources. Their primary functions are the organization and provision of access to knowledge and information. They are the primary locations in which to plan and organize research. An enormous wealth of research material is held in library and information collections in Turkey. The NL is at the center of the library network in the country. In its various reference divisions it holds the national collection of printed materials. Broadly speaking, the researcher can expect to find there any significant publication printed in Turkey. It stands in relation to other libraries in Turkey just as the Library of Congress, the British Library and the Bibliothèque Nationale stand in relation to other libraries in the United States, Britain, and France. Since 1946, along with Beyazıt State Library in İstanbul, this library has received a copy of everything published in Turkey. The NL's strongest collections are in bibliography, political, economic, and social science, public law and legislation, the fine arts, as well as Turkish history, and biography. Its collections comprise the national archive and contain rare and valuable materials many of which are unique.

The Beyazıt State Library is located close to the former BOA building and just around the corner from İstanbul University. It holds a wide collection of newspapers and journals in Ottoman Turkish.[13]

The NL is of key importance as it is the official repository for all books published in Turkey. It retains its preeminent position as the country's most valuable deposit of manuscript and published material available for research purposes. The NL is open to the public. The widest and freest possible use of the library is permitted.

Some material—mainly general reference and bibliographic material, as well as science and business information—is held in open access in the reading rooms, and can be browsed freely. However, most items in the collections are held in closed access stores so one must order them using the catalog. Collection items can only be consulted in reading rooms. They cannot be removed from reading rooms and must be returned to the Issue Desk before departure. Copying services are in reading rooms. The NL's website—http://www.mkutup.gov.tr—is a useful source of information about its services and collections. Many NL catalogs are accessible through the website.[14]

The NL catalogs are primarily lists of books and serials. They do not as a rule list the contents of books or periodicals. Other materials that often may not be listed include—for example—government documents and the contents of microform sets which are not usually cataloged. The automated catalogs do not often include the entire stock of the NL; they hold only acquisitions since a specified date. Earlier holdings of the NL have to be sought in the older card, guard book, microfiche or other catalogs.

The range of reference sources is very extensive—specialist encyclopedias, directories, dictionaries, periodicals' indexes, catalogs of national imprints, current bibliographies, critical specialized bibliographies, subject guides to sources, national and special library catalogs, abstracting services, citation indexes, biographical sources, and book review indexes, among others. It is a constant surprise to the NL staff, who are more fully aware of the burgeoning range of reference sources, that so few scholars know of the existence—let alone use of—a number of reference tools which would greatly strengthen their grasp of the potential sources and literature. It is in this area of reference tools that developments of computerization and information technology are having greatest impact. Many of the catalogs, indexes and bibliographies about to be referred to in the NL are available in both printed form and on CD-ROMs, but may cover only the more recent years of the reference source. The printed version of earlier volumes may have to be consulted to complete a search.

The breadth and depth of the collections held by the NL have made it central to humanistic scholarship—especially historical scholarship—in Turkey. Historians have quickly come to claim the NL as their own. Librarians have always viewed the NL as "the librarian's library" and have looked to Ankara for innovation and leadership in the continuing effort to foster the nation's library system.

NOTES

1. For a discussion of the work of the THS, see Uluğ İğdemir, *Yılların İçinden Makaleler, Anılar, İncelemeler* (Inside the Years: Articles, Recollections, Studies), (Ankara: Türk Tarih Kurumu Basımevi, 1976), pp. 193–205.

2. Uluğ İğdemir, *Cumhuriyetin 50. Yılında Türk Tarih Kurumu* (Turkish Historical Society in the Fiftieth Anniversary of the Founding of the Republic), (Ankara: Türk Tarih Kurumu Basımevi, 1973), pp. 37–51; idem, *Yılların İçinden*, pp. 205–207; Fahri Çoker, *Türk Tarih Kurumu: Kuruluş Amacı ve Çalışmaları* (Turkish Historical Society: Purpose of Its Foundation and Activities), (Ankara: Türk Tarih Kurumu Basımevi, 1983), p. 142; *Türk Tarih Kurumu Yayınları Kataloğu 2011* (Publications Catalog of the Turkish Historical Society 2011), (Ankara: Türk Tarih Kurumu Basımevi, 2011), p. xii; Semih Yalçın, *Türkiye Cumhuriyeti Tarihinin Kaynakları* (Sources on the History of the Turkish Republic), (Ankara: Berikan Yayınları, 2003), pp. 45–46; Yunus Koç, "Türk Tarih Kurumu ve Türk Tarihçiliğindeki Yeri" (Turkish Historical Society and Its Place in Turkish Historianship), in Öz, *Cumhuriyet Döneminde Türkiye'de Tarihçilik ve Tarih Yayıncılığı Sempozyumu Bildiriler Ankara, 18–20 Mart 2010*, pp. 655–656.

3. Uluğ İğdemir, "Belleten Yirmibeş Yaşında" (Belleten at Its Twenty-fifth Year), *Belleten*, Vol. 25, No. 100 (January 1961), pp. 536–537; idem, *Yılların İçinde*, pp. 207–209; Yalçın, *Türkiye Cumhuriyeti Tarihinin Kaynakları*, pp. 180–182; Yüksel Özgen, "Belleten Dergisinin Türk Tarihçiliğindeki Yeri" (Place of the Belleten Journal in Turkish Historianship), in Öz, *Cumhuriyet Döneminde Türkiye'de Tarihçilik ve Tarih Yayıncılığı Sempozyumu Bildiriler Ankara, 18–20 Mart 2010*, pp. 619–626.

4. İğdemir, *Cumhuriyetin 50. Yılında Türk Tarih Kurumu*, pp. 40–41; *Türk Tarih Kurumu Yayınları Kataloğu 2011*, p. xi; Yalçın, *Türkiye Cumhuriyeti Tarihinin Kaynakları*, pp. 168–170.

5. For details of Enver Pasha's military career, see Hülya Toker and Nurcan Aslan, eds., *Birinci Dünya Savaşına Katılan Alay ve Daha Üst Kademedeki Komutanların Biyografileri* (Biographies of the Regiment and More Senior Level Commanders Who Participated in the First World War), Vol. 3, (Ankara: Genelkurmay Basımevi, 2009), pp. 8–10.

6. Erickson, *Ottomans and Armenians*, p. 113; Şevket Süreyya Aydemir, *Makedonya'dan Ortaasya'ya Enver Paşa* (From Macedonia to Central Asia: Enver Pasha), Vol. 3: 1914–1922, (İstanbul: Remzi Kitabevi, 1972), pp. 15–25.

7. "1972 Yılı Çalışma Raporu"(Annual Report of the Board of Governors of the Turkish Historical Society for 1972), *Belleten*, Vol. 37, No. 147 (July 1973), p. 425.

8. Çiçek, *War and State Formation in Syria*, p. 25.

9. Although many of Enver Pasha's papers have long been available, relatively few scholars have written substantially about his activities. The most detailed coverage is by Aydemir, *Makedonya'dan Ortaasya'ya Enver Paşa*, 3 Vols. See also Şükrü Hanioğlu, *Kendi Mektuplarında Enver Paşa* (Enver Pasha in His Own Letters), (İstanbul: Der Yayınları, 1989); Masayuki Yamauchi, *Hoşnut Olmamış Adam Enver Paşa: Türkiye'den Türkistan'a* (Discontented Man Enver Pasha: From Turkey to Turkestan), (İstanbul: Bağlam, 1995); Arı İnan, ed., *Enver Paşa'nın Özel Mektupları* (Enver Pasha's Private Letters), (Ankara: İmge Kitabevi, 1997); Yusuf Gedikli, *Enver Paşa: Nutukları, Makaleleri, Bazı Beyannameleri ve Mektupları* (Enver Pasha: His Speeches, Articles, Some Declarations and Letters), (İstanbul: Ufuk Ötesi Yayınları, 2005).

10. For a brief biographical sketch of Kazım Orbay, see *Türk Parlamento Tarihi Cumhuriyet Senatosu Üyelerinin Özgeçmişleri* (History of the Turkish Parliament: Curricula Vitae of the Members of the Republican Senate), Vol. 1: 1961–1964, (Ankara: Türkiye Büyük Millet Meclisi Vakfı Yayınları, 1998), pp. 668–670.

11. İğdemir, *Cumhuriyetin 50. Yılında Türk Tarih Kurumu*, p. 51; Çoker, *Türk Tarih Kurumu: Kuruluş Amacı ve Çalışmaları*, p. 143.

12. Mustafa Aksakal, "Why Did the Ottomans Enter a European War in 1914? New Sources, New Views," *The Journal of Ottoman Studies*, No. 36 (2010), pp. 187–193.

13. Selim Efe Erdem, ed., *İstanbul'un Yaşayan Efsanesi Semavi Eyice Kitabı* (The Living Legend of İstanbul: The Semavi Eyice Book), (İstanbul: Timaş Yayınları, 2014), p. 366.

14. Mahmut Şakiroğlu, "La bibliothèque nationale d'Ankara," *Turcica*, Vol. 20 (1988), pp. 243–246.

Chapter Nine

Muslim Court Records and Others

MUSLIM COURT RECORDS

In 1991 the NL became the home of indispensable Muslim court records exceeding ten thousand items. Other than the BOA and the ATASE, this repository has to be regarded as the major resource for an Ottoman historian. Through concrete stories and events recorded contemporaneously by locals, the material gives a vivid sense of how society actually worked, of the pursuits, practices, strategies, conflicts and accidents that wove the fabric of daily life. Women and ordinary people, who scarcely figure in most other sources, appear on virtually every page of the records. With a sufficiently large body of cases in hand it is possible to draw larger patterns out of the bits and pieces of detail. Muslim court records remained in place in many of the former provinces—now nation-states—of the Middle East and the Balkans. Whereas various sources contribute much to particular aspects of Ottoman history, local judicial registers have proven the most useful in exploring Muslim society and economic endeavors.[1]

The court and the kadi who presided over it were among the most important administrative institutions in Ottoman cities. Kadis were appointed by the sultan upon the recommendation of the highest religious officials and were in effect civil servants of the Ottoman state. A kadi's responsibilities were many. He was the holder of religious authority and expected to be an expert on Islamic law, Ottoman administrative ordinances or regulations—which theoretically conformed to or at least did not contradict the precepts of Islamic law—and local customary law, usually unwritten but recognized by judges as binding precedent. He served as judge, notary, and supervisor of religious endowments, and was responsible for the distribution of legacies. As representative of the central government he was, in effect, responsible for administration of the city and was charged with enforcement of the law, as well as division of the tax burden and its collection. Decrees issued by the central authorities were addressed to the kadi, whose responsibility it was to see that they were copied into his record books, brought to the attention of the populace, and carried out. The kadi served as an intermediary between the local population and the state. It was through him that petitions were presented to the sultan and the grand vizier, and he was responsible for checking their details. Due to the kadi's many functions, his court became the venue in which he came into contact with residents of all religious persuasions. It was generally located in an accessible site, such as the courtyard of a mosque or near the central market place. Non-Muslims did not refrain from turning to the Muslim court. Their faith and confidence in the court is clear from the fact that they presented petitions to the kadi.[2]

In all the major urban centers of the Ottoman Empire, proceedings of the Muslim court were recorded and stored. Although these must have been kept since early in the empire's history, the largest number of them have been preserved from the eighteenth and nineteenth centuries. Many of the records in the NL's Rare Books and Manuscript collection were brought there from the following provincial museums in Turkey, with the notable exception of İstanbul: Adana, Afyon, Antalya, Bursa, Diyarbakır, Hatay, İzmir, Konya, Kütahya, Manisa, Niğde, Sivas and Van. The İstanbul records consist of approximately 12,000 pieces, dating back to the early sixteenth century and continuing through the early twentieth, housed in the office of this city's mufti in the Süleymaniye quarter. The wealth of information in these makes them one of the most complete, continuous, and enlightening sources for the history of the Ottoman capital. Records formerly kept in the Topkapı Palace Museum Archive were also included in the NL's collection. The whole collection could be consulted in the İbni Sina Reading Room on the third floor of the library.[3] Some 8,934 copies of Muslim court records were moved in 2006 to the BOA in İstanbul.[4]

Muslim court records consist of transcriptions—often abbreviated—of cases involving a wide range of issues, including imperial administration, city government, the affairs of townspeople, and villagers. They deal with almost every aspect of the lives of the people, be it personal status, taxes, loans and credits, sales of houses and other real estate, property rights, commercial dealings, marriage payments, divorce, child custody and support, inheritance, family trusts, market and guild regulations, water supply, appointments to public office, charitable endowments, business partnerships, conversion to Islam, communal institutions, official abuses, construction, crime, public morals, complaints, flight, or theft. Any matter requiring official resolution, registration, verification, or adjudication was potentially the domain of the Muslim judge. Cases are listed in chronological order and present a full account of the social life and actual legal conditions of the non-

Muslims under Ottoman rule. This happened not only because the non-Muslims were under the jurisdiction of Muslim judges for so many areas of the law, but also because the former often preferred to seek the latter's decision or certificate. The use of Muslim courts provided greater assurance, or the means to escape the more rigid stipulations of their own religious law in such matters as marriage, divorce, and parenthood rights, which were supposed to be under the exclusive jurisdiction of the non-Muslim authorities. Muslim court records abound in decisions, as well as contracts, transactions, certificates, and other kinds of documents, drawn up not only between Muslims and non-Muslims but also between non-Muslim parties.[5]

The materials in the administrative archives previously mentioned were written by members of a scribal institution rigorously trained in certain methods of writing and penmanship. The script in which they wrote was regular in form throughout the centuries of Ottoman rule. However it appears that scribes in the Muslim courts were not similarly trained in a regular system of calligraphy. The scripts in which the Muslim court records are written vary widely, and are far more difficult to decipher than those in the administrative registers. However the material contained in these records is of such importance for the study of the political, social, and economic structure and development of the Ottoman Empire, that these difficulties must be surmounted and the materials in these records consulted during the course of research.[6]

ARMENIANS IN MUSLIM COURT RECORDS

In the Muslim court records Armenians were not mentioned merely in passing, but as individuals involved in actual cases—either with Muslims and Jews or with other Christians, including other Armenians. This abundance of cases encompasses an impressive range of topics and covers most aspects of life. These aspects include, (1) Family matters: marriage and divorce; relations between husband and wife; education of children; death and inheritance; (2) Demographic data and trends; (3) Economic activity: financial and commercial agreements; real estate; debts; professional organizations; rich and poor; fund-raising for charitable purposes; (4) Religious life: churches, cemeteries, and other religious institutions; religious functions and functionaries; customs and rituals; (5) Intercommunity relations: the Armenians' relations with their Muslim, Jewish and other Christian neighbors; relations with the central and local authorities; contacts with other Armenian communities; channels of communication with İstanbul; (6) Community life and organization: community institutions; social stratification; housing and communications; (7) Cultural aspects: the use of Armenian and other languages; terminology; names and personal adjectives.[7]

SCHOLARS AND MUSLIM COURT RECORDS

Muslim court records have become increasingly popular among scholars eager to obtain large amounts of material in a more or less uniform format from periods and areas poorly reflected in the BOA collection of tax registers. They were first used to good effect by Halit Ongan in 1958.[8]

The importance of extant Muslim court records has long been recognized by historians of the Ottoman realm as evidenced by the numerous original investigations which have been done relying on them. Hundreds of books and articles have appeared in which the authors make extensive use of these records from the Balkans to the Arabian Peninsula. Their increasing availability and use have greatly enhanced our understanding of the social and economic life of the empire. Many of our old conceptions about Ottoman society have been reevaluated. In some cases Ottoman history was (and still is) being reshaped.[9]

During the last four decades, a number of scholars from North America, Europe, the Middle East, and Japan have turned their attention and efforts to the Muslim court records of various Ottoman cities. Historians have used them alongside chronicles, biographical dictionaries, and European travelers' reports, to provide a deeper and more accurate portrait of provincial life under Ottoman rule than was available before. Ronald Carlton Jennings, Jr. was among the first non-Turkish scholars to draw attention to the potential richness of such material. He was more closely associated with the fruitful use of the Muslim court records than perhaps any other historian on the other side of the Atlantic. Beginning with his "Loans and Credit in Early Seventeenth Century Ottoman Judicial Records," and continuing with articles on women, wealth, taxation, slaves, and urban demography, among other topics, his work has confirmed the richness of Muslim court records as a source for economic and social history of the Balkans and the Middle East in the Ottoman era.[10]

A new generation of scholars has been challenged to reexamine the history of the peoples of the Ottoman Empire, using previously neglected authentic archives. It was hoped that the results would supplement—and even revise—earlier studies of the period that had relied on such traditional mainstays of Western historiography of the Ottoman Empire as travelers' accounts, European consular reports, and local chronicles. Thanks to the wave of research in Muslim court records beginning in the 1970s, many books and doctoral dissertations published since provide detailed treatments of provincial judicial systems, as well as discussions of court buildings, the manner in which a court record was compiled, and the status of non-Muslims. *Morality Tales: Law and Gender in the Court of Aintab* makes use of Muslim court records, in this instance the 3,000 civil and criminal cases heard in the court of Aintab in the twelve months from September 1540 to October 1541.[11]

Leslie Peirce of Columbia University, a former Peace Corps volunteer, was grateful to the staff of the NL, who facilitated her work in their collections. She was especially indebted to Dursun Kaya, director of the Rare Books and Manuscripts division, who together with his staff assisted her in numerous ways as she read the Muslim court records of Aintab.[12]

Turkish scholars have employed these registers extensively for Anatolian regional studies. But their work has not yet gained the recognition it deserves beyond the ranks of specialists in Ottoman and Middle East history.[13]

Several works of Professor Halil İnalcık are in some degree based upon the same sources. From these sources he has extracted an abundance of information about Ottoman society and the ways it functions. He is at home with Muslim court records and actively takes on the role of historian as evaluator—and not merely chronicler—offering colorful portraits of dozens of his *dramatis personae*. The innovation of using these records represented a breath of fresh air in the craft of writing the history of Ottoman Turkish provinces. Some of the material used confirmed or expanded our knowledge based on other places and times; some provided us with new insight.[14]

Unfortunately, much of this wealth is unknown to the scholastic world and under-exploited by academic researchers. The bulk of the present material remains to be explored. They constitute the focal resource for much new analytic and interpretive research. Using court documents, however, requires special skills: one must be familiar with Islamic law and with the organization and culture of these courts.[15]

The best, though certainly not definite, description of the contents of Turkish Muslim courts series and its various uses for historiography thus far to appear has been Ahmed Akgündüz's *Şer'iye Sicilleri:Mahiyeti, Toplu Kataloğu ve Seçme Hükümler*.[16] It allows the prospective user to determine the years covered by each record in addition to the call number. Moreover this guide contains a selection of reproduced documents. A complete inventory of Muslim court records is the aim, and it is to be hoped that this three-volume work will stimulate efforts to fill in the gaps.[17]

Although the Muslim court records are certainly a major source for the study of Ottoman societies, their importance greatly decreases with regard to the second half of the nineteenth century. Late nineteenth-century judicial reforms largely limited the legal and administrative responsibilities and functions of the Muslim court. The records clearly reflects this marginalization.[18]

MANUSCRIPTS AND SPECIAL COLLECTIONS: MAPS, PHOTOGRAPHS, AND ENGRAVINGS

The NL's Rare Books and Manuscripts division includes thousands of prints, engravings, lithographs, and photographs. There is a splendid collection of old war maps. Much valuable historical matter is contained in the files of newspapers, some of which are hundreds of years old. The newspapers, however, form only part of the records that line the long shelves. There are also hundreds of periodicals currently being published and many of older date. Additional construction at the NL increased materially the accommodations for books and branch facilities. The public is able to access the digital archive at the institution.[19]

Beyazıt and Süleymaniye Libraries in İstanbul have exhaustive holdings of government documentation, and hold popular and short-lived material not available elsewhere. Many researchers frequently resort to these collections.

İstanbul Atatürk Library has significant potential research material, with a particularly rich trove of current and past periodicals. Backfiles of newspapers are often held in bound folios, in clipping collections, or on microfilm. They include major newspapers holding different political opinions. Few newspapers are indexed retrospectively. The staff at the İstanbul Atatürk Library is knowledgeable and helpful, and answers all inquiries about the location of newspapers and periodicals.

Libraries in Turkey are in a period of rapid transition. New automated facilities appear almost daily to supplement and sometimes replace traditional hard-copy versions of reference resources.

THE REPUBLICAN ARCHIVE

A great number of archival materials regarding the Turkish Republic are gathered, cataloged, and made available in the RA at İvedik Sokağı in the Yenimahalle district of Ankara.[20] The RA has recently been swollen by the addition of hundreds of boxes of documents released from several government departments. These materials amount to 30 million documents and are arranged either chronologically, according to subject matter, or by their institutional provenance. Most sets are bound into volumes classified by subject. The RA provides reading rooms, equipped with microfilm readers and reader-copiers, and supported by a reference library of handbooks, directories, and other works based on the documents in the archive. The former building had long been overcrowded, with inadequate space for those who wished to study the records. Additional features in reading rooms such as extra filing cabinets, cupboards, tables and chairs permits more storage and greater accessibility. The records of the Republic, which also include several *fonds* belonging to the periods of the First World War and the War of Independence, cover a huge variety of subjects. A complete and accurate catalog of all holdings exists. These include those concerning the Decisions of the Council of Ministers, Joint Ministerial Decrees, Directorate of the Private Cabinet of the Prime Minister, Directorate General of the Administrative

Transactions of the Prime Minister's Office, Ministry of Public Works, Directorate General of the Land Settlement, Presidency of the Department of Religious Affairs and the Republican People's Party. Publications are available to help researchers orient themselves. There is open access to archival materials at Yenimahalle.[21]

The RA is consulted by such users as historians, genealogists, educationalists, students, journalists, filmmakers, geophysicists, environmentalists, and individuals concerned with their rights and entitlements. Working in the RA is comfortable and convenient. The Director and staff, often historians themselves, are friendly, helpful and anxious to serve. They guide the researchers to the right cabinet, carton, or file and to pertinent holdings elsewhere. Requests are normally handled expeditiously. Unsurprisingly, Marc David Baer, professor of history at the University of California, Irvine, writes: "In Ankara, Director Ahmet Ceylan and the helpful and earnest staff of the Archive of the Republic enabled me to successfully conduct my research in a very short period of time."[22] Sarah Shields, associate professor of history at University of North Carolina, owed a great deal to archivists and librarians of the RA who have helped her locate the materials on which her *Fezzes in the River: Identity Politics and European Diplomacy in the Middle East on the Eve of World War II* is partly based.[23]

The Statutes of Regulations, as a general rule, provide for the regular transfer of records to the DGSA for research by all government bodies thirty years after their creation and upon declassification. By setting this time limit, Turkey has put a considerable amount of material of crucial importance to the Armenian affairs at the disposal of the academic community. Today more and more archival evidence from the RA is opening up to scholarly examination. It seems certain that no serious student of twentieth-century Turkish history will be able to disregard these resources.[24]

OTHER ARCHIVE COLLECTIONS

Less well known, although just as significant, are the archives of various universities, museums, and other Turkish scientific or cultural organizations. University manuscript departments, often located within university libraries, hold valuable research collections. They have wide-ranging materials of national importance, sometimes accumulated over many centuries. They may also yield relevant documentation in the search for contingent records of Turkish-Armenian contacts in many fields. These repositories are widely scattered over the country. All this material is available for the public to read.[25]

NOTES

1. İsmail Hakkı Uzunçarşılı, "Şer'i Mahkeme Sicilleri" (Muslim Court Records), *Ülkü Halkevleri Mecmuası*, Vol. 5, No. 29 (1935), pp. 365–369; Halil İnalcık, "Osmanlı Tarihi Hakkında Mühim Bir Kaynak" (An Important Source on Ottoman History), *Ankara Üniversitesi Dil, Tarih-Coğrafya Fakültesi Dergisi*, Vol. 1, No. 2 (1942), pp. 89–96; Çaykara, *Tarihçilerin Kutbu Halil İnalcık Kitabı*, p. 127; Özel and Çetinsaya, "Türkiye'de Osmanlı Tarihçiliğinin Son Çeyrek Yüzyılı," pp. 31–32; Ahmed Akgündüz, *Osmanlı Devletinde Gayrimüslimlerin Yönetimi* (The Governance of Non-Muslims in the Ottoman State), (İstanbul: Timaş Yayınları, 2008), pp. 64 and 87; Ali Birinci, *Tarihin Hududunda Hatırat Kitapları, Matbuat Yasakları ve Arşiv Meseleleri* (Reminescences Books, Press Prohibitions and Archival Questions on the Boundary of History), (İstanbul: Dergah Yayınları, 2012), p. 71; Abraham Marcus, *The Middle East on the Eve of Modernity: Aleppo in the Eighteenth Century* (New York: Columbia University Press, 1989), p. 11; Faroqhi, *Approaching Ottoman History*, p. 55.

2. Ortaylı, "Osmanlı Kadısı (Tarihi Temeli ve Yargı Görevi)," pp. 117–128 and idem, *Osmanlı'yı Yeniden Keşfetmek*, pp. 127–134; Ben-Naeh, *Jews in the Realm of the Sultans*, pp. 33–34.

3. Halaçoğlu, "Osmanlı Devletinde Arşivcilik," p. 89; Fethi Gedikli, "Osmanlı Hukuk Tarihi Kaynağı Olarak Şer'iyye Sicilleri" (Muslim Court Records as a Source of Ottoman History of Law), *Türkiye Araştırmaları Literatür Dergisi*, Vol. 3, No. 5 (2005), p. 188n3.

4. Gönül Büyüklimanlı et al., *Geçmişten Geleceğe Köprü: Milli Kütüphane* (A Bridge from the Past to the Future: The National Library), (Ankara: Milli Kütüphane Yayınları, 2011), p. 65.

5. İnalcık, "Ottoman Archival Materials on *Millets*," p. 437; Amy Singer, "Tapu Tahrir Defterleri ve Kadı Sicilleri: A Happy Marriage of Sources," *Tarih*, Vol. 1 (1990), pp. 95–125 and Yvonne Seng, "The Şer'iyye Sicilleri of the Istanbul Müftülüğü as a Source for the Study of Everyday Life," *The Turkish Studies Association Bulletin*, Vol. 15, No. 2 (September 1991), pp. 309–325.

6. Shaw, "Archival Sources for Ottoman History," p. 8.

7. Ali Özgökmen, Konya Şer'iyye Sicilleri Işığında Müslim-Gayrımüslim Münasebetleri (Muslim-Non-Muslim Relations in the Light of the Konya Muslim Court Records), Selçuk University, Doctoral Dissertation, 1996, Konya and Fethi Gedikli, "Şer'iyye Sicillerinin Hukuk Tarihi Açısından Önemi ve Sicillere Dayalı Araştırmalar" (Importance of the Muslim Court Records As Regards the History of Law and Studies Based on Muslim Court Records) in Ali Akyıldız, Tufan Buzpınar and Mustafa Sinanoğlu, eds., *Dünden Bugüne Osmanlı Araştırmaları Tespitler-Problemler-Teklifler Sempozyum* (Ottoman Studies From Yesterday to the Present Diagnoses-Problems-Proposals: Symposium), (İstanbul: İsam Yayınları, 2007), pp. 73–96.

8. Halit Ongan, *Ankara'nın 1 Numaralı Şer'iye Sicili 14 Mayıs 1583–12 Şubat 1584* (Muslim Court Records of Ankara Number 1, 14 May 1583–12 February 1584), (Ankara: Ankara Üniversitesi Dil ve Tarih-Coğrafya Fakültesi Yayınları, 1958).

9. Dror Ze'evi, "The Use of Ottoman Shari'a Court Records as a Source for Middle Eastern Social History: A Reappraisal," *Islamic Law and Society*, Vol. 5, No. 1 (1998), p. 35.

10. See Ronald Carlton Jennings, Jr., The Judicial Registers ('Şer'i Mahkeme Sicilleri') of Kayseri (1550–1630) as a Source for Ottoman History, Doctoral Dissertation, University of California at Los Angeles, 1972; idem, *Studies on Ottoman Social History in the Sixteenth and Seventeenth Centuries Women, Zimmis and Sharia Courts in Kayseri, Cyprus and Trabzon* (İstanbul: The Isis Press, 1999); idem, "Loans and Credit in Early Seventeenth Century Ottoman Judicial Records," *Journal of the Economic and Social History of the Orient*, Vol. 16 (1973), pp. 168–216; idem, "Women in Early 17th Century Ottoman Judicial Records: The Shari'a Court of Anatolian Kaiseri," *Journal of the Economic and Social History of the Orient*, Vol. 18 (1975), pp. 53–114; Marco Salati, "The Prayer and the Bread: A Document on the Mevlevi Order from the Qadi Court Registers of Aleppo (1154–1741)," *Eurasian Studies*, Vol. 10 (2012), p. 2. Also Suraiya Faroqhi, *Men of Modest Substance: House Owners and House Property in Seventeenth-Century Ankara and Kayseri* (New York: Cambridge University Press, 1987).

11. Leslie Peirce, *Morality Tales: Law and Gender in the Ottoman Court of Aintab* (Berkeley and Los Angeles, CA: University of California Press, 2003).

12. Ibid., p. xi.

13. See, for instance, among others Hülya Canbakal, *Society and Politics in an Ottoman Town: 'Ayntab in the 17th Century* (Leiden: E. J. Brill, 2007); Boğaç Ergene, *Local Court, Provincial Society and Justice in the Ottoman Empire: Legal Practice and Dispute Resolution in Çankırı and Kastamonu* (Leiden: E. J. Brill, 2002); Işık Tamdoğan-Abel, Les Modalités de l'Urbanité dans une Ville Ottomane: Les Habitants d'Adana au XVIIIème Siècle d'après les Registres des Cadıs, Ecole des Hautes Etudes en Sciences Sociales, Doctoral Dissertation, 1998, Paris and Hayri Erten, *Konya Şer'iyye Sicilleri Işığında Ailenin Sosyo-Ekonomik ve Kültürel Yapısı (XVIII. Yüzyıl İlk Yarısı)* (Socio-Economic and Cultural Structure of the Family in the Light of the Konya Muslim Court Records [First Half of the Eighteenth Century]), (Ankara: Türkiye Cumhuriyeti Kültür Bakanlığı, 2001). For a critical review on studies based on Muslim court records see Ze'evi, "The Use of Ottoman Shari'a Court as a Source for Middle Eastern Social History," pp. 35–36.

14. On studies using the Muslim court records as a source and for an assessment of these, see Yunus Uğur, "Mahkeme Kayıtları (Şer'iyye Sicilleri): Literatür Değerlendirmesi ve Bibliyografya" (Muslim Court Records: Assessment of Literature and Bibliography), *Türkiye Araştırmaları Literatür Dergisi*, Vol. 1, No. 1 (2003), pp. 305–344.

15. For insightful discussions on the use and importance of Muslim court records, see Güçlü Tülüveli, "Mikrotarihçilik ve Kaynak Kullanımı Problemi: Kadı Sicilleri Örneği" (Microhistorianship and the Problem of Source Use: Example of Muslim Court Records), in Zeynel Abidin Kızılyaprak, ed., *Tarih Yazımında Yeni Yaklaşımlar: Küreselleşme ve Yerelleşme Üçüncü Uluslararası Tarih Kongresi* (New Approaches in Historiography: Globalization and Localization: Third International History Congress), (İstanbul: Türkiye Ekonomik ve Toplumsal Tarih Vakfı Yayınları, 2000), pp. 271–273; Cahid Baltacı, "Şer'iye Sicillerinin Tarihsel ve Kültürel Önemi"(Historical and Cultural Importance of the Muslim Court Records), in *Osmanlı Arşivleri ve Osmanlı Araştırmaları Sempozyumu 17 Mayıs 1985*, pp. 127–132; Jon Mandaville, "The Jerusalem Shari'a Court Records: A Supplement and Complement to the Central Ottoman Archives," in Moshe Maoz, ed., *Studies on Palestine During the Ottoman Period* (Jerusalem: The Magnes Press, the Hebrew University and Yad Izhak Ben-Zvi, 1975), pp. 517–524 and Amy Singer, *Palestinian Peasants and Ottoman Officials: Rural Administration Around Sixteenth-Century Jerusalem* (Cambridge and New York: Cambridge University Press, 1994), pp. 20–21.

16. Ahmed Akgündüz, *Şer'iye Sicilleri: Mahiyeti, Toplu Kataloğu ve Seçme Hükümler* (Muslim Court Records, Its Comprehensive Catalog and Selected Rulings), 3 Vols., (İstanbul: Türk Dünyası Araştırmaları Vakfı, 1988).

17. Ahmed Akgündüz, "Shari'ah Courts and Shari'ah Records: The Application of Islamic Law in the Ottoman State," *Islamic Law and Society*, Vol. 16 (2009), pp. 202–230.

18. I am indebted to Professor Şükrü Hanioğlu for indicating this point, though I bear sole responsibility for any shortcomings in my interpretation and presentation of it.

19. For an American scholar's impression of the manuscript collections in the NL in Ankara, see Leslie Peirce, "The Milli Kütüphane in Ankara," *The Turkish Studies Association Bulletin*, Vol. 18, No. 2 (Fall 1994), pp. 137–140.

20. İsmet Binark, *Arşiv ve Arşivcilik Bilgileri* (Archives and Information on Archival Administration), (Ankara: Başbakanlık Basımevi, 1980), pp. 34–35; Fikret Ar, *Arşivlerin Organizasyonu Hakkında Araştırma Raporu* (Research Report on the Organization of Archives), (Ankara: Türkiye ve Orta Doğu Amme İdaresi Enstitüsü Yayınları, 1971), p. 149.

21. Şakir Gürsoy et al., *Başbakanlık Devlet Arşivleri Genel Müdürlüğü Cumhuriyet Arşivi Daire Başkanlığı Rehberi* (Guide to the Prime Minister's Office Directorate General of State Archives Department of the Republican Archive), (Ankara: Başbakanlık Basımevi, 2nd expanded ed., 1996), pp. v–vi; Rahim Erişti, "Cumhuriyet Arşivi Daire Başkanlığının Kuruluşu ve Çalışmaları" (Establishment and the Activities of the Republican Archive), in Erişti, Yıldırım, Atik and Yay, *Birinci Milli Arşiv Şurası (Tebliğler-Tartışmalar) 20–21 Nisan 1998*, pp. 401–418; Mehmet Çanlı, "Cumhuriyet Arşivi Tasnif Çalışmalarına Bir Bakış" (A Glance at the Declassification Activities of the Republican Archive), in ibid, pp. 391–399.

22. Marc David Baer, *The Dönme: Jewish Converts, Muslim Revolutionaries, and Secular Turks* (Stanford, CA: Stanford University Press, 2010), p. xix.

23. Sarah Shields, *Fezzes in the River: Identity Politics and European Diplomacy in the Middle East on the Eve of World War II* (New York: Oxford University Press, 2011), pp. ix–x.

24. Sarınay, "Türk Arşivleri ve Ermeni Meselesi," pp. 289–290. For details see İsmet Binark, *Cumhuriyet Döneminde Arşiv Hizmetlerinin Geliştirilmesi Konusunda Yapılmış Çalışmalar ve Cumhuriyet Arşivi* (Activities Relating to the Development of Archival Services in the Republican Period and the Republican Archive), (Ankara: Başbakanlık Basımevi, 1991) and idem, *Türk Arşivlerinin Kısa Tarihçesi ve Devlet Arşivleri Genel Müdürlüğünün Faaliyetleri* (A Brief History of the Turkish Archives and the Activities of the Directorate General of State Archives), (Ankara: Başbakanlık Basımevi, 1994).

25. Bahaeddin Yediyıldız, "Türkiye'de Osmanlı Araştırmaları II-Cumhuriyet Dönemi Türkiye'sinde Osmanlı Tarihi Araştırmaları" (Ottoman Studies in Turkey II-Studies on Ottoman History in the Republican Period Turkey) in *XIII. Türk Tarih Kongresi Ankara, 4–8 Ekim 1999 Kongreye Sunulan Bildiriler*, Vol. 1, pp. 177–183; Kenan Ziya Taş, "Arşiv Malzemesi Olarak Şer'iyye Sicilleri ve Taşra Üniversitelerinde Tarih Araştırmaları" (Muslim Court Records as Archival Materials and Historical Studies in Provincial Universities), in Erişti, Yıldırım, Atik and Yay, *Birinci Milli Arşiv Şurası (Tebliğler-Tartışmalar) 20–21 Nisan 1998*, pp. 175–186.

Chapter Ten

The Armenian Archives

ARMENIAN DEPOSITORIES

To achieve a full understanding of the Turkish-Armenian conflict, studies in the Ottoman archives alone would be insufficient. Also important is the need to do research in the archives of the Armenian revolutionary committees and bands that were active in the Ottoman Empire during and after the First World War. They are kept at the repositories of the Dashnak Party and the First Republic of Armenia in the Hairenik Association Building in Watertown, Massachusetts. The First Armenian Republic supported Antranig's ravages in eastern Anatolia following the Soviet revolution. One of the most important Armenian nationalist organizations at the time, the ARF, provided most of the men and money for Antranig's campaign. Their archives have to be made fully available to all researchers, not merely to Armenian supporters of "the Armenian National Cause," as they have been until now.[1]

According to Yervart Pamboukian, historian and former ARF Bureau member from Lebanon,

> most of the material found in these archives comes from Tsarist Russia and the Ottoman Empire and it includes thousands upon thousands of letters and reports, sometimes written in secret codes or by invisible ink. After the war, they were moved to Boston, where they were kept in perfect condition. . . . Not only do these archives contain party-related issues, but also a wealth of information about the recent history of the Armenians, statistical and demographic data, etc. I can say that no archives of any Armenian organization are as rich as the Armenian Revolutionary Federation archives. In fact, we sometimes have more material about other Armenian organizations than those organizations themselves.[2]

The ARF announced at the beginning of 2009 that it had established a central archive institute that would be digitizing the vast archives of the 118 year-old political party. The project would be headed by the ARF Archives Institute in Montebello, California, authorized by a decision of the previous year's ARF World Congress. The institute had offices in Watertown, Massachusetts and Beirut and was being headed by former *Azbarez* editor Vatche Proodian. Proodian said the current priority of the institute was to digitize the archives to facilitate academic research and study. The remainder of the archives would be organized and cataloged gradually. It would also prepare the processed material for publication. An extensive effort had been exerted during the last several decades to organize the archives, Proodian explained, adding that thus far, five volumes had been published under the heading of "Topics for the History of the Armenian Revolutionary Federation." The volumes covered the period between 1890 and 1907 through the Fourth ARF World Congress and included, among other things, meeting minutes, reports, and letters. The first four volumes were edited by the late Hratch Dasnabedian, while the fifth volume was edited by Yervant Pamboukian. Among the archives were the first and original ARF Manifesto, hand-written letters from the ARF founders, World Congress minutes, circulars and regional organizational reports, as well as maps, and an extensive collection of photographs. Among the maps housed in the Archives, was the one of the Caucasus in 1907—during the Czarist period—that delineated the demographic breakdown of Armenians in each administrative region. Also included in the archives was the hand-written Declaration of Independence of the First Republic of Armenia and hundreds of thousands of other documents, which Proodian described as important historical and political treasures.[3]

Professor Ara Sanjian of the University of Michigan-Dearborn remarked on 21 November 2010 that for the post-1924 period of the history of the ARF, not only did historians not have access to the party's own archives, but they were also told that the archives for this particular era were not only out of bounds because of an administrative decision, but that they were still poorly organized, if at all. Moreover, the party itself had not undertaken any real effort to publish collections of primary documents pertaining to developments after 1924. Sanjian found more curious the fact that the ARF leaders had themselves been reluctant to pen their memoirs of this period. Famous ARF leaders, who were active both before and long after 1924, rarely touched on post-1924 developments in their voluminous writings of autobiographical nature. Ruben Ter Minasian, Simon Vratzian, Vahan Papazian and Garo Sasuni were prominent examples of this group. Among members of roughly the same generation, it seemed that Vahan Navasardian, Dro, and Kapriel Lazian never wrote memoirs. The next two generations of the ARF leaders, Gobernig Tandurdjian, Adour Kabakian, Papken Papazian, and Hratch Dasnabedian, also had no published autobiographies.[4]

In contrast to open Ottoman archives, the ARF collections and the archives of the Armenian patriarchate in Jerusalem (the Monastery of Saint James [Surp Hagop]) and the Catholicosate (seat of the supreme religious leader of the Armenian people) in Echmiadzin, remain closed to non-Armenian researchers. No foreseeable date for access to them is suggested.[5] The archives of the Armenian patriarchate in Jerusalem is said to have over a half million documents in its own archival collection. According to Bedross Der Matossian, assistant professor of history at Nebraska University, due to different reasons from its unorganized nature to the lack of professional staff, these archives have not been open to historians.[6] It is clear that the closure is not reasonable and is likely to prejudice the work of the serious historian. The boxes that had remained sealed at the patriarchate for almost a century must now be opened and made available to researchers in their entirety.

Taner Akçam wrote:

> The archive (archives of the Armenian patriarchate in Jerusalem) is unfortunately not open to all researchers. For this reason it is difficult to state with any authority the extent of its holdings. There is no need to emphasize the wrongness of such an indefensible policy as the denial of access to such a potentially valuable source.[7]

Whereas there is available a superfluity of unpublished and published Turkish material on which to base a history, the problems in drawing on Armenian sources are very different. Of archive material, which is the lifeblood of history, little has been made available. The Armenian documentation is often inaccessible or difficult to get at. In many instances, access is restricted for political or other reasons. Often records have not been adequately cataloged, which also severely limits access for the researcher. Full accessibility to Armenian archives most certainly would be welcome to all scholars interested in the field.

APPLICATIONS BY NON-ARMENIAN SCHOLARS TO USE THE ARMENIAN ARCHIVES

When Stefano Trinchese of the University of Chieti in Italy wrote to the ARF archives, they did not respond. Professor Şükrü Hanioğlu wrote, too, and also obtained no reply. Unfortunately, they could not gain access to these repositories.[8]

In this connection, the case of Associate Professor Göknur Akçadağ of İnönü University at Malatya, Turkey, deserves particular attention. In response to his letter of 20 June 2008, requesting the opportunity to use sources available in the Armenian archives in Watertown, the Turkish academic was informed that although the repositories (1890–1922), until very recently, were open for research to qualified scholars, access to them has been temporarily suspended, as they were in process of implementing necessary repairs in the facilities and upgrading of technology. Akçadağ, whose scholarly credentials carry convincing stature, was told that it was difficult, at this stage, to assess the time that would be required to complete the planned improvements.[9]

Nothing has changed since then. In August 2014, The French scholar Maxime Gauin sent an email to the ARF archives asking for access to their depository. He was not answered. He repeated the mail without any success. He later wrote to Dikran Kaligian, an Armenian-American historian affiliated with the ARF, but he did not reply. Eventually, Gauin called the ARF Archives Institute, but nobody responded. This was hardly a surprise—if the official website of the institute is consulted, no information for researchers such as the working hours and the opening days is found. Moreover, this was not Gauin's first bad experience with the Armenian archives. He tried twice to work in the Nubarian Library in Paris, which is not affiliated with the ARF, but the curator first said that he would be out of France when Gauin would be in the French capital, and the second time he simply did not reply Gauin's emails.[10]

The Dashnaksutiun archives are also not available to those Armenians who do not toe the party line. Garabet Moumdjian indicates that only a few people have been able to do research there.[11] Levon Thomassian was unable to gain access to the archives of the ARF.[12] In the words of Vahakn Dadrian and Taner Akçam, "Boston's Dashnak archive operates on the basis of restrictive access."[13]

Matossian writes:

> Unfortunately, these archives (the archives of the ARF) have not been easily accessible to all scholars. Historians who work on this time period (1908–1918) need access to these archives in order to evaluate the period and understand the extent to which these sources contribute to our understanding of the Armenian Genocide.[14]

Historian and publisher Ara Sarafian, director of the Gomidas Institute in London and an Armenian who has been working for the past decade in the BOA, complained that

> some Armenian archives in the diaspora are not open to researchers for a variety of reasons. The most important ones are the Jerusalem Patriarchate archives. I have tried to access them twice and [been] turned away. The other archives are the Zoryan Institute archives, composed of the private papers of Armenian survivors, whose families deposited their records with [it] in the 1980s. As far as I know, these materials are still not cataloged and accessible to scholars.[15]

And he revealingly went on,

> key "Armenian archives" on the Armenian Genocide remain closed to critical scholars. This matter concerns all scholars and should be subject to scrutiny. The most important examples are the archives of the Jerusalem Patriarchate, which include materials from Ottoman Turkey related to the Genocide. Partisan scholars have used archives in their work, though their assertions cannot be checked. In the 1980s the Zoryan Institute collected the private papers of individuals in the diaspora, yet the materials have remained under lock and key. Such standards should not be acceptable within our communities. We should object to them as we object to any manipulations of Ottoman archives in Turkey today.[16]

Beyond the closure of Armenian archives to non-Armenian and even to some Armenian scholars, few of these allow the public to access catalogs detailing their holdings.

THE TÜRKYILMAZ CASE: A TURKISH SCHOLAR HARASSED IN YEREVAN

Ara Sarafian also says that the archives in Armenia are inadequate. Even so, after a Turkish historian gained access to them in 2005, he was detained upon leaving the Zvartnots airport by Armenia's National Security Service on the ground that the books he was carrying could not be exported from Armenia. These, however, were reported to be publications dating from after the Second World War which would not normally be regarded as under an export ban. Yektan Türkyılmaz, whose academic views are more pro-Armenian than pro-Turkish, was the first Turkish scholar to gain access to the archives and was held in isolation for two months before his trial. All of his research materials, including some 20,000 images saved on more than thirty CDs, were confiscated, along with a backup set of CDs that he had left with a friend. He was asked to prove that he had permission to reproduce every one of those images, which were then scrutinized, one by one, to see whether they revealed state secrets. He was interrogated about his politics, dissertation topic, motivations for learning the Armenian language, and knowledge of the Turkish military and intelligence communities.[17]

Academics worldwide joined in protest of Türkyılmaz's arrest. Organizations like international PEN, which is a worldwide association of writers, the Human Rights Action Network of the American Association for the Advancement of Science, and the Society for Armenian Studies argued on behalf of Türkyılmaz—speaking for several communities of scholars. In a typical sentiment, the Middle East Studies Association of North America said the case violated the notion that "scholarship, free exchange of ideas, and international collegiality can help lessen political tensions between states and increases mutual respect and understanding amongst peoples."[18]

A number of Türkyılmaz's local friends in Yerevan were also reportedly harassed and intimidated. Having been given a suspended sentence and released only after the intervention of prominent historians and United States Senator Bob Dole, Türkyılmaz still considers that the real reason for his arrest was to give the National Security Service access to his research notes.[19]

CALLS TO OPEN THE ARMENIAN ARCHIVES TO SCHOLARS

This incident brought the integrity of the NAA into question and is of considerable significance for the Turkish-Armenian historical debate. Some historians have felt uneasy that the NAA was too willing to withhold documents which revealed indiscretion in Armenian policy. They could no longer have complete confidence that no omissions have been made simply to conceal embarrassing errors of judgment. In order that historians can regain full confidence in the NAA, it is to be hoped that deletions from the records should be rare and should occur only after a thorough and informed review by competent historians to ensure that the omissions are necessary.

On 16 September 2005, Turkish Prime Minister Recep Tayyip Erdoğan stated emphatically:

> We clearly say that Turkey's archives are open and Armenia should open its archives, if it has any. We shall speak on the basis of documents and concrete information. I do not understand the grounds on which unrelated countries make decisions about the so-called Armenian genocide. The decisions are all political in character and do not serve world peace.[20]

"Turkey is not afraid of its history and is ready to begin the discussion, but in this case Armenia should open its archives," said Minister of Turkey's relations with the EU, Egemen Bağış, on 9 January 2012. "Turkey has always called on Armenia to open its historical archives. Other countries that agree or disagree with the position of Turkey in this matter, should open their archives along with Armenia and Turkey," the Minister remarked.[21] Bağış's call proved of no avail.

The Armenian government appears to use the archives strictly for public relations purposes. In 2011, in various ways they announced that the archives on the Armenian issues are open. Yet, they fail to publicize that the wrong archives are open or the restrictions that prevent any incriminating documents from coming to light. For example, on 9 January 2012, Hayk Demoyan, director of the Armenian Genocide Museum Institute in Yerevan, stated that his archives were available for everyone, but he did not open those on relevant First World War years.[22] An examination shows that he refers only to material concerning massacres of Armenians, not that involving the murderous activities of Antranig's armed bands which were condemned by reports from American and Russian as well as Ottoman military men serving in eastern Anatolia during and after the First World War.

Matossian stresses that

> to better understand and evaluate the Armenian Genocide material lying in different Armenian archives, historians in general should have equal access to them. The Armenian archives should follow the regular procedures that exist in other archives, such as the FO Archives in London and the Zionist Archives in Jerusalem.[23]

Indeed in virtually all the National Archives in democratic countries, the granting of research permission is almost automatic for scholars, and is usually granted within a week (often the same day) of the initial application. Most National Archives give temporary permits on demand to enable the applicant to begin his work while waiting for the completion of formalities.

There has been a steady trend toward more open records in Turkey and toward more closed records in Armenia. Just as the one is encouraging, the other is discouraging and can only arouse—and should arouse—only concern. If documented history is to be written, then the Armenian archives should also be fully opened to scrutiny and research.

Samuel Weems, an American jurist and historian, writes that the archives in İstanbul are very much open and have been so for some time. The irony is that the files in Armenia's capital of Yerevan, as well as the ARF offices in Boston, are still closed to researchers and the public. Weems, therefore, asks the pertinent question: What are they hiding?[24]

THE ARMENIAN RESOURCE MATERIALS

Armenia is situated in an area of high temperatures and high humidity, with the result that its records deteriorate rapidly, since temperature and humidity are major determinants in the self-destruction of paper. The lack of resources for the proper care of records hastens the process as do major hydroelectric projects which raise the humidity in countries like Armenia. If Armenia keeps its records closed, it eventually will face the ironic situation in which the only records of its past available to historians are likely to be those papers of its former Russian rulers which were generated before the introduction of wood acetate paper in the late nineteenth century.

ARMENIAN NATIONAL ARCHIVES

Surprisingly, little is known about the history of the NAA in Yerevan and close to nothing about the exact methods in which records are deposited, distributed, classified, and cataloged. There is no scholarly publication dedicated specifically to the Armenian archives.

Far too little has been written on the modern history of Armenia. This may be because it is hard, if not impossible, to get research clearance and the archives seem chaotic.

Scholars must not be inhibited from conducting research in Armenia's archives and libraries. They must have full and open access to the cataloged documentary collections in the archives. They should be able to use these in the same fashion they utilize archives in other countries, e.g., the BOA in İstanbul, the National Archives in Washington, the NA in London, and the Ministry of Foreign Affairs Archives in Paris. Implementing a policy of giving researchers in the Armenian archives the same free access that they enjoy in these other national archives is urged. In İstanbul, Washington, London, and Paris, researchers need only personally to present some proof of their identity in order to receive research permission. Such permission usually is granted instantly and always within 24 hours. These archives place no restrictions whatever on the research topics, the nature of the research or the amount of photocopying. Scholars are free to look at any and all cataloged documents without restriction. Such procedures should be adopted and implemented by the Armenian government.

The procedures presently in force at the Armenian archives make the task of researchers more difficult, often preventing completion of the planned research. Present policies are discouraging many scholars of international reputation, whose voices are heard with respect in many parts of the world, from carrying out research. If the present trend continues, there will be little future research on Armenia and its past carried out by the international academic community. If scholars who are trained in the languages and who are familiar with Armenia and its people continue to be prevented from carrying out research, then fewer accurate facts about Armenia and the Armenians will be uncovered.

From both historical and historiographical perspectives—in matters concerning Armenian actions, policies, and experiences—Armenian sources must be consulted. One would think, therefore, that it is incumbent on the Armenian people to do what they can to help in the process of opening all the archives so that the scholarly community will have a far clearer picture than it presently does of what precisely happened in the Ottoman Empire during the First World War. To the extent that some of the Armenian archives are already open and available, catalogs and descriptions should be published telling people where they are and how they could be used. To the extent that some of these archives are not yet open or available or cataloged, efforts should be made to change the situation as soon as possible.

International Crisis Group, a Brussels-based civil advocacy organization, following its survey on Turkey and Armenia, recommended on 14 April 2009, that the government of Armenia encourage universities and institutes to (1) pursue more research on matters relating to the events of 1915, preferably with the engagement of Turkish and third-party scholars; (2) modernize history books and remove all prejudice from them; and (3) organize the cataloging of known Armenian archives pertaining to the events in and around 1915 wherever they may be located. The Group also recommended that the United States, Russia, the EU and its Member States, support Turkey-Armenia reconciliation with projects to encourage region-wide interaction, heritage preservation and confidence building; and support as requested any new bilateral historical commission or subcommission, development of archive management, as well as independent Turkish- or Armenian-led scholarly endeavors to research aspects of the 1915 events.[25]

NOTES

1. Stanford Shaw, "Archival Sources on the Ottoman Empire I," in *International Symposium on Turkish Archives 17–19 November 2005 (Presentations and Discussions)*, pp. 106–112.
2. Khatchig Mouradian, "Pamboukian Talks about ARF Archives," *The Armenian Weekly*, 29 April 2009, p. 1.
3. "ARF Archives Institute Aims to Digitize Party's 118-Year History," *Asbarez*, 15 January 2009, p. 1.
4. Ara Sanjian, The ARF's First 120 Years: A Historian's Perspective; Comments Delivered at the Public Forum Held in the New York Hilton Hotel, 21 November 2010.
5. Halaçoğlu, *Tarih Gelecektir*, p. 97.
6. Bedross Der Matossian, "The Genocide Archives of the Armenian Patriarchate of Jerusalem," *The Armenian Review*, Vol. 52, No. 3–4 (Fall–Winter 2011), p. 22.
7. Akçam, *The Young Turks' Crime Against Humanity*, p. 6n10.
8. "Prof. Hanioğlu'na İzin Verilmedi" (Professor Hanioğlu Is Not Allowed), *Vatan*, 15 January 2009, p. 1.
9. Letter from Tatul Sonentz-Papazian, ARF archivist, to Göknur Akçadağ, Associate Professor of İnönü University at Malatya, Turkey, 30 June 2008.
10. Maxime Gauin, "The Turkish-Armenian Dispute: Who Has Something to Hide," Daily Sabah, 14 October 2014. http://www.dailysabah.com/opinion/2014/10/14
11. Garabet Moumdjian, "From Millet-i Sadıka to Millet-i Asiya," in Hakan Yavuz with Peter Sluglett, eds., *War and Diplomacy: The Russo-Turkish War of 1877–1878* (Salt Lake City, UT: University of Utah Press, 2011), p. 336n3.
12. Levon Thomassian, *Summer of '42 A Study of German-Armenian Relations During the Second World War* (Atglen, PA: Schiffer Publishing Ltd., 2012), p. 11.
13. Dadrian and Akçam, *Judgment at Istanbul*, p. 9n8.
14. Matossian, "The Genocide Archives of the Armenian Patriarchate of Jerusalem," p. 20.
15. Ara Sarafian, "Génocide arménien et la Turquie,"*Nouvelles d'Arménie*, September 2008, p. 1.
16. "Study the Armenian Genocide with Confidence, Ara Sarafian Suggests," *The Armenian Reporter*, 20 December 2008, p. 2.

17. "Diaspora: Ara Sarafian Responds," *The Caucasian Knot*, 22 January 2009, pp. 3–4; "Turk Held for 2 Months in Armenia," *The Moscow Times*, 18 October 2005, p. 1 and Robert Bliwise, "The Strange Case of Yektan Turkyılmaz: An International Incident," *Duke Magazine*, Vol. 91, No. 6 (November–December 2005), p. 1. Amatuni Virabyan, director of the NAA, said in July 2009 that Yektan Türkyılmaz, working on his doctorate in anthropology at Duke University in the United States, was the Turkish citizen who first entered the archives in Yerevan in 2005. The first Turkish historian, coming directly from Turkey and belonging to a Turkish university, who did research in these repositories was Candan Badem. He has been assiduous in tracking down unpublished Armenian material. See Candan Badem, *Çarlık Rusyası Yönetiminde Kars Vilayeti* (The Province of Kars under the Tsarist Russian Rule), (İstanbul: Birzamanlar Yayıncılık, 2010), p. 10n1 and "Ermenistan Arşivinde Bir Türk Akademisyen" (A Turkish Academic in the Archive of Armenia), *Milliyet*, 18 August 2009, p. 5.

18. Bliwise, "The Strange Case of Yektan Turkyılmaz," p. 2.

19. "Diaspora: Ara Sarafian Responds," pp. 3–4.

20. Anatolian News Agency, 16 September 2005.

21. Ibid., 9 January 2012.

22. Hayk Demoyan, "Armenian Archives Open for Everyone, Including Turkish Officials," 9 January 2012. http://www.news.am

23. Matossian, "The Genocide Archives of the Armenian Patriarchate of Jerusalem," p. 33.

24. Samuel Weemes, *Armenia Secrets of a "Christian" Terrorist State* (Dallas, TX: St. John Press, 2002), p. xviii.

25. http://www.crisisgroup.org/home/index.cfm?id=6053&1=1

Chapter Eleven

The British Archives

MAJOR BRITISH DEPOSITORY

The major depository in Britain is the NA at Kew in London. The NA (of England, Wales and the United Kingdom) was formed in April 2003 by bringing together the Public Record Office and the Historical Manuscripts Commission. It holds the shared public archive created by the central government of the United Kingdom in its various historic forms over the past thousand years. The NA holds about 375 separate collections of records from government departments, the armed services and the courts, occupying about 178 kilometers of shelving.[1]

There the prospective reader will find the major collections of the papers of the Cabinet, Prime Minister, Foreign Office, the three service departments, some important personal papers, and a great deal more, all covered by "class lists" from which one selects the files needed and then calls them up via a computer.[2] Kenneth Bourne and David Cameron Watt suggest that the British archives are fuller and much less damaged by the ravages of war and time than the archives of any other major European power. Those of France on national defense were widely destroyed in 1940. Those in Rome are excellent on those parts of the world they cover, but much is omitted. The German records were divided by the accident of Allied occupation and their dispersal to escape damage by bombing. According to Bourne and Watt, the British alone remain accessible and undamaged by bombing; and in the nineteenth and early twentieth centuries British diplomatic reporting was worldwide in its coverage.[3]

The bulk of British First World War era records have been opened, but there are disappointing exceptions.[4] For instance, the materials left from the British occupation of İstanbul and other parts of Turkey following the First

World War, including evidence regarding the returning Armenian refugees, and the dossiers of the British intelligence organizations, have been withheld from research by the British government under the authority of the Official Secrets Act of 1958 (amended in 1967) as well as other pretexts, and are only partially available in the archives of the Government of India in Delhi.[5] Even so British policy is more liberal than that of most other governments, except those defeated powers who have had their documents made public by the victors or where new regimes have considered it to their advantage to make public the "sins" of their predecessors.

BRITAIN'S UNOPENED ARCHIVES AND THE EASTERN MEDITERRANEAN SPECIAL INTELLIGENCE BUREAU

Files of the British Eastern Mediterranean Special Intelligence Bureau (EMSIB) are still locked away ninety-seven years after the end of the First World War—and still subject to "extended closure." This subdivision of the Military Intelligence Directorate of the Egyptian Expeditionary Force, headquartered in Port Said, specifically invented to coordinate the British operations in the Ottoman Levantine lands during the First World War, was founded on the networks of prewar consular officers and was headed by Major "R." Major (later Lieutenant Colonel) Rhys Samson had been consul at Edirne since 1907, but his diplomatic status was a cover for his military intelligence operation. He was later, under the codename "R" to be in charge of the British Secret Service in the Aegean. By the beginning of 1915 Samson was head of the EMSIB in Port Said.[6] The EMSIB was staffed by such officers as Robert Graves, William Stanley Edmonds, Ian Smith, Leonard Woolley, Harry Gordon-Pirie, H. C. Slater and Richard Hadkinson. Perhaps the least known British actions against the Ottoman Empire were those sideshows undertaken by the EMSIB in southern Anatolia in 1914–1918. Although the flood of books on the conduct of the First World War shows no signs of abating, this subject has unfortunately been neglected by scholars. Some very brief references occasionally appear in intelligence histories.[7] A few memoirs by veterans of the EMSIB exist but they do not elaborate the work of landing and reembarking agents on the Cilician coastal areas.[8]

The EMSIB's archive remains one of the outstanding exemptions to the British practice of opening records to public access under the current 30- or 50-year rule. This in itself is a testimony to the sensitivity and importance of the information they contain. Access to this repository will enable historians—and others researching the British espionage and sabotage, demoralizing propaganda, and attempts to provoke treason and desertion from Ottoman ranks during and immediately after 1914–1918—to find more extensive, more revealing and, in some cases, more chilling, details about the misuse of many native individuals in the region by British officials at that time.

The American journalist/historian Patricia Goldstone opened her work on *Aaronsohns's Maps: The Untold Story of the Man Who Might Have Created Peace in the Middle East* in 2003. Like other researchers, she was denied access to the British archival material relating to the EMSIB on the grounds that the same methods are still in use today.[9]

BRITISH MILITARY INTELLIGENCE DOCUMENTS OF THE FIRST WORLD WAR

Added to this, generally deemed unworthy of preservation, once the information British military intelligence reports contained had ceased to be current, most of them were not retained for any length of time by the War Office and, thus, are no longer to be found in their rightful place among the files of the Directorate of Military Intelligence. Those that still exist—and many seem to have been permanently destroyed—are only available because, at one time or another, copies were sent for reference to one of the other Whitehall departments, most of which, fortuitously, had a more generous policy regarding documentary preservation than that employed by the War Office. Nevertheless, locating these duplicate memoranda is, in itself, no small task, involving as it does rooting them out from various obscure resting places within the public records. To date, this has not been done in any systematic way. The very fact that these documents have not hitherto been subject to proper scrutiny is an oversight crying out for rectification. New sources on the British military intelligence activities of the First World War are, after all, uncommon.[10]

The Secret Office of War Propaganda, a branch of the British Foreign Office (known only by the name of the building where it was located, Wellington House), was in charge of developing propaganda used against the Central Powers during the First World War, under the direction of Viscount Bryce and Arnold Toynbee. Documents stored here, have likewise, for the most part, been concealed from researchers. They must instead be made fully available for examination. When an archive is kept so firmly closed, it naturally raises questions in inquiring minds about the reasons for and the nature of its existence.[11]

The apparent reason for retaining and keeping under extended or indefinite closure of these records is that they contain material of a personally sensitive nature, or information obtained under a pledge of confidence, or material whose disclosure might affect the security of the state.[12] According to the British official publication *Guide to the Contents of the Public Record Office*, papers withheld are "those whose disclosure could endanger national security or cause distress or embarrassment to the persons, or the immediate descendants of the persons named in them."[13] This policy was endorsed in 1998 by the then British Foreign Secretary Robin Cook.[14] Meanwhile it is to be reminded that in the United States legal title to the military personnel records transfers to the National Archives sixty-two years after a veteran's discharge, death in service, or retirement. After this transfer of ownership, the records are referred to as "archival" or "accessioned" holdings. In the United States, archival records are open to the public; researchers do not need the consent of the veteran (or the next of kin) in order to view or obtain copies of the record.[15]

Some ninety-seven years later, the First World War (or *The Great War*, as it was known in contemporary parlance) continues to haunt the British imagination. Memories of it are, in effect, still living and breathing. The War is not a closed chapter but a living past. The history of the First World War is emotionally charged, full of political and moral meaning, and more than ever reproduced in popular stories and iconic images. Any persons interested in this war can be forgiven entirely if they are bewildered by the conflict's huge bibliography, which has increased enormously since the 1960s, when the fiftieth anniversaries resurrected popular and academic attention. Keeping up with the literature is a hard task indeed, particularly when the spectrum of available material is so broad. Enter "First World War" on the London Library's computer and 890 titles come up. The Imperial War Museum has thousands of Great War diaries, letters, interviews and memoirs as well as its library. There are also Great War archives at Leeds University, Birmingham University, and King's College, London.

The recent rush of British publications on the Great War shows no sign of abating. It has been fueled by the declassification programs of several western countries and access to the records of Eastern European intelligence agencies after the political changes of 1989–1991. A century after the First World War, scholarly interest in its history appears to be as vigorous as ever. This centenary, if anything, is marked by increased attention and publication of a spate of new books. Despite this fact, both professional military historians and general readers are still poorly informed on the war as waged in the Ottoman Levant.

Likewise, intelligence history is currently one of the most rapidly developing fields of historical research in Britain. In ways that were essentially unthinkable as little as a decade ago, historians are now able to study intelligence in a scholarly manner previously out of the question. The unprecedented ability of researchers to study intelligence is derived from a growing sense of openness on the part of intelligence services on both sides of the Atlantic.[16] Following a century of official non-existence and government denial, Britain's intelligence services were finally given statutory recognition in the early 1990s, and, following the Waldegrave Initiative on Open Government in 1992, Britain's Security Service (MI5) began to release records on a rolling approximately fifty-year rule of declassification. By 2009 there were more than 3,000 MI5 records released to the NA, London, many of them multivolume, ranging from MI5's official establishment in 1909 to the early Cold War, relating to people, organizations and places which MI5 investigated, as well as MI5's policies on various national security concerns.[17]

In short, more intelligence records are now available for researchers than ever before. These declassified intelligence records are useful not just for intelligence historians, but also for political and military historians; for historians of international relations; and even for social historians. Intelligence services reflect the societies from which they draw their recruits, and their records thus often contain useful material for social and cultural history. Intelligence records are also indispensable for biographers: the MI5 records on individuals whom MI5 investigated often contain unique material, such as intercepted communications, that cannot be found in any other historical archive.[18]

EMSIB RECORDS MUST BE OPENED

All this raises the questions of why the EMSIB records are not yet available and where they are secreted. Perhaps those people who would like to leave the Armenian question for another 100 years of historical consideration know the answer. The events concerned are already history. How long does an event take before it becomes history? As long as fifty years? Or, perhaps, seventy-five? Turkey has already released page after page of documents on the Armenian issue, documents that have not been contradicted, documents that indicate clearly and convincingly that no genocide occurred in Anatolia during the First World War.

There are reasons for protecting the secrecy of current and recent intelligence operations. There are grounds also for protecting the identity of some intelligence officers (such as penetrating agents) throughout their lifetime. But since the EMSIB records, by definition, are now a century old, their continued classification serves only to discredit the whole concept of "national security." Surely there is no need to cover events now from scrutiny by a long-since defeated Ottoman Empire. Against what and whom are the secrets of the First World War being protected now? In Britain, the guardians of archivism still rule. They inevitably create the impression that they are hiding something.

On the centennial of the First World War, Whitehall's position on the EMSIB must be changed and restrictions covering the records relating to British propaganda activities and military and naval intelligence operations in the eastern Mediterranean in the period must be reviewed, with emphasis on new openness, rather than continued closure. The British government has no reasonable grounds for keeping them secret. These have nothing in them that can significantly affect British national security. Beyond a doubt much source material is to be found here. There is a wealth of material in the EMSIB files to document and substantiate the broader picture. The historian, therefore, will want to go there to examine various pieces of the vast picture, particularly as specific episodes and periods begin to take on special significance. It is almost certain that in this new collection there will be many substantial new sources.

The release of the EMSIB material will change what we know about the Turkish-Armenian past. It is obvious that any new evidence that can be brought to bear upon this hotly contested area of debate is strongly to be welcomed. They are an untapped source of primary information. The opening of the EMSIB files will doubtless lead to many new books and articles.

Since the relevant records in all the archives are on paper that is deteriorating and will disintegrate entirely before many more years, one can only hope that they will be opened and microfilmed before they disappear forever. Many of these paper-based records are endangered due to the fragility or instability of the materials used, or because of deliberate decisions not to preserve them. Even in those repositories where the documentation is well maintained, many paper documents are at risk due to the acidity of the low-grade paper manufactured at the time they were written. The process of deterioration that is tied to the quality of wartime paper threatens to cut off those who still guard them from their own history. If the EMSIB documents are kept closed for as long a period of time as the British governments preferred, all or almost all of them will yellow and crumble into dust by the time historians are finally allowed access to them. The paper of all the belligerents was particularly bad in those years of wartime shortages. This is as true for Britain as it is for other nations.[19]

Gerhard Weinberg, professor emeritus of history at University of North Carolina, has two comments concerning records that are still closed to all research. First, it becomes increasingly ridiculous to assert that records which are a century old have anything to do with any country's security today. He acknowledges that there are undoubtedly some records, which pertaining to private matters, such as medical and court martial records, which need to be kept closed for the obvious protection of privacy (but in some cases could surely be made accessible under protective rules requiring the omission of names). For the rest of the documentation, however, "national security" sounds quite hollow. The second point, according to Weinberg, relates to the physical quality of paper. The records of the war (both those of the First and the Second World Wars), in so far as they have not been microfilmed, are literally disappearing as the original paper deteriorates. In all countries, the quality of paper was deliberately made worse during the war in order to conserve resources needed elsewhere in stressed and stretched wartime economies; the result of this is that the wood acetate paper of the war period is disintegrating rapidly. If it is not microfilmed, it will literally vanish. If it is not made accessible to scholars very soon, it will have deteriorated beyond use before anyone can see it, with the effect that countries that keep such material closed will cut themselves off from an important part of their past.[20]

THE MALTA DEPORTATIONS AND EARLY ATTEMPTS AT PROSECUTION

There is another topic which needs to be specifically mentioned when British documents are discussed in the context of the end of the Ottoman Empire and its immediate aftermath, the occupation of İstanbul by Britain, France, and Italy. This is the "Malta deportations and trials."

It will be recalled that the attempt to bring a case like Nuremberg against the Turks collapsed after a two-year investigation, led by the British during the occupation of İstanbul. It became clear that neither Britain nor the United States would be able to produce any evidence to support the prosecution. In 1919 and 1920, a total of 144 senior Ottoman statesmen and officials were arrested and deported to the island of Malta on charges of Armenian massacres. The principal sources of information about the accused that the British High Commission in İstanbul relied upon in doing this were local Armenians and the Armenian patriarchate itself. Among the deportees were the grand vizier, the speaker of the parliament, the chief of the general staff, state ministers, army commanders, sheikh-ul-Islam, deputies, generals, governors, university professors, editors, and well-known journalists. While the deportees were interned on Malta, the British appointed an Armenian scholar, Haigazn Khazarian, to conduct a thorough examination of documentary evidence in the Ottoman archives to substantiate the charges. There was no problem about access to the Ottoman records as the British and French occupied and controlled the Ottoman capital at the time. The figurehead government in İstanbul undertook to furnish to the Allies "all documents and information of every kind" which would be considered necessary to ensure the full knowledge of the alleged incriminating acts. And there were no allegations that records had been purposefully destroyed. Khazarian's corps of investigators discovered complete lack of evidence demonstrating that Ottoman officials either sanctioned or encouraged the killings.[21]

The Foreign Office in a cypher telegram to Sir Auckland Geddes, the British Ambassador to Washington, informed him on 31 March 1921 that a number of Turks arrested for alleged complicity in the Armenian massacres were in the hands of the British government at Malta. There was considerable difficulty, according to the British authorities, in establishing proofs of guilt owing to disappearance or dispersion of victims and other causes. The Ambassador was asked to ascertain if the United States government were in possession of any evidence that would be of value for purposes of prosecution.[22]

Robert Leslie Craigie, a diplomat in the Embassy, replied on 13 July 1921 that a member of his staff visited the United States State Department a day earlier in regard to the Turks who were presently being detained at Malta with a view to a trial in connection with the Armenian massacres. He was permitted to see a selection of reports from the United States Consuls on the subject of the atrocities committed in eastern Anatolia during the Great War—reports chosen from among several hundred, and judged by the State Department to be most useful for the purposes of the British government. There was nothing therein which could be used as evidence against the Turks who were being detained for trial at Malta. The reports seen made mention of only two names of the Turkish officials in question—those of Sabit Bey and Süleyman Faik Pasha—and these cases were confined to personal opinions of these officials on the part of the writer, no concrete facts being given which could constitute satisfactory incriminating evidence. Craigie added that the officials of the State Department expressed the wish that no information supplied by them in this connection should be employed in a court of law. Having regard to this stipulation and to the fact that the reports in the possession of the State Department appeared not to contain evidence against these Turks which would be useful even for the purpose of corroborating information already in the possession of the British government, Craigie feared that nothing was to be hoped for in addressing any further inquiries to the United States government on this matter.[23]

The Foreign Office official who read the above dispatch minuted that it seemed very unlikely that they should be able to obtain additional evidence from Washington. They were waiting for the Attorney General's opinion as to whether there was a reasonable prospect of convicting any of the prisoners charged with massacres, but it appeared that the chances of obtaining convictions were almost nil.

ABSENCE OF EVIDENCE

In response to the Foreign Office's letter of 31 May 1921, asking his opinion as to which of the Turkish prisoners interned at Malta could be prosecuted with a reasonable prospect of success, Raymond Wybrow Woods of the British Procurator General's Department said on 29 July 1921 that up to that date no statements had been taken from witnesses supporting the truth of the charges against the prisoners. It was indeed uncertain whether any witnesses could be found and it was hardly necessary to dwell upon the difficulty of finding witnesses in a region so remote and inaccessible as eastern Anatolia, especially after so long a lapse of time and so many political changes. Even if the charges made were substantially true, Woods continued, it seemed more than probable that the great majority of those who could appear as witnesses against the accused were dead or had been irretrievably dispersed. It seemed "improbable that the charges made against some of the accused [would] be capable of legal proof in a Court of Law."[24]

The Foreign Office official who read the above opinion minuted that it appeared that the chances of obtaining convictions were almost nil.

Sir Lindsey Smith, judge in the British Supreme Court in İstanbul, minuted on 24 August 1921 that it did not appear from the files what, if any, evidence the British authorities already had, but it was evident from the Attorney General's dispatch that it would not, in his opinion, be sufficient to secure the conviction of the Turks detained at Malta in a Court of Law. Smith accepted that as conclusive. It appeared to him that an abortive trial would do more harm than good as it would give the prisoners the opportunity of claiming that they had been wrongfully detained or imprisoned.[25] The British High Commissioner in İstanbul, Sir Horace Rumbold, was in general agreement with the views of Smith and considered that "failing the possibility of obtaining proper evidence against these Turks which would satisfy a British Court of Law, [they] would seem to be continuing an act of technical injustice in further detaining the Turks in question."[26]

No Ottoman official was ever prosecuted or convicted of anything close to an Armenian genocide by an impartial court following customary due process (while 1,673 soldiers and civilians were prosecuted and punished in 1915–1916 for killing and abusing Armenians), and some Armenians have stooped to fabricating incriminating telegrams and similar bogus evidence in seeking to prove their case.[27] Armenians have never sought a genocide ruling from the International Court of Justice (ICJ) at The Hague, the main United Nations judicial organ.

NOTES

1. Amanda Bevan, *Tracing Your Ancestors in the National Archives* (Kew, Richmond: The National Archives, 7th ed., 2006), pp. 2 and 5.

2. R. J. Olney, *Manuscript Sources for British History: Their Nature, Location and Use* (London: University of London, Institute of Historical Research, 1995); Janet Foster and Julia Sheppard, *British Archives: A Guide to Archive Resources in the United Kingdom* (London: Macmillan, 1995); L. J. Butler and Anthony Gorst, eds., *Modern British History: A Guide to Study and Research* (London and New York: I. B. Tauris Publishers, 1997).

3. Kenneth Bourne and David Cameron Watt, "General Introduction," in Kenneth Bourne and David Cameron Watt, eds., British Documents on Foreign Affairs: Reports and Papers From the Foreign Office Confidential Print, Part I: From the Mid-Nineteenth Century to the First World War, Series B: The Near and Middle East, 1856–1914, Volume 1: The Ottoman

Empire in the Balkans, 1856–1875 (Frederick, MD: University Publications of America, 1984), p. xi.

4. Stephen Twigge, Edward Hampshire and Graham Macklin, *British Intelligence: Secrets, Spies and Sources* (Kew, Richmond/Surrey: The National Archives, 2008), p. 8 and Ian Beckett, *The First World War: The Essential Guide to Sources in the United Kingdom National Archives* (Kew, Richmond/Surrey: National Archives Public Record Office, 2002), p. viii.

5. Jaeschke, *Kurtuluş Savaşı İle İlgili İngiliz Belgeleri*, p. 259; Metin Hülagü, *Yurtsuz İmparator Vahdeddin İngiliz Gizli Belgelerinde Vahdeddin ve Osmanlı Hanedanı* (Vahdeddin Emperor Without a Country: Vahdeddin and the House of Ottomans in Secret British Documents), (İstanbul: Timaş Yayınları, reprinted, 2010), p. 13. On the subject of intelligence documentation in the British archives, see Yigal Sheffy, "British Intelligence and the Middle East, 1900–1918: How Much Do We Know?" *Intelligence and National Security*, Vol. 17, No. 2 (Spring 2002), pp. 33–52. Also Salahi Sonyel, "Armenian 'Massacres';The 'Great Lie' Re-Visited; A Good Yarn That the British Weaved," *Impact International*, Vol. 20:10, 25 May–7 June 1990, p. 10. On the archives of the Government of India consult *Index to the Foreign and Political Department Records* (Delhi: National Archives of India, 1957).

6. Richard Popplewell, "British Intelligence in Mesopotamia 1914–16," *Intelligence and National Security*, Vol. 5, No. 2 (April 1990), pp. 142 and 168n20; Percival George Elgood, *Egypt and the Army* (London: Oxford University Press, 1924), pp. 299–300.

7. On the EMSIB consult the letter book and diary of John de Vere Loder in St. Antony's College Middle East Center Archives at Oxford/Britain; Yigal Sheffy, *British Military Intelligence in the Palestine Campaign 1914–1918* (London: Frank Cass, 1998), pp. 83–87, 124, 135, 146–147, 150–159, 162–163, 179–180, 301, 303, 312–313 and 323; Anthony Verrier, ed., *Agents of Empire: Anglo-Zionist Intelligence Operations 1915–1919 Brigadier Walter Gribbon, Aaron Aaronsohn and the NILI Ring* (London: Brassey's Ltd, 1995), pp. 2, 12, 96–100, 133, 207 and 211; Priya Satia, *Spies in Arabia: The Great War and the Cultural Foundations of Britain's Covert Empire in the Middle East* (New York: Oxford University Press, 2008), pp. 48, 54, 56–57 and 284; Bruce Westrate, *The Arab Bureau: British Policy in the Middle East, 1916–1920* (University Park, PA: Penn State University Press, 1992), p. 40; Ronald Florence, *Lawrence and Aaronsohn: T.E. Lawrence, Aaron Aaronsohn, and the Seeds of the Arab-Israeli Conflict* (New York: Viking Penguin, 2007), p. 264 and Keith Jeffery, *MI6 The History of the Secret Intelligence Service 1919–1949* (London: Bloomsbury, 2010), pp. 18, 68, 92, 126, 131–132 and 206.

8. See Lewen Francis Barrington Weldon, *"Hard Lying" Eastern Mediterranean 1914–1919* (London: Herbert Jenkins Limited, 1925); Leonard Woolley, *As I Seem to Remember* (London: George Allen and Unwin Ltd., 1962) and Compton Mackenzie, *Greek Memories* (Ann Arbor, MI: University Publications of America, 1987, orig. London: Cassel, 1932).

9. Patricia Goldstone, *Aaronsohn's Maps: The Untold Story of the Man Who Might Have Created Peace in the Middle East* (Orlando, FL: Harcourt, Inc., 2007), p. 9.

10. Matthew Seligmann, " 'A Barometer for National Confidence': A British Assessment of the Role of Insecurity in the Formulation of German Military Policy before the First World War," *English Historical Review*, Vol. CXVII, No. 471 (April 2002), p. 336.

11. Shaw, "Archival Sources on the Ottoman Empire I," pp. 106–112. The British government instigated an inquiry, much of it carried out by historian Arnold Toynbee—the findings of which were published at the Bryce Report in October 1916. Viscount Bryce had some experience of producing unvarnished propaganda, having previously been responsible for a similar report concerning German atrocities committed during the invasion of Belgium in 1914. See Roger Ford, *Eden to Armageddon: World War I in the Middle East* (New York: Pegasus Books, 2010), p. 440n8.

12. Louise Atherton, *Top Secret: An Interim Guide to Recent Releases of Intelligence Records at the Public Record Office* (London: Public Record Office Publications, 1993).

13. *Guide to the Contents of the Public Record Office*, Vol. 2: *State Papers and Departmental Records* (London: Her Majesty's Stationery Office, 1963), p. vi.

14. See Richard Aldrich, "Policing the Past: Official History, Secrecy and British Intelligence since 1945," *English Historical Review*, Vol. CXIX, No. 483 (September 2004), pp. 922–953.

15. William Seibert, Wanda Williams, and Nancy Schuster, "1 Archives Drive Personnel Records Are Consolidated at New Location in St. Louis," *Prologue*, Vol. 43, No. 3 (Fall 2011), p. 9.

16. Christopher Moran and Christopher Murphy, eds., *Intelligence Studies in Britain and the US: Historiography Since 1945* (Edinburgh: Edinburgh University Press, 2013).

17. Calder Walton, Reviews of Christopher Murphy's *Security and Special Operations: SOE and MI5 during the Second World War* and R.A. Ratcliff's *Delusions of Intelligence: Enigma, Ultra, and the End of Secure Ciphers* in *English Historical Review*, Vol. CXXIV, No. 506 (February 2009), pp. 241–242.

18. Ibid., p. 242.

19. On the deterioration and disintegration of the First World War-era records, see Gerhard Weinberg, *Germany, Hitler, and World War II: Essays in Modern German and World History* (New York: Cambridge University Press, 1995), pp. 329 and 332.

20. Gerhard Weinberg, *A World at Arms* (New York: Cambridge University Press, 2nd ed., 2005), p. 942; idem, "The End of Ranke's History? Reflections on the Fate of History in the Twentieth Century," *Syracuse Scholar*, Vol. 9, No. 1 (1988), pp. 51–59.

21. Haigazn Khazarian was an Ottoman academic who, beginning in March 1920, served on staff at the headquarters of the British navy in İstanbul as an officer of the British occupation forces. He worked under the direction of the Chief Dragoman of the British Embassy, Andrew Ryan, on the archives of the Sublime Porte. Khazarian had access to, and copied, certain of the documents preserved there. See Kévorkian, *The Armenian Genocide*, p. 984n6.

22. Foreign Office Papers, NA, Kew/London (henceforth referred to as FO) 371/6500. E 3352/132/44. Evidence Against Turks Detained at Malta. FO to Sir Auckland Geddes (Washington), 31 March 1921.

23. FO 371/6504. E 8519/132/44. Evidence Against Turks Accused of Massacres. Sir Auckland Geddes (Washington) to FO, 13 July 1921.

24. FO 371/6504. E 8745/132/44. Prosecution of Turks Detained at Malta. Raymond Wybrow Woods (Procurator General's Deparment) to FO, 29 July 1921.

25. FO 371/6504. E 9779/1/44. Prosecution of Turks Detained at Malta. Sir Lindsey Smith (Supreme Court) to British High Commission (Istanbul), 24 August 1921.

26. FO 371/6504. E 9779/1/44. Prosecution of Turks Detained at Malta. Sir Horace Rumbold (Istanbul) to FO, 30 August 1921.

27. Şinasi Orel and Süreyya Yuca, *The Talat Pasha Telegrammes: Historical Fact or Armenian Fiction?* (Nicosia: Rustem, 1986); Yusuf Sarınay, "The Relocation (Tehcir) of Armenians and the Trials of 1915–1916," *Middle East Critique*, Vol. 20, No. 3 (Fall 2011), pp. 308–314; Maxime Gauin, "Aram Andonian's Memoirs of Naim Bey and the Contemporary Attempts to Defend Their 'Authenticity'," *Review of Armenian Studies*, No. 23 (2011) pp. 233–292.

Chapter Twelve

The Russian Archives

RUSSIAN DEPOSITORIES BEFORE *PERESTROIKA*

Those who received their academic training in Russian and Soviet history before the collapse of the communist regime worked under a considerable handicap: lack of access to the bulk of primary source materials in the libraries and archives of the Soviet Union. Even medievalists were routinely denied access to archives, even to those that had already appeared in print. Archives could—and often did—refuse admission or deny access to catalogs and finding aids.[1] The historical archive, party and state alike, remained a cardinal and constrictive bastion that aimed at nurturing an official ideology that would rest on selective history(ies). Access to its holdings and the rules of research within them were stringently regulated by the secret police, rather than an academic institution. In the principles that governed perusal of its contents, historiography that buttressed the official version of history and discursively lauded the advance toward communism retained an uninterrupted primacy. In the quest for permission for academic investigation within the archive, the aspirant's political status usually outweighed the criterion of scholarly potential or accomplishment.[2]

On 5 May 1927, a top secret resolution of the Soviet Politburo proclaimed "the old tested principle that secret matters must be known only to those who absolutely need to know." Until *perestroika* (restructuring) the Soviet archives strictly observed this principle. A Soviet historian could undertake research in the state archives only with permission from his institute, and could use only files directly dealing with a specific topic. The topic had to be approved by both the institute and the archives. More secret files were kept in special collections, and could be seen only if the reader had the right level of security clearance. Some files could be consulted but not cited. Very frustrating to the reader was the fact that a particularly secret category could be inspected, but without taking any notes. Only trusted party members were allowed to use the Communist Party archives, which were separately organized. In the central party archive, the historian's notes from the files were vetted for accuracy and orthodoxy. "Inappropriate" material was removed with scissors; notebooks were sometimes literally cut into ribbons. Some depositories were even more inaccessible. As late as 1990, five years after Mikhail Gorbachev took office, the foreign affairs archive was praised by one of its senior archivists as "a temple, where the sanctuaries—i.e., the documents of which only one copy exists—can be approached only by those who have proved by their publications that they can work properly." In the state archives, foreign citizens, including people from other communist countries, were segregated in a special reading room. For the Soviet period, they could not select files for themselves because they were not shown any inventories. Instead they were handed small batches of files chosen by the archivists after a careful security check behind the scenes.[3]

OPENING OF THE RUSSIAN ARCHIVES

Russian archives were being opened unevenly and sporadically, with some sensitive material available for brief periods and then withdrawn, and made available only to a few favored scholars. The whole process was complicated by the material poverty of the archival system and continuing political controversy over what should be known or remain unknown.

Beginning in 1988, democrats encouraged by the public, fought to widen access to the Russian archives. They were fiercely resisted by conservative administrators, the party *apparat* and the Committee of State Security (KGB). On a memorable day in 1989, foreigners were first admitted to the normal reading room in the state archives; in the same year a few privileged foreigners were let into the central party archive. But most restrictions still remained.[4] Historians by 1989 gave mixed reports, with some being granted almost unlimited access to materials while others were able to view but not cite materials. Millions of sheets of valuable archival material were crumbling in appalling storage facilities, as in the depository on Pirogovskaya Street in Moscow. The director of the Chief Archive Administration (Glavarkhiv), F. Vaganov, showed little interest in improving the situation.[5]

As a result of an agreement signed on 29 July 1988 with the United States Holocaust Memorial Council (USHMC), the Soviet Union announced that it would grant Western scholars access to its vast collection of archives of Nazi and other Holocaust-related materials. Involved were several million Nazi documents, photographs and other records of Nazi atrocities seized by the Red Army in the former German occupied territories of the Soviet Union and

Eastern Europe at the end of the Second World War. United States officials credited the unlocking of the Holocaust papers—which included perhaps one-third of all contemporary records of the Holocaust—to the new spirit of *glasnost* inside the Soviet Union. These were documents the Western eye had not seen before. A USHMC mission to Moscow in 1979 had received an unfavorable answer from Leonid Brezhnev's Kremlin when it made a request for similar access. Previously, Holocaust-related documents had typically been released only on a case-by-case basis, usually for trials of accused war criminals. This breakthrough agreement called for the mutual exchange of Holocaust-related collections between the USHMC and the main archival administration of the Soviet Council of Ministers. "They [these documents] will become the building blocks from which we are fashioning our collective memory," said a leading Holocaust scholar and a member of the USHMC delegation that signed the agreement.[6]

The more open regime in the archives was established at a time when public interest in revelations about the past was at its maximum. Historians poured into the archives. The general reading room of the state archives was usually half-empty. But in 1990 there was a flood of Soviet and foreign researchers; there were no free places; there was nowhere to keep the files which had been issued to readers. These relaxations did not satisfy many archivists and most historians. Vaganov, the director of Glavarkhiv, was regarded with great suspicion in view of the extreme orthodoxy of his contributions to the historical debates of 1987. By 1990, only a handful of files classified as secret had been released.[7]

The story of what happened to the Russian archives after the collapse of Soviet communism in 1991 is in itself worthy of historical investigation. Roughly speaking, the use and control of the Russian archives went through three different stages: In 1991 and 1992, a phase of euphoria, of show and tell, irregular access, and a hunt for sensations. Then 1993–1994, a period of slow and hesitant regularization of declassification, some of it enlightened, some not quite so enlightened. Archival facilities were improved—often with foreign assistance—and the use of the archives began to be a matter for public debate. In all, this was the most positive phase so far. From late 1994 on, however—in tune with general political developments in Russia—progress toward the implementation of internationally accepted standards for the use of Russian archives all but stopped.[8]

After the defeat of the August 1991 coup President Boris Yeltsin announced that the former Communist Party and the KGB archives were to be transferred to the normal archival system. The recently appointed Director General of the Russian Archival Administration (Roskomarkhiv), Rudolf Pikhoia, announced triumphantly that all problems of access would be removed. This was a revolution. The central party archive, renamed the Russian Center for the Study and Preservation of Documents of Recent History, was opened to the public within two months, and inventories were readily available to foreign and Russian readers alike. In the state archives, "confidential files"—the lowest level of secrecy—and their inventories were freely accessible.[9]

The opening of the Russian archives in Moscow and St. Petersburg in 1991 has transformed research opportunities and scholarship in many fields. The new Russian Law on State Secrets of July 1993 established a maximum period of secrecy of thirty years, with a longer period—fifty years—only for documents of intelligence services and materials relating to the Soviet nuclear program. Personal information could legally remain classified for up to seventy-five years. Declassification would proceed on documents thirty years old or older. These provisions were included in the Law on Archival Collections of July 1993 to regulate all the far-flung repositories in the Russian Federation. This was considered a significant step in the policy of *glasnost*. When specialists broke down the official wall of secrecy that had stood for decades, they gained access to intriguing new knowledge they had previously only been able to speculate about.[10]

The veil of secrecy was lifted for earlier periods (including the Stalin period), which could now be studied systematically. As mentioned above, previously, the lack of access to archives and other indispensable sources of information made studying Russian history a very frustrating and arduous enterprise. Coming across data that contained useful pointers, or hitting upon a well-documented Russian publication, was a signal event. So when Russian archives became accessible, historians had to take advantage of them.[11]

By the end of 1993, several of the most important Soviet period archives had been opened, albeit on a limited and sporadic bases for scholarly inquiry. This opening of floodgates had a major impact on historical scholarship. The sheer volume of literature published during the first post-Cold War decade and beyond shows that many took the opportunity to study the Russian past. The ability to sift through files in both party and state archives has had a profound effect on recent historiography, an effect that is likely to continue for some time to come.[12]

Historians of eastern Europe, prior to the fall of the Soviet Union, rightly stressed that their interpretations were restrained by the fact that Russian archives were virtually closed to foreign research. This implied that if they ever were opened, exciting new historical interpretations were to be expected. Sean McMeekin's latest book, *The Russian Origins of the First World War*, illustrates this expectation. He has taken advantage of the partial opening of Russian archives to uncover fresh material—and has incorporated the recent documentary evidence published in Russia since 1991, having already absorbed the extensive secondary literature on the subject. Despite McMeekin's efforts, important gaps remain in the record. Not all the materials are accessible and scholars do not know what has been held back. Much material has been destroyed but again we do not know how much.[13]

Not all Russian archives have been opened to independent scholars, and it is probably illusory to think that when and if that happens, all mysteries will be solved. But there can be little doubt that the contribution of collections to our understanding of the world of the nineteenth and twentieth centuries will be massive.

GUIDES TO THE RUSSIAN ARCHIVAL SOURCES

As mentioned earlier, among the many benefits of the fall of the Soviet Union was the opening of the Russian archives to scholars. The boon was qualified, however, by the continuing lack of adequate published archival guides to major repositories. This lack had long been an obstacle to Soviet and foreign researchers alike. Not only were guides to larger repositories sketchy, but smaller facilities sometimes had no published guides, and their in-house lists were not available to researchers.[14]

Some help was provided by Patricia Kennedy Grimsted, Research Associate at the Harvard Ukrainian Research Institute and the West's leading authority on archives of the former Soviet Union. Her publications on the history of Russian, Ukrainian, and other archives and her lists of guides to various repositories were and continue to be invaluable. Soviet archivists, badly served by their own central archival administration, translated her publications for their own use. But these were not detailed references to specific collections of the kind being produced in 1994 by the Russian Archive Series (RAS).[15]

The RAS includes basic reference works for the principal central repositories, including the Russian Center for Preservation and Study of Documents of Contemporary History (the former Central Party Archive), the Central State Archive of Ancient Acts, the Russian State Archive of the Economy, the State Archive of the Russian Federation (the former Central State Archive of the October Revolution) (GARF), the Central State Archive of the Russian Republic, and others. In addition, the project includes a set of six volumes (in ten parts) of "Special Files" from the Ministry of Internal Affairs, the first four of which are the special files, respectively, of Joseph Stalin, Vyacheslav Molotov, Nikita Khrushchev, and Georgi Malenkov. The last two volumes are archival guides to correspondence between the Ministry of Internal Affairs and the Ministry of Foreign Affairs from 1944 to 1959 and correspondence between the Ministry of Internal Affairs and the Ministry or Committee of State Security during much of the Soviet period.[16]

The guide for the Russian State Archive of the Economy is a first of its kind. Until 1994, the only guides for this important archive were a 1973 imprint that included a listing of less than half the collections (and was for all practical purposes an in-house guide because of its press run of only 450 copies). In 1987, the archive published a list of some of its collections of personal papers (*lichnye fondy*) but, again, in a very limited press run. By contrast, the new guide prepared for the RAS contains information on 81 percent of the archive's document collections (covering 3,861 Soviet economic institutions) and is widely available. Holdings that were still classified could not be included, and some recently declassified collections did not make the press date for the volume. Listings of collections of personal papers are likewise not included in this volume. But information on them and on the recently declassified collections is planned for a separate guide.

The guide to the history of Russian Jewry, compiled by Genrich Deych, is a labor of four decades. Deych began to assemble references to Jewish materials in the Russian State Historical Archive in Leningrad at the end of the Second World War in preparation for the publication of a comprehensive guide to the holdings of this institution, the principal repository for state papers from the nineteenth century. Although the guide appeared in 1956, the editors decided to excise most of the references to Jewish materials (a common censorship practice in the postwar Soviet Union into the late 1980s). At considerable personal risk, Deych continued his research for archival materials on Jews, and when he emigrated in 1989, he was able to bring out his notes. These notes form the basis of the volume, which details the holdings on Jews in the archives of the central government ministries, the reports of the offices of provincial administrations in regions belonging to the Jewish Pale of Settlement, and a large number of personal archival collections from such well-known figures as Leon Trotsky and Isaac Babel and also less prominent Jewish doctors, teachers, historians, and artists.

The disintegration of the Soviet Union and the spirit of openness that accompanied it made this publication project possible and necessary. With Russian and foreign researchers suddenly permitted to work in collections previously restricted, archivists and researchers understood that they needed a clearer picture of what was now available to them. It should, however, be pointed out that the euphoric moment of openness soon passed. A decree of September 1993 set in motion a process of reclassification of some collections. This process affected highly sensitive material in the former Central Party Archive more than the holdings of other repositories, but historians were rightly concerned about how far restrictions might ultimately extend.

Patricia Kennedy Grimsted indicated in 1997 that large segments of the GARF, the Russian State Military-Historical Archive (RGVIA), the Archive of Foreign Policy of the Russian Empire (AVPRI) and the Russian State Military Archive (RGVA later renamed TsGASA) (formerly the Special Archive or Central State Archive of Soviet Army and Central State Archive of Red Army)—previously among the most closed in the world—were now becoming among the most open, in terms of expanding reference information. But the foreign and military intelligence archives and the defense ministry archive were never open to most researchers. The greatest untapped repositories were the central and regional archives of the former Cheka (All-Russian Extraordinary Commission for Combating Counter-Revolution, Sabotage and Speculation), GPU (State Political Directorate of the People's Commissariat of the Interior), OGPU (Unified State Political Administration), NKVD (People's Commissariat of State Security) and KGB, to which foreign researchers had limited access. Wide access to such documents would open new vistas and perspectives for inquiry.[17]

The GARF, the main archive of central state institutions, was established in 1992 on the basis of the combined holdings of the former Central Archive of the October Revolution, High Organs of State Power, and Organs of State Administration of the Union of Soviet Socialist Republics (USSR) and the Central State Archive of the Russian Socialist Federated Soviet Republics. By 1994, it had accumulated over 3000 *fonds* (with over five million file units), dating from 1800 to 1993. Its most substantial holdings are from the Soviet period, including records of commissariats and ministries, both of the USSR and the Russian Republic in the USSR, from the Revolution to the demise of the USSR in 1991. The pre-revolutionary holdings comprise records of the apex central judicial, penal, political and criminal investigative agencies of the former empire, and personal papers of the imperial family and members of the court.[18]

The Third Section collections housed in the GARF hold the fascinating and hitherto unknown reports of the police on public opinion regarding all matters of domestic and foreign policy. They are particularly comprehensive on the Russian campaigns against the Ottoman Empire and reveal the educated public of the European capitals to have had a far keener understanding of the Eastern Question and foreign and military policy generally than might have been expected.[19]

The private papers of the czarist military commanders are found in the TsGASA. The Russian military archives are voluminous but fragmented in nature. Besides the TsGASA located in Moscow, which contains army military records from 1918–1940, there exist numerous branch archives at other locations associated with various ministries and their subordinate entities. The Russian armed forces maintain a network of archives, which include the Central Archives of the combined Armed Forces (TsAOVS) (formerly the Central Archives of the Union of Soviet Socialist Republics Ministry of Defense—TsAMO), located at Podolsk, near Moscow; the central Archives of the Navy, located at Gatchina near St. Petersburg; the archives of military medical records of the Military-Medical Museum located in St. Petersburg; and the archives of military districts, army groupings, fleets, flotillas, and military naval bases scattered across the country. The latter turn over the key records to the appropriate Central Archives after a specific period of time. The Central Archives (TsAOVS) is the largest storehouse of military documentation in Russia (and the Commonwealth of Independent States). It contains more than 18 million records, with documents from other central military command bodies: the *Stavka*; force branches; armies, special forces headquarters, operational commands, large formations and units; and military institutions, organizations, and enterprises (excluding the Navy). The Central and Navy Archives supervise the work of the remainder of the military archival system.[20]

The manuscript collection of the military-scientific section of the RGVIA comprises the former archive of the tsarist General Staff and the orderly, thematic organization of the material greatly facilitates its use. Some significant documents from this collection were published in the prominent czarist nineteenth-century periodicals such as *Russkaia starina* and *Russkii arkhiv*, though a great deal of material has remained undiscovered. In addition, some archival material has gradually been published in the Russian general press, professional political and military journals, and revivified archival periodicals. The publication of these has done much to clarify long-standing factual issues.[21]

RELEASE AND ORGANIZATION OF THE RUSSIAN ARCHIVAL MATERIALS

The American historians, David Glantz and Jonathan House, wrote in 1995 that the recent flow of Russian archival materials to the West was heartening but must be viewed in perspective. Collectively, it represented only the tip of the iceberg, and the release had been selective in nature. Some of the materials had been accurate and candid; others had been as inaccurate as some of the existing open source materials published over the past forty years. All of this, according to Glantz and House, conveyed the clear message that some "archival" materials were not really archival at all; instead, they were the products of the system that was so effective at managing information.[22]

Although release of archival materials was welcome, the larger question regarding direct archival access, in the Western sense of the word, remained unanswered. Russian authorities had frequently announced that the archives were open for foreign scholars. Glantz and House said in 1995 that they had seen no evidence to date that this was, in fact, true. When archival access had been tested and published as in many cases, the documents were brought to researchers rather than giving researchers the freedom to hunt for documents in the actual archive locations. To 1995, scholars who claimed to have access usually had been limited to peripheral materials or had been provided selected materials on request.[23]

Although a few major segments of Russian archival holdings were opened in 1997, of most areas of Soviet internal and foreign policy, only selected portions or subject files— or even only individual documents—had been made available. In very few areas did one have open access to "the archives." Such scattered materials did help to provide some information and at least a broad range of illustrative samples of the kinds of material held in particular archives. At the same time, they often did not permit one to be sure a given subject was being covered in a representative way. Moreover, in many cases selection of documents remained in the hands of Russian archivists and access to archival lists of files and documents (or, often in Russia, to boxes of hand-penned index cards listing individual documents called a *kartoteka*) was restricted or denied.[24]

By 1997 the archives of the Soviet ministry of defense were closed unless special permission for access could be obtained from the chief of staff. Some holdings were, however, available at the military archives, which came under the direct control of the State Archival Service of Russia (Rosarkhiv). These archives also contained Russian military intelligence material, but access appeared to be unobtainable. The KGB archives were officially closed, but in fact they were partially and indirectly open in restricted form on terms to be negotiated.[25]

Public funding for operating the Russian archives was probably at an all-time low in 1997, resulting in dismal working conditions even in those repositories that attempted to uphold some standards of public access. With the exception of the Ministry of Foreign Affairs Archive, the international community had made no comprehensive attempts to render plans for long-term assistance to the Russian foreign affairs archives. The Ministry of Foreign Affairs Archive was also the only foreign affairs archive in Moscow that held to a set of fixed regulations concerning declassification and access, a system that enabled scholars to work on a fairly wide range of top-level materials from 1917 up to the early 1960s. The other important archives—the Presidential Archive, the two archives of the Soviet Communist Party Central Committee, the KGB archives, and the military archives—had very limited access and irregular procedures of declassification.

The British historian, Zara Steiner, remarked in 1999 that the Soviet diplomatic and military archives had recently been opened, but only on a very restricted and selective basis—still presenting problems of access and availability—the number of books using primary Soviet sources was still quite restricted. A few scholars had made extensive use of the valuable published Soviet sources or had explored previously unavailable non-Soviet archives.[26]

The most recent reorganization of the Russian archives took place in March 1999. After Vladimir Putin came to power in 2000, historians noticed a gradual imposition of limitations to access to archives. For instance, many files were stalled in "declassification commissions" and were not given to scholars. As those who have worked with Russian materials attest, their condition is far from satisfactory. Indexes of documents are poor and sometimes unavailable. Some files are missing, and many of the most important have been withdrawn to the so-called presidential archives, which remains closed to all but a handful of privileged and well-connected native Russian scholars.[27]

The organization of the Russian archives on the basis of political sensitivity helps explain selectivity in the opening of their contents. Under increasing restriction, generally, was the Central State Archive of the October Revolution and Socialist Construction (Ts-GAOR), the main source for the Western research on Soviet social and economic history that burgeoned from the 1960s on. Far more restrictive, if not totally closed, was the Central Party Archive at the Institute of Marxism-Leninism (now the Russian Center for the Preservation and Study of Documents of Contemporary History), along with the military, security, and foreign relations archives. Separate from all these was the supersensitive Central Committee archive.[28]

As previously noted, the new Russian Archival Service under Rudolf Pikhoia, an old friend of Boris Yeltsin's, had promised a sweeping declassification of historical materials in these archives, though the most sensitive materials (including most Politburo documents) were already reserved by Mikhail Gorbachev in a presidential archive. This latter was inherited by Yeltsin and released only on a selective basis for political effect (e.g., the documents proving Soviet responsibility for the Katyn massacre of Polish officers during the Second World War). But ever since the political crisis of 1993, access to archives at all levels has been progressively tightened, and Pikhoia was forced to resign amid complaints that he had been too forthcoming with Western interests early in 1997.[29]

The contributors to *Adventures in Russian Historical Research*, a collaborative volume by American scholars, were emboldened to write about their research experiences because the frustrations most of them experienced during the Cold War period and the changes that occurred after 1991 illustrate the larger historical changes that took place in the former Soviet Union.[30] Norman Naimark noted in 1995 that despite the passage of a state law in 1993, gaining access to the Russian archives was a haphazard and uneven undertaking. Some were able to use the archival guides and to see almost all of the documents they requested. However, at other times and in other circumstances, researchers were denied access—partial or total—to the same collection. One had frequently to seek permission to consult sensitive files.[31]

R. W. Davies, collaborator and successor to E. H. Carr in their multivolume history of the Soviet Union between the wars—and past director of the Center for Russian and East European Studies at the University of Birmingham in Britain—suggested in 1997:

> Access has been more difficult for historians concerned with sensitive issues of foreign policy and with more recent periods. But with this important reservation, the story of the archives is a success story. Improvements before August 1991 were transformed into a revolution thereafter, [which remained, however,] an unfinished revolution. . . . The battle for the archives has not yet been won.[32]

Although the situation for historians of Russia and the Soviet Union is vastly better now than it was less than two decades ago, access to archives in Moscow and St. Petersburg remains uneven for a variety of reasons ranging from the political to technical and budgetary. The world has moved on, but minds are slower to change.[33]

The poor scholarly output on tsarist Russia's First World War effort is not surprising, in view of the difficulty of archival access in Russia until very recently and the fact that so few Russian-language monographs exist to guide researchers on their way. During the past few years, there has been a boom in research on the Russian army—its command structure, logistics and supply, the education of officers and institutional culture, strategic doctrine and efforts to update it.[34] Dramatically easier access to archives in Moscow and St. Petersburg is one reason. As a generation of young American scholars has applied Western historical training and methods to the vast holdings in the archives of the former Soviet Union, Russia's officials and soldiers, have all come in for new scrutiny. The principles that guided the soldiers, the strategies they adopted, and the tactics they used have been reexamined and, in the former Soviet Union and in the West, there is a new mass of scholarship about what these men struggled to accomplish and why they failed.[35]

Michael Reynolds's *Shattering Empires* represents one of the first important results of multiarchival work that draws on records so unattainable until recently but so critical to historical reconstruction. The Russian archives will never finally resolve issues of historical intention and responsibility, any more than British archives, but they are the basis for informed inference and argumentation. Reynolds uses them precisely in that scholarly spirit.

IMPORTANCE OF THE RUSSIAN ARCHIVES TO TURKISH HISTORY

Russian imperial history has come of age in the past three decades. The collapse of the Soviet Union and the emergence of new states and putative states pushed the imperial dimension of Russian history to the fore; the opening of the archives allowed the question to be investigated at a level of detail hitherto inconceivable.

During the past few decades, studies on the nationality question have become perhaps the most innovative field of Russian studies. In the Soviet

Union discussion of national problems were considered taboo, while mainstream Western interpretations considered them resolved. The transformation of the Soviet republics into national states and the emergence of ethnonational conflicts in the post-Soviet space led to a fundamental reevaluation: nation instead of class has become the main focus of interest. This trend was reinforced by the turn of the historical profession to cultural and ethnic studies and the elaboration of new postmodernist theories of nationalism during the last three decades. With the partial opening of the Russian archives, a lot of new material on national problems has become accessible for the first time.[36]

About the time that the Soviet Union ceased to be a union, scholars became more interested in the non-Russian peoples that were tearing apart the world's largest state. That contrasts dramatically with the studied neglect of earlier times, when Soviet historiography could not, and Western scholarship would not, give more than passing attention to nationality matters. The opening of Russian archives at roughly the same time made it possible for historians to investigate the past of Armenians and Turkic peoples whose experiences had been absorbed into a general Russo-Soviet history. The Czarist Empire was composed of diverse nationalities, as was the revolutionary movement that sought to overthrow it. Armenians and Turkic peoples played their part in both the evolution of the empire and the revolutionary movement.

Until now, however, the most obvious and fascinating question of all has gone understudied. In a nation ruled by an autocrat whose predecessors included such monumental historical figures as Ivan the Terrible, Peter the Great, Catherine II, and Alexander II, how did Nicholas II, Emperor and Autocrat of All the Russias, react to the Armenian events of 1915 that threatened to destroy the territorial integrity of the Ottoman Empire and reshape Russia's future? What meaning did Nicholas II see in the relocation of the Ottoman Armenians during the First World War? And what guided the Soviet leader Vladimir Ilyich Lenin in establishing the course Russia would follow in this regard as it entered a new era of Communist government? These are critically important questions.

The Russian archives are essential for a comprehensive understanding of Turkish and Ottoman history. This reality, however, has not yet been sufficiently appreciated. Modern historiography was born in Western Europe and exhibits a natural and inevitable bias toward European sources. And whereas a knowledge of European history could be assumed even of experts on Russian and Ottoman history, few in working in the latter two fields were acquainted with, let alone trained in, the other.[37]

Yet just as the histories of the Turkic and Slavic people have been intertwined for centuries, so, too, are the histories of the Ottoman and Romanov empires inextricably linked. The Russian empire has played an outsize role in

Ottoman history. It can be fairly stated that the Russians were the Ottomans' greatest rivals. Between 1568 and 1918 the two empires fought twelve wars. The Treaty of Küçük Kaynarca of 1774 that ended one of those wars is commonly cited as marking the eclipse of Ottoman power and the beginning of Ottoman decline. Russia's expansion into the Balkans and Caucasus presented a chronic challenge not only to Ottoman statesmen, but indeed also of the Western European Powers, and of Britain in particular. More than any other power, it was the rising Romanov Russia that shaped the "Eastern Question," the predominant problem of European diplomacy in the nineteenth century. Russia likewise played an absolutely central role in the genesis and development of the related "Armenian Question" following the 1878 Treaty of Berlin through the Armenian Reform plan of 1914. To write Ottoman history without attention to Russia would be akin to narrating the history of France without reference to Germany and the German states.[38]

Russia's importance for the history of Ottoman diplomacy and foreign relations thus is clear. But it should be emphasized that the utility of the Russian archives for understanding Ottoman history goes well beyond documenting the movement of armies, the drafting of treaties, the shifting of borders, and the application of diplomatic protocols. First, Russian subjects were keen observers of developments within the Ottoman Empire. The imperial Russian state devoted considerable resources toward this end. The perspectives of Russian diplomats, spies, and police officials, along with those of the merchants, clerics, academics, and travelers who served as their informants, can be invaluable for making sense of Ottoman internal political and social realities. Second, the Ottoman and Russian empires shared mixed populations along with borders. The flow of goods and people across their borders was considerable, and went beyond the borderlands to the imperial centers. Needless to say, any history of those peoples along the borderlands—Armenians, Assyrians, Azerbaijani Turks, Circassians, Crimean Tatars, Kurds, Pontic Greeks, to name a few—cannot be written in any comprehensive fashion without making use of both Ottoman and Russian archives. Third, given their shared physical and human geographies, the two empires make natural comparisons for the study of the developments of imperial techniques of rule, including everything from border control through land use and taxation to the administration of religious and ethnic differences. As dynastic regimes ruling over multiconfessional and multiethnic populations, the Ottomans and Romanovs faced many of the same challenges. Comparative study of each can therefore yield important insights unavailable otherwise. Fourth, and finally, just as the Russian archives make possible comparative study of imperial techniques of rule and management of populations, they also make possible rich comparative studies of social change. Historians of the Ottoman Empire and Turkey, for example, have long acknowledged the contributions of Russian imperal émigrés to intellectual and religious currents in the late Ottoman Empire and the Turkish Republic. Studies of the Volga Tatars, Turks of Central Asia, Azerbaijani Turks, and of the Peoples of North Caucasus under Russian rule have much to offer to students of social, intellectual, and religious trends in the late Ottoman Empire and the Middle East more broadly. Indeed, it is perhaps in these domains of social, cultural, and intellectual history that Russian archives can be exploited for the greatest gains.[39]

Lastly, it should be noted that the term "Russian archives" does not apply solely to the central imperial archives located in Moscow and St. Petersburg but rather to all Imperial Russian archives. These include, for example, the Central Historical Archive of Tbilisi, which houses the records of the Imperial Russian Viceroyalty of the Caucasus, the National Library of Finland in Helsinki, which contains a copy of nearly every book published in the Russian Empire, the archives of former Soviet republics, such as Azerbaijan, and the archives of autonomous and regional entities such as the archives of the Tatarstan and Dagestan republics.[40]

According to İlber Ortaylı, there can be no doubt that for study of Ottoman history today the archives of Moscow are not less important than the archives of such centers as London (the NA), Paris (the Quai d'Orsay; now housed at Courneuve, in the northern Paris suburbs), Berlin (the Preussische Geheime Staatsarchiv), Bonn (the Auswärtigen Amtes), Potsdam (the old Zentral Archiv Deutsche Demokratische Republik), and Vienna (the Haus-, Hof und Staatsarchiv). Besides the Turkish documents in the Moscow archives, the holdings for Russian history itself are important for Turkey. Russia's origins, and its foreign relations, have taken on an increased significance for Turkey. In this sense, every archival collection recording the history of Russia is also important for Turkish history. Ortaylı maintains that examination of these archives sometimes seems to yield new information even on the types of material and paper the Ottomans used. From the point of view of diplomatics, issues such as titulature (*elkab*) can be illumined by striking new evidence. And we gain a new understanding of the character of the Russian chancery. Thus these archives are essential for the establishment and development of a subfield like Russo-Turkish history, and the immense value of both these two countries' archives for the joint history of these two empires.[41] One can only regret that Ortaylı did not do more to tap these sources.

Our understanding of the reasons for the Armenian relocation of 1915 and its aftermath depends crucially upon research in Russian documents. It is therefore incumbent upon professors of history in Turkish universities who teach, research, and train graduate students, to encourage the study of the Russian language.

After the Ottoman repositories, the quest for truth about the Armenian events of 1915 must be sought with a look at the situation in Russian archives. In the 1990s, this improved greatly for scholars who wanted to consult documents from that period. The declassification of hitherto secret papers led to the publication of many works, some of high quality. But as the years passed, political developments made things more difficult. It was much easier to gain access to sensitive material under Boris Yeltsin than it is today. Rudolf Pikhoia, who headed the Russian Federal archive service from 1990 to 1996, has stated that in Soviet times up to 90 percent of the documents in the archives of the Communist Party, and 20 percent of those in state repositories, were considered secret or were otherwise subject to restrictions. The regulations on release of official documents to the public domain are not adhered to. Many are kept under lock and key.[42]

Fortunately, a number of dedicated scholars have persisted in their efforts to use the now available letters, correspondence, records, notes, telegrams, and minutes of meetings to confirm, clarify, or reject previous assertions about the czarist and Soviet role in Armenian affairs during and immediately after the First World War. One of the most effective laborers in this vineyard is Mehmet Perinçek of İstanbul University. Perinçek, like a growing number of foreign researchers, has benefited from the open access of Russian archives granted in the last two decades or so. He has had the chance to discover new material and scrutinize its prior use by Russian historians. He has examined a wide array of archives and document collections and in his recent products, collected key documents on the Turkish-Armenian conflict. The net result is a body of works that can fairly be said to be the only ones in Turkish on the Armenian question to blend Russian military and foreign policy in such breadth and depth using a great deal of unpublished documentation.[43] The evidence the author marshals demonstrates conclusively that the Armenian events of 1915 had no genocidal intent or effect.[44]

Although Perinçek's works provide a great deal of stimulating material there seems more ground for future researchers. Fortunately, these documents are exact, precise, and rich in historical value, and those following in Perinçek's tracks should be able to mine the veins he has uncovered with relative ease. But the author's books, not translated into English, have had little to no impact on general English-language scholarship on the First World War. They deserve translation into Western languages.[45]

Research in the Russian archives continues and new documents are uncovered every day. Although archival revelations have not, to date, supported any radically new interpretations of Czarist or Soviet history, they have served to clarify important issues and strengthen one or another long-standing argument on the causes or consequences of the Armenian relocation of 1915. Moreover, new documentary sources have contributed much to works that shed light on various aspects of the Ottoman Armenian history.

Understandably the archival work in Seyit Sertçelik's *The Emergence of the Armenian Question 1678–1914* has been limited by the scale of the study and by continuing restrictions on access—for instance, to intelligence or military records.[46] No doubt, this book will in due course be supplanted as more records are unearthed, but this is the norm in the historical profession, and if historians were to postpone writing until every relevant document is made accessible, very few histories would ever be published. Sertçelik would admit that, although much of his work has withstood the archival test, he would have preferred to have had greater access to Russian archives when his book was written. Nonetheless the available Russian documents, taken in conjunction with a careful combing of Ottoman and British sources, have made possible a much more detailed and nuanced view of this subject than has ever been possible before.

Sertçelik is aware of the fact that much remains unknown about the Armenian relocation of 1915 in imperial Russia, although one wishes that he had pointed out more clearly that there are reams and reams of archival materials on this and related subjects in the former Soviet Union that are as yet untouched by historians. But it is more than unlikely that further archival discoveries will merely reinforce and document those already known.

The Armenian Question in the Caucasus: Russian Archive Documents and Publications was issued by the European Azerbaijan Society in 2011 in a three-volume collection as a special topic of study for the first time in world historiography. The work is a complex presentation based on rare documents and publications which were long stored as "secret" and "top secret" in the RGIA and the RGVIA. The volumes (dealing chronologically with the periods 1724–1904, 1905–1906 and 1906–1914) provide analyses of documents and materials and contain copies of the originals in the archives and publications. Most of the documents and materials presented are made publicly available here for the first time. A large proportion of the documents can, in one way or another, be traced back to the governing circles of the Russian empire and this allows one to suppose that they reflect the state point of view on related subjects. To guarantee academic objectivity, the contextual integrity of the archive documents has been preserved. The collection provides the reader with the opportunity to undertake a critical review of current theses on the Armenian question. It also assists the application of contemporary academic methods to a comprehensive study of the essence of this issue.[47]

What has been outlined earlier barely skims the surface. It is hoped that historians can now plunge much deeper. Some files have recently been accessioned or declassified, while others were closed for re-cataloging or microfilming. The continued availability of documents in the Russian archives is subject to the vagaries of Russian politics. Access is still arbitrary in more than one sphere.

The historian of the Ottoman Empire will need to consult Russian sources—both primary and secondary—seriously, critically, and with a special understanding of its characteristics. They are of substantial value for the course of military operations, in particular.

NOTES

1. Abby Smith, "Russian History: Is It in the Archives?" in Francis Blouin, Jr. and William Rosenberg, eds., *Archives, Documentation and Institutions of Social Memory* (Ann Arbor, MI: University of Michigan Press, 2006), p. 451.

2. Ziva Galili, "Archives and Historical Writing," in Blouin, Jr. and Rosenberg, *Archives, Documentation and Institutions of Social Memory*, p. 443; Arup Banerji, *Writing History in the Soviet Union: Making the Past Work* (New Delhi: Social Science Press, 2008), p. 225.

3. "Russian History; The Battle for the Moscow Archives; With the End of Communism in Russia, Long-secret State Archives Were Thrown Open. Or Were They?" *The Economist*, Vol. 338, No. 7955 (2 March 1996), p. 88.

4. Ibid.

5. Richard Sakwa, *Gorbachev and His Reforms* (Englewood Cliffs, NJ: Prentice Hall, Inc., 1991), pp. 75–76; Stephen White, *After Gorbachev* (New York: Cambridge University Press, 1993), p. 93.

6. Raffi Shoubookian, "Holocaust Unlocked. When Will the Genocide Be?" *Asbarez*, 9 October 1988, p. 18.

7. R.W. Davies, *Soviet History in the Yeltsin Era* (London: Macmillan Press Ltd., 1997), p. 90.

8. Odd Arne Westad, "Secrets of the Second World: The Russian Archives and the Reinterpretation of Cold War History," *Diplomatic History*, Vol. 21, No. 2 (Spring 1997), pp. 259–260.

9. "Russian History," p. 88.

10. Alter Litvin, trans. and ed., John Keep, *Writing History in Twentieth-Century Russia: A View from Within* (London and Basingstoke: Palgrave Macmillan, 2001), p. 34.

11. Badem, *Çarlık Rusyası Döneminde Kars Vilayeti*, p. 10; Odd Arne Westad, "The Foreign Policy Archives of Russia: New Regulations on Declassification and Access," *Society for the History of American Foreign Policy Newsletter*, Vol. 23 (June 1992), pp. 1–10.

12. Patricia Kennedy Grimsted, "Russian Archives in Transition: Caught Between Political Crossfire and Economic Crisis," *American Archivist*, Vol. 56 (Fall 1993), pp. 614–662. See also Cemil Hasanlı, *Tarafsızlıktan Soğuk Savaşa Doğru Türk-Sovyet İlişkileri 1939–1953* (From the Neutrality Toward the Cold War: Turkish-Soviet Relations 1939–1953), (Ankara: Bilgi Yayınevi, 2011), pp. 7–14 and idem, *Stalin and the Turkish Crisis of the Cold War, 1945–1953* (Lanham, MD: Lexington Books, 2011), pp. vii–xiv. Hasanlı's books are based on research in Russian archives as well as published works in Russian and English, and a few in Turkish.

13. See Sean McMeekin, *The Russian Origins of the First World War* (Cambridge, MA and London: Belknap Press of Harvard University Press, 2011).

14. David Ransel's review of William Chase et al.'s, eds., *A Research Guide*, Vol. 1: *Guide to Collections*; Genrich Deych's, *A Research Guide to Materials on the History of Russian Jewry (Nineteenth and Early Twentieth Centuries)* in Benjamin Nathans, ed., *Selected Archives of the Former Soviet Union*; Gregory Freeze and S. V. Mironenko's, eds., *A Research Guide*, Vol. 1: *Collections of the State Archive of the Russian Federation on the History of Russia in the Nineteenth and Early Twentieth Centuries*; Arch Getty and V. P. Kozlov's, eds., *A Research Guide*; V. A. Kozlov and S. V. Mironenko's, eds., *Archive of Contemporary Russian History*, Vol. 1: *The "Special Files" for I. V. Stalin: From Materials of the Secretariat of the NKVD-MVD SSSR 1944–1953* and idem, eds., *Archive of Contemporary Russian History*, Vol. 2: *The "Special File" for V. M. Molotov: From Materials of the Secretariat of the NKVD-MVD of the USSR, 1944–1956*, in *The American Historical Review*, Vol. 12, No. 2 (April 1997), pp. 486–487.

15. See, for example, Patricia Kennedy Grimsted, ed., *Archives of Russia: A Directory and Bibliographic Guide to Holdings in Moscow and St. Petersburg* (New York and London: M. E. Sharpe, 2000) and idem, *Handbook for Archival Research in the USSR* (Washington, DC: Kennan Institute for Advanced Russian Studies, 1989).

16. Ransel's review of Chase et al.'s, Deych's, Freeze and Mironenko's, Getty and Kozlov's, Kozlov and Mironenko's books. This and the following pertinent paragraphs are mainly based on this source.

17. Patricia Kennedy Grimsted, "Increasing Reference Access to Post-1991 Russian Archives," *Slavic Review*, Vol. 56, No. 4 (Winter 1997), pp. 718–756. See also Badem, *Çarlık Rusyası Yönetiminde Kars Vilayeti*, p. 10.

18. Özhan Kapıcı and İbrahim Köremezli, "Osmanlı Askeri Tarihçiliğinin Eksik Aynası: Rusya Federasyonu Arşivleri" (The Imperfect Mirror of the Ottoman Military Historianship: Archives of the Russian Federation), in Şayin and Yıldız, *Osmanlı Askeri Tarihini Araştırmak*, pp. 147–149; Eftal Şaşmaz, "Rusya Federasyonu Arşivi" (State Archive of the Russian Federation), *Kebikeç*, No. 16 (2003), pp. 433–442.

19. Eftal Şaşmaz, "Rusya Devlet Askeri Arşivi" (Russian State Military Archive), *Kebikeç*, No. 17 (2004), pp. 114–115.

20. David Glantz and Jonathan House, *When Titans Clashed: How the Red Army Stopped Hitler* (Lawrence, KS: University Press of Kansas, 1995), p. 311.

21. Kapıcı and Köremezli, "Osmanlı Askeri Tarihçiliğinin Eksik Aynası," pp. 134–139.

22. Glantz and House, *When Titans Clashed*, p. 311.

23. Ibid., p. 314.

24. Raymond Garthoff, "Some Observations on Using the Soviet Archives," *Diplomatic History*, Vol. 21, No. 2 (Spring 1997), p. 244.

25. Jonathan Haslam, "Russian Archival Revelations and Our Understanding of Cold War," *Diplomatic History*, Vol. 21, No. 2 (Spring 1997), pp. 219–220.

26. Zara Steiner, "The Soviet Commissariat of Foreign Affairs and the Czechoslovakian Crisis in 1938: New Materials from the Soviet Archives," *The Historical Journal*, Vol. 42, No. 3 (September 1999), pp. 751–752.

27. Steven Merritt Miner, *Stalin's Holy War: Religion, Nationalism, and Alliance Politics, 1941–1945* (Chapel Hill, NC and London: University of North Carolina Press, 2003), p. xv.

28. Robert Daniels, "The Soviet Union in Post-Soviet Perspective," *The Journal of Modern History*, Vol. 74, No. 2 (June 2002), pp. 386–387.

29. Ibid., p. 387.

30. Jeremy Popkin, *History, Historians and Autobiography* (Chicago and London: University of Chicago Press, 2005), pp. 168–169; Samuel Baron and Cathy Frierson, eds., *Adventures in Russian Historical Research: Reminiscinces of American Scholars from the Cold War to the Present* (New York: M. E. Sharpe, 2003).

31. Norman Naimark, *The Russians in Germany* (Cambridge, MA and London: The Belknap Press of Harvard University Press, 1995), pp. 475–476.

32. Davies, *Soviet History in the Yeltsin Era*, pp. 95 and 114.

33. Author interview, Cemil Hasanlı, professor of history at Baku State University, 13 December 2011.

34. McMeekin, *The Russian Origins of the First World War*, pp. 2 and 246n3.

35. See, among many others, Peter Holquist, *Making War, Forging Revolution: Russia's Continuum of Crisis,1914–1921* (Cambridge, MA: Harvard University Press, 2002); Eric Lohr, *Nationalizing the Russian Empire: The Campaign against Enemy Aliens during World War I* (Cambridge, MA: Harvard University Press, 2003); Ronald Park Bobroff, *Roads to Glory: Late Imperial Russia and the Turkish Straits* (London: I.B. Tauris, 2006); Reynolds, *Shattering Empires*.

36. See, in particular, Ronald Grigor Suny and Terry Martin, eds., *A State of Nations: Empire and Nation-Making in the Age of Lenin and Stalin* (Oxford: Oxford University Press, 2001) and Terry Martin, *The Affirmative Action Empire: Nations and Nationalism in the Soviet Union, 1923–1939* (Ithaca, New York: Cornell University Press, 2001).

37. Michael Reynolds, Personal Communication, 31 July 2014.

38. Ibid.

39. Ibid.

40. Ibid. For a useful overview of the Russian archives to Ottomanists and others working on Muslims and Islamic civilization in Eurasia, see the following by Sean Pollock and several other articles in the same issue of *Ab Imperio*: Sean Pollock, "Historians and Their Sources: Discourses of Empire and Islam in Eurasian Archives," *Ab Imperio*, Vol. 4 (2008), pp. 234–252.

41. İlber Ortaylı, "Rusya Arşivleri ve Osmanlı Tarihi" (Archives of Russia and Ottoman History), in *Tarih Boyunca Türk Tarihinin Kaynakları Semineri, 6–7 Haziran 1996 Bildiriler* (Seminar on Sources of Turkish History Throughout History, 6–7 June 1996 Communications), (İstanbul: Edebiyat Fakültesi Basımevi, 1997), p. 145.

42. Alter Litvin and John Keep, *Stalinism: Russian and Western Views at the Turn of the Millenium* (London and New York: Routledge, 2005), p. 3.

43. Mehmet Perinçek, *Ermeni Devlet Adamı B. A. Borian'ın Gözüyle Türk-Ermeni Çatışması* (Turkish-Armenian Conflict Through the Eye of the Armenian Statesman B. A. Borian), (İstanbul: Kaynak Yayınları, 2006); idem, *Rus Devlet Arşivlerinden 100 Belgede Ermeni Meselesi* (Armenian Question in 100 Documents from the Russian State Archives), (İstanbul: Doğan Kitapçılık, 2007) and idem, ed., *Rus Kafkas Ordusu Kurmay Başkanı Tuğgeneral L.M. Bolhovitinov 11 Aralık 1915 Tarihli Resmi Ermeni Raporu* (Chief of Staff of the Russian Caucasian Army Brigadier General L. M. Bolhovitinov: Official Armenian Report of 11 December 1915), (İstanbul: Doğan Kitapçılık, 2009).

44. Mehmet Perinçek, "Sovyet Arşivleri Türkiye'nin Tezlerini Doğruluyor" (The Soviet Archives Corroborate the Theses of Turkey), in Şenol Kantarcı, Kamer Kasım, İbrahim Kaya and Sedat Laçiner, *Ermeni Araştırmaları 1. Türkiye Kongresi Bildirileri*, Vol.1, p. 127.

45. Russian and Persian translations of *Rus Devlet Arşivlerinden 100 Belgede Ermeni Meselesi* exist.

46. Seyit Sertçelik, *The Emergence of the Armenian Question 1678–1914* (Ankara: Council of Culture, Art and Publications of the Grand National Assembly of Turkey, 2010).

47. Tale Heydarov, ed., *The Armenian Question in the Caucasus: Russian Archive Documents and Publications*, 3 Vols., (Reading: Ithaca Press, 2011).

Chapter Thirteen

Whither the Turkish-Armenian Debate?

A TASK FOR HISTORIANS

The Armenian question occupied a prominent place in twentieth-century Middle Eastern historiography and remains controversial at the beginning of the twenty-first. Exceptionally intense debates about what actually took place in 1915 have been going on for almost a century and show no sign of resolution.

No one denies, or seeks to deny, that the Armenian people suffered terribly during the last years of the Ottoman Empire. This is made clear, but in the context of Ottoman history. What may be overlooked is that the experience of the Armenians, however terrible it undoubtedly was, was not unique to them. It was part of a general tragedy that engulfed all the people of the empire—Turks, Greeks, Armenians, Arabs, Jews, and others, all of whom have traumatic memories of the period. This was the terrible result of the final breakup of a multinational society as the consequence of a whole series of brutal and destructive foreign invasions, terroristic attacks, national revolts, massacres and counter massacres, and famine and disease, in which all the empire's people, Muslim and non-Muslim alike, had their victims and criminals. One appreciates, understands, and sympathizes with the sensitivity of the Armenians and others on this issue. But it is in the interest of all concerned that all sources be examined without preconceptions or prejudice. As additional research uncovers new information, it is inevitable that studies on the subject will be modified. Only through consultation of all relevant records by different researchers, with each giving his own differential weight to the sources at his disposal to present his interpretation, will a definite picture emerge. The many facets of truth will appear only when the inquiring mind of the reader examines all the interpretations and reaches its own conclusions.[1]

Discussions in Turkey are not limited to the Armenian allegation of genocide. Rather, Turkish historians and others in Turkey have long discussed the experience of the Ottoman Armenians in the context of general Ottoman history. Nonetheless, many Turkish historians have conducted earnest research, subject to peer review, that has revealed evidence tending to disprove the genocide allegation. Indeed, there has been a steady increase in interest in Ottoman history from this period, partly due to the broad assault on Turkey via accusations of genocide in parliaments and state houses motivated by politicians with anti-Turkish constituencies.

Marc David Baer indicates that "the published books and research and fellowship proposals promote the entire six hundred year existence of the Ottoman Empire as a model of tolerance and coexistence for the world to emulate." Baer then asks himself the pertinent question why the Armenians were privileged in the early nineteenth century but forcefully displaced a century later. He concludes that he has yet to read a convincing argument that explains how this change in Ottoman policy happened.[2]

A particular historical event may be interpreted in many different ways. To truly understand isolated occurrences, they must be evaluated within a larger context. This is the task that historians now face. They must discover the truth of what took place, and more importantly, how those events fit into the overall picture of the world at war. Only those with something to fear from the truth would limit the scope of the investigation.[3]

Official disclosure has important historical consequences. It exposes a mass of detail, and even if the details in themselves are not always crucial, the accumulation of them is. In particular, the historian's ability to wallow in these details helps him to enter into the minds of those who guided, or tried to guide, or thought they were guiding, the march of events; to understand—whether sympathetically or not—why they thought and acted as they did; and to readjust their interpretation of the kaleidoscope of circumstances.

In opening up a vast and rich store of official records, any historian has a primary responsibility to observe the spirit as well as the letter of the truth with respect to the character of officials and the nature of policies. The full story of any incident, of the actions of individuals, or the application of policy to any given situation can be obtained only by using as wide a range of available documents as possible. The proliferation of documents will beget a proliferation of interpretations—old questions will be reopened, and new questions will arise. And this, all to the good. New questions, approaches and concepts are more likely to enhance our understanding of the origins of the Armenian relocation. These will enable us to review well-known primary sources in a fresh light. A student of Ottoman Armenian history consequently must follow a trail through all the documentation if he or she is to avoid the pitfall of passing erroneous judgments.[4]

Historians must use all kinds of materials, and seek them even in unlikely places. Ottoman history peculiarly requires such wide-ranging research. Because the empire included so many different peoples, had hostile or friendly contact with so many other states, and was in its later years so susceptible to great power influence and intervention, the historian ideally will approach Ottoman affairs not only from the Turkish records, but from Russian, British, French, German, Austrian, American and Armenian archives as well.[5]

The task for historians of the region is then to discover as much source material as exists about the Armenian episode, to work together to put it all together, and simply to find out what happened. It is only after all these materials have been examined, published, studied, and discussed that a definitive history of the tragedy of the First World War can be written. Archival revelations either confirm or challenge understanding of particular events. Since the important thing for scholars of all persuasions is to look at all documents before reaching their conclusions—not simply doing research to "prove" preconceived ideas and to ignore sources which disagree with those ideas—that a great amount of research must still be done.[6]

Historians in all countries need to be able to say that the archives where materials exist on the topic are now open, completely—and without reservation—to anyone who wishes to examine them. Only by this means will we be able to guarantee that the real history of the First World War becomes fully known.

Much information regarding the First World War has become available in the past years through published Armenian works. But doubt remains as to its truth which can never be verified until Armenians throw open their archives to the public.

Historians are duty-bound to look at all the evidence, whether from İstanbul, Ankara, Moscow, London, Paris, or Yerevan. Their business is not automatically to dismiss evidence because it comes from one particular source or another. Rather, it is to examine any particular piece of evidence and come to their own judgment about its credibility and cogency in the light of all the evidence at their disposal. This is one of the simplest and perhaps one of the most outstanding principles that should guide any investigator. To the extent that he fails to do this he weakens his position. This challenge is already being taken up by a new generation of international historians, who have benefited from the increased attention being paid to language training and cultural studies over the past few decades.

A great deal remains to be done. Further research may reveal additional sources and lost accounts. Likewise, additional information may be uncovered in the libraries and manuscript collections that have thus far been overlooked.

Any scholarly investigation is a search for truth, for facts, for certainties. By *truth* is meant that which is in exact accordance with what is, or has been—in short, a verified fact. *Fact* means an act, an event, a circumstance, or anything which has come to pass. A *certainty* is unquestionable; and a truth may be said to be established when there is a coincidence of the observed sequence of events with the laws of experience as recognized by competent scholars.

A historian may expect to be confronted with documents and records of every description: new and old, well preserved and mutilated, originals and copies, the carefully written and carefully published, and the poorly written and the poorly published. Often the documents may be copies of copies, several steps removed from the original, and in some cases—especially in the case of ancient and mediaeval documents—the copies may be very poor and very inaccurate. It thus becomes quite clear that no careful historian will accept his documents without a sound examination of them.

The historian must always raise three questions: (1) What is the place of origin of the documents? (2) Who is its author? (3) What is its date? A document is worthless as a source of information if the historian is in absolute darkness on these points. To answer these questions is the purpose of the sound investigation of authorship. Its purpose is to rid ourselves of documents that would have misled us. It is a necessary preliminary step to serious work upon the major problem in hand. The historian's job is important.

Like historians, politicians also have a duty to truth. If they make pronouncements on history, they assume the duties of historians. They must look honestly at the historical record, the whole historical record. They must not accept that what they are told is true because political pressure groups tell them it is true. They must not accept that something is true just because their fathers believed it was true. They must not accept as truth what their own prejudices tell them is true. If politicians speak about history, if politicians pass resolutions on history, then they must follow the rules of history.

TURKEY'S PROPOSAL TO ESTABLISH AN INTERNATIONAL HISTORIANS' COMMISSION

A number of foreign lawmakers have long urged the government of Turkey to open its archives. Now that Turkey has responded positively and in good faith to these requests, the very least the foreign parliaments could do is to set aside their attempts to legislate historical questions and allow scholars time to study and write the history of the tragedy which affected Ottoman citizens during the First World War. Indeed, this was the position espoused by the American President George H.W. Bush in the autumn of 1989. In testimony before the House of Representatives Subcommittee on Europe and the Middle East on 31 October 1989, President Bush's Assistant Secretary of State for European and Canadian Affairs, Raymond Seitz, outlined the administration's policy in the following terms:

> The administration strongly opposes the Armenian resolution. We are not insensitive to the concerns of Armenian-Americans. But historians themselves disagree about what precisely occurred in eastern Anatolia in the waning days of the Ottoman Empire. The historical records of that period are now open for research. We should await that judgment.[7]

For the first time in the history of the Turkish-Armenian conflict, one now had the United States administration on record as agreeing that: (1) the historical record is unclear; (2) the key to resolve these questions is the Ottoman archives which have now been opened by the Turkish government; and (3) we should await the judgment of scholars before characterizing the events.

So, one ought to act with great care before using the term "genocide" in any kind of legislative expression. And, above all, one should give scholars—who now for the first time have the opportunity to research the issue in question—all available documentation that would help them make some final decisions about it; and give scholars an opportunity to conduct their research before legislators—in the political process—rush to judgment on a consensus that has not yet developed in the scholarly community.

As United States Congressman John McCain aptly put it on the floor of the Senate on 21 February 1990, one has to agree with the Secretary of State James Baker III that history should be the judge of the Armenian episode. And history is not entirely settled on this question. With the opening of the historical archives of the period for scholarly research, it would be well to heed Secretary Baker's advice and await the subsequent findings of historians.[8] Congressman Timothy Wirth, in cogent, lucid, and well-thought-out remarks made the same date in the same body, did not consider that it was appropriate at all for the Senate to get into an intense historical dispute. The genocide charge was a hotly debated one and he thought immediately the assumption was: "Something happened; the Turks were guilty; the Armenians were the ones wronged in this situation." That, he thought, has been the conventional wisdom. In preparing for this speech, however, Wirth discovered, to his surprise, that there was a very significant division and a great deal of scholarship about the charges of genocide. "The issues, given this division, [were] certainly better left to historians and not to politicians and governing bodies like the U.S. Senate."[9]

Again, on 21 February 1990, Senator Robert Byrd said that ascertaining whether or not the crime of genocide had occurred was not a task for the Senate. He remarked:

> We have not conducted hearings. We have not conducted investigations. We do not have the records before us. We are politicians. We are not historians. And we should not put ourselves in the position of making the Senate an instrument of determination of what is genocide and what race or what nation now or in the far distant past committed the inexplicably horrific crime of genocide [...] The Senate is in no position to do that. We are politicians. We are not historians. Some of us try to be scholars of history. I think we all try to be scholars of history. There are no historians in this body that I know of. And, if there are, they have not studied the records which need to be opened and studied and evaluated before any such criminal determination can be made.[10]

In the House of Representatives on 24 April 1990, Congressman Greg Laughlin went a step further on the subject stating eloquently:

> Genocide is the most highly charged indictment that can be made against a country. However, if the term is to retain its meaning, it must not be applied to the events of 1915 in the Ottoman Empire, no matter how tragic they were for the victims. No one denies that a civil war within a global war, intercommunal hostilities, famine, epidemics and banditry took a heavy toll on all sides. The Armenians suffered and the Turkish people did as well. However, no matter how painful this was, historians tell us there is insufficient evidence to apply the term genocide. Tragedy, suffering, loss of life and genocide are not synonymous. Until further research is done by bona fide scholars, the allegation that there was a systematic state-directed program of the Ottoman Empire's Government to exterminate the Armenian people is not sustainable.[11]

McCain, Byrd and Laughlin were all right. The floor of the Congress was not the appropriate place to determine the truth of a matter that ought to be researched, evaluated, and decided by historians. The volume of archives surviving from the First World War is enormous. This issue should be left to historians to decide. It is to the First World War and its records that we must now return.

NOTES

1. Shaw and Shaw, *History of the Ottoman Empire and Modern Turkey*, Vol. 2, p. x.
2. Marc David Baer, Ussama Makdisi, and Andrew Shryock, "Tolerance and Conversion in the Ottoman Empire: A Conversation," *Comparative Studies in Society and History*, Vol. 51, No. 4 (October 2009), pp. 936–937.
3. İlber Ortaylı, *Kırk Ambar Sohbetleri* (Forty Store Conversations), (Ankara: Aşina Kitaplar, 2006), p. 203.
4. Oktay Özel, "Ermeni Meselesi Tarihçisini Arıyor" (The Armenian Question Is Looking For Its Historian), *Kebikeç*, No.19 (2005), pp. 8–9.
5. Roderic Davison, "European Archives as a Source for Later Ottoman History," in Kathleen Brown, ed., *Report on Current Research 1958: Survey of Current Research on the Middle East* (Washington, DC: The Middle East Institute, 1958), p. 33.
6. The research worker in the field of history should find it profitable to consult Ahmet Yaşar Ocak, "Usta Tarihçiler Nasıl Çalışıyorlar?" (How Do Master Historians Work?), in

Ahmet Şimşek, ed., *Tarih Nasıl Yazılır? Tarihyazımı İçin Çağdaş bir Metodoloji* (How Is History Written? A Modern Methodology for Historiography), (İstanbul: Tarihçi Kitabevi, 2011), p. 378.

7. Developments in Europe, October 1989. Hearing Before the Subcommittee on Europe and the Middle East of the Committee on Foreign Affairs, House of Representatives 101st Congress, 1st Session, 31 October 1989 (Washington, DC : U.S. Government Printing Office, 1990), pp. 2 and 7.

8. Congressional Record-Senate, Proceedings and Debates of the 101st Congress, 2nd Session, Vol.136, No.14, 21 February 1990, S 1356.

9. Ibid., S 1321.

10. Ibid., S 1335.

11. Congressional Record-House of Representatives, 24 April 1990, H 1681.

Chapter Fourteen

The First World War and Its Archival Records

ARMENIANS AND THE TURKISH-RUSSIAN CONFLICT IN THE FIRST WORLD WAR

During the First World War, the eastern provinces of the Ottoman Empire were invaded by Russia, the twelfth time the Turks had fought the Russians. Incited by the Russians, Armenians in the region launched an armed uprising to establish an exclusively Armenian state in an area that was predominantly non-Armenian.[1] The Armenian masses greeted the advancing Russian armies as liberators. Many Armenians deserted the Ottoman army, and assisted the Russian advance. There is no doubt that, as a whole, the Armenian elements in the villages of Asia Minor were hostile to the Turks and that their loyalty was highly doubtful. Little wonder that *The Chicago Sunday Tribune* wrote on 8 November 1914 that "the most significant development to date of the Russo-Turkish war is the announcement that the Armenians are rising against Turkey." And it continued:

> Realizing that the present is an opportune time to throw off Turkish yoke and to get revenge for past outrages, the Armenians are offering their services to the Russian Caucasian army which had invaded Turkey. The Russian forces have already proceeded westward from Passine, Dendine, and Barazet, where the first actual fighting of the war took place.[2]

Nor do we have to rely solely on American press reports to establish that the events of 1915 were not a one-sided Turkish-perpetrated genocide, but were rather the result of communal strife precipitated by the fact that many Ottoman Armenians chose to betray their state at the time of the outbreak of the First World War and fight with the invading Russians against their lawful government. One such individual was Garekin Pasdermadjian who fought under the *nom de guerre* "Armen Garo." Pasdermadjian, a former member of the Ottoman Chamber of Deputies for Erzurum, deserted to the Russians and became the commander of the "Second Battalion of the Armenian Volunteers on the Caucasian Front." In his book, *Why Armenia Should Be Free Armenia's Role in the Present War* he proudly revealed the war-time role played by Ottoman Armenians:

> In the early days of August, 1914, when civilized nations took up arms against the German aggression, only three of the smaller nations of Europe and the Near East had the courage, from the very first days of the war, to stand by the Allies without any bargaining or dickering, and they still stand at their posts on the ramparts, in spite of the immense sacrifices they have already made [...] The third member of this heroic triad was the Armenian people, who for four years and without an organized government or a national army, played the same role in the Near East by preventing the Turco-German advance toward the interior of Asia as the Belgians played in the West by arresting the march of Germany toward Paris.[3]

It was therefore hardly surprising that the Italian *Tribuna* of 14 May 1915 read:

> Enver Pasha accused the Armenians as traitors and this accusation was probably correct, for the Armenians never failed under any circumstances, to desire the triumphant march of Russia and to help toward it. They hoped to see their salvation reborn from the embers of Europe in conflagration.[4]

On 24 May 1915, the Russian, British, and French governments agreed to publish the following joint declaration:

> For the past month, Kurds and the Turkish population of Armenia have been engaged in massacring Armenians with the connivance and help of the Ottoman authorities. Such measures took place about the middle of April at Erzurum, Dertshav [Derjan], Mush, Zeytun, and in all Cilicia. The inhabitants of about a hundred villages near Van were all assassinated. In the town itself, the Armenian quarter is besieged by Kurds. At the same time, the Ottoman government at Constantinople is raging against the inoffensive Armenian population. In the face of these fresh crimes committed by Turkey, the Allied Governments announce publicly to the Sublime Porte that they will hold all members of the Government, as well as such of their agents as are implicated, personally responsible for such massacres.[5]

On 3 June 1915, the Ottoman government publicly refuted the arguments and information included in the above-mentioned announcement. The reply is worth quoting extensively:

It is entirely incorrect that massacres against the Armenians have taken place in the territory of the Turkish state. The following explanations are supplied to establish the truth based on facts. Armenians in Erzurum, Terjan, Agn, Sasun, Bitlis, and Mush, and the Armenians of Cilicia have never been the subject of special measures by the Imperial Government, because they do not engage in behavior that could disrupt public order and peace. This truth is already well known to the consuls of neutral states. Therefore, the accusations raised by the Allied states are purely lies, invented by the agents of the Triple Alliance, especially Russia and England, which take advantage of every opportunity to provoke the Armenian population to revolt against the Imperial Government.[6]

These unending conspiracies became intensified after hostilities started between the mentioned countries and the Ottoman Empire. Thus, their consuls and agents in Bulgaria sent to the Caucasus groups of Ottoman Armenian youths by way of Varna, Sulina, and Constantza; the Russian government accepted these young men into its armed forces, or it sent them—armed with weapons and bombs—to the parts of the Ottoman empire with a concentrated Armenian population, also supplying them with [pamphlets] and platforms calling for a revolution. These young men intend [ed] to create secret revolutionary societies in those centers, and they succeeded, in particular, in provoking the Armenians of Van, Shadakh, Hayots-Tsor, Kavash [Gevash], and Timar to revolt against the Imperial Government. They also provoked and organized massacres against Turks and Kurds.

In this regard, it is important to cite the following example. When hostilities started between the Ottoman state and Russia, erstwhile Ottoman deputy Karekin Pastermajian, also known as "Karo," joined the *chetehs* organized by the leaders of the Armenian *komitehs* [revolutionary committees], Dro and Khecho. He, together with the two mentioned leaders, assumed the leadership of the Armenian volunteers armed by Russia, and these crossed the Ottoman frontier. During the time the Russians occupied Bayazid, [Karo] destroyed all the Muslim villages on his way and massacred their inhabitants. When the Russians were expelled from that region, he was wounded, and the Tashnagtsagan delegate of Erzurum, Suren, was killed by his side. Pastermajian is now active on the Caucasian front. The Tashnagtsagan organ [official publication] in the United States, *Asbarez*, published a picture in which he, Khecho, and Dro are seen participating in a religious oath-taking ceremony before an expedition.

This separatist movement was soon revealed more clearly through the activities of other Armenians, among whom was Toros Oghlu Agop. Papers found on him established indisputably their criminal purpose. These Armenians were brought on shore near Alexandretta by British officials from Cyprus. The provocation planned in this manner led, among other things, to the derailing of a train. On the other hand, high-level officials of the Anglo-French naval forces entered into relations with the Armenians of the areas of Adana, Deort-Yol, Yumurtalek, Alexandretta, and other coastal villages and incited them to revolt. As for what pertains to Zeytun, it should be said that, with the propaganda of the English and French governments, the revolutionary organization in Zeytun set to work directly. Already in February, the inhabitants of that town raised arms against the Imperial Government's officials and surrounded the government building. Faced with such developments, the Imperial Government was compelled to suppress the revolt to maintain public peace and order.

The Imperial Government's authority to take all measures to suppress such a revolutionary and separatist movement follows directly from its incontestable sovereign right. In addition, it is all the more important and necessary to take such measures during times of war, such as the present. Because of this, the Imperial Government found it necessary, on the one hand to send troops to subdue these movements, and, to arrest the Armenian agitators, who were in communication with the [revolutionary] committees abroad and the agents of the Triple Alliance. Contrary to the arguments of the three above-mentioned states, the subjugation operation was accomplished without the slightest participation of the local Muslim population. In searches conducted in the Armenian revolutionaries' homes, revolutionary flags and important writings pertaining to revolt were found, and the separatist intent of this movement is evident from these objects. Furthermore, these writings confirmed that the revolutionary committees, presently having their centers in Paris, London, and Tiflis, are enjoying the protection of the English, Russian, and French governments. During searches conducted in the countryside, thousands of bombs and Russian arms were found in the hands of Armenians. Understandably, these people were arrested and delivered to the appropriate courts, just like others who deserted from military service under the provocation of English and French agents and committed assaults on the military police in favor of these foreign countries.

Today, the Imperial Government has in its hands writings that confirm that these movements were planned under the high-level protection of the Russian, English, and French governments and that the latest revolutionary assembly of the Armenians, held in Constanza, had decided to resume its work at the most opportune moment, while outwardly giving the impression of having abandoned rebellious activities.

The Sublime Porte will publish, at the proper time, all these documents in detail, in order to inform public opinion.

Thanks to the measures employed by the full force of the Imperial Government for the protection of the public order, the Armenian revolutionary movement was suppressed without any massacres taking place. The measures taken were necessary because of the circumstances, and they do not signify that there is a movement against Armenians. This is evident from the fact that there are 77,836 Armenians resident in Constantinople, of whom only 235 have been arrested, and these were people helping the revolutionary movement; all the other Armenians are continuing with their affairs comfortably and enjoying complete security. If it was necessary to remove a few Armenians from their native lands, it was because they were living in areas in the theater of war, and the presence of Armenians in these areas touches upon the Imperial Government's legitimate concerns for the protection of its land.

In addition, the Sublime Porte considers it its duty to take whatever measures it considers necessary for the security of the land and sea frontiers, for which it is not accountable to any foreign government.

Is it not surprising that the English, French, and Russian governments are appealing to humane feelings, when the Anglo-French navy's command at the

Dardanelles bombs the stations and hospitals of the wounded, and the Russian government allows the Armenians to massacre thousands of peaceful Muslims in the region of Kars, or brings Turks captured on the Caucasus front and has them massacred at the hands of the same Armenians?

Such unqualified savagery was not seen, even in ancient times—times which are generally not lacking in merciless acts. The English, French, and Russian governments, which felt themselves obliged to suppress the revolts and uprisings in the Caucasus, Morocco, Egypt, India, and other places with brutal force and necessarily inhumane behavior, do not have the right to shove in the Ottoman government's face those measures of restraint that it was obliged to implement and that it implemented with great moderation and justice. In this instance, the Ottoman government has performed only the most fundamental actions concerned with its authority. The announcement, according to which members of the Imperial government and other officials are considered responsible for the measures employed in suppressing the revolt, is not worthy of any response. The entire responsibility for the majority of these incidents—about which the Triple Alliance think that it should protest—falls upon their shoulders, because they are the very states that organized and directed these revolutionary movements. Their announcement has no significance other than protecting and encouraging the instigators of Armenian revolutionary movements.

Not in Turkey but in Russia were the consuls of the fighting states subjected to hardships and torments. English, French, and Russian statesmen were not satisfied with the preparations of the Armenian revolt, but they also attempted to deceive the Muslim element into rebelling against the Sultan's government. The Sublime Porte has in its hands evidence that they even organized conspiracies against certain persons to attain their goals.

Heinrich Bergfeld, the German consul in Trabzon, was in favor of the relocation of the Armenians, even still at the end of 1918 when he, too, was aware of all the consequences. "Based on the Armenians' attitude and convictions at the beginning of the war, their evacuation—not just that of the men, but of entire families—was, in my opinion, a compellingly necessary military measure."[7] It is clear from German diplomatic sources that Hans Humann, Lieutenant Commander and Naval Attaché, and Colonel Otto von Lossow, Authorized Military Representative, both at the German Embassy in İstanbul, and General Fritz Bronsart von Schellendorff, Deputy Chief of the General Staff of the Ottoman Army in the field, also favored the Armenian population displacement, which was necessary for military reasons.[8]

As already related, war, brigandage, famine and epidemics took a heavy toll on all sides. Armenians suffered, as did approximately two million Turks who perished during this period. It is morally wrong to recognize the suffering of Armenians without acknowledging that much of it was the result of communal strife initiated by Armenian revolutionaries in collaboration with invading Czarist Russian armies. The goal of these revolutionaries was to create an exclusively Armenian state in an area of the Ottoman Empire where

Armenians were a minority. There was no government-planned-and-implemented scheme to exterminate the Empire's Armenian population. In fact, hundreds of thousands of Armenians in the western provinces of the Ottoman Empire were unaffected by events in eastern Anatolia.[9] It must be pointed out here, and kept in mind all along, that the British military historian John Grainger has recently concluded on the human deaths in Asia Minor in the First World War as follows: "It [the Armenian relocation] was not genocide since plenty of Armenians survived, and some served in the Ottoman army."[10]

DOCUMENTS KEY TO HISTORY

The true history of Turkish-Armenian conflict can be retrieved only through archival work. Documents are the key to historical truth. Documents that were produced at the time of the event by competent and responsible officials and that are accessible at well-organized archival collections facilitate the accurate reconstruction of the manner in which a government formed and implemented policy. In historical investigation, there is little substitute for solid research in the written archives. This approach will put an end to superficial and arbitrary historical narratives and, instead, assist in revealing the truth. For one thing, the Turkish authorities have not denied that deaths took place in that period of 1915-1916. The argument centers on the scale of, and the responsibility for, these casualties.

The methods and principles of historical research can be fully applied to Ottoman history. Ottoman studies should no longer be solely limited to examination and comparison of the reports of foreign diplomatic representatives and missionaries in the Ottoman Empire. However, these reports can still make a valuable contribution in supplementing, enriching, confirming, and sometimes explaining the information available in the Ottoman chronicles and archives concerning the political, diplomatic and commercial developments in the Ottoman Empire.[11]

NOTES

1. BOA, Babıali Evrak Odası (Records Office of the Sublime Porte), No. 326758. Communication from the Ministry of the Interior to the Grand Vizier's Office, 26 May 1915.
2. "Armenians Against Turkey," *The Chicago Sunday Tribune*, 8 November 1914, p. 1.
3. Garekin Pasdermadjian, *Why Armenia Should Be Free: Armenia's Role in the Present War* (Boston, MA: Hairenik Publishing Company, 1918), p. 15.
4. Robin Bidwell, ed., *The Arab Bulletin Bulletin of the Arab Bureau in Cairo, 1916–1919*, Vol.1: 1916, (London: Archive Editions, 1986), p. 30.
5. Havas Agency, 24 May 1915.
6. This and the following pertinent paragraphs are based on "Fictitous Judgment of the Triple Alliance: A Trustworthy Turkish Description of the Conspiracy Prepared by the Triple Alliance Regarding the Armenian Massacres," *Neue Freie Presse*, 6 June 1916, pp. 10–11, as

cited in Zaven Der Yeghiayan, trans. Ared Misirliyan, *My Patriarchal Memoirs* (Barrington, RI: Mayreni Publishing, 2002), pp. 68–70.

7. Wolfgang Gust, ed., *The Armenian Genocide: Evidence from the German Foreign Office Archives, 1915–1916* (New York and Oxford: Berghahn Book, 2014; origin in German, 2005), p. 85.

8. Ibid., pp. 107–108.

9. The potential bibliography is vast. A true angle on this theme can be obtained by reading Guenter Lewy, *The Armenian Massacres in Ottoman Turkey: A Disputed Genocide* (Salt Lake City, UT: University of Utah Press, 2005); idem, *Outlawing Genocide Denial: Dilemmas of Official Historical Truth* (Salt Lake City, UT: University of Utah Press, 2014); Justin McCarthy, Esat Arslan, Cemalettin Taşkıran, and Ömer Turan, *The Armenian Rebellion at Van* (Salt Lake City, UT: University of Utah Press, 2006); Hikmet Özdemir, trans., Şaban Kardaş, *The Ottoman Army 1914–1918: Disease and Death on the Battlefield* (Salt Lake City, UT: University of Utah Press, 2008); Salahi Sonyel, *The Great War and the Tragedy of Anatolia: Turks and Armenians in the Maelstrom of Major Powers* (Ankara: Turkish Historical Society, 2nd ed., 2001); Shaw, *The Ottoman Army in World War I*; Erickson, *Ordered to Die*; idem, *Ottomans and Armenians*; Yücel Güçlü, *Armenians and the Allies in Cilicia 1914–1923* (Salt Lake City, UT: University of Utah Press, 2010) and idem, *The Holocaust and the Armenian Case in Comparative Perspective* (Lanham, MD: University Press of America, 2012). Despite the increasing number of works written about the subject, there remains much to consider.

10. John Grainger, *The Battle for Syria 1918–1920* (Woodbridge, Suffolk: The Boydell Press, 2013), p. 25n2.

11. Shaw, "Archival Sources for Ottoman History," p. 12. This is, in essence, also the conclusion drawn by Davison, "European Archives as a Source for Later Ottoman History," pp. 33–45.

Chapter Fifteen

From Historical Controversy to Political Campaigning

The Armenians and Greeks have been lobbying against Turkey among Western politicians and parliaments since the nineteenth century. This started again on a new scale in the 1990s, drawing on the lobbying resources of expatriate groups. History was the first casualty in this war.

DEBATES IN THE BRITISH AND EUROPEAN PARLIAMENTS

In a speech on 14 April 1999 in the House of Lords, the upper chamber of the British Parliament, Lord Monson thus set the Ottoman scene in perspective and he was fairly correct. By the standards of most of the past 600 years, the Ottoman Empire was generally pluralist and reasonably tolerant, more so than most of Christian Europe during most of that time. Sephardic Jews expelled from Spain in 1492 by Ferdinand and Isabella were welcomed to the Ottoman Empire in their tens of thousands. They settled in İstanbul, Salonika, and elsewhere, where they prospered hugely. Provided that they obeyed the rules and did not rock the boat, the Armenians and other Christians could rise to senior and well-paid positions in the government as well as make money commercially. What happened to Ottoman Armenians in the First World War was, however, terrible. But it is not genocide as most people understand the word. It was not, for instance, comparable to the Chinese attempt totally to exterminate Tibetan identity and culture. Still less is it comparable to the Nazi attempt from 1942 onwards to exterminate the Jewish race the world over. The Jews had always been good German citizens and fought bravely for Germany during the First World War; indeed, many won

Iron Crosses, whereas some Armenians were indeed subversives. The Jews never retaliated against German civilians, whereas on occasion, when the Armenians had the upper hand, they took reprisals upon Muslim civilians. Most importantly, the Jews were hunted down and murdered everywhere in Germany and on the German-occupied continent, even during the last days of the war in Europe, whereas atrocities against Armenians were confined largely to eastern Anatolia. The substantial Armenian community in and around İstanbul survived reasonably intact.[1]

Lord Monson went further and said that while the policy of the Ottoman government of forcibly deporting Armenians away from Russian frontier regions to Syria undoubtedly involved an enormous amount of suffering (in the same way as the Japanese forced marches of prisoners of war and European and Asian civilians during the Second World War led to terrible suffering), the deaths involved were incidental to—rather than the prime purpose of— those marches. Meanwhile, the murder of many thousands of Armenians by Kurdish and other civilians was not organized by the government even if the government may have lost little sleep over it. Those massacres were partly fuelled by the sort of religious hatreds seen in the Balkans over the past 150 years or more, and partly fuelled by resentment against economically successful groups, comparable to the hatred vented periodically against the Chinese minority in those parts of Southeast Asia where Muslims predominate.[2]

In the same debate the Foreign and Commonwealth Office spokesperson, Baroness Ramsay of Cartvale, stated that the position of the British government on the Armenian issue was well known and understood, but it certainly bore repeating there. The British government condemned the massacres of 1915–1916 at the time and viewed the sufferings of the Armenian people then as a tragedy of historic proportions. The British government of today, like their predecessors, in no way dissented in any form from that view. But in the absence of unequivocal evidence to show that the Ottoman administration took a specific decision to eliminate the Armenians under their control at the time, British governments have not recognized the events of 1915 and 1916 as genocide. Baroness Ramsay drew attention to the fact that the vast majority of other governments were in a similar position. Very few of them have officially attributed the term genocide to these events. In the British government's opinion that was rightly so, because they did not believe it was the business of governments of today to review events of over eighty years ago with a view to pronouncing on them.[3]

Lord Moynihan, Opposition Spokesman on Foreign Affairs in the House of Lords, wrote on 11 June 1999 that successive British governments have not recognized the events of 1915 as genocide, in the absence of unequivocal evidence to demonstrate that the Ottoman administration took a specific decision to eliminate the Armenians under their control at the time. This remained the view of the Conservative Party. There was little doubt that the First World War saw the occurrence of a vast tragedy in Anatolia and Lord Moynihan took this as his starting point. However, although it remained his view that these were largely matters of historical and legal debate, he hoped to make it clear in his comments that he fully appreciated the sensivity on both sides which still surrounded this emotive issue.[4]

Armenag Topalian, a British citizen of Armenian descent, through his Member of Parliament, asked Keith Vaz, Minister for Europe, on 5 February 2001, which sources the Foreign and Commonwealth Office were relying on to support Britain's view that, in the absence of unequivocal evidence to the contrary, the massacres of 1915–1916 should not be described as genocide. Topalian had a response dated 12 March 2001 from Vaz, which ran as follows:

> Bernard Lewis said in 1993 that it was extremely doubtful that the Turks had carried out a systematic policy of annihilation. Heath Lowry and Justin McCarthy both dispute that the evidence supports a verdict of genocide. Other historians, among them, John Fox, Vahakn Dadrian and Helen Fein, take a very different view, supporting the argument that the massacres should be classified as genocide. Erik Zürcher and A. L. Macfie take an intermediate view. The first says that "there are indications that, while the Ottoman government as such was not involved in genocide, an inner circle within the Committee of Union and Progress under the direction of Talat Pasha wanted to solve the Eastern question by the extermination of the Armenians and it used the relocation as a cloak for this policy (*Turkey: A Modern History*, London: I. B. Tauris, 1995).

Macfie said:

> Documentary evidence, such as it is—many of the documents concerning the Armenian massacres were destroyed by the Ottoman government at the end of the First World War—would appear to support the Turkish view that Armenian deaths were unplanned and unintended consequences of the policy of deportation. Yet it is difficult, if not impossible, to escape the conclusion that, once the deportations were instituted, the Ottoman leadership, or at least elements within it, were not averse to exploiting the opportunities offered to resolve a problem that for decades caused the empire so much difficulty (*The End of the Ottoman Empire 1908–1923*, London: Longman, 1998).

The ongoing historical debate was—the British government felt—the correct place for addressing the question.[5]

Representatives of Turkish citizens of Armenian origin protested on 16 November 2000 against a European Parliament resolution calling on Ankara to recognize as "genocide" the Ottoman Armenian deaths in the First World War. A statement from the Armenian patriarchate, carried by the Anatolian

News Agency, said the Armenian minority in Turkey had always chosen to resolve their problem through "[D]irect dialogue with the [Turkish] state. . . . For this reason, we do not approve, find it right or beneficial that our problems are taken up by irrelevant parties and used in a manner which could prevent our country's integration with Europe," it said. It added that the report's reference to the Armenian minority in Turkey was "odd" since "[T]here have been no such demands by Turkey's Armenians." The statement was issued after a meeting in İstanbul of some sixty representatives of the Armenian community, which was chaired by the Armenian Patriarch in Turkey, Mesrob II. In the report, adopted on 15 November 2000, the European Parliament urged Turkey "[G]ive fresh support to the Armenian minority, as an important part of Turkish society, in particular by public recognition of the genocide which that minority suffered before the establishment of the modern state of Turkey." Turkey swiftly denounced the resolution, warning that relations with the European Parliament would suffer.[6]

Upon passage of the European Parliament's resolution, *The Wall Street Journal Europe* commented in a lead article on 20 November 2000 that

> perhaps the Parliament should also call on Greece to officially "recognize"—and apologize for—its invasion of Turkey following World War I. France and Britain might do the same with respect to the 1920 Treaty of Sévres, which consigned most of historic Armenia to the Soviet sphere and so to the horrors that followed. . . .Whether the majority of these [Armenian] deaths were the result of a deliberate policy of extermination or of other factors is a matter of contentious scholarly debate. What seems clear, however, is that the present amendment has less to do with the claims of memory and justice than it does with the politics of EU enlargement. It's a foolish ploy.[7]

TURKEY AND THE EUROPEAN UNION

It needs to be stressed that the European Parliament—though it has no binding powers over the EU and does not speak on its behalf, nor on behalf of the various individual EU member states and national legislatures that have passed Armenian genocide resolutions—has permitted a full hearing on whether the accusation of genocide was valid. But they acted, as politicians and not as scholars—accepting the pleas and charges of the anti-Turkish factions as correct without consulting or providing a meaningful due process of reply to the accused. Furthermore, the few EU members that have defined the Armenian case as genocide, have not complied with the United Nations Convention on the Prevention and Punishment of the Crime of Genocide (UNCG) of 1948 in seeking a judicial determination, either in the form of an advisory opinion or legal action against Turkey.[8] Most likely they understood that they did not have a case that could withstand scholarly scrutiny under the law and facts. Moreover, after having tried to satisfy the political demands of their various anti-Turkish constituents, these countries resumed constructive relations with Turkey, notwithstanding the fact that Turkey accepted the Armenian case purely as an unproven allegation of genocide and was ready to see it fully examined in an objective light.

Perhaps one may clarify here the issue of EU membership. The conditions which all applicants for membership of the EU, including Turkey, must fulfil were laid down by the Copenhagen European Council in 1993. These criteria include stable institutions guaranteeing democracy, the rule of law, human rights and respect for and protection of minorities. The Council has not laid down any additional conditions relating to recognition of an Armenian genocide. The EU accession rules or the Copenhagen criteria did not make any references to this issue. Thus, on behalf of the British government, Secretary of State for Foreign and Commonwealth Affairs, Douglas Alexander said in the House of Commons on 17 October 2005:

> There is no consensus among EU member states that the massacres of 1915–16 should be categorised as genocide as defined by the 1948 UN Convention on Genocide and there is no reference to the issue in the Negotiating Framework agreed by EU member states that will guide Turkey's accession negotiations. The Turkish government does not accept that there was any intention or act that constituted genocide.[9]

The Parliamentary Under Secretary for the Foreign and Commonwealth Office, Lord Triesman, could make a similar declaration in the House of Lords on 22 January 2007: "For this government, recognition of the so-called Armenian genocide is not a condition of Turkey's membership of the EU. I wish to be straightforward and clear about that."[10]

It is not surprising to hear the speaker of Armenia's National Assembly saying on 30 August 2005 he supports neighboring Turkey's application to join the EU and suggesting the eventual accession to the EU of other countries in the South Caucasus. "What's wrong with having a neighboring country a member of the EU?" Artur Baghdasarian replied when asked about Turkey's possible entry into the twenty-five-nation organization. Baghdasarian, leader of the center-right Orinats Yerkir (Country of Law) party in Armenia's governing coalition stated that if Turkey could comply with the EU standards and join the organization, then other countries of the region should seek accession. "I see the future of our region in an expanded EU," he remarked at a meeting of the Center for Strategic and International Studies, a policy research group in Washington, DC. He also said Turkey and Armenia, which did not have diplomatic relations, should "not set barriers to cooperation but sit down and talk, not avoiding past problems but moving forward with constant dialogue."[11]

It should be recalled that Turkish President Ahmet Necdet Sezer had already stated on 1 October 2003 that Turkey would normalize its relations with Armenia, on the condition that this country adopt a foreign policy in line with principles of law, and resolve its problems with neighbors. Addressing the TGNA on the first session of its new legislative year, Sezer stressed that Armenia must finally make a choice "to reconcile with its past, and leave judgment on history to historians,"[12] and rightly so.

TURKEY AND THE UNITED NATIONS CONVENTION ON GENOCIDE

When the first UN General Assembly affirmed that genocide is a crime under international law and called for a convention on the crime of genocide to be prepared, the bitter experiences of the Second World War were still very much alive. The drafting of a convention on the elimination and punishment of the crime of genocide, which was mainly a response to the Holocaust, was completed in a short time and adopted by a roll call vote at the third session of the UN General Assembly with fifty-six states, including Turkey, voting in favor. Turkey was one of the earliest countries acceding to the convention on 31 July 1950, whereas the United States did not ratify it until 25 November 1998. Turkey could honestly and proudly affirm its abhorrence of genocide by agreeing to the convention. For half a century the United States Senate refused to consent to ratification, first because of fears that it would be accused of genocide because of segregation, and later because of similar fears concerning its actions in Vietnam. Upon its entry into force this convention became binding Turkish law, and of equal stature to any other criminal statute enumerated in the Turkish Code. The wording in the Turkish criminal code's definition of responsibility for genocide is in accordance with the UNCG.[13]

On 26 January 2004, in his keynote speech to the Stockholm International Forum: Preventing Genocide; Threats and Responsibilities, the UN Secretary General suggested that the states party to the UNCG should consider setting up a committee on the prevention of genocide, which would meet periodically to review reports and make recommendations for action. He suggested that those States should also consider establishing a special rapporteur on the prevention of genocide, to be supported by the High Commissioner for Human Rights but reporting directly to the Security Council—making clear the link between massive and systematic violations of human rights and threats to international peace and security. The Stockholm Forum was the first international conference on the question of genocide prevention since the adoption of the UNCG. On 7 April 2004, in an address to the Commission on Human Rights in Geneva on the occasion of the International Day of Reflection on the 1994 Genocide in Rwanda, the Secretary General announced his wish to launch an action plan to prevent genocide that would involve the whole UN system, and his decision to create a new post of Special Advisor on the Prevention of Genocide.[14]

As a follow-up to the Secretary General's initiative, on 4 March 2004, the Office of the High Commissioner for Human Rights sent notes verbales to states party to the UNCG seeking their views on the Secretary General's proposals concerning a committee on the prevention of genocide. The majority of replies indicated support, in principle, for the proposed initiative but stopped short of providing detailed explanations for their positions. The United States of America and the Russian Federation expressed opposition to the proposal. Several others raised concerns about the following elements: (1) the lack of clarity about the type of mechanism that could be envisaged to monitor the UNCG, (2) the possible duplication of the mandates of the proposed committee vis-à-vis other existing bodies, such as special rapporteurs, the Special Advisor to the Secretary General on the Prevention of Genocide or the International Criminal Court (ICC), (3) the challenges that would be faced in making such a committee an effective tool in the prevention of genocide.

The reply received from Turkey on 9 July 2004 was as follows. The UNCG was an example of the determination of founding members of the UN to prevent future generations from reexperiencing this scourge in the future. This convention expanded the boundaries of international law in more than one respect. First and foremost, the convention introduced to international law a crime with a clear distinction. Second, the convention held everybody responsible—including the constitutional rulers, public officials and individuals—without distinguishing whether there was a state of war or peace. Third, the crimes defined in the convention were placed outside the scope of political crimes for the purpose of extradition. Last, this convention envisaged that the criminals would be tried by a national or an international tribunal, thus upholding one of the most important principles of international criminal law, i. e.,"try or extradite." Along with other states party to this convention, Turkey affirmed the significance of the convention as an effective international instrument for prevention and punishment of the crime of genocide in the future. Turkey supported the steps taken by the international community.

The conclusion of the UNCG was no doubt a historic development. However, Turkey believed that it was high time for its universalization and full and comprehensive implementation. On 12 July 2004 Turkey welcomed the appointment of Juan Mendez of Argentina, as Special Advisor to the UN Secretary General on the Prevention of Genocide, with a mandate to collect existing information on violations of human rights that could lead to genocide and to bring potential genocidal situations to the attention of the UN

Security Council. The new office was a complementary step towards effective implementation of the UNCG. Turkey was confident that the Special Advisor would undertake his responsibilities meticulously and with impartiality in conformity with the letter, spirit and aim of the UNCG and thus constructively contributing to the UN's common efforts to ensure that this scourge does not occur. It was Turkey's understanding that the work of the Special Advisor would constitute a qualified mechanism to detect potential threats and to address them to the appropriate organs of the UN.

Turkey was among the cosponsors of the UN resolution entitled "Fiftieth Anniversary of the Convention on the Prevention and Punishment of the Crime of Genocide" adopted by the General Assembly on 27 March 2008. The resolution drew the attention of all states to the significance of the Convention and invited them to redouble their efforts for the prevention and punishment of the crime of genocide. It might, however, be worthwhile to ask whether the international community had succeeded in addressing the root causes of such crimes. Turkey was of the opinion that it would be difficult to give an affirmative answer. Hatred, intolerance, discrimination on the basis of race, gender and religion were still among the causes for various conflicts which carried the potential for triggering such crimes. Therefore Turkey considered that the promotion and dissemination of the culture of tolerance worldwide was of utmost significance. Combined efforts to live together in multicultural environments should be continued vigorously. The concept of "the other" should be removed from man's cultural references as well as from national educational systems and politics. Mutual understanding, respect for others and tolerance should be the guiding principle in countries'common efforts in international forums.

NOTES

1. Lord Monson's remarks in House of Lords Hansard Text for 14 April 1999 (190414-08), Columns 814–816.
2. Ibid.
3. Baroness Ramsay of Cartvale's remarks in House of Lords Hansard Text for 14 April 1999 (190414-09), Columns 826–827.
4. Letter from Lord Moynihan, Opposition Spokesman on Foreign Affairs in the House of Lords, to Özdem Sanberk, Turkish Ambassador to Britain, London, 11 June 1999.
5. Armenag Topalian, Reader's Letter, Armenian News Network/Groong, 21 March 2001, p. 1.
6. Anatolian News Agency, 16 November 2000; "Turkish Armenians Disapprove Euro MPs' Call for Genocide Recognition," Agence France Presse, 16 November 2000. There are about 60,000 Armenians in Turkey, nearly all of them in İstanbul. They form the country's largest minority, maintaining thirty-three churches, sixteen schools, several hospitals and a variety of other institutions.
7. "Stop Trashing Turkey EU Sanctimony Ignores Turkey's Importance for Europe," Editorials Opinion, Review and Outlook, *The Wall Street Journal Europe*, 20 November 2000, p. 8.

8. The UNCG, the first and most important international law defining genocide, was adopted and opened for signature, ratification or accession by Resolution 260 A (III) of the UN General Assembly on 9 December 1948. It entered into force on 12 January 1951 in accordance with its Article 13, the ninetieth day following the date of deposit of the twentieth instrument of ratification with the UN Secretary General. By 29 October 2013, 143 states are party to it. The purpose of the UNCG is to codify international law relative to genocide and, second, to require signers to deter acts of genocide and punish those who commit genocide.

9. Douglas Alexander's remarks in the House of Commons Hansard Text for 17 October 2005, Column 739W.

10. Lord Triesman's remarks in House of Lords Hansard Text for 22 January 2007, Column 891.

11. Harry Dunphy, Associated Press, 1 September 2005.

12. Anatolian News Agency, 1 October 2003.

13. More than fifty states have not yet ratified the UNCG, including states such as Somalia and Japan. This does not mean, however, that these states can commit genocide without violating international law. Instead these states are bound by what is called customary international law, building on the long-standing general practice and legal opinion of the international community of states pursuant to which genocide is a crime under international law. This has been confirmed in numerous international judgments. Indeed, the prohibition of genocide is said to enjoy *jus cogens* (compelling law) status. See Martin Mennecke, "The Crime of Genocide and International Law," in Barbara Boender and Wichert ten Have, eds., *The Holocaust and Other Genocides: An Introduction* (Amsterdam: Amsterdam University Press, 2012), p. 148.

14. This and the following four paragraphs are based on UN Economic and Social Council Commission on Human Rights Sixty-first session Item 17 of the Provisional Agenda, Promotion and Protection of Human Rights, Views of States Party to the UNCG on the Secretary General's Proposal that They Consider Setting Up a Committee on the Prevention of Genocide, Note by the Secretariat, E/CN. 4/2005/46, 10 December 2004.

Chapter Sixteen

The Quest for Facts

TURKISH PRIME MINISTER RECEP TAYYİP ERDOĞAN CALLS FOR UNBIASED INVESTIGATION INTO ARMENIAN CLAIMS

On 8 March 2005, Turkish Prime Minister Recep Tayyip Erdoğan called for an impartial study by historians of Armenian claims that their people suffered genocide at the hands of Turkish troops during and after the First World War.

"We have opened our archives to those people who claim there was genocide. If they are sincere, they should also open their archives," Erdoğan told a news conference in Ankara. "Teams of historians from both sides should conduct studies in these archives. We are ready to take steps on this issue. We do not want future generations to have a difficult life because of hatred and resentment," he added.

Erdoğan's appeal for an unbiased investigation was issued jointly with Deniz Baykal, the leader of the main opposition Republican People's Party. "We are facing a political campaign against Turkey," Baykal said. In his statement to the TGNA, Baykal declared, " It is time to put an end to insinuations on the Armenian genocide," describing it as a product of a "morbid imagination." He announced that his party would host a symposium, under the auspices of the United Nations Educational, Scientific and Cultural Organization (UNESCO), with the participation of the world's most famous scholars in this area. "If the Armenian scholars really have serious arguments and facts on the genocide, they should display them here. Those who talk about the Armenian genocide by the Ottoman government must present documentary proofs. If the events are nothing but insinuations, however, the international community should be aware of that," he said.[1]

The next development came on 10 April 2005, when the Turkish Prime Minister Recep Tayyip Erdoğan extended an invitation to the Armenian President Robert Kocharian to establish a joint commission consisting of historians and other experts to study the developments and events of 1915, not only in the archives of Turkey and Armenia, but also in the archives of all relevant third countries such as Russia, Britain, France, Germany, Austria and the United States, and to share their findings with the international public. Scholars from other countries would be welcome to participate in this commission. The TGNA lent explicit and broad support to the Prime Minister's appeal. It was hoped that an initiative of this kind would shed light on a disputed period of history and also constitute a step toward the normalization of relations between Turkey and Armenia. Turkey did not fear its past and was prepared to face the outcome of the proposed joint historical commission. Erdoğan proclaimed openness to accept a judgment of genocide if records prove it.[2]

One cannot ignore the broader context to the events of 1915; not least the catastrophic way in which eastern Anatolia, where most Armenians lived, was turned into a war zone leading also to the death of one million of Muslims. In this regard Ahmet Tevfik Pasha (Okday), until recently Grand Vizier of the Ottoman Empire, gave an interview to the *Giornale d'Italia* on 10 March 1919, in which he said:

> I have asked for the constitution of an international commission to ascertain the facts about the Armenian massacre. In this way Europe will begin to know the truth. We not only do not deny the painful fact of the occurrences in Armenia [eastern Anatolia], but deplore them deeply. We are now trying those responsible for them. At the same time, I wish that the facts be known in their true light. . . . Ever since 1876, Russia did its utmost to breed ill-feeling between the Armenians and their Muslim compatriots. This was a historical fact, as demonstrated by the publication of the secret Russian archives by the revolutionists in Petrograd. . . . Armenian committees organized a general uprising, instigated by Russian agents, the moment the war broke out. The Ottoman army attacked in front by the armies of the Czar, saw itself also attacked in the rear by the Armenian bands. Consequently, the Supreme Command ordered the deportations. Unfortunately this order was executed under bad conditions. Crimes were here committed by both sides. The Mussulman criminals have been arrested and will be punished, as public opinion in Turkey demands, with the extreme rigor of law. I demand, however, that the heads of the Armenian bands, who were guilty of all kinds of crimes and destruction among the Mussulman population of one million souls, shall also be judged and punished. Justice must make no difference between Christians and Mussulmans. It must be the same for all.[3]

Ahmet Tevfik Pasha's request for the establishment of an international commission to inquire into the facts about the Armenian events of 1915 proved of no avail among the Allied powers.

Ahmet Tevfik Pasha was the last Ottoman grand vizier. He received a military education before entering the civil service, served as ambassador in Athens and Berlin before becoming minister of foreign affairs in 1895 for thirteen years. Briefly grand vizier after the mutiny of 13 April 1909, then ambassador in London, and grand vizier during the armistice in 1918–1919 and 1920–1922 until the dissolution of the Ottoman state.[4]

It is worthwhile to recall here that the following statement, in the form of an appeal to the Turkish and Armenian communities of America, was jointly issued on 4 April 1985 by Professor Talat Halman, prominent Turkish scholar and journalist, and Professor Vazken Parsegian, a retired nuclear physicist holding the title of Rensselaer Professor Emeritus at Rensselaer Polytechnic Institute, where he was dean of engineering:

> The early decades of this century brought events that continue to breed hate and to threaten the Armenian and Turkish communities. The conflicts are not being resolved by the passing of time or by the involvement of third parties. Clearly the burden for reducing the conflict falls heavily on responsible members of the two communities, to face the issues realistically and comparatively. We believe that such a cooperative effort is timely, and that it should be undertaken without delay. What might be the steps for such an effort? The seared memories of those events find their sorest wounds in the extreme disparity of claims, denials, and counterclaims that persist with respect to the history of those tragic events. Although the official and unofficial records of the period are very extensive, they have yet to be studied and presented in a form that provides perspective as well as details on the national and international conditions that brought, and that continue to bring, so much suffering to the people of the region. The cooperation can begin best therefore, with a thorough-going analysis of the history of those decades by a team of Turkish, Armenian and other historians. The study will be difficult to conduct with academic objectivity and perspective. Every event will invite moral judgment, but the study must limit itself to factual analysis and leave the exercising of moral judgment to the world at large. The objective must be to reveal the truths of history, not to resolve the related political issues. To that end, we suggest that there be assembled a group of responsible Turks, Armenians and others to serve as the project study board whose functions would be to: (a) assemble a task force of Turkish, Armenian and other historians, consultants, including experts in authenticating of documents; (b) convene an international commission to oversee the progress and approve the products of the studies before they are published; (c) undertake the translation and distribution of the products of the study; and (d) seek the required financial support.[5]

The appeal went unheeded in Armenian circles and the *Armenian Mirror Spectator*, published by the Baikar Association in Watertown, Massachusetts, in its edition of 6 April 1985 felt that the act was untimely and unnecessary.[6]

Donald Miller, director of the School of Religion at the University of Southern California, indicated on 28 April 1985 that the task on the Armenian issue now was to turn to the enormous archives of diplomatic and other materials that were present in Turkey, Britain, France, Germany and the United States. The time had come for scholars to examine more intensely the historical record.[7] Caro Martin of Don Mills, Ontario in Canada urged on 30 January 1989 that if the Turkish government was genuine and intended to resolve the Armenian matter amicably and equitably, it should have no difficulty in accepting the proposal for an international commission consisting of Turkish, Armenian and foreign scholars with a broad mandate to deliberate on this issue, taking into consideration all international documents and evidence available since 1895. The commission could then submit its findings and recommendations on the basis of a protocol or a letter of understanding, to be entered into by the Turkish government, the Armenian government and representatives of the three Armenian political parties which were actively functioning in the Middle East, North America and other countries where large Armenian communities existed. Martin advanced that Turkey should surely accept this formula if it wanted to project and protect its international credibility in a statesmanlike manner.[8]

Maynard Wishner, chairman of the Jewish Community Relations Council in Chicago, suggested on 30 November 1989 that with regard to the Armenian issue the Turkish government approach a respected body of scholars. The participating scholars might be subject to approval as to objectivity and qualifications by the Turkish government and whoever might be deemed to be appropriate representatives of Armenian interests. This agreed-upon group of scholars would be given access in a public way to all relevant documents and archives that might be in possession of the government of Turkey and such other places where relevant documentation might exist. The charge to such a body of scholars, Wishner pointed out, would be to deliver a report of historic findings dealing with the troublesome period in question.[9]

In order to be fair, aspects warranting examination should include acts committed by both sides in the conflict. Such aspects include: Armenian groups who massacred Turkish villagers; Armenian militias that collaborated with invading Russian and French armies; the share of provocations made by the British who used the Armenians in order to undermine the Ottoman state; the share of the German General Staff and its stance vis-à-vis the Armenian relocation.

Regarding the last point a few clarifications are in order. The borderlands of the eastern Mediterranean constituted the prime area of German imperial ambitions. The German bureaucrats and businessmen, officers and diplomats, intellectuals and pastors, kaisers and chancellors, had their gaze fixed tightly on the Ottoman Empire. Through all the political upheavals of modern German history, the German rulers thought of the Ottoman Empire as the prime site of German imperial influence abroad. The widely strewn territory of the empire, including its Anatolian lands, would provide investment opportunities and markets for the German economy and, no less important, a place for Germany to assert its powerful stature and contest British, French, and Russian power.[10]

Never had Germany been connected so intimately with the Armenian relocation as in the testimony of Alpheus Newell Andrus, senior missionary for the Congregational Station at Mardin, southeastern Anatolia. The plan to move Armenians from the Ottoman Empire was "made in Germany and suggested to the Turks by the German officials," he declared. The far-sighted Germans, he explained in the *New York Post*, were looking forward to the time when

> [T]hey expected to gain complete dominion in Turkey, and they wanted to eliminate the Armenian question by getting rid of the Armenian race. [...] At first the Turkish Government objected to the German suggestion of the removal of the Armenians on the grounds that they were valuable as artisans and businessmen and necessary to the economic life of the country, but the Germans promised to supply men to take their place. Having persuaded the Turks, the Germans then left it to them to put the plan into effect.[11]

It is to be noted that Andrus had begun his work as a missionary in Mardin in 1868. He was charged with the supervision of the whole mission field, and, since he spoke Turkish as well as Arabic, it was part of his duty to conduct all business connected with the government. His wife was a frail woman, greatly beloved for her unfailing sympathy with the people, who brought all their troubles to her, and respected by her fellow-workers who found her a wise and steady counsellor.[12]

Unlike the judicial affirmations of the Holocaust or the Rwandan genocide, there has never been an impartial, independent tribunal or commission that has evaluated the Armenian genocide thesis. That glaring omission is not due to the absence of an available judicial forum. The ICJ enjoys jurisdiction to determine genocide accusations under the UNCG. The ICJ adjudicated Bosnia's claim of genocide against Serbia and Montenegro on 26 February 2007.

World public opinion should endorse the need for conducting a thorough and objective investigation of the full historical facts relating to the Armenian conflict, before branding the Turkish government with accusations of "genocide denial" and placing the collective onus of "genocide" on the Turkish people.

TURKEY'S PARLIAMENT GIVES ITS BACKING

Due to its crucial importance, the full text of the declaration issued unanimously on 13 April 2005 by the TGNA on the subject of establishing an international historians' commission to investigate the Armenian events of 1915 is given below:

> The TGNA believes that it is in the interests of both Turkey and Armenia to establish peace between their two nations which have lived side by side on the same soil down the ages on a basis of mutual respect and tolerance, to deliver themselves from deep-rooted prejudices and to create an environment in which they will be able to share a common future based on friendship and cooperation. To this end, the ruling and opposition parties of Turkey put forward a proposal aiming to shed light on the historical facts through scholarly research and relieving both nations from the burden of history. This proposal envisages that both Turkey and Armenia set up a joint commission made up of their historians; that they open their national archives without restrictions; that they also disclose findings and results of the studies that will be made in the archives of the third countries to the international public; and that both countries decide on the establishment and working methods of the commission. The TGNA fully adopts and supports this historical proposal. In order to implement this initiative, the active cooperation of the Armenian government is needed on the matter. In this regard, if Turkey and Armenia do not succeed in perceiving history from a common perspective, they will have nothing to leave but hard feelings of prejudice, hostility, and revenge to their children and posterity as their legacy. Reason and logic dictate that Turkey and Armenia need not fear the destruction of taboos with a joint iniative and that they get ready to settle accounts with their history by exposing all aspects of the human tragedy they experienced together. It is the only way to prevent our past from obscuring our today and tomorrow. The TGNA wishes to emphasize that, in the appraisal of this proposal, this move, in principle, should be considered a peace iniative. If Armenia wants to establish good relations and develop its cooperation with Turkey, it should not hesitate to accept this proposal for joint assessment of historical facts. Another point that the TGNA wishes to emphasize is that all statesmen and all countries that are well-intentioned and are eager to contribute to world peace and stability need to approach affirmatively Turkey's proposal, that is based on compromise and common sense, by leaving aside their domestic policy concerns. Therefore, it is expected that those countries that sincerely wish that the relations between Turkey and Armenia improve and that desire that peace and stability reign in the Caucasus, also support this iniative and avoid activities that may undermine this venture. On this subject, the responsibility, before all else, lays upon the countries that passed resolutions regarding Armenian allegations on the so-called Armenian genocide in their parliaments. If these countries attach importance to the development of relations between Turkey and Armenia as they claim to, they need to prove their goodwill and support our proposal to set up a joint Turkish-Armenian commission of history. The TGNA considers it improper, meaningless, arbitrary and unjust that foreign parliaments pass politically motivated

> resolutions on certain chapters of the history of the Ottoman Armenians that are still a subject of debate among world historians, and decide through parliamentary legislation the outcome or aspects of a historical problem on which enough light has not yet been shed. The TGNA declares that those who think they can, through intensive lobbying efforts, get Turkey to reconstruct its history on the basis of one-sided and misleading appraisals based on a number of propaganda documents, are grossly mistaken. International circles that think thus, and that make their calculations accordingly, will find that their designs never materialize—under any circumstances.[13]

ARMENIAN RESPONSES TO THE TURKISH PROPOSAL

In reply to the question asked by Turkish journalists on 24 January 2005, "If the issue is first discussed by historians and specialists, who find some common ground, would not that ease the process," the Armenian Minister of Foreign Affairs Vartan Oskanian stated that there was nothing new to say on this. According to him, there were countless studies on the subject and the events of 1915 had very clearly emerged. If the historians were to gather again, no one's point of view would change. The specialists had been working. They were done with their work. Now, Oskanian said, it was essential that the Turkish government enter into this discussion. Why were they [Armenians and Turks] afraid of these discussions? Today, around the world, there are many countries with similar problems. Japan and South Korea, China and South Korea, the United States and Japan, the United States and Mexico, and others. These countries continue to have relations with each other, even as they continue to discuss these events. And they have fine relations.[14]

Armenia on 9 March 2005 rejected the Turkish proposal for an impartial panel of historians to test Armenian claims that their people suffered genocide at the hands of Ottoman Turkey. "The historians have already said their piece and it is now up to Turkey to determine its attitude," Minister of Foreign Affairs Vartan Oskanian said in an interview with Reuters. "It is no longer a question for historians; they have already done their work. But since Turkey denies genocide, the matter has become a political issue that needs a political solution," he said. Ankara was keen to show it had nothing to hide amid growing calls—including some from members of the European Union it sought to join—for it to recognize that genocide took place.[15]

In a written reply of 25 April 2005, President Robert Kocharian effectively rejected the idea and came up with a counterproposal to set up a Turkish-Armenian intergovernmental commission that would deal with this and other issues of mutual concern.[16] Other Armenian officials, backed by local and Diaspora scholars, dismissed Prime Minister Recep Tayyip Erdoğan's move as a Turkish ploy designed to scuttle international recognition of the Armenian genocide. They also said that by agreeing to the proposed study, the Armenian side would play into Turkey's campaign of denial, which attempts to question the very fact of the genocide.[17] In a speech in Baku, the capital of Azerbaijan, Prime Minister Erdoğan reiterated his position that conducting historical research was not an issue for politicians: "Let historians, political scientists, archaeologists, lawyers and art historians study this question." He then suggested that the Armenians were not responding because then they would have to answer for the Hocalı massacre in which 683 Azeri civilians were killed by Armenians on 25–26 February 1992 during the fighting over Mountainous Karabagh: "There is still no answer because they will have to face the Hocalı massacre."[18]

On 28 March 2007, the Turkish Deputy Prime Minister and Minister of Foreign Affairs Abdullah Gül affirmed this offer:

> We eagerly await a positive response from Armenia, agreeing to establish this joint commission and declaring its readiness to accept its conclusions. . . . I hereby extend an invitation to any third country, including the United States, to contribute to this commission by appointing scholars who will earnestly work to shed light on these tragic events and open ways for us to come together.[19]

In a gesture toward dialogue, the Turkish government published full-page advertisements in major Western newspapers on 23 April 2007 calling for a joint Turkish-Armenian historical commission. It said let us unearth the truth about what happened in 1915 together and invited Armenia to study historical facts jointly. To this end, Turkey proposed to Armenia the establishment of a joint commission of historians which would also be open to third parties. Turkey ensured full access to all its archives.[20] And in February 2008, the Turkish Prime Minister Recep Tayyip Erdoğan reiterated this position at an international security conference in Munich. On 24 June 2008, the Armenian President Serzh Sargsyan was quoted as saying, "[W]e are not against the creation of such a commission, but only if the border between our countries is opened."[21]

NOTES

1. Anatolian News Agency, 8 March 2005; "Erdogan Calls for a Study About Armenian Genocide Insinuations," *Asbarez*, 9 March 2005, p. 1; Amberin Zaman, "Turkish Leader Calls for Study of Genocide Debate—Erdogan Seeks Review of Archives Amid Challenges to the Nation's Official Denial of Blame in the Deaths of Armenians During and After WWI," *Los Angeles Times*, 9 March 2005, p. 12 and Katia Peltekian, "Turkey to Open Archives for Probe Into Alleged WWI Genocide," Armenian News Network/Groong, 12 March 2005, p. 1.
2. Anatolian News Agency, 10 April 2005. Full text of the Turkish Prime Minister Recep Tayyip Erdoğan's letter addressed to the Armenian President Robert Kocharian is in Appendix 2.

3. "Wants an Armenian Inquiry: Tewfik Pasha Asserts That Atrocities Were Not Confined to Turks," *The New York Times*, 13 March 1919, p. 3.

4. On Ahmet Tevfik Pasha's character see Süleyman Kani İrtem, *Sultan Abdülhamid ve Yıldız Kamarillası* (Sultan Abdülhamid and the Yıldız Camaraderie), (İstanbul: Temel Yayınları, 2003) and İsmail Müştak Mayakon, *Yıldız'da Neler Gördüm* (What I Saw in Yıldız), (İstanbul: Sertel Matbaası, 1940). A lengthy discussion of his career can be found in İbnülemin Mahmud Kemal İnal, *Osmanlı Devrinde Son Sadrazamlar* (The Last Grand Viziers in the Ottoman Era), Sect. 11, (İstanbul: Maarif Matbaası, 1940–1944), pp. 1704–1762.

5. "Prof. V. L. Parsegian Joins Turkish Scholar in Plea to Armenians and Turks of America," *The Armenian Reporter*, 4 April 1985, p. 1; Talat Halman, "Bir Çağrı" (An Appeal), *Milliyet*, 8 April 1985, p. 2.

6. "An Untimely Appeal," *Armenian Mirror Spectator*, 6 April 1985, p. 1.

7. Donald Miller, "Why Armenians Can't Forget What the World Doesn't Remember," Opinion, *Los Angeles Times*, 28 April 1985, Part 4, p. 5.

8. Caro Martin, "Archives on Armenians," Letters to the Editor, *The Globe and Mail*, 30 January 1989, p. 13.

9. Letter from Maynard Wishner, chairman of the Jewish Community Relations Council in Chicago, to Jak Kamhi, president of Profilo Holding, Mecidiyeköy/İstanbul, 30 November 1989.

10. Eric Weitz, "Germany and the Ottoman Borderlands," in Omer Bartov and Eric Weitz, eds., *Shatterzone of Empires: Coexistence and Violence in the German, Habsburg, Russian, and Ottoman Borderlands* (Bloomington and Indianapolis, IN: Indiana University Press, 2013), p. 152.

11. "German Guilt for Armenian Blood," *The Literary Digest*, Vol. 55, No. 17 (27 October 1917), p. 29.

12. Caleb Frank Gates, *Not to Me Only* (Princeton, NJ: Princeton University Press, 1940), p. 33.

13. "İktidar ve Ana Muhalefet Partileri Bildirisi" (Declaration by the Ruling and Main Opposition Parties), Anatolian News Agency, 13 April 2005.

14. Cumali Önal and Süleyman Kurt, "Kars Antlaşmasını Tanıyoruz" (We Recognize the Kars Treaty), *Zaman*, 25 January 2005, p. 1.

15. "Armenia Rejects Turkish Proposal for Genocide Study," Reuters, 9 March 2005.

16. Anatolian News Agency, 25 April 2005; Halaçoğlu, *Tarih Gelecektir*, p. 73. Armenian President Robert Kocharian's official response to the letter of the Turkish Prime Minister Recep Tayyip Erdoğan is in Appendix 3.

17. Turkey and Armenia: Opening Minds, Opening Borders: Crisis Group Europe Report No.199, 14 April 2009, p. 6.

18. "PM Erdoğan Attends Turkish Diaspora Meeting in Baku," *Briefing*, 12 March 2007, pp. 4–5.

19. Anatolian News Agency, 28 March 2007.

20. See, for instance, *Los Angeles Times*, 23 April 2007, p. A18.

21. Emil Danielyan, "Sarkisian Signals Support For Turkish Genocide Proposal," Armenia Liberty, 26 June 2008.

Chapter Seventeen

What Next?

RELATIONS BETWEEN TURKEY AND ARMENIA

Armenia and Turkey coexist in peace, Armenian Minister of Foreign Affairs Vartan Oskanian remarked in an interview with the Armenian Public TV on 16 October 2006. "Turkey is a big country and our neighbor. We should resign ourselves to the thought that we live next to a nation, whose ancestors perpetrated the Genocide," Oskanian said. In his words, the Armenian genocide problem should be considered not at the historical but at the political level. "Taking into account the current political situation within Turkey, the proposal of the Prime Minister Erdogan on formation of a historical commission is insincere and not serious," the Armenian Minister of Foreign Affairs claimed. According to him, this proposal was made merely for public relations purposes to show Europe that Turkey was ready to discuss the issue. "If a commission of historians is formed, nothing will change. It will consist of Turks denying the Genocide and of Armenians pressing for its recognition," Oskanian asserted. "This issue cannot be considered at the historical level with Turks, who themselves politicized the problem," the Minister said. He contended that the response of the Armenian President on formation of an intergovernmental commission was more logical and corresponded to political reality, reported newsarmenia.ru.[1]

On the establishment of a commission of historians, the Armenian historian Ara Sarafian proposed the following as alternative to Prime Minister Recep Tayyip Erdoğan's suggestion: (1) Relevant archives in Turkey should be open to researchers, with special procedures to allow them ready access to records; (2) Independent groups of specialists from different disciplines should be funded to collaborate on specific projects related to 1915; (3) The work of such groups should be open to the scrutiny of third parties; (4)

Academic excellence should be the governing criterion in putting research teams together, not ethnicity, citizenship, or horse-trading among Turkish and Armenian bureaucrats; and (5) The examination of archival records should not be limited to Ottoman records but include other archives outside of Turkey.[2]

Many universities and civil society organizations in Turkey were prepared to facilitate cooperative efforts between Turkish and Armenian scholars interested in exploring all aspects of their history. In addition, they would facilitate participation by qualified scholars from the two countries at academic conferences abroad dedicated to a scholarly exploration of the historic aspects of the Armenian issue. Some contacts were happening already.

Turkey earnestly rejoiced at Armenia's independence after the demise of the Soviet Union in 1991 and it was one of the first countries to recognize Armenia's statehood, a country with which it shares a 268-kilometer border. As a token of friendship, the Turkish government provided wheat to the Armenian people who were then in dire need. Turkey integrated Armenia into the Black Sea Cooperation Council, although it is not a littoral state. But the two countries never established diplomatic relations and Turkey closed the common border in 1993 in solidarity with fellow Turkic country Azerbaijan, which was fighting Armenian-backed separatists in the breakaway region of Mountainous Karabagh.

Both Turkey and Armenia have expressed a desire to normalize relations. One believes that true progress toward normalizing relations will stem from an approach that stresses reconciliation and understanding. Peace, cooperation and stability in the Caucasus will benefit Armenia. In addition, Armenia will derive immediate economic benefits from normalized relations with Turkey.

INTERNATIONAL RESPONSES

Of the Council of Europe at Strasbourg, 97-members of the Parliamentary Assembly signed a declaration on 27 April 2005 calling on Armenia to accept the Turkish proposal. This statement is so significant that we quote it in full:

> The Turkish and the Armenian people have shared a common history and geography for centuries. The First World War, as in other parts of Europe, was a dark period with tragic consequences for the peoples of the Ottoman Empire, including Turks and Armenians. They suffered huge losses due to war, intercommunal fighting, massacres, diseases and famine. 90 years after these events, the two peoples have diverging interpretations of this historical period which hamper the development of relations between Turkey and Armenia. To transcend the heavy legacy of the past, we call on Turkey and Armenia to

> undertake a joint study of the events of the First World War in the Ottoman Empire, using the historical material available in all national archives. We welcome and support the recent proposal of the Prime Minister Erdogan of Turkey to President Kocharian of Armenia to this effect. We call on President Kocharian to respond positively to this proposal, which, we hope, will pave the way to the normalisation of relations between the two countries. [3]

That is wholly appropriate. A study of the entire situation in the Ottoman Empire during the First World War would be the best way to understand what happened in 1915.

Turkey's invitation drew strong praise from EU governments. The United States applauded Turkey's initiative as a move to promote a spirit of tolerance and cooperation and hoped that this would mark the beginning of a new and fruitful dialogue. [4]

In his annual commemoration message to the Armenian American community on 24 April 2005, President George W. Bush expressed support for Turkey's proposal.

> I applaud individuals in Armenia and Turkey who have sought to examine the historical events of the early 20th century with honesty and sensitivity [...] We look to a future of freedom, peace, and prosperity in Armenia and Turkey, and hope that Prime Minister Recep Tayyip Erdoğan's recent proposal for a joint Turkish-Armenian commission can help advance these processes. Armenian expatriates in the United States and elsewhere should support this endeavor aimed at a reconciliation that would allow us to look forward—together—to a peaceful and prosperous future. [5]

The president's statement concerned current policy more than historical remembrance, and presented the policy in a positive manner for Turkey, emphasizing the need for further research and efforts toward reconciliation. It explicitly endorsed the Turkish Prime Minister's plan, which had been turned down by Armenia.

The United States Deputy Assistant Secretary of State for European and Eurasian Affairs, Laura Kennedy, endorsed Prime Minister Recep Tayyip Erdoğan's proposal for a joint history commission during a visit to Ankara on 5 May 2005. Switzerland and other countries acted similarly. The Swiss Embassy in Ankara issued a statement on 2 May 2005: "The claims in question should be researched by historians. The Swiss government supports the Turkish government's quest to set up and carry out a joint commission to look into the Armenian claims." Swiss President Joseph Deiss indicated on 3 October 2006, "The Swiss Federal Council welcomes the proposal of Prime Minister Erdoğan to establish a joint commission of Turkish and Armenian historians to shed light on the tragic events of the past." [6]

Replying to a letter by Faruk Loğoğlu, the Turkish Ambassador in Washington, DC, regarding Prime Minister Recep Tayyip Erdoğan's initiative to establish a joint commission of historians from Turkey and Armenia to reexamine the events of the early twentieth century, Secretary of State Condoleeza Rice said on 25 May 2005 that the United States applauded these recent moves to promote a spirit of tolerance and cooperation. They hoped that this marked the beginning of a new and fruitful dialogue. Their mutual objectives of peace and stability in the Caucasus could only result from honest and productive exchanges, including between Turkey and Armenia, with the goal of reconciliation. In his April 24 statement marking Armenian Remembrance Day, President George W. Bush recognized Prime Minister Recep Tayyip Erdoğan's recent proposal and commended the individuals in Armenia and Turkey who have worked to support these efforts. To help in this process, they continued to encourage scholarly, civic and diplomatic dialogue between the governments and civil society leaders. The United States was committed to strengthening its long-standing ties with Turkey. They would continue to work together to achieve common objectives.[7]

In response to the Turkish Deputy Prime Minister and Minister of Foreign Affairs Abdullah Gül's letter of 5 July 2005 concerning House Resolution 316—the "Affirmation of the United States Record on the Armenian Genocide Resolution"—which was recently referred to the House of Representatives Committee on International Relations for consideration, Secretary of State Condoleeza Rice made it clear on July 19 that the Administration did not support the passage of this resolution. Rice stressed that as President Bush acknowledged in his April 24 statement, the suffering that befell the Armenian people in 1915 was a tragedy for all humanity. The United States continued to encourage Turkey and Armenia to reconcile and normalize relations and to engage in scholarly, civil society, and diplomatic discussion of the forced exile and killings of 1915. The United States applauded efforts by Turks and Armenians to examine the historical events of the early twentieth century with honesty and sensitivity.[8]

Secretary of State Rice made the same points forcefully on 21 March 2007:

> I think that these historical circumstances require a very detailed and sober look from historians. And what we have encouraged the Turks and the Armenians to do is to have joint historical commissions that can look at this, to have efforts to examine their past, and in examining their past to get over their past. . . . I believe that this [whether genocide occurred] is something that Turks and Armenians are best able to address through their own process of coming to terms with their history. Lots of people have had to come to terms with their history in order to move forward.[9]

In her reminiscences, Rice characterizes the Armenian events of 1915 as "something that had happened almost a hundred years before" and about which "there are many historical interpretations." She notes that the Armenian relocations are better left to scholars. "Tragic" as these deaths were, "it was a matter for historians—not politicians—to decide how best to label what had occurred," the former Secretary of State observed.[10]

These are admirable sentiments, and we shall return to these considerations in our conclusion. But we wish to emphasize one point: we are perfectly aware that historical research is a difficult undertaking and it seems to us crucial that it be conducted in a dispassionate and unbiased fashion. Ironically, however, there is an insistence on the part of many Armenian writers on the "authenticity" of purely Armenian sources as reflecting the reality of the "indigenous" population; as a corollary, Ottoman Turkish sources originating with the government are ignored, or in several cases, dismissed, as reflecting nothing more than the agenda of the Muslim rulers in the Sublime Porte.

Furthermore, regardless of which sources Western or Armenian historians are able to or choose to employ, they must take the Ottoman context into account. This, of course, implies the possession of a thorough knowledge of the Ottoman environment, including developments at the imperial center and in other provinces. Indeed, it is clearer today than ever before that we simply cannot grasp the history of the Anatolian Armenians between the Battle of Malazgirt in 1071[11] and the First World War without a full understanding of Ottoman history and institutions. This means more than just a pageant of governors and judges imposed upon a supposedly supine indigenous population. It means acknowledgment and appreciation of the manner in which the Armenian-populated areas were administered by the Ottoman system politically, militarily, agriculturally, fiscally, commercially, and socially.

Ahmet Üzümcü, Deputy Under Secretary at the Turkish Ministry of Foreign Affairs, during the talks with Arman Kirakossian, Armenian Deputy Minister of Foreign Affairs, in Vienna on 14 July 2005, reiterated Prime Minister Recep Tayyip Erdoğan's proposal for a joint history commission, offering terms of reference including its mandate, composition, procedures for opening archives in Turkey, Armenia, and other countries, and publishing findings with a respected third party such as UNESCO. Armenian diplomats indicated that their archives merely consisted of eyewitness accounts, memoirs, and copies of archives from different countries. The archives of greatest value were in Turkey, where the alleged "genocide" had occurred. They focused on the need for a confidence-building process to address all bilateral issues rather than to wait for the commission to do its work.[12]

Douglas Silliman, director of the Office of Southern European Affairs at the United States State Department, in response to a letter from Kürşad Doğru, chairman of the Turkish-American Association of Northern Texas, regarding Turkish-Armenian relations, said on 10 August 2005, that his government continued to encourage scholarly, civil society and diplomatic discussion of this issue, as well as economic and political dialogue between the Turkish and Armenian governments in order to help all parties come to terms with the past. The United States welcomed recent overtures from Turkey and Armenia to begin a discussion with one another on this sensitive topic. They were pleased by the Turkish government's positive approach to the letter exchange between Prime Minister Erdoğan and President Kocharian, and hoped to see continued effort at establishing a dialogue. They continued to believe that a productive dialogue on the tragic events of the past was a key to achieving lasting peace and stability in the region. Silliman assured Doğru that the United States continued to consider Turkey a friend, ally and partner in the North Atlantic Treaty Organization and the Global War on Terrorism.[13]

The United States Assistant Secretary of State for Legislative Affairs, Matthew Reynolds, wrote on 15 September 2005 to the Chairman of the Committee on International Relations of the House of Representatives, Henry Hyde, that he found it especially promising that Turkey would host an unprecedented conference on Ottoman Armenians in İstanbul on 23–25 September 2005. Reynolds said the United States continued to encourage scholarly, civil society and diplomatic discussion of the events of 1915, as well as the nascent economic and political dialogue between the Turkish and Armenian governments to help all parties come to terms with the past. They were pleased by the Turkish government's positive approach to the letter exchange between Prime Minister Recep Tayyip Erdoğan and President Robert Kocharian and hoped to see continued effort at establishing a dialogue.[14]

Douglas Alexander, the British Minister of State for Europe, declared in the House of Commons on 17 October 2005 that they welcomed open discussion of the Armenian genocide allegations and related matters at a recent conference in İstanbul, and the Turkish Minister of Foreign Affairs' statement to that conference expressing hope that research into the era could improve relations between Turkey and Armenia. They also welcomed the fact that, on March 9, the Turkish Prime Minister and the leader of the main opposition party had called for an impartial investigation into the genocide allegations by Turkish and Armenian historians under the supervision of an international organization such as UNESCO. The Armenian President rejected the proposal on the grounds that establishing diplomatic relations was a necessary prior step, Alexander added.[15]

Denis MacShane, Douglas Alexander's predecessor as the British Minister for Europe, had raised the need for an independent inquiry on the events of 1915 at an EU ministerial meeting with Turkey in March 2005, in an attempt to promote a truth and reconciliation process. Geoffrey Hoon, MacShane's successor, shared the view on 7 June 2006 that the work of establishing truth, if it was indeed to help towards reconciliation, must be conducted as a joint exercise by the parties directly involved. Although outsiders could commend the idea to them, doing of the work by the parties themselves was an important part of the confidence-building and reconciliation process.

Hoon understood that the Armenians felt unable to accept the Turkish Prime Minister Recep Tayyip Erdoğan's call for an impartial investigation by Turkish and Armenian historians of the allegations at that time, but the British government believed the Turkish proposal to be a welcome signal that Turkey wished to engage with its neighbor and reexamine the issue. The British Minister's conclusion was that the idea, or some variant of it, was not at an end, but that further developments in the international situation would be needed before the idea could be explored again and constructively developed.[16]

In the discussion of the report on the establishment of a European remembrance center for victims of forced population movements and ethnic cleansing in the Committee on Migration, Refugees and Population of the Parliamentary Assembly of the Council of Europe on 6 October 2006, Ahmet Özal stated as follows:

> Population transfers and examples of ethnic cleansing are not new phenomena and cannot be attributed specifically to any political or economic system. It is also a fact that in the past international reactions to such population movement have been limited and, in general, evaluated in light of the ideologies and alliances of the parties concerned. The goal of overcoming prejudice and favoring reconciliation by promoting the impartial study of history will certainly contribute to the creation of a common European memory. Remembering tragic historical events objectively will certainly contribute to the prevention of their recurrence. However, objectivity should be carefully maintained, especially given the contentious issues that fall in the center's area of interest. In other words, with an objective approach, the center will be rightly established to stop the misuse of such population movements by some populist politicians. Approaching contentious issues in an objective and impartial manner may have a vital role in the credibility and, therefore, the success of the center. The center should promote a comprehensive and impartial study of European history, because it is only through such that a common history and reconciliation can be achieved and respect for the rights of victims maintained. On the other hand, the center should avoid creating new enmities among nations by reviving historical problems. Otherwise, the noble goal of the center—reconciliation and building a common history—will disappear and the center will itself become a subject of conflict.[17]

Ahmet Özal also wished to respond to claims made by some of his colleagues about the Armenian events of 1915. The tragedy that was imposed on both Armenians and Turks during the First World War was sad enough. The Turkish government's call for a joint study of the period by international historians should be accepted, so that the truth may be known. Özal opposed political manipulation of the center and declared it should be protected from attempts to do so, which could undermine its entire credibility. If the center gave way to those who judged history in their own interests, it would become useless and harm efforts towards reconciliation.[18]

In a press release of 14 April 2005, the Presidium of the Conference of European Churches welcomed the announcement of Prime Minister Recep Tayyip Erdoğan opening Turkish archives and allowing Armenian and Turkish, as well as independent researchers to have full access to documentation.[19]

On 27 September 2006, the General Assembly of the European Parliament in Strasbourg took note of the proposal by Turkey to establish a committee of experts under the auspices of the UN in order to overcome the tragic experience of the past, and the position of Armenia regarding that proposal, urged both the Turkish government and the Armenian government to continue their process of reconciliation leading to a mutually acceptable proposal; welcomed the fact that, with the recent debates in Turkey, a start has been made in the discussion of the history with Armenia; and called on the Turkish authorities to facilitate the work of researchers, intellectuals and academics working on this question, ensuring access for them to the historical archives and providing them with all relevant documents.[20]

On 25 October 2006, the mass daily, *Globe and Mail*, cheerfully announced that Peter MacKay, Minister of Foreign Affairs and Minister of the Atlantic Canada Opportunities Agency, had stated that Canada supports a Turkish plan to convene an academic panel to study the Armenian events of 1915. MacKay endorsed an independent inquiry of the question, with third-party participation, in order for all possible facts to be looked at.[21] In a speech he delivered during the inauguration ceremony of the Parliamentary Canada Turkey Friendship Association on 18 October 2006, MacKay said directly that his government supported the Turkish government's practical proposal to establish a joint commission composed of Turkish and Armenian historians as well as historians from third countries to look into the events of 1915, and encouraged the Armenian government to participate in this body.[22]

On 3 May 2007 Susan Cartwright, Foreign and Defense Policy Advisor to the Prime Minister of Canada and Deputy Secretary to the Cabinet, agreed with the Turkish position that the events which affected Armenians during the First World War need to be addressed through proper investigation. This was reflected in Canadian support for Turkey's proposal to establish a joint historical commission. As indicated in the Prime Minister Stephen Harper's recent message to the Armenian community, Canada encouraged individuals on both sides of this issue to examine the historical events of this time in order to develop a common understanding with honesty and in a spirit of reconciliation.[23]

Peter MacKay, the Canadian Minister of Foreign Affairs, wrote on 21 June 2007 that there needs to be a fully open, honest, and dispassionate examination of the events of 1915. For that reason, MacKay reconfirmed that

Canada continued to endorse Turkey's proposal to establish a joint commission of historians to shed light on every aspect of those events. To the extent that a jointly agreed historical commission could contribute to this, Canada was fully supportive.[24]

Replying to a written question by Philip Claeys, a member of the European Parliament for Northern Ireland, Olli Rehn, on behalf of the EU Commission, said on 24 November 2006 that the French bill making illegal the denial of the Armenian genocide stirred a vibrant debate across the EU and in Turkey. As the adoption of such a law might have considerable repercussions on the overall dialogue between the EU and Turkey—and even on the process of the accession negotiations— Rehn, the member of the Commission responsible for its enlargement, expressed publicly his views on it. In an article published in the French newspaper *Libération* on 12 October 2006, Rehn reiterated the Commission's position that only an open and democratic debate within Turkish society, between Turkey and Armenia and between the Turkish and Armenian communities at large could lead to reconciliation in relation to the tragic events of 1915. Some steps had been taken in this respect. In 2005, the Turkish Prime Minister proposed to set a joint commission composed of independent historians and other experts with unconditional access to all relevant archives. A conference on the issue, during which all points of view could be expressed, also took place in autumn 2005 in İstanbul. In general, open debate had increased in Turkish society on issues linked to Armenia and the events of 1915. Rehn added that the Commission would continue to follow developments and to encourage the Turkish government's efforts in this area.[25]

Baroness Nicholson of Winterbourne, member of the House of Lords in Britain, wrote on 22 August 2007 that at the end of the Ottoman Empire Turkish and Armenian history was shaped by numerous tragic events during that critical time. The British peer believed historians and academics play an important role in analyzing the history of Turkish-Armenian relations of that time and help people understand the contemporary situation. This particular issue reflected an important and sensitive matter affecting contemporary political tensions between both countries. Hence, she appreciated the work and commitment of organizations that have promoted reconciliation and mutual understanding between nations and cultures to solve contested subjects in a fair and balanced way.[26]

In Britain's House of Commons, an Early Day Motion titled "Establishment of a Turkish-Armenian Historical Commission" was introduced by Bob Laxton on 12 November 2007, which read:

> This House welcomes the proposal to establish a Joint Historical Commission comprised of Turkish, Armenian and independent third-party historians and experts to research and examine all relevant historical materials to try and

> uncover the true nature of the events of 1915 between the Turks and Armenians in Anatolia; recognizes that this proposal provides a constructive step to reach agreement about the said period of history; and urges the establishment of the proposed commission in the hope that the commission's findings will act as a catalyst in the normalisation of Turkish-Armenian relations.[27]

Many Members of Parliament from both the government and the opposition expressed their opinions freely and supported the motion.

Timothy Ryback and Elazar Barkan, codirectors of the Institute for Historical Justice and Reconciliation in The Hague, supported the idea of establishing a formal Turkish-Armenian historical commission with full access to the historical record. Their comments made on 25 February 2008 are worth quoting at length:

> Unlike the Nazi persecution of the Jews, which was determined to have constituted genocide by an international tribunal in Nuremberg, and subsequent tribunals that made similar determinations for Rwanda and for Srebrenica in the former Yugoslavia, the Armenian genocide, or "events of 1915," has never been subjected to similar international historical or legal scrutiny. There has never been a formal independent historical commission that has had access to the complete historical record or involved teams of scholars from Turkey and Armenia, like the Czech-German historical commission established to resolve historical disputes between those two countries or similar commissions. . . . Perhaps the time has come to take Turkey up on its offer and establish an independent, international historical commission that can explore the historical facts and legal definitions in a neutral and sustained manner and render an independent and informed opinion. Such a commission would need to have historical authority and legal expertise to review the historical facts and deliberate on their legal implications. It would need the cooperation of Turkey and Armenia, as well as Russia, France, Britain, the United States, and other countries, to provide access to pertinent archives. It would benefit from access to private archives that contain relevant documents. History is best researched and debated before it is lobbied and legislated.[28]

In the House of Lords, Baroness Finlay of Llandaff asked the British government on 4 March 2008 whether it recognized the existence of genocide in Armenia in 1915. The Minister of State at the Foreign and Commonwealth Office, Lord Malloch-Brown, replied:

> The position of the Government on this issue is long-standing. Neither this Government nor previous Governments have judged that the evidence is sufficiently unequivocal to persuade us that these events should be categorised as genocide as defined by the 1948 UN Convention on Genocide. As my right honourable friend, the then Minister for Europe (Geoffrey Hoon), said in a debate in Westminster Hall on 7 June 2006 (Official Report, col. 137WH) the work of establishing the truth must be conducted as a joint exercise by the parties directly involved if it is to help towards reconciliation. There needs to

> be a truth and reconciliation process owned by the people of Armenia and Turkey. Outsiders can commend the idea to the parties but they should not try to do the work for them—undertaking this is an important part of the confidence-building and reconciliation process for the parties themselves. The Government will continue to encourage the parties to embark on such a process. In the mean time we should resist the temptation to preempt its conclusions.[29]

This remark found a receptive audience.

Ed Whitfield and Virginia Foxx, members of the United States House of Representatives, in a "Dear Colleague" letter of 4 October 2011, wrote that six years ago the Turkish Prime Minister Recep Tayyip Erdoğan proposed the establishment of a joint historical commission where historians from both countries would work together to present the facts of what took place during the First World War, utilizing the archives of both parties, and vowing that Turkey would accept the findings of the commission. This historic proposition was unanimously endorsed by the TGNA. Whitfield and Foxx continued to believe that a bilateral approach to the issue, as opposed to the passage of resolutions by third-party legislatures, remained the best way to move forward and should continue to be encouraged by the United States.[30]

Indeed, the majority of other governments were in a similar position. Few of them have officially ascribed the label "genocide" to these events. And rightly so, because it is not the business of governments today to review events of more than 100 years ago with a view to pronouncing on them. These events took place in a time of massive and dramatic upheaval in Europe and the former Ottoman territories in the first decades of the last century. These should not, in countries not involved in the events concerned, be matters of political controversy today. Moreover, it has not been established whether the terms of the UNCG can be applied retroactively.

DEFINITION OF GENOCIDE AND RETROACTIVE APPLICATION OF THE UNCG

To understand the definition of genocide it is important to understand the history of the notion. Genocide is a legal concept that was invented and developed after the Holocaust. It is true that, in 1915, the concept of genocide had not emerged. To a remarkable extent, it was the product of one man's work. Raphael Lemkin, an attorney and Holocaust survivor—who would later serve as an advisor to Nuremberg chief counsel Robert Jackson—coined the term "genocide" with the Jews in mind. He had lost at least forty-nine members of his family, including his parents, aunts, uncles, and cousins, in the Warsaw ghetto, in concentration camps, or on Nazi death marches.

In November 1944, the Carnegie Endowment for World Peace published Lemkin's *Axis Rule in Occupied Europe: Laws of Occupation, Analysis of Government, Proposals for Redress*—by then a 712-page volume of the rules and decrees imposed by the Axis powers and their client states in nineteen Nazi-occupied countries and territories in Europe. Having begun gathering these laws while in Sweden, Lemkin had continued the compilation as part of his service to the United States government. It included proposals for post-war restitution of property to the dispossessed and for the reimbursement of millions to foreign workers who had been forced into labor in Germany. He also stated his proposal to outlaw the targeted destruction of groups and urged the creation of an international treaty that could be used as a basis for trying and punishing perpetrators.[31]

Guenter Lewy believes that Lemkin used the concept of genocide to describe the systematic annihilation of Europen Jewry by Hitler's "Final Solution of the Jewish Question," also known as the Holocaust.[32] Indeed, in his seminal book, Lemkin focuses almost exclusively on the Holocaust. He explained "the practice of extermination of nations and ethnic groups as carried out by the invaders [Nazis] is called by the author 'genocide,' a term driving from the Greek word *genos* (tribe, race) and the Latin *cide* (by way of analogy, see homicide, fratricide)."[33] It is worth noting that Lemkin made no reference to the Armenian case in his same work, in which he cites "the destruction of Carthage in 146 B.C.; the destruction of Jerusalem by Titus in 72 A.D.; the religion wars of Islam and the Crusades; the massacres of the Albigenses," rounding off his list with the horrors committed by Tamerlane.[34]

In one of his articles Lemkin, an assiduous chronicler of Nazi occupation policies, admits, "...Germany's practices actually provided the basis for developing the concept of genocide."[35] The concept of genocide—and the resultant UNCG—entered the domain of international law in 1948, in response to the horrors of the Holocaust and other Nazi crimes against humanity that were proscribed by the Nuremberg trial judgments.

As a legal concept it has not matured significantly since then. Other than the primary international conventions defining the crime, little new law on the matter has been promulgated in any country. Moreover, cases applying the international conventions and the sparse domestic law are few. Despite calls for enlarging the definition of genocide, this has not been done. The ICC, International Criminal Court for the Former Yugoslavia, and International Criminal Tribunal for Rwanda, have not made any changes to the definition that appears in the UNCG. These tribunals were the first international mechanisms of their kind to have been established since the postwar international military tribunals of Nuremberg and Tokyo. The ICC Treaty definition mirrors the UNCG definition in every respect.[36]

Article 6 of the Rome Statute of the ICC defines genocide in the exact words as the UNCG. In Bosnia and Herzegovina v. Yugoslavia, (1993 ICJ 325, 431) the ICJ applied the Article 2 definition of the UNCG. Again, in Legality of Threat and Use of Nuclear Weapons, (1996 ICJ 226, 502) ICJ used the UNCG definition. Nevertheless, the word genocide has achieved broad usage in common parlance to refer to amorphous tragedies in which many perish or even to cases in which death does not result but in which a language or culture is changed or eliminated. Because the legal concept of genocide has remained largely untested, the commonplace, spoken language version of the term has come to overshadow and, in effect, to pollute the legal concept. Indeed, it is this trend towards the muddling of the genocide concept that poses the greatest challenge when allegations of the crime of genocide are made. Rather, the UNCG and the subsequent legal history of the prosecution of genocide by international tribunals should form the backbone of our contemporary understanding of the term.

The language of the UNCG neither excludes nor requires its retroactive application; there is nothing in the text of the convention that would either prohibit or allow its retroactive application. Yet Article 28 of the 1969 Vienna Convention on the Law of Treaties provides that "(U)nless a different intention appears from the treaty or is otherwise established, its provisions do not bind a party in relation to any act or fact which took place or any situation which ceased to exist before the date of the entry into force of the treaty with respect to that party."[37]

Because of the general principle of law *nullem crimen sine lege* (no crime without law) the UNCG cannot be applied retroactively to events before 12 January 1951, when it came into force. This principle has its bases in numerous laws and documents, chief among them the United States Constitution, which in Article 1, Sections 9 and 10 prohibits *ex post facto* laws. Article 38 of the Turkish Constitution is similar in effect. It can also be found in Article 7 of the European Convention on Human Rights and Fundamental Freedoms, Article 22 of the Statute of the ICC, Article 11(2) of the Universal Declaration of Human Rights, Article 15 of the International Covenant on Civil and Political Rights, Article 7 (2) of the African Charter, and Article 9 of the American Convention on Human Rights.

On 7 June 2006, the British Minister for Europe Geoffrey Hoon stated that it is not possible to apply the term genocide retrospectively:

> The fact is that the legal offence of genocide had not been named or defined at the time when the [Armenian] atrocities were committed. The UN convention on genocide came into force in 1948, so it was not possible at the time of the events that we are considering legally to label the massacres as genocide within the terms of the convention. I recognize that it is perfectly possible intellectually to try to apply the definitions of genocide from the convention to appalling tragedies that occurred, in this case, some thirty years before. The

> common practice in law is [, however,] not to apply such judgments retrospectively. It is not possible for us properly to provide a substitute today for the submission of evidence, cross-examination or arguments that necessarily would have arisen in mitigation in a court of law, whether a local or international one, had there been one with the necessary jurisdiction and had the crime already been recognized and defined.[38]

Yet, since both Turkey (31 July 1950) and Armenia (23 June 1993) are states party to the UNCG, it would be possible to invoke Article 8, which provides that any contracting party may call upon the competent organs of the UN to take such action as they consider appropriate for the "suppression" of genocide. Armenia may also invoke Article 9 of the convention, which stipulates, "(D)isputes between the Contracting Parties relating to the interpretation, application, or fulfillment of the present Convention, including those relating to the responsibility of a State for genocide or for any of the other acts enumerated in Article 3, shall be submitted to the International Court of Justice at the request of any of the parties to the dispute." A legal dispute such as those required by Article 9 of the UNCG for bringing a case before the ICJ, must consist of (1) a clash of legal views concerning the interpretation or the application of a treaty or customary rule of international law, and (2) the State against whose conduct or views a protest has been made by another state must reject that protest at least implicitly. In addition, the legal conflict between two states must be such as to bring to a settlement that is capable of effective and practical application— in other words— must not be merely historic or theoretical.[39]

PRACTICAL OUTCOME OF A GENOCIDE DECLARATION

Looking beyond historical and legal issues, what would be the practical outcome of a declaration by any government that the events of 1915 constituted genocide? A foreign government taking a public position on an issue as contentious and sensitive as these events of a century ago will severely hamper their ability to help the southern Caucasus realize its potential. And who will benefit from foreign governments' taking such a position? That is a problem.

On 28 September 2000, Nitzan Horowitz reported from Washington for his Israeli daily *Haaretz* that the American State Department recently published a condemnation of House Resolution 398 which called upon the president to "define as genocide the systematic and intentional murder of a million-and-half Armenians," and asked the State Department to pass on this material to American diplomats. "Historians, not lawmakers, are the ones who should be concerned with this matter," explained the State Department spokesman. "We are prepared to assist the efforts of the Turkish and Armenian experts, together with academics from other countries, to study their joint history." The State Department had clear instructions not to use the expression "Armenian genocide." In the announcements concerning the congressional initiative, the spokesman was careful to use the word with quotation marks, gesturing with his fingers to signify this.[40]

The events of 1915 remain a painful issue and a source of tension between Turkey and Armenia. One would hope that it is better to look forward than back. It is also to be hoped that these two countries will be able to overcome the historical legacy of bitterness and pursue better relations, in their own interests and in the interests of their region and the international community.

Parliamentarians of the Organization for Security and Cooperation in Europe, in their Seventeenth Annual Session held in Astana, Kazakystan 29 June–3 July 2008, encouraged the establishment of joint history commissions between participating states, composed of their historians and experts, including where necessary those of third countries, to conduct research in the relevant historical, political and military archives in order to shed objective and scientific light on contentious episodes in the history of participating states, with a view to contributing further to transparency and mutual understanding.[41]

NOTES

1. "Peaceful Coexistence of Armenia and Turkey Possible," PanARMENIA. Net, 16 October 2006.

2. Ara Sarafian, "Study the Armenian Genocide with Confidence, Ara Sarafian Suggests," *The Armenian Reporter*, 20 December 2008, p. 2.

3. "Joint Study of the Events of World War I in the Ottoman Empire," Parliamentary Assembly of the Council of Europe, Written Declaration No. 363, Doc. 10532, 27 April 2005.

4. For an appraisal on the subject, see "Turkey and Armenia: When History Hurts," *The Economist*, Vol. 376, No. 8438 (6–12 August 2005), p. 26.

5. "Presidential Message," 24 April 2005. The White House, Office of the Press Secretary.

6. David Phillips, Diplomatic History: The 2009 Protocol on the Establishment of Diplomatic Relations between the Republic of Armenia and the Republic of Turkey and The 2009 Protocol on the Development of Bilateral Relations between the Republic of Armenia and the Republic of Turkey, March 2012. http://hrcolumbia.org, p. 1.

7. Letter from the United States Secretary of State Condoleeza Rice to the Turkish Ambassador Faruk Loğoğlu in Washington, DC, 25 May 2005.

8. Letter from the United States Secretary of State Condoleeza Rice to the Turkish Deputy Prime Minister and Minister of Foreign Affairs Abdullah Gül, Washington, DC, 19 July 2005.

9. Congressional Transcripts, Congressional Hearings, 21 March 2007. United States House of Representatives Appropriations Subcommittee on State-Foreign Operations.

10. For Condoleeza Rice's reminiscences see her, *No Higher Honor: A Memoir of My Years in Washington* (New York: Crown Publisher Group, 2011), p. 598. In it, she shares the wisdom she gained from her first-hand experiences, providing valuable guidance and relevant lessons for the diplomats. Rice is currently a professor of political science at Stanford University.

11. In the year 1071, the Turks coming from Central Asian lands first entered Asia Minor.

12. Phillips, Diplomatic History, p. 25.

13. Letter from Douglas Silliman, director of the Office of Southern European Affairs at the United States State Department, to Kürşad Doğru, chairman of the Turkish-American Association of Northern Texas, Washington, DC, 10 August 2005.

14. Letter from the United States Assistant Secretary of State Matthew Reynolds to the Chairman of the Committee on International Relations of the House of Representatives Henry Hyde, Washington, DC, 15 September 2005.

15. Douglas Alexander's remarks in House of Commons Column 739W, 17 October 2005.

16. Geoffrey Hoon's remarks in House of Commons Column 137WH, 7 June 2006.

17. 2006 Ordinary Session: Thirtieth Sitting, Parliamentary Assembly of the Council of Europe, AACR30 AS(2006) CR 30, 5 October 2006.

18. Ibid.

19. "Statement on the Occasion of the 90th Anniversary of the Armenian Genocide," Press Release No.05–16/efg, 14 April 2005. The Conference of European Churches is a fellowship of some 125 Orthodox, Anglican and Catholic Churches from all countries of Europe. It has offices in Geneva, Brussels and Strasbourg.

20. European Parliament Resolution on Turkey's Progress Towards Accession (2006/2118 [INI]), 27 September 2006.

21. Brian Langhi, "Ottawa to Soothe Turks' Anger Over Genocide Tag," *The Globe and Mail*, 25 October 2006, p. 1.

22. http://www.turkishembassy.com/II/O/MacKay-Speech.htm.

23. Letter from Susan Cartwright, Foreign and Defense Policy Advisor to the Canadian Prime Minister and Deputy Secretary to the Cabinet, to Aydemir Erman, Ambassador of Turkey in Ottawa, 3 May 2007.

24. Letter from Peter MacKay, the Minister of Foreign Affairs of Canada, to Aydemir Erman, Ambassador of Turkey in Ottawa, 21 June 2007.

25. EU Commission E-4505/06EN P-4709/06EN, Answer by Olli Rehn on behalf of the Commission, 24 November 2006.

26. Letter from Baroness Nicholson of Winterbourne to Yiğit Alpogan, Ambassador of Turkey in London, 22 August 2007.

27. House of Commons Early Day Motions EDM185, 12 November 2007.

28. Timothy Ryback and Elazar Barkan, "A $12 Billion History Lesson," Views, *International Herald Tribune*, 25 February 2008, p. 12.

29. Lord Malloch-Brown's remarks in House of Lords 2001 Column WA166, 4 March 2008.

30. Ed Whitfield and Virginia Foxx, "What You Should Know About H. Res. 304, the Armenian Genocide Resolution," Congress of the United States House of Representatives, Washington, DC 20515, 4 October 2011.

31. See Raphael Lemkin, *Axis Rule in Occupied Europe: Laws of Occupation, Analysis of Government, Proposals for Redress* (Washington, DC: Carnegie Endowment for World Peace, 1944). Also Samantha Power, *"A Problem From Hell" America and the Age of Genocide* (New York: Harper Perennial, 2007), pp. 38–39.

32. Lewy, *Outlawing Genocide Denial*, p. 154.

33. Lemkin, *Axis Rule in Occupied Europe*, p. 79.

34. Ibid., p. 80.

35. Raphael Lemkin, "Genocide as a Crime in International Law," *The American Journal of International Law*, Vol. 41, No. 1 (January 1947), p. 149.

36. The idea behind the Rome Statute of the ICC of 17 July 1998 was to establish a standing court capable of acting on a complementary basis to the domestic organs of a State party where the State party might be unwilling or unable to prosecute crimes under international law. The Court's competence was intended to cover the most serious violations of human dignity whether they occurred during or outside armed conflict, and irrespective of who perpetrators or victims might be. During the drafting of the ICC's statute, a number of parties sought to change the definition of genocide, war crimes, and crimes against humanity. These efforts failed (UN, "Report of the Ad Hoc Committee on the Establishment of an International Criminal Court,"

UN Document A/50/22, para. 61). The ICC came into being on 11 April 2002. The court was opened on July 1.

37. Vienna Convention on the Law of Treaties, 23 May 1969, United Nations Document A/CONF. 39/27 (1969).

38. Official Report, House of Commons, 7 June 2006; col. 136 WH.

39. For a discussion of the scope of Article 9 of the UNCG, see William Schabas, "Genocide and the International Court of Justice: Finally, a Duty to Prevent the Crime of Crimes," *Genocide Studies and Prevention*, Vol. 2, No. 2 (August 2007), pp. 101–122.

40. Nitzan Horowitz, "Turks and Armenians Corner Jews in Debate Over Genocide," *Haaretz*, 28 September 2000, p. 3.

41. Astana Declaration of the Organization for Security and Cooperation in Europe Parliamentary Assembly and Resolutions Adopted at the Seventeenth Annual Session, Astana, 29 June–3 July 2008.

Chapter Eighteen

Attempting to Overcome History

Signing of the Protocols

ROAD MAP TO NORMALIZE TURKISH-ARMENIAN RELATIONS

After two years of talks in Switzerland, Turkey, Armenia and Switzerland announced on 22 April 2009 that they had reached a road map to normalize Turkish-Armenian relations:

> Turkey and Armenia, together with Switzerland as mediator, have been working intensively with a view to normalizing their bilateral relations and developing them in a spirit of good-neighbourliness, and mutual respect, and thus to promoting peace, security and stability in the whole region. The two parties have achieved tangible progress and mutual understanding in this process and they have agreed on a comprehensive framework for the normalization of their bilateral relations in a mutually satisfactory manner. In this context, a road map has been identified. This agreed basis provides a positive prospect for the on-going process.[1]

Javier Solana, EU High Representative for the Common Foreign and Security Policy, welcomed the move saying that it was good news for both Turkey and Armenia and for Europe as a whole. Solana stressed that it was an important contribution towards stability and security in a crucial region of Europe and he commended both parties for their courage and vision. He encouraged them to take this opportunity to proceed with the agreed framework and road map, and normalize their relations in the near term.[2]

The United States, with its large Armenian American community and strategic alliance with Turkey, threw its weight behind the deal. The Assistant Secretary of State for European and Eurasian Affairs, Philip Gordon, on 17 June 2009 indicated that the Obama Administration supports the establishment of a Turkish-Armenian historical commission, the Armenian National Committee of America (ANCA) reported. Gordon, during testimony earlier the same day before the Europe Subcommittee of the United States House of Representatives Foreign Affairs Committee, fielded a question from the panel's chairman, Robert Wexler about how the Department of State intends to "nagivate the course of the engagement between Turkey and Armenia so that Azerbaijan comes out a winner." In his response to this inquiry, Gordon voiced support for the Turkey-Armenia roadmap, a document publicly welcomed by the State Department on April 22 the last, noting, in particular an element of this agreement stipulating the establishment of a commission to examine historical issues between the two nations. His comments read, in part:

> You have two parallel but separate tracks [Turkey-Armenia dialogue and the Mountainous Karabagh peace process] going on, a Turkey and Armenia normalization reconciliation process that we do think is quite potentially historic, where the two countries have agreed on a framework for normalizing their relations that would include opening the border, which has been closed far too long, which would establish diplomatic relations and would provide commissions in key areas including history, and we encourage that process and we support it.[3]

TURKISH-ARMENIAN PROTOCOLS OF COOPERATION SIGNED ON 10 OCTOBER 2009

In a press release issued on 31 August 2009 simultaneously in Berne, Yerevan and Ankara by the Swiss Federal Department of Foreign Affairs, the Ministry of Foreign Affairs of the Republic of Armenia and the Ministry of Foreign Affairs of the Republic of Turkey, it was announced that Armenia and Turkey had agreed to start their internal political consultations on the Protocol on the Establishment of Diplomatic Relations and the Protocol on Development of Relations, and that these have been initiated in the course of their efforts under Swiss mediation. Article 2 of the Protocol on Development of Relations requires, besides other matters, the implementing of "a dialogue on the historical dimension with the aim to restore mutual confidence between the two nations, including an impartial scientific examination of the historical records and archives to define existing problems and formulate recommendations." The Turkish Minister of Foreign Affairs, Ahmet Davutoğlu, said the two nations were at the beginning of a long process. He spearheaded a policy aimed at resolving disputes with Turkey's neighbors in order to restore Turkey's influence as a regional player and smooth its path towards joining the European Union.[4]

There are two important observations to be made here. The first is that, the joint historical commission defined by the Protocol on Development of Relations was correctly charged with a broad mandate to discover facts that would lead to reconciliation based on truth. The second point is that, the goal was to depoliticize what is really a question for historians. This matters greatly.[5]

Roger Smith, the chairman of the Academic Board of Directors of the Zoryan Institute, in an open letter he sent to President Serzh Sargsyan on 29 September 2009, expressed his concerns regarding Article 2 of the Protocol on Development of Relations. Smith claimed that "numerous distinguished historians, political scientists, sociologists, legal scholars, and authoritative institutions around the world have investigated the Genocide many times over, issued academic publications, and even made public declarations." "These scholars," he went on, "have devoted their professional lives to conducting scientific research with the highest levels of academic integrity. As a result of their work, scholars have identified the Armenian Genocide as the archetypal case of modern genocide, whose pattern has many similarities with subsequent cases." Therefore, according to him, "any commission that purports now to conduct 'an impartial scientific examination of the historical records and archives' in effect dismisses all of the extensive research that has already been conducted for decades and implies that none of it was impartial or scientific."[6] Smith's letter was not replied to by its addressee.

The Turkish Minister of Foreign Affairs, Ahmet Davutoğlu, and his Armenian opposite number broke new ground by signing the previously initialed protocols on 10 October 2009 in the Swiss city of Zurich.[7] After they put their signatures on several pages, they stood up and shook hands to applause and exchanged hugs and handshakes with the other ministers. The Turkish and Armenian ministers of foreign affairs signed the agreement after a dispute over the final statements they would make. In the end, the signing took place about three hours later and there were no spoken statements. The Armenians were concerned about wording in the Turkish statement that was to be made after the signing ceremony and had expressed those concerns at the last minute before the scheduled signing ceremony.[8]

The Armenian diplomat Rouben Shougarian likened the ceremony attended by the United States Secretary of State, Russian and Swiss Ministers of Foreign Affairs, and the EU's High Representative for Common Foreign and Security Policy to a miniature replica of the signing of the Declaration of Principles for Peace between the Arabs and Israelis at the White House in 1993.[9]

United States Secretary of State Hillary Rodham Clinton stated her country would build on the milestone that had been achieved, but admitted concerns on both sides had delayed the signing. "Your political courage, your relentless efforts and your generous vision have made this agreement possible," Swiss Federal Councillor and Minister of Foreign Affairs Micheline Calmy-Rey said. Thus a potential historic start has been made toward Turkish-Armenian reconciliation. The developments that took place about a year earlier when the Turkish President Abdullah Gül visited Yerevan were the backdrop for the advance in Turkish-Armenian relations. During his historic visit on 8 September 2008, Gül watched a soccer match between Turkey and Armenia, part of the World Cup preliminaries. "Soccer diplomacy" was the highlight of a process lasting for more than a year of secret negotiations between the two countries over the signing of the protocols. The landmark agreement is backed by many countries and international organizations, including Switzerland, the United States, Russia, Britain, the UN, the EU, the Council of Europe, and the Organization for Security and Cooperation in Europe. Both the Turkish and Armenian parliaments had to ratify the protocols before they could enter into force. As part of the agreement, the two countries pledged to establish an international commission to research the First World War era archives to clarify the extent of the Armenian events of 1915. The protocols omitted any reference to the Armenian "genocide." The countries were to open their borders within two months after ratification, and establish the historical commission within four months.[10]

In an annex to the protocols, where a timetable for the implementation of the protocols is detailed, the importance of the subcommission on historical issues in the overall negotiations is clearly demonstrated. In "Step 5," the annex refers to different subcommissions to be established after the ratification of the protocols by both national parliaments. It is mentioned that six different subcommissions on the issues of transport/energy, legal matters, science/education, economic cooperation, environmental protection, and the historical dimension will be established. The first five subcommissions are defined in one or two lines, whereas the subcommission on the historical commission is explained in ten. This points towards the intense diplomacy behind the protocols as well as both sides' divergent views on how to label the events of 1915.[11]

The protocols were the result of painstaking work and, at times, very difficult negotiation processes. They were designed not only to normalize relations between the two countries and thus seek reconciliation on long-standing issues, but also, in a larger context, to contribute to the strengthening of peace and stability in the volatile Caucasus by creating a favorable atmosphere for tackling frozen conficts.

The text of the protocols does not explicitly mention Mountainous Karabagh, but the dispute looms large in the background. When the accord was signed, Ankara hoped that there would be a breakthrough in the peace talks over the conflict.

The Prime Minister Recep Tayyip Erdoğan declared on 10 October 2009 that Turkey was demonstrating its goodwill and added that it was also keen on seeing Armenian troops withdrawn from Mountainous Karabagh. He stated: "We are trying to boost our relations with Armenia in a way that will cause no hard feelings for Azerbaijan." Armenian President Serzh Sargsyan said that his government was taking a responsible decision in normalizing relations with Turkey, despite what he maintained were "the unhealable wounds of genocide." He continued that "there is no alternative to the establishment of relations with Turkey without any precondition. It is the dictate of the time."[12] Despite the protests, a majority of the people in Armenia supported Sargsyan's stance, arguing that it would boost trade and living standards for the landlocked republic's impoverished citizens. Many Armenians were already traveling to Turkey to buy and sell goods.[13]

On 14 October 2009, the Armenian president journeyed to Turkey where the Turkish president hosted him in the ancient Ottoman capital of Bursa for a final round of soccer diplomacy. There Serzh Sargsyan specifically explained that his recent meeting with representatives of the powerful but skeptical Armenian diaspora was merely a briefing process, and that he was not "seeking permission" from them to reconcile with Turkey. Turkish President Abdullah Gül declared: "We are not writing history, we are making history."[14]

Turkey seeks to attain a just memory of the suffering that the Turkish and Armenian nations experienced in the past. To that end, it signed the Zurich Protocols that were expected to overcome all hurdles in relations with Armenia, and jointly consider with that country the historic controversy.

NOTES

1. Anatolian News Agency, 22 April 2009.
2. http://www.consilium.europa.eu/uedocs/cmsdata/docs/pressdata/en/declarations/109899.pdf.
3. PanARMENIAN.Net, 17 June 2009.
4. Media reports to this effect are numerous. See, among others, Şebnem Arsu, "Turkey and Armenia to Establish Diplomatic Ties," *The New York Times*, 1 September 2009, p. A4; "Turkey, Armenia Agree to Form Ties," *The Wall Street Journal*, 1 September 2009, p. A8; "Armenia-Turkey; Plan to Normalize Ties Advances," *Los Angeles Times*, 1 September 2009, p. A22; "Turkey Armenia Ties," *The Times*, 1 September 2009, p. 31; Suzan Fraser, "Turkey and Armenia Embark on Normalizing Relations," *The Jerusalem Post*, 2 September 2009, p. 8; "Türkei und Armenien vereinbaren Normalisierung," *Westdeutsche Zeitung*, 1 September 2009, p. 3.
5. Guillaume Perrier, "Turquie et Arménie vont normaliser leurs relations," *Le Monde*, 3 September 2009, p. 7; Laure Marchand, "Début de réconciliation turco-arménienne," *Le Figaro*, 2 September 2009, p. 6; Marc Semo, "Turquie-Arménie: réchauffement sur le feu," *Libération*, 2 September 2009, p. 9; Jean-Christophe Ploquin, "Turquie-Arménie, espoir de détente," Editorial, *La Croix*, 2 September 2009, p. 1; Alain Guillemoles, "La Turquie et l'Arménie vont nouer des relations diplomatiques," *La Croix*, 2 September 2009, p. 8; Hassane Zerrouky, "Accord historique entre Ankara et Erevan," *l'Humanité*, 2 September 2009, p. 15; "Turquie-Arménie: la diplomatie du football," *Les Echos*, 3 September 2009, p. 12.

6. "Prof. Roger Smith's Open Letter to President Sarkissian," *The Armenian Weekly*, 1 October 2009, p. 1.

7. The full texts of the Protocol on the Establishment of Diplomatic Relations Between the Republic of Turkey and the Republic of Armenia and the Protocol on Development of Relations Between the Republic of Turkey and the Republic of Armenia are in Appendices 4 and 5 respectively.

8. Marc Semo, "Le turc Ahmet Davutoglu signe en silence," *Libération*, 12 October 2009, p. 1. The full text of the statement that was to be made but not pronounced by the Turkish Minister of Foreign Affairs, Ahmet Davutoğlu, after the signing ceremony of the Turkish-Armenian protocols of 10 October 2009 is in Appendix 6.

9. Rouben Shougarian, "Armenian-Turkish Diplomacy: Track I Failures and Track II Prospects," *The Armenian Review*, Vol. 54, No. 1–2 (Spring–Summer 2013), p. 40. Rouben Shougarian was Armenia's first ambassador to the United States (1993–1999), Deputy Minister of Foreign Affairs (1999–2005) and ambassador to Italy, Spain and Portugal (2005–2008).

10. These are described in detail in Mary Beth Sheridan, "Armenia, Turkey Reach Accord; Swiss Broker New Diplomatic Ties," *The Washington Post*, 11 October 2009, pp. A12 and A16; Mark Landler and Şebnem Arsu, "Long-Bitter Turkey and Armenia Sign Pact to Normalize Relations," *The New York Times*, 11 October 2009, pp. 5 and 12; Samantha Shields, Nicholas Birch and Marc Champion, "Hurdles to Turkey-Armenia Pact; Territorial Dispute Is One Problem on Path to Ratification by Both Parliaments," *The Wall Street Journal*, 12 October 2009, p. A6; "Clinton Helps Turkey, Armenia on Accord; With Nudging, the Nations Agree to Open Border, Establish Ties," *Los Angeles Times*, 11 October 2009, p. A29; Delphine Strauss, "Turkey-Armenia Accords Aim to Dispel Hostility," *Financial Times*, 12 October 2009, p. 4; Guillaume Perrier, "L'Arménie et la Turquie établissent des relations diplomatiques," *Le Monde*, 10 October 2009, p. 1; Laure Marchand, "Un compromis historique," *Le Figaro*, 10 October 2009, p. 1; Marc Semo, "La Turquie et l'Arménie s'appuient sur la détente," *Libération*, 10 October 2009, p. 1; Alain Guillemoles, "La diaspora arménienne est inquiète," *La Croix*, 12 October 2009, p. 1; Hassane Zerrouky, "Turquie et Arménie signent un accord historique," *l'Humanité*, 12 October 2009, p. 1; Jean-Michel Demetz, "Turquie-Arménie L'enjeu caucasien," *Le Vif/L'Express*, 16 October 2009, p. 82; "Türkei und Armenien bereit zur Versöhnung," *Rheinische Post*, 12 October 2009, p. 3; "Entspannung: Türkei und Armenien," *Westdeutsche Zeitung*, 12 October 2009, p. 3.

11. Aybars Görgülü, Alexander Iskandaryan and Sergey Minasyan, *Assessing the Rapprochement Process* (İstanbul: Caucasus Institute, 2010), p. 13.

12. Anatolian News Agency, 10 October 2009.

13. Tony Halpin, "Football Diplomacy Seals the Deal Between Armenia and Turkey," *The Times*, 10 October 2009, p. 6.

14. Anatolian News Agency, 14 October 2009.

Chapter Nineteen

The Collapse of the Protocols

REACTION TO THE PROTOCOLS IN ARMENIA AND IN THE ARMENIAN DIASPORA

The purpose and meaning of the subcommission on the historical dimension generated heated and divisive debate within both countries and their respective diasporas. There were several reasons for this debate, but one crucial aspect was that since the announcement of the protocols at the end of August 2009, the presidents of both countries have expressed diametrically opposing views on the meaning of this subcommission. On October 1, in Yerevan, Armenian President Serzh Sargsyan answered questions posed by the editors of the *Armenian Reporter* regarding this subject. He said this was not the historians' commission proposed years ago. This was a subcommission of an intergovernmental commission, which was suggested by the Armenian side in its response to that proposal. The purpose of the subcommission was to generate a dialogue on history, in order to increase mutual trust. Armenian President contended that this was a long-term process, which would encompass a broad range of issues: issues of the Armenian heritage in Turkey, issues of restoring and preserving that heritage, issues of the heirs of the victims of the "genocide." It was not possible to establish relations with a country without having dialogue about issues of mutual interest. And historical research should scare only those who falsified history. The agenda of the commission and its subcommissions would be set by the two sides, Armenia and Turkey.[1] A day earlier, at a meeting with members of the Public Council of Armenia, Sargsyan had stressed that the subcommission would be formed on a parity basis and both parties would be able to express their positions. "I perfectly understand any political process has a price. I am ready to pay. Time will show if we gain or lose," he added.[2]

On October 3, in New York, Sargsyan explained to the assembled representatives of the Armenian diaspora organizations that the subcommission was not to judge whether or not genocide took place, but rather "to discuss the issues of Armenian heritage in Turkey, issues of restoring and preserving that heritage, issues of heirs of victims of Genocide." However, Turkish President Abdullah Gül defined the subcommission's objective as one which would provide a historical judgment. On October 6, in İstanbul, he stated:

> There are all sorts of allegations about what happened a century ago. It is clear that people who do not know what happened where or how are not able to take decisions on this matter. What we hope is that historians, archive specialists study this matter and we are ready to accept the conclusions of this commission. To show that we are sincere, we even said that if a third country is interested in this matter, if French historians, for example, want to take part in this commission, they are welcome.[3]

In response to an 13 October 2009 open letter from the president of the International Association of Genocide Scholars, William Schabas, Armenian President Serzh Sargsyan said on 13 November 2009 that any relation with neighboring Turkey did not question "the fact of the Armenian Genocide and deprivation of Homeland." As for the matter of the establishment of the intergovernmental subcommission aimed to discuss the historical dimension, envisaged by the protocols signed by Armenia and Turkey, Sargsyan assured Schabas that it was not a commission of historians. The purpose of that commission was to give an opportunity to Armenian and Turkish peoples to find common grounds for mutual trust and dialogue. The Armenian President claimed that the contribution to the elimination of the consequences of "the Genocide" should be the goal of the subcommission's work, and "the fact of the Genocide" itself could in no way become a subject of discussion within the agenda of the subcommission. Sargsyan added that with this perception, Armenia signed the protocols with the Turkish side, and this was what he stated in his address to the nation prior to the signing.[4]

According to David Phillips of Columbia University, Yerevan saw the joint historical commission as an opportunity for Turks to engage in a discussion about their own history. A structured dialogue affirming the "genocide" could provide political cover for Ankara to apologize, while the submission on legal issues also opened the door to reparations. In exchange, the Armenian side was also prepared for the joint historical commission to consider a broad sweep: events in the nineteenth century; the role of righteous Turks who saved Armenians; and the assassination of Turkish diplomats in the late twentieth century by the Armenian Secret Army for the Liberation of Armenia. Yerevan viewed the protocols as a way to end the embargo by Turkey, boosting Armenia's economy and facilitating exports, such as electricity sales, to Turkey. By omitting reference to negotiations with Azerbaijan,

Yerevan expected that the protocols would contribute a new dynamic and sense of urgency to the work of the Minsk Group.[5] The joint historical commission would buttress the "genocide's" validity, boosting recognition. The protocols also represented a legacy opportunity for the Armenian President Serzh Sargsyan, who saw the diplomatic breakthrough as a way of securing his place in history. Sargsyan, however, received withering criticism in Armenia and from some elements in the Diaspora. Accusing the government of a diplomatic failure, the Dashnaks and its sixteen members of Parliament withdrew from the governing coalition on 27 April 2009, after the protocols were initialed. Dashnak Chairman Hrant Markarian blasted the deal for undermining Armenia's national interests by making major concessions to Ankara with nothing in return. Other opposition parties were also critical. Armen Martirosyan, Parliamentary leader of the Heritage Party, called it too vague and a cause for deep concern, which would undermine recognition of the genocide. The Armenian National Congress called the protocols very dangerous and defeatist. Stepan Demirchyan, Chairman of the People's Party, criticized the protocols for giving Ankara a say in the Mountainous Karabagh negotiations and putting unprecedented international pressure on Yerevan to make further concessions.[6]

These critics lambasted the historical dialogue as a vehicle for investigating the facts of the genocide. The Armenian government countered that the mandate of the historical commission was not defined, but even many of those who supported opening the border believed that Turkey would manipulate the historical dialogue. Questioning the Armenian genocide was equated with betraying the Armenian state. According to paragraph 11 of the 1990 Declaration of Independence, "The Republic of Armenia stands in support of the task of achieving international recognition of the 1915 Genocide in Ottoman Turkey and Western Armenia."[7]

There was opposition to the signing of the protocols from the vast majority of the Armenian Diaspora that continues to demand that Turkey accept "the killing of up to a million and a half Armenians amounted to genocide."[8] Diaspora Armenians were especially incensed by a plan for a joint commission of historians to investigate the events leading up to 1915. They fumed that this called the genocide into doubt and might make it harder to seek compensation.[9]

Before the signing there were demonstrations in Beirut and Paris, as well as in New York, Montreal and Los Angeles, by local Armenians opposed to a rapprochement. Despite noisy street protests, however, some influential expatriate groups in the United States—Western and Eastern Dioceses of the Armenian Church, the Armenian General Benevolent Union (AGBU), the Knights of Vartan and the Armenian Assembly of America (AAA)—announced they would back the agreement. In a joint statement issued on 1 October 2009, these major Armenian-American institutions said the protocols initialed by Armenia and Turkey presented new opportunities and posed new challenges to generations-old issues. They welcomed the initiative of the President of the Republic of Armenia in taking a positive approach to the process of normalizing relations with Turkey. The protocols announced on August 31 represented a marked change from the past. Western and Eastern Dioceses of the Armenian Church, the AGBU, the Knights of Vartan and the AAA supported the public discourse and welcomed a vigorous debate regarding this historic development within the parliaments of Armenia and Turkey, as well as throughout the Diaspora. They believed, however, that ongoing mischaracterizations of the general principles and guidelines of the protocols as potential concessions, and then attacking the protocols and the best intentions of the president of the Republic of Armenia based on these mischaracterizations, misguided public opinion and did not serve the best interests of the Armenian people. According to them, the path ahead would not be easy and would undoubtedly involve new twists and turns along the way. They considered that made it all the more important to understand that this was not the time to advance other agendas at the expense of Armenia's future.

The AGBU was one of the first organizations that took a stand in support of the Turkey-Armenia normalization process, and it was also one of the five signatories of a joint statement in support of the process. The Montreal-based Congress of Canadian Armenians also supported the accord. It said the agreement would hopefully lead to the resumption of normal diplomatic ties and the reopening of the shared border between the two countries. This would improve the national security of Armenia and the flow of trade for the landlocked country, and it would be seen as a responsible action by Turkey facilitating its entry into the EU.

The more than 10,000 participants of a public rally in opposition to the Turkey-Armenia Protocols organized by the Social Democratic Hunchakian Party, the ARF, the Ramkavar Azadagan Party and the Unified Armenian Youth, on 27 September 2009 unanimously adopted a strongly-worded resolution directed at the Armenian authorities, demanding the government put an immediate end to the protocols. They found unacceptable that within the context of implementing dialogue on the historical dimension any examination of historical records and archives by a commission or subcommission on any level. Such an examination not only would irrevocably halt the process of international recognition of the Armenian "genocide," but also completely diminish the Armenian people's achievements resulting from decades of immense and continuous efforts, as well as reality of the recognition of the Armenian "genocide" by numerous countries.[10]

The ANCA condemned the agreement ferociously. Its chairman, Kenneth Hachikian, in a letter of 30 September 2009 he wrote to the Secretary of State, Hillary Rodham Clinton, said these agreements which were imposed upon a landlocked Republic of Armenia, threatened its security, jeopardized the freedom of Mountainous Karabagh, and compromised the inalienable rights of all Armenians. In light of Clinton's powerful track record as a United States Senator and Presidential candidate in support of recognition of the Armenian "Genocide," the ANCA was particularly troubled by the role that she played in pressuring Armenia to accept these protocols. Rather than keeping faith with her principled stands on this human rights issue, the letter went on, Clinton has, since taking office, aggressively pressured Armenia into a process that effectively provided President Barack Obama with a rationale for failing to honor his clearly stated pledge to recognize the Armenian "Genocide."[11]

The Armenian National Committee of Canada (ANCC) felt the international community had put Armenia in a corner. "In the opinion of the ANCC, as well as the vast majority of the Armenian diaspora," read a statement from the organization released the day the protocols were signed, "this agreement was the result of immense and undue pressure on landlocked and blockaded Armenia by leading powers within the international community, and in full disregard of historical facts, human rights and justice, and self-determination rights."

"We have to understand that the protocols came as a total surprise not only to the Diaspora, but to everyone, including Armenians in Armenia," told the Republic of Armenia's Consul General to Los Angeles, Grigor Hovhannisyan, in a panel organized at Sherman Oaks, California on 17 December 2009. "Negotiations of that type and caliber do normally take place in an atmosphere of utmost secrecy. Only very few people are involved in those things." "I was in Yerevan in a meeting with the diplomatic corps when the Foreign Minister revealed the protocols," said the Consul General, explaining how he had come to find out about the document. "When I got back to Los Angeles, I did not have enough of a background on these negotiations and the issues on the table." Hovhannisyan stated that the Republic's first administration had kept dialogue with Turkey a secret. It was not until the current administration that the public was informed about the diplomatic dialogue. Revelation of the document was an "eye opening" experience to him and his colleagues, leaving them unprepared to address questions by friends and local Armenians about the Kars Treaty[12] and the recognition of Armenia's and Turkey's borders. "I was unprepared, which is no credit to our diplomatic service," said the Consul General very frankly. "But this is how it works, especially when we're talking about top secret negotiations."[13]

The consul general reiterated what President Serzh Sargsyan has stated repeatedly and offered no new justifications or explanations about the protocols. Hovhannisyan also reiterated the president's claims that the protocols were indeed initiated by Armenians and included many conditions that the Armenian government put on the table. Speaking about the process since the revelation of the protocols, the consul general said public policy must be debated openly in a civil society, and no one can argue against the dialogues taking place throughout the Diaspora. "The Diaspora is part of global Armenian civil society," remarked Hovhannisyan. "We should think of ways on how to make that happen." Hovhannisyan also negated fear that the validity of the Armenian Genocide would be questioned as part of the proposed Historical Commission. He said the commission was not designed to debate the validity of the Armenian Genocide but to settle the consequences and property claims.[14]

Chargé d'Affaires of the Armenian Embassy in Ottawa, Arman Akopian, acknowledged strong opposition from some segments of his country's approximately 80,000-strong diaspora in Canada. And that was to be expected, he said. Akopian related that for many members of the diaspora getting Turkey to recognize the genocide was their top priority. The problem was, the Armenian government had other considerations to take into account as well. "For the diaspora, it seems to be more important than for the Armenians, at least they think it is. Because for Armenia there are other issues, like the economic situation of Armenia, good relations with our neighbors," he explained. "So obviously the burden of responsibility for the Armenian president or the Armenian government is much, much heavier." However, contrary to the ANCC's assertions, Akopian indicated, the diaspora was not unanimous in its position on the accords. "I've seen a lot of people who are opposed and they've come to the embassy and expressed their concerns," he added. "There were protests in Montreal and Toronto. But there are those who expressed their support because they understand there are some priorities back in the old country." According to Akopian, the genocide issue had not been shelved. He said this would continue to be communicated to members of the diaspora, though he acknowledged there were some who would not be persuaded.[15]

Several American and French Armenian academics have also expressed their views on the historical subcommission through comments and interviews to local media outlets, with very few coming out in support of it. In the document, compiled and edited by *The Armenian Weekly* editor Khatchig Mouradian, Diasporan Armenian scholars share their opinions.[16]

Richard Hovannisian wrote that the international commissions had significant value in easing historical tensions and promoting mutual understanding. Such commissions, presently at work in Central Europe and elsewhere, had registered noteworthy progress. But these commissions were based on acknowledgment of particular human tragedies and injustices. They could not function if one of the parties was a "denialist state, intent on obfuscating the truth and deceiving not only the world community but also its own people." Hovannisian claimed that the proper order must be 1) recognition of the crime then—and only then—2) the formation of commissions to seek the means to gain relief from the suffocating historical burden.

Raymond Kévorkian, Associate Professor at the Institut Français de Géopolitique of the Université de Paris VIII and director of the Nubar Library in Paris, contended that although the mission entrusted to the historical subcommission in the protocols did not explicitly raise the genocide issue, it was that it would be discussed within that framework one way or the other. In an effort to delay qualifying the events of 1915 as genocide for a few more years, he asserted, Ankara had tried to make it seem like this was an adoption of the previous Turkish proposal to establish a committee of historians. By assigning this issue back to the undertakings of a subcommission, which was itself operating within the context of official bilateral relations, and by avoiding a direct reference to the genocide, the Armenian road map negotiators had clearly attempted to anticipate the bitter criticism of their opposition. Kévorkian maintained that "insofar as this subcommission has at least partly lost its initial mission to throw doubt on the facts of 1915," exchanges could prove to be useful, provided that the required experts were competent and of an adequate level. Its formation and working methods should be subject to scrutiny.

Ara Sanjian, associate professor of Armenian and Middle Eastern History and director of the Armenian Research Center at the University of Michigan in Dearborn, said the subcommission was a victory for Turkey, arguing as follows: Agreeing to the formation of a subcommission on the historical dimension of relations between Armenia and Turkey was a concession, which Sanjian was afraid Armenian diplomacy would come to regret deeply. At present, he had no reason to share the optimism of President Serzh Sargsyan and his entourage that this subcommission would increase international awareness of the Armenian Genocide. One should expect the current Turkish government to fill its allotted share in the subcommission with proved and experienced "deniers." Assisted by an army of diplomats, as well as American and other public relations firms, these Turkish representatives would in all likelihood use the subcommission "to engage the Armenian side in protracted yet unproductive exchanges." Their objective—to give to the outside world an impression that Turkey was not afraid of investigating the truth and that it was committed to a serious endeavor in this regard—was unlikely to change. According to Sanjian, Ankara would use the subcommission to continue to discourage outside parties from taking a principled stand on the Armenian Genocide issue and to delay indefinitely any meaningful discussion with Armenians on the legal, political, social, economic, and cultural repercussions of that genocide. Because of these Turkish tactics, "professional" historians had long been careful not to get dragged into direct exchanges with "deniers," and thus provide the latter with undeserved academic legitimacy. Sanjian stressed that the protocols negotiated by the authorities in Yerevan had lent Turkey this "long-sought opportunity." He expected Ankara to use the subcommission card effectively in its quest to keep this episode from the late Ottoman period solely within the realm of an academic dispute.

Sanjian did not place any hope in the possible participation of Swiss and other international experts in the workings of this subcommission. He held that in this highly charged politicized atmosphere involving many nations, independent-minded experts from third countries would either prefer to stay away or Ankara would try hard to exclude them, perhaps with the tacit support of fellow western governments, which maintain deep strategic, military, and financial interests in Turkey. Those who would end up on the subcommission would always be under constant pressure from their respective ministries of foreign affairs to be careful of the political ramifications of what they would say, both during the meetings of the subcommission or outside them, and not incur Ankara's ire.

Hovann Simonian, an Armenian author, wrote that the historical subcommission could be considered a major success of Turkish and other "deniers" of the Armenian Genocide. According to him, it brought to fruition their objective of casting a shadow on the objectivity and quality of the historical works affirming the veracity of the genocide. Simonian developed his case as follows. Unable to discredit these works with their own studies, "deniers" would from now on hide behind the subcommission and insist on waiting for its conclusions to block any discussion of the Armenian Genocide in international forums. Another constituent that would be comforted by the creation of this subcommission included the waverers and bystanders who, rather than bothering to read the Armenian literature published on the topic, would adopt a neutral or objective stance, stating that there were two sides to the story—the Armenian version and the Turkish one. By agreeing to the establishment of the subcommission on the historical dimension, the Armenian government had with one signature offered the Turkish government what the latter had failed to achieve for decades.

Dikran Kaligian, a historian and the managing editor of *The Armenian Review*, said the proposal to have an "impartial scientific examination of the historical records and archives" was dangerous on a number of grounds. Firstly, no matter the composition of the commission or how its mandate was framed, its mere existence would be exploited by the Turkish government in its genocide denial campaign. Turkey would ensure that the examination "drags on" for years, and neither the United States Congress nor any other legislature would consider recognizing the Armenian Genocide during such an ongoing examination. Likewise, Turkey had ensured that the genocide would not be raised during its negotiations to join the EU. This replicated what happened in 2001, when the European Commission—citing the formation of the Turkish-Armenian Reconciliation Commission—excluded all mention of recognition of the genocide from the resolutions of Turkey's accession to the EU. Secondly, the decades of research and dozens of books already written on the Armenian Genocide would be immediately discredited as biased and unscientific because the impartial and scientific examination would have begun. Thirdly, because all the past genocide research had been discredited, all past decisions made based on it would be brought into question. There would not be a state board of education that included the genocide in its curriculum, or a newspaper that changed its policy and began allowing its reporters to use the words Armenian Genocide, or a university that hosted a panel or a course that included the genocide, that would not be pressured by the Turkish government and its lobby to reverse its position because even Armenia agreed that the issue needed more study.

Armenian author Razmik Panossian wrote that many Armenians in the diaspora were dead against a historical commission. They assumed that it would question the very existence of the genocide. According to Panossian, this was a correct assumption insofar as Turkey's intentions were to use the commission to deny the Armenian Genocide—or at the very least to use it to minimize international pressure for recognition. But this did not have to be the case, he argued, and the denial of the genocide was not an inevitable outcome of the commission. Commissions did not work if there was no political will on all sides to make them work. Armenians must come to the commission with the starting point of the reality of the genocide. The questions they should put on the table must therefore center on the effects of 1915, Panossian said. He also pointed out that the Turkish side would naturally want to examine a different set of questions. If there was no common ground for discussion, so be it. A commission could easily be rendered irrelevant, it could be dragged on and on; in short, it could fail. Let Armenians and Turks not be afraid of the commission, Panossian concluded, but engage with it based on their multiple interests.

Bedross Der Matossian claimed that the inclusion of the historical commission as part of the Armenian-Turkish protocols was one of the most serious blows to the historical research of the Armenian genocide. From the perspective of a historian, the establishment of a joint commission by two governments in order to investigate the events of 1915 as part of their normalization package contradicted the craft of historianship. The involvement of governments in iniating and promoting this kind of understanding defied the basic tenets of writing history. In this instance, Der Matossian argued, the "victimized" group agreed to establish a historical commission with the "perpetrator" group in order to examine the veracity of an event that had long been accepted by international scholars as "the mass murder" of the indigenous Armenian population of the Ottoman Empire. The Armenian Genocide was a fact; it could neither be subject to a historical compromise nor be the victim of a Machiavellian diplomatic plan. In addition, the Armenian Nebraska assistant professor of history went on, attempting to question the veracity of the research conducted thus far was itself "a travesty of colossal magnitude" that mainly aimed at serving the regional interests of international powers. This did not mean that the motives, processes, and factors that led to the genocide could not be the subject of an honest academic discussion by all historians, regardless of their ethnic background.

Der Matossian indicated that he said "regardless of their ethnic background" because in the past decade the meetings between Turkish and Armenian historians had resembled a soccer game in which a third party always got involved as the mediator. Historians who were interested in debating the history of the Armenian genocide should participate in conferences and workshops by first representing themselves as historians and not as Armenians or Turks. Ethnicity should not be a criterion for their historianship in venues where they talked as Armenians or Turks. The Armenian assistant professor of history believed that the aim of the Turkish government in this initiative was clear: to reach some kind of a historical compromise about the Armenian genocide that satisfied the Turkish side. A sincere discussion of the Armenian genocide required the involvement of honest scholars who treated their material with utmost professionalism, integrity, and sobriety in their understanding of the historical, political, legal, and ethical dimensions of "several shades of state-sanctioned denialism."

INTERNATIONAL REACTION

UN Secretary General Ban Ki-moon welcomed the signing of the two protocols aimed at normalizing the relations between Turkey and Armenia. The spokesperson for Secretary General, Michele Montas, stated on 10 October 2009 in New York:

> This historic decision constitutes a milestone toward the establishment of good neighbourly relations and the development of bilateral cooperation between both countries. The Secretary-General is confident that this development will also contribute to peace, security and stability in the South Caucasus. The Secretary-General hopes that protocols will be swiftly ratified by the parliaments of Armenia and Turkey to ensure full normalization of their bilateral relations.[17]

The EU welcomed the signing. "The signature of the protocols confirms the desire of both Turkey and Armenia to turn a page and build a new future. This opens new perspectives for the solution of conflicts, notably in Nagorno-Karabakh," EU External Relations Commissioner Benita Ferrero-Waldner said in a statement. Significantly for Turkey's EU hopes, EU High Representative for Common Foreign and Security Policy Javier Solana thanked

Turkey and declared: "This is an important cooperation, no doubt, of Turkey, to solve one issue that pertains to a region which is in our neighborhood." [18]

The Swedish presidency declared as follows on 15 October 2009 to the Permanent Council of the Organization for Security and Cooperation in Europe on behalf of the EU on Armenia and Turkey:

> The EU would like to draw the attention of the Permanent Council to the declaration by the presidency on behalf of the EU on Armenia and Turkey as issued on 10 October 2009. The EU welcomes the signature by Armenia and Turkey, in Zürich on 10 October, of the two protocols relating to the establishment of diplomatic relations and the development of bilateral relations between the two countries, including the opening of the common border. The EU encourages Armenia and Turkey to remain committed to the process of normalisation and calls for the ratification and implementation of the protocols as soon as possible. The EU believes that the full normalisation of bilateral relations between Armenia and Turkey would be an important contribution to security, stability, and cooperation throughout this crucial region and will continue to offer its political and technical support to this process. The candidate countries Crotia and the former Yugoslav Republic of Macedonia, the Countries of the Stabilisation and Association Process and potential candidates Albania, Bosnia and Herzegovina, Montenegro, Serbia and the EFTA countries: Iceland, Liechtenstein and Norway, members of the European Economic Area, as well as Ukraine, the Republic of Moldova and Georgia, align themselves with this declaration. [19]

The Minister of Foreign Affairs of Slovenia, Samuel Zbogar, in his capacity as Chairman of the Committee of Ministers of the Council of Europe, welcomed the signing of the protocols and stressed that this was a historic event since Turkey and Armenia had decided to put distrust behind them, and overcome their painful history. The minister welcomed the decision of the two countries to create a better future for both nations, and emphasized that the protocols would also help improve security, stability and prosperity in the region. Zbogar expressed appreciation to the Swiss Minister of Foreign Affairs, Micheline Calmy-Rey, for the role of mediator that Switzerland had played in this process. He also indicated that the Turkish and Armenian authorities can count on the Council of Europe's assistance if they wish to draw on its expertise, as well as Slovenia, which continues to have an intense interest in finding solutions to problems in the South Caucasus. [20]

In answer to a written question on the recent rapprochement between Turkey and Armenia by Conservative and Reformist member of the European Parliament from Britain Charles Tannock, the EU Council stated on 18 January 2010 that it welcomed the signature in Zurich on October 10, of the two protocols relating to the establishment of diplomatic relations and the development of bilateral relations between the two countries, including the opening of the common border. The Council believed that full normalization of bilateral relations between Turkey and Armenia would be an important contribution to security, stability and cooperation throughout this crucial region. It encouraged Turkey and Armenia to remain committed to the process of normalization and called for the ratification and implementation of the protocols as soon as possible.[21]

AMERICAN RESPONSES

The United States Secretary of State Hillary Rodham Clinton noted that the agreement established a commission to examine Turkish-Armenian history and argued "[I]t is not for any other country to determine how two countries resolve matters between them."[22] That is true. In an interview with Vladimir Pozner of First Channel Television at Moscow on 19 March 2010, she further commented:

> The work going on between Turkey and Armenia is of great import. In fact, I was in Zurich last fall with the foreign ministers of Turkey, Armenia, Russia, France, and other countries, to witness the signing of a set of protocols to normalize relationships between Armenia and Turkey. And in these protocols, there was an agreement between the two countries to establish a historical commission that would look at all of the issues that are part of the past. And I think that's the right way to go to have the two countries and the two peoples focusing on this themselves.[23]

It should be added that Ottoman source materials for such studies are abundant. The entire Turkish archival repositories have been thrown open to systematic scrutiny. Access is limited only by the speed of the declassification process. Turkish and Armenian scholars, and those from other areas of the world, have an opportunity to study and develop a full account of the period. It will be appropriate for everybody to encourage that scholarly research. Let us learn all we can about that period.

On 3 October 2009, the United States Senator Bob Menendez, Foreign Relations Committee member and an outspoken advocate of the Armenian genocide claims, called provisions in the Turkey-Armenia protocols which would create a historical commission "frankly absurd." The New Jersey legislator went on to state that "I do not think that Armenia should be pressured into anything that is not in their interests or in the long-term national interests of the United States." Expanding on his concerns about the protocol's historical commission provision, Senator Menendez called such an action "an insult to the Armenian people. It is an insult to the memory of the victims. It is an insult to the top scholars who have clearly spoken on this issue and issued their unequivocal conclusions."[24]

Ergun Kırlıkovalı, West Coast director of the Assembly of Turkish American Associations, argued on 4 October 2009 that a historical commission would allow experts to come to a nonpolitical verdict on the issue, and said that was why Armenians were opposed to the creation of such a panel. It could debunk their main indictment against Turks, he remarked. Gunay Evinch, the Assembly's Washington, DC-based president and a Fulbright scholar, said that despite the concerns over the consequences of the accord between Turkey and Armenia, the agreement presented a unique opportunity to move forward for these countries and their people, but not without risks.[25]

Representative Mark Kirk, co-chairman of the congressional Armenian Caucus, on 19 October 2009 sharply criticized the Obama Administration's support for the creation of an official commission on the Armenian events of 1915. In reference to the president's many pledges to recognize the Armenian "Genocide" and his record in the Senate calling for the full and proper condemnation of this "crime," Kirk stated, "Despite repeated pledges to recognize the Armenian Genocide, the State Department now supports the establishment of an official commission to review whether a genocide happened at all. The United States should be leading the world in calling for recognition of the Armenian Genocide—not supporting efforts to rewrite history." Kirk, who had emerged as a leading contender for the Illinois Senate seat vacated by President Barrack Obama, joined with his Armenian Caucasus Co-Chairman Frank Pallone and Armenian Genocide Resolution sponsors Adam Schiff and George Radanovich, on the eve of the October 10th signing of Turkey-Armenia Protocols, in describing the establishment of a historical commission as "a thoroughly discredited idea." The four legislators stressed that, "Turkey cannot be allowed to re-invent this tragic part of its history as a price for normal relations with Armenia. To do so means acquiescence in a charade that demeans the memory of so many victims."[26]

In a 30 October 2009 letter to ANCA-Nevada activist Razmig Libarian, the Senate Majority Leader Harry Reid reported that he had recently written to Secretary of State Hillary Rodham Clinton to pass along the concerns of his state's citizens of Armenian heritage, and to encourage her to meet directly with the national leadership of the Armenian American community regarding the state of Turkey-Armenia relations. In his letter to Secretary Clinton, dated 20 October 2009, Senator Reid wrote:

> I am sure you are aware that this agreement has raised concerns in the Armenian community inside the United States. I have received many letters from Nevadans who do not support the creation of an international commission to examine the historical record on the genocide and who believe that the agreements are unfair to Armenia. Given the serious nature of the community's concerns, I felt it was important to raise them directly with you. The commission is particularly sensitive to the Armenian American community since the Armenian genocide has never been recognized by Turkey.

Despite the high profile of Turkey-Armenia ties in the Obama-Biden Administration's foreign policy agenda, neither President Obama nor Secretary Clinton met the Armenian American community leadership.[27]

The nature of the events of 1915 is a matter of legitimate scholarly debate. Accepting the Armenian nationalist narrative as uncontested fact, therefore, is both legally and historically problematic. Turkey does not deny that Armenian civilians suffered; however, it objects to considering this in a vacuum, ignoring the suffering of millions of other Ottoman citizens in these same events. Turkey's archives and reliable scholarly research lead it strongly to oppose defining the tragic suffering of civilians in the Ottoman Empire during the First World War as genocide. Turkey has conveyed this message to the United States government, which has in turn resisted calls to extract the Armenian experience from its historical context and then label it as genocide. The genocide allegation is of the utmost importance to Turkey, both as a matter of foreign policy and as a matter of domestic concern. Turkey has firmly and repeatedly stated that it considers legislation by any United States governmental body or official statement that proclaims that events in its history qualify as genocide, to be an impediment to its relations with the United States. It has conveyed this message to the United States government at the highest level and in the plainest possible terms and with corresponding actions.[28]

The United States Congress should not take a position, one way or the other, on the Armenian genocide claims question and should leave the writing of Turkish-Armenian history to scholars possessing the necessary skills and training. Legislators have no qualifications to judge acts committed about a century ago. Investigating, analyzing and interpreting history is a matter for historians.[29] Let historians decide. The Turkish government has been saying this for years. It is the Armenians who refuse to take part in a joint historical review, even when organized by impeccably neutral academics. This review is the logical and most sensible path forward. Passage of an Armenian genocide bill by Capitol Hill would constitute an act of legislative vengeance and would cast shame upon well-meaning scholars who want to explore this history from any vantage point other than the one foisted upon the world by Armenians.[30]

The most succinct statement of the problem comes in *The Chatham House Version* by the late Elie Kedourie of the London School of Economics and Political Science. This is—as the Turkish government says—an historical matter that should now be left to historians.[31]

All United States administrations, both Democrat and Republican, have opposed proposed Armenian genocide legislation in the past. They believed historians rather than legislators should deal with the issue. They were prepared to facilitate efforts by Turkish and Armenian experts along with academics from other countries to explore their common history.

Jim Moody, member of the United States House of Representatives from Wisconsin, in a "Dear Colleague" letter of 6 March 1987, said that some of his colleagues, with the best of intentions, were asking for cosponsors for an "Armenian Genocide Resolution," House Joint Resolution 132, that would have serious repercussions for the United States-Turkish relations. He urged caution as they considered this resolution. A similar resolution had failed three times in the Ninety-ninth Congress, even after more than four hours of debate prior to the last vote. And not without good reason. Representative Moody emphasized that House Joint Resolution 132 asked Congress in effect to endorse a specific historical version of tragic events that occurred between 1915 and 1923 in one region of the old Ottoman Empire about which there remained considerable controversy among historians and scholars. He went on to point out that no doubt, thousands of Armenian and non-Armenian civilians died—many of starvation—as a result of the terrible conditions and actions of the time, including a civil war within a world war. But reputable scholars disputed whether there was a government policy of genocide. More than sixty distinguished United States scholars of Turkish and Middle East studies have specifically criticized the historical assumption of the House Joint Resolution 132.[32]

Moody put it clearly on 7 August 1987 that genocide was the most dastardly charge one could level against anyone because it implies systematic, premeditated murder of a whole group of people. That was not what was happening in the Ottoman Empire in the First World War. He asked the question: "What was the context?" and went on to answer it:

> The context was a civil war within a world war. The Armenians in Asia Minor rose up in this period of chaos. There was no effective government at all, much less a context to carry out premeditated murder. They rose up, declared independence, and they were being armed by the Russian-Armenian factions. There was fighting going on behind the lines of Ottoman troops protecting the country against an invasion by Russia, and in that context the Ottoman government attempted to deport the Armenian population from that area, very much the way Americans attempted to deport the Japanese-Americans from America. In that context there was no effective control. Armenians were killing one another, villages were killing one another and 4 to 5 million civilians—that is non-Armenian Ottoman citizens—were killed. There was chaos, there was killing all around, there was starvation. People were moved without adequate provisions for health care or food. It was wintertime and people died of exposure. No one doubted the suffering, almost no one had suffered more than the Armenians. But the term genocide was just far too strong to apply.[33]

Stephen Solarz, member of the United States House of Representatives from the Thirteenth District of New York and chairman of the Subcommittee on Asian and Pacific Affairs said in the Foreign Affairs Committee, on 12 December 1985, that he had talked to dozens of people in an effort to determine what really happened in the eastern parts of the Ottoman Empire in the second decade of the twentieth century, and he had listened very carefully to the debate on the House Joint Resolution 132, both now and when it was brought up before the House a few months ago. There were, indeed, some very significant arguments which had been advanced against this resolution. Every member of the House had received a telegram concerning the House Joint Resolution 132 which was signed by a majority of the leading academic specialists on Turkey, the Ottoman Empire, and the Middle East in the United States. The signatories included such prestigious academics as Bernard Lewis, perhaps the preeminent specialist in the entire United States on these questions at Princeton University, and Jacob Coleman Hurewitz at Columbia. Solarz read to his colleagues the following two paragraphs of that telegram which addressed precisely the point he was trying to develop.[34]

The academic specialists wrote:

> As for the charge of "genocide": No signatory of this statement wishes to minimize the scope of Armenian suffering. We are likewise cognizant that it cannot be viewed as separate from the suffering experienced by the Muslim inhabitants of that region. The weight of evidence so far uncovered points in the direction of serious intercommunal warfare (perpetrated by Muslim and Christian irregular forces), complicated by disease, famine, suffering and massacres in Anatolia and adjoining areas during the First World War. Indeed, throughout the years in question, the region was the scene of more or less continuous warfare, not unlike the tragedy which has gone on in Lebanon for the past decade. The resulting death toll among both Muslim and Christian communities of the region was immense, but much more remains to be discovered before historians will be able to sort out precisely responsibility between warring and innocent, and to identify the causes for the events which resulted in the death or removal of large numbers of the Eastern Anatolian population, Christian and Muslim alike. As the above comments illustrate, the history of the Ottoman Armenians is strongly debated among scholars, many of whom do not agree with the historical assumptions embodied in the wording of House Joint Resolution 192. By passing the resolution, Congress will be attempting to determine by legislation which side of a historical question is correct. Such a resolution, based on historically questionable assumptions, can only damage the cause of honest historical inquiry, and damage the credibility of the American legislative process.[35]

Solarz stressed on 7 August 1987 that there was a distinction between massacres and genocide. Nobody denies that hundreds of thousands of Armenians lost their lives. Their fate was bemoaned, but whether or not it constituted a systematic effort to exterminate an entire race was apparently open to dispute. He thought it would, therefore, be a mistake for American legislators to insert themselves into the midst of this raging historical debate.[36]

In the United States Senate debates of 21 May 1985, James Hansen had already submitted for the record that the statement of the sixty-nine scholars demonstrated that the Armenian events of 1915 were a complex, historical issue, the facts of which were not as clear or well defined as they were sometimes represented to be in presentations to the House. The statement raised a serious question as to whether the tragic events they had been asked to comment on could, in justice, be labeled a genocide.[37]

In his speech in the House of Representatives on 23 April 1996, Dan Burton stated that much has been said in the Congress regarding events in the eastern part of the Ottoman Empire toward the end of the First World War. Yet he urged his colleagues to consider all sides and not rush to judgment. Many of Burton's colleagues condemned Turkey and its predecessor, the Ottoman Empire, for perpetrating genocide against its Christian Armenian population eighty-one years earlier. Genocide is the most heinous of crimes and before taking such charges, one should be absolutely certain of facts. Many renowned United States historians and academics specializing in Ottoman history declared that the events in question required more scholarly study. Historical evidence did not justify the genocide charge. While it was not disputed that Armenians died in eastern Anatolia during the period from 1915 to 1922, over two million Turks and other non-Christians also died. Although many died as a result of intercommunal fighting, many more died because of starvation and epidemic disease. Burton remarked that no reasonable person could dispute the unfortunate events in eastern Anatolia some eighty years ago. But did the House of Representatives dare ignore the deaths of two million non-Christian people, many at the hands of Armenian revolutionary groups who had allied themselves with Russian forces which were invading Ottoman land for territorial gains? Ottoman responsibility lay in the Empire's inability to protect its civilian population, Christian and Muslim alike, from threats of wide-scale fighting, famine, and disaster.[38]

The American congressman said there was little to be gained from inflaming past animosities, that were invariably grounded in the complex political and military dynamics of the time. It was far more productive for all parties to look toward the future. Armenia and Turkey would only benefit from improved relations. Turkey was among the first countries to recognize Armenia upon its secession from the Soviet Union. Just after taking office, Turkish Prime Minister Mesut Yılmaz emphasized Turkey's readiness to develop close relations and cooperation with Armenia in every field once the Mountainous Karabagh conflict was resolved. He also expressed his government's determination and willingness to open the border posts with Armenia once the declaration of principles was reached with Armenia and Azerbaijan regarding settlement of the conflict. Armenian President Levon Ter Petrossian, while addressing the Association of Armenian Manufacturers and Businessmen in March 1996 noted Turkey's importance as an economic partner for his country, referring to Turkey as Armenia's closest gate to the outside world. The United States Congress, according to Burton, should encourage progress in Turkish-Armenian relations. Any efforts which would hinder these developments threatened Armenia's economic viability. Western interests are better served through the stabilization of the Caucasus. The Caspian Sea region contains oil and gas reserves second only to the Middle East. A pipeline passing from Azerbaijan through Armenia and Turkey to markets in the West would not only create an important alternative energy source for the West, but also would create conditions necessary for economic growth and development for the region. Commercial cooperation would lead to enhanced relations. By providing economic strength, this pipeline would also ensure the independence of new states, and would help bolster democracy and democratic institutions. Burton concluded that, the time had come for all states in the Caucasus, Muslim and Christian, to put their differences behind them and work together for a prosperous future. He urged his colleagues interested in stability in the Caucasus to oppose any efforts to undermine regional cooperation.[39]

AMERICAN SCHOLARS AND THE DEBATE

At least forty-five of the above sixty-nine scholars who signed the statement on House Joint Resolution 192 were historians, and twenty-two of these had published extensively on the time period covered by and on the specific charges made in this resolution. Of the other scholars, the academic speciality of each was identified in the original declaration. They were political scientists, anthropologists, experts in language, literature, art, history, folklore, and other specialties. Whatever their speciality, they all had extensive knowledge of the issues involved, and they all agreed that the charge of genocide needed closer examination. None of them denied what happened to the Armenians. They simply pointed out that the kind of research necessary to reach a decision on the charge of genocide had not been carried out. Also, despite the wishful thinking of the Armenian lobbying groups, none of these sixty-nine scholars had withdrawn support for the declaration. These scholars should be afforded the credit that they deserve.

Besides the sixty-nine scholars, the following reputable experts either take issue with the genocide characterization, or provide an historical narrative which clashes with the Armenian version of events: Arend Jan Boekestijn, Youssef Courbage, Bertil Dunér, Gwynne Dyer, Edward Erickson, Philippe Fargues, Michael Gunter, Eberhard Jäckel, Yitzchak Kerem, Guenter Lewy, Andrew Mango, Michael Meeker, Stephen Pope, Michael Radu, Jeremy Salt, Norman Stone, Hew Strachan, Elizabeth-Anne Wheal, Brian Williams, Gilles Veinstein, and Malcolm Yapp. Thus, contrary to popular belief, the genocide appelation for the Armenian tragedy does not command a consensus in the community of Middle East and Ottoman scholars.

SUPPORT FOR THE TURKISH-ARMENIAN PROTOCOLS IN THE BRITISH AND AUSTRALIAN PARLIAMENTS

In the British House of Commons an Early Day Motion titled "Relations between Republic of Turkey and Republic of Armenia" was introduced by Bob Laxton, Lindsay Hoyle, Andrew Dismore, Paul Rowen, Peter Bottomley, Sir Nicholas Winterton, Lynne Jones and Bob Spink on 13 October 2009, which read:

> This House welcomes the recent Protocols on the Development of Relations and the Establishment of Diplomatic Relations between the Republic of Turkey and the Republic of Armenia, signed by the Turkish Foreign Minister, Ahmet Davutoglu and his Armenian counterpart, Edward Nalbandian in Zurich on 10 October 2009; finds these developments very encouraging for the creation and maintenance of an atmosphere of trust and confidence between the two countries; applauds the desire by both sides to develop bilateral cooperation in political, economic, cultural and other fields; notes the mutual commitment to respect equality, sovereignty and non-intervention in the internal affairs of other states, territorial integrity and inviolability of frontiers and condemnation of all forms of terrorism, violence and extremism irrespective of their cause; welcomes the agreement to open the common border between the two countries and establish an intergovernmental bilateral commission for regular political consultations between the two countries; notes the agreement to implement dialogue on the historical dimension with the aim of restoring mutual confidence between the two nations; and believes these developments will strengthen peace, security and stability in the region as a whole.[40]

Again in the House of Commons on 20 October 2009, in reply to Bob Laxton's question "[W]hat assessment has been made of the implications for government policy in the region of the conclusions of protocols on (1) development of relations and (2) establishment of diplomatic relations between Turkey and Armenia?" Chris Bryant, the Minister for Europe, replied, "The government welcome the signing of protocols between Armenia and Turkey. That is important not only for those countries, but for peace in the wider region." And in answer to Laxton's next query, "[W]hat further steps can the Government take to encourage both Turkey and Armenia to ratify and implement these protocols, because the benefits will be immense for the region?" Minister Bryant stated, "We need to ensure that momentum in this process is maintained. My honorable Friend is right: we need to ensure that ratification is proceeded with by the parliaments, and two months after that it will be possible to open the border. That is such a significant change from the position that we were in only a few years ago that all members will wholeheartedly welcome it."[41]

In the House of Lords on 17 October 2013, in response to Lord Hylton's question of asking the British government whether they will make representations to the governments of Turkey and Armenia about reopening their common frontier, Baroness Warsi, the Senior Minister of State, Department for Communities and Local Government and Foreign and Commonwealth Office, said that the United Kingdom supported the 2009 Turkey-Armenia Protocols on the Development of Relations and Establishment of Diplomatic Relations, and continued to encourage their ratification without preconditions. They have called on the governments of both Turkey and Armenia to work together to take forward the normalization process including the reopening of their common border, for the benefit of both countries and the wider region, and will continue to do so. The United Kingdom has also engaged with both Turkey and Armenia about the need to promote reconciliation between the peoples of both countries. The EU's Instrument for Stability program was supporting efforts to normalize relations between Turkey and Armenia.[42]

On 29 October 2009 in the Australian House of Representatives, Maxine McKew, Parliamentary Secretary for Infrastructure, Transport, Regional Development and Local Government, put on the record and called attention to the recent signing of two protocols between the governments of Turkey and Armenia in Zurich. McKew was hopeful that they might see the beginning of a more normal bilateral relationship between the two countries. It might be that they were at a point in the twenty-first century where the two parties could begin the long, hard process of reconciling what happened during the first two decades of the twentieth century. She stated that the October protocols were an agreement to start internal political consultations in two areas: the establishment of diplomatic relations and the development of bilateral relations. Significantly, Turkey and Armenia also agreed to form a historical commission which would investigate the tragic events of the First World War. She welcomed this first step in what had been a long history of tragedy and hostility. The Australian Parliamentary Secretary noted in particular the comments of the Turkish Minister of Foreign Affairs, Ahmet Davutoğlu, who had said in the Turkish parliament only a short time before: "We aim at reconciliation between Turkish and Armenian communities in diaspora and at opening healthy communication channels through the elimination of exploitation based on historical sufferings." She noted as well the comments of the Armenian President Serzh Sargsyan, who said just prior to the signing of the protocols: "It's important that our nations are able to establish normal relations." These protocols had the support of the Australian government.[43]

Julie Bishop, the Australian Minister of Foreign Affairs, in a letter of 15 May 2014 to Ahmet Davutoğlu, the Turkish Minister of Foreign Affairs, about the recent statements in Australia concerning the events of 1915–1923 involving the Armenian and other communities, assured him that there had been no decision to change the long-standing position of successive Australian governments on this issue. Bishop clearly said that the Australian government did not recognize these events as "genocide." They did not seek to intervene in this sensitive historical debate. They believed the issue was best resolved through dialogue between the communities and governments concerned. She acknowledged the recent positive messages from the Turkish government on this matter. Australia continued to encourage ratifications of the Protocols, signed on 10 October 2009, to normalize relations between Turkey and Armenia.[44]

NOTES

1. "All the Countries That Have Not Yet Recognized the Armenian Genocide Will Do So Sooner Or Later: An Interview With President Serge Sargsian," *Armenian Reporter*, 1 October 2009, p. 1.
2. "President Meets With Armenia's Public Council," *Armenian Reporter*, 7 October 2009, p. 1.
3. Greg Sarkissian, "The Pitfalls of a Historical Commission," *Asbarez*, 20 November 2009, p.1; "An Interview with Serge Sargsian," *Armenian Reporter*, 3 October 2009, p. 4; "Gul Invites Historians to Study Genocide," *Asbarez*, 6 October 2009, p. 1.
4. "Sarkisian to IAGS President: No to Commission of Historians, Yes to Eliminating Consequences of Genocide," *Asbarez*, 15 December 2009, p. 1.
5. The Minsk Group was created in 1992 by the Conference on Security and Cooperation in Europe to encourage a peaceful, negotiated resolution to the conflict between Azerbaijan and Armenia over the Mountainous Karabagh. The Minsk Group is headed by a cochairmanship consisting of the United States, Russia, and France.
6. Phillips, Diplomatic History, p. 60.
7. Ibid., pp. 60–61.
8. Razmig Shirinian, "Reflections on the Turkish-Armenian Protocols," *Journal of the Society for Armenian Studies*, Vol. 19, No. 1 (June 2010), pp. 7–13 and Joseph Kéchichian, "The Turkish-Armenian Protocols: Perceptions in the Diaspora," ibid., pp. 15–19.
9. "Bones to Pick," *The Economist*, Vol. 393, No. 8652 (10–16 October 2009), p. 44.
10. "Resolution Urges End to Protocols Process," *Asbarez*, 28 September 2009, p. 1.
11. Armenian National Committee of America, Letter, 30 September 2009.
12. Text of the Kars Treaty of 13 October 1921, signed between Turkey and the Soviet Republics of Armenia, Azerbaijan, and Georgia, can be found in *Türkiye Dış Politikasında 50 Yıl Kurtuluş Savaşımız (1919–1922)* (Fifty Years in the Foreign Policy of Turkey: Our War of Liberation [1919–1922]), (Ankara: Dışişleri Bakanlığı Matbaası, 1973), pp. 137–146. It delineated the borders established by the Moscow Treaty of 16 March 1921 and was ratified in Yerevan.
13. "Armenia's Consul General Comes Face-to-Face with American-Armenians: The Semantics of the Turkish-Armenian Protocols Discussed in the Valley," *Asbarez*, 23 December 2009, p. 1.
14. Ibid.
15. Lee Berthiaume, "Diaspora Split on Armenia-Turkey Accords," *Embassy*, 28 October 2009, p. 3.
16. Khatchig Mouradian, "Leave It to the Historians: Scholars from the Diaspora Reflect on the Commission," *The Armenian Weekly*, 19 October 2009. The following description of the views of the American and French Armenian academics is based on this source.

17. "Statement Attributable to the Spokesperson for the Secretary-General on the Armenian-Turkish Normalization Process," New York, 10 October 2009.

18. http://ec.europa.eu/archives/commission 2004–2009/ferrero-waldner/speeches/index en.htm.

19. "Declaration by the Presidency on behalf of the EU on Armenia and Turkey," Swedish Presidency of the EU, Organization for Security and Cooperation in Europe Permanent Council No. 776, Vienna, 15 October 2009.

20. http://www.coe.int/t/de/press/news/20091013 CM slovenia en.asp.

21. EU Council Reply E-5944/09, 18 January 2010.

22. "Making Sense of Genocide," Editorial, *Los Angeles Times*, 8 March 2010, p. A16.

23. http://www.state.gov/secretary/rm/2010/03/138712.htm; "Armenia Denies Clinton Remarks on 'History Commission' Creation," *Asbarez*, 23 March 2010, p. 1.

24. "Senator Menendez Calls Protocols "Insult" to Armenian Nation," *Asbarez*, 3 October 2009, p. 1.

25. Ann Simmons, "Tentative Deal Between Armenia, Turkey Brings Opposition From Both Sides," *Los Angeles Times*, 4 October 2009, p. A16.

26. "Kirk Challenges Obama Support for Historical Commission," Press Release, Armenian National Committee of America, 19 October 2009.

27. "In Letter to ANCA-Nevada, Senator Reid Reports that He Has Shared Community Concerns over Protocols with Secretary Clinton," *Asbarez*, 2 November 2009, p. 1.

28. In the United States Court of Appeals for the Ninth Circuit Movsesian, et al., Plaintiffs and Appellees, v. Victoria Versicherung Ag, et al., Defendants and Appellants. On Appeal From an Order of the United States District Court for the Central District of California, No. CV-03-9407 CAS. Motion for Leave to File Brief of Amicus Curiae the Republic of Turkey in Support of Appellants' Petition for Rehearing *en Banc*, p. 12.

29. There is a full discussion of this point in Heath Lowry, "Leave Armenia's History to Armenians," *The Wall Street Journal*, 15 November 1989, p. A25.

30. Norman Stone, "Armenian Story Has Another Side," *Chicago Tribune*, 17 October 2007, p. 6.

31. See Elie Kedourie, "Minorities," in *The Chatham House Version and Other Middle-Eastern Studies* (London: Weidenfeld and Nicolson, 1970), pp. 286–300.

32. Jim Moody, "Let's Not Legislate History on the Armenian Resolution," Congress of the United States House of Representatives, Washington, DC 20515, 6 March 1987.

33. Congressional Record, House of Representatives, Proceedings and Debates of the 100th Congress 1st Session, 7 August 1987, H 7323.

34. Congressional Record, House of Representatives, Proceedings and Debates of the 99th Congress 1st Session, Vol.131–Part 26, 11 December 1985 to 17 December 1985, pp. 36157–36158.

35. For more details, see the text of the sixty-nine scholars' statement on House Joint Resolution 192 in *The New York Times* and *The Washington Post*, 19 May 1985. The text is reproduced in Appendix 7. For Turkish press reports on the statement see, for example, Tuna Köprülü, "Bilim Adamları Ermenileri Yalanladı" (Scholars Have Negated the Armenians), *Hürriyet*, 19 May 1985, p. 7; Turan Yavuz, "69 Amerikalı Bilim Adamı Mektup Yayınlayarak Ermeni Katliamı İddialarına Karşı Çıktı" (69 American Scholars Have Opposed the Armenian Genocide Claims by Publishing a Letter), *Tercüman*, 19 May 1985, p. 1; "69 Tarih Uzmanı Tasarıya Karşı Bildiri Yayınladı" (69 Specialists on History Have Issued a Statement Against the Resolution), *Cumhuriyet*, 19 May 1985, p. 5; "Ermeni Tasarılarına Karşı Çıktılar: ABD'li 69 Bilim Adamından Destek" (They Have Opposed the Armenian Resolutions: Support from 69 American Scholars), *Milliyet*, 19 May 1985, p. 3; "Ermeni Tasarısına ABD'li 69 Bilim Adamı Sert Tepki Gösterdi: Tarihi Hata İşleniyor" (69 American Scholars Have Reacted Sharply to the Armenian Resolution: A Historical Mistake Has Been Committed), *Son Havadis*, 19 May 1985, p. 1.

36. Congressional Record, Proceedings and Debates of the 100th Congress 1st Session, 7 August 1987, H7320.

37. Congressional Record, Proceedings and Debates of the 99th Congress 1st Session, Vol. 131, No. 67, 21 May 1985.

38. Congressional Record—Extension of Remarks. 24 April 1996, E 808.
39. Ibid.
40. The text of this statement is to be found in House of Commons Early Day Motions EDM2019, 13 October 2009.
41. http://www.publications.parliament.uk/pa/cm200809/cmhansrd/cm091020/index/91020-x.htm.
42. Baroness Warsi's remarks in the House of Lords Column WA111, 17 October 2013.
43. Australian House of Representatives, Speech, 29 October 2009, p. 84.
44. Letter from Julie Bishop, the Australian Minister of Foreign Affairs, to Ahmet Davutoğlu, the Turkish Minister of Foreign Affairs, Canberra, 15 May 2014.

Chapter Twenty

The International Debate and the Archives

Since the mid-nineteenth century, the United States has been closely involved in the Turkish-Armenian controversy. Its role remains very important today, though unlike the period before 1945, there are many scholars and statesmen today who can see a Turkish angle to the problem. They do so largely because of the increasing growth of scholarship in this area drawing on the archives in Turkey and elsewhere.

TURKISH-ARMENIAN PROTOCOLS AND THE AMERICAN PUBLIC

It is worthwhile noting that Gerry Rankin, a person with no tie to either Turkey or Armenia, in his letter published in Glendale News Press on 13 October 2009, wrote that the signing of the Turkish-Armenian protocols sounded like progress to him and believed that the agreement was reason for celebration and congratulations to Armenians everywhere. While some Armenians, he said—safe in America—might want their former homeland to maintain a belligerent posture with its most important neighbor, those who lived in Armenia were the ones who would face the consequences of continuing failed relations with Turkey. Obviously, they were the vulnerable ones. As a nation, Armenia might be strong in heart, but it was relatively weak in economic and military power, and potential adversaries surrounded it on every side. Peace was everybody's business. To his Armenian friends Rankin offered an opinion, as a disinterested observer, that they should let the historians decide about genocide. After all, their judgment, in the centuries to come, would serve as the ultimate verdict in this matter. It was time for

Armenia to be pragmatic about its relations with its most important neighbor.[1]

A JOINT COMMISSION—THE KEY TO NORMALIZATION

Establishing a joint commission between Turkey and Armenia, for which the interpretation of history has been the primary source of dispute, is the key to the normalization of bilateral relations.[2] Hayk Demoyan, director of the Armenian Genocide Museum Institute in Yerevan, told Radio Free Europe/ Radio Liberty on 7 September 2009 that he supports the scheme because the research will provide Armenian members with access to Ottoman archives from the First World War and enable them to uncover more historical information.[3] In this sense, Demoyan is correct. Very little new serious research on Ottoman Armenians can be conducted without drawing extensively on Ottoman sources.

The *Los Angeles Times* was surely justified when it said in its edition of 13 October 2009 that the joint historical commission would "offer an opportunity for the two sides to face the issue together." This piece was written by a senior member of the newspaper's editorial board, and appeared on the editorial leader page. It demonstrates the serious view taken by that paper in the matter of a Turkish-Armenian historical commission. As the dominant leader of public opinion in the state of California, The *Los Angeles Times* has a readership that is already well-informed about the problem.[4]

Through the objective eye of the trained observer, Gwynne Dyer came to realize on, 19 October 2009, that the creation of a joint historical commission to determine what actually happened in 1915 is "a triumph for reason and moderation."[5] He is right. It is necessary to study the question with an open mind and see both sides of the coin. No wonder that throughout the world, many countries, organizations, groups, and individuals share this belief.

In a written answer to a parliamentary question, on 15 January 2010—announced by the Foreign Office Minister Lord Brett—the British government held that its

> main concern is how we can ensure that the lessons are learnt and relationships are rebuilt to ensure a peaceful and secure life for everyone living in the region. For this reason, we believe that it is first and foremost for the Turkish and Armenian people to address their common history. We welcome the recent signature of protocols on establishing and developing relations between Turkey and Armenia as an important step in this direction. In particular, we welcome the fact that the protocols provide for an intergovernmental subcommittee to examine historical issues. It is important that this process is owned by the parties directly concerned.[6]

This was basically an accurate assessment.

Hans Wilhelm Longva of the Norwegian Ministry of Foreign Affairs emphasized in a paper he delivered at the Conference on the Turkish-Armenian Relationship, organized by the University of Oslo on 1 February 2010, that the Armenian tragedy during and after the First World War is today history and should be left to historians rather than to politicians. History should be written on the basis of historical research and not according to political decisions. The approach adopted by the governments of Turkey and Armenia in the Protocol on the Development of Relations, namely to set up a commission of historians to address this issue, deserved their support.[7]

On 27 February 2010, Mike Hammer, a White House spokesman, in a carefully worded statement said:

> Our interest remains the achievement of a full, frank and just acknowledgment of the facts. We continue to believe that the best way to advance that goal is for the Armenian and Turkish people to address the facts of the past as a part of their ongoing efforts to normalize relations.[8]

There is much merit to Hammer's position. The Ottoman Empire no longer exists, but its history remains highly relevant—perhaps more so today than ever. Contrary to the picture painted by the Armenian writers, Turkey has a long history of religious tolerance. During centuries when there was religious warfare and persecution in Europe, Turkey operated a social system which permitted diverse religious beliefs to exist side-by-side. Jews fleeing the Inquisition found refuge in Turkey, as did those fleeing the rise of Adolf Hitler in the twentieth century. As noted earlier, today over 60,000 citizens of Armenian descent live, work and worship in Turkey, as do members of many other Christian denominations.

On 8 March 2010, Sarah Ludford, a liberal democrat member of the European Parliament for London and her party's European justice and human rights spokeswoman—as well as vice-chair of the European Parliament delegation to the United States—strongly criticized the vote by the Foreign Affairs Committee of the United States House of Representatives to label the treatment of Armenians in 1915 as genocide. Her reasoning was sound. She spoke her mind with clarity, conviction, and effect. Ludford said:

> Both the United States and the European Union have backed the welcome moves to set up a joint commission of historians from Turkey and Armenia to try and establish the truth about the tragic and large-scale wartime deaths almost a century ago. It makes no sense for outsiders in Europe or America to wade in with hobnail boots and prejudge the outcome of that sensitive exercise. That there were deportations which entailed atrocities and deaths of many Christian Armenians is not in doubt. But the precise actions, the 1915 war context, and the extent of reciprocal killings of Muslim Turks, all need to be

> better understood. The term genocide has a very narrow meaning under the 1948 Convention: the deliberate intent to destroy an ethnic, national, racial or religious group. It is deeply irresponsible to use that term without establishing the full facts about the Armenian case and to leave the suspicion that politics or even religious prejudice is a motive. That is why as a Member of the European Parliament I have always refused to define the events of 1915 and preferred to await the conclusion of honest and objective research. That is not a cop-out; it is acting with integrity. The Congressional vote was won by the narrowest of margins, 23 to 22. I hope that in those circumstances wisdom will prevail, with Congressmen heeding the call of President Obama and Secretary Clinton not to bring this to a vote of the full House.[9]

Ludford's advice was heeded.

To term as genocide a series of events that happened almost a century ago is something that should not be done without great care. Labeling a series of events a genocide is not something the United States Congress should undertake without serious study, deliberation, and careful examination of the evidence. Until that kind of careful examination of all pertinent documents has been done by trained historians, the Congress should not address this issue. It was ironic, just as the necessary documentary evidence in light of which the history of Turkish-Armenian relations will ultimately be written, to have the United States Congress attempt to legislate a skewed, faulty, narrow Armenian-generated version of events as historical fact.

Members of the Committee on Foreign Affairs of the United States House of Representatives, as articulated during consideration of House Resolution 252 (the "Affirmation of the United States Record on the Armenian Genocide Resolution") on 4 March 2010, were encouraged by the willingness of the leadership of the governments of Turkey and Armenia to agree for the establishment of a joint historical commission to review the Armenian events of 1915, as laid out in the two protocols they signed on 9 October 2009. This was an effort worthy of support. Therefore, any archives that might contain relevant documents regarding the events in the Ottoman Empire in that period, which had not been fully opened, should be made immediately available to both countries, to a joint historical commission described in the two protocols, and to interested parties researching the events of that time. Philip Gordon, Assistant Secretary of State for European and Eurasian Affairs, stated on 16 March 2010:

> As President Obama has said, our interest is in a full, frank and just acknowledgement of the facts related to the events of 1915. But the best way to do that, we believe, is for the Armenian and Turkish people themselves to address this history as part of their efforts to build a future of shared peace and prosperity.

The Committee on Foreign Affairs should take steps to encourage such transparency and cooperation. Ultimately, congressional action on issues addressed in House Resolution 252 affecting Turkey and Armenia, should focus on encouraging the governments of the two countries to reinvigorate their earlier, tentative agreement, embodied in the protocols of 2009, to establish a joint historical commission to conduct an impartial inquiry, toward improvement of relations between the governments and the people of Turkey and Armenia.[10]

Mark Meirowitz, who has taught politics, history and law in the New York Metropolitan area, aptly pointed out on 23 April 2010: "The historical commission is the proper platform for this [Turkish-Armenian conflict] discussion and analysis."[11] Meirowitz does not label the events of 1915 as genocide and supports research into the historical truth by the parties directly involved. This American scholar has until now received less attention than he deserves.

In a report submitted on behalf of the Political Committee by Michael Hancock, Vice Chairman and Rapporteur (United Kingdom, Liberal Group), to the Assembly of the Western European Union on frozen conflicts and Europe's security on 5 May 2010, it was stated that the Turkish-Armenian protocols of 10 October 2009—the first intergovernmental texts to be signed between the two countries since the Kars Treaty of 13 October 1921—were a positive development in the South Caucasus in a situation characterized by conflicts, blockades and trade restrictions. It was pointed out that it would be naïve and mistaken to imagine that the texts could fully normalize relations or settle all the problems between Turkey and Armenia overnight. Nonetheless, the ratification of the protocols by the two countries' parliaments would mark the beginning of a reconciliation process. The report went on as follows: The protocols, among other things, made provision for setting up a number of subcommissions, including one on trade, tourism, and economic cooperation, and another on the historical dimension. The tasks of the latter were two-fold: to carry out an impartial, scientific examination of the historical records and archives in order to define existing problems and formulate recommendations; and to open up a channel for dialogue enabling Turks and Armenians to look back jointly on their common history and bridge progressively the historical gap currently symbolized by the sealed border between the two countries. The report concluded that both sides had much to gain in the regional and international arenas from this proactive approach to solving their problems.[12]

In its reply to a parliamentary question of 16 February 2011, the Swiss Federal Government stated that the Federal Council (Council of Ministers) continued to maintain its position that it was the task of historians to work through and clarify the Armenian events of 1915 as comprehensively as possible. It said the interest shown by Turkey and Armenia to normalize their relations paved the way for the signing of Zurich Protocols. Despite all the difficulties, the Federal Council was confident that dialogue and cooperation between the parties would contribute to a mutual rapprochement of the two countries, from which both could profit. In any case, no means should be left unused on this issue and the Federal Council was determined to continue its engagement for peace, stability and development in the region. The Federal Council said it stood by its opinion that it was the task of historians to work out the events of 1915 and to clarify them as comprehensively as possible. Switzerland wanted to encourage both Turkey and Armenia to handle historical questions on a constructive basis within the framework of the rapprochement between the two countries. The invitation of historians to deal with the events of 1915 aimed to encourage an open and responsible debate, which would lead to a better understanding, knowledge and greater acceptance of the tragedy of 1915.[13]

On 13 April 2011 in Ankara, Francis Ricciardone, the United States Ambassador to Turkey, voiced Washington's support for the 2005 call by Turkish Prime Minister Recep Tayyip Erdoğan to the then-Armenian President Robert Kocharian to establish a joint commission of historians and experts from Turkey and Armenia to study the events of 1915 in the archives of Turkey, Armenia and other countries around the world. Ricciardone also said:

> One must also not forget the feelings of Armenian people whose relatives suffered during that period. If parties can manage to understand each other's pain, then, you are going to have a different perspective on what happened in 1915. So it seems to me, Armenians and Turks, and third country people, America and France and both sides need to participate in this scholarly examination in an honest way.[14]

And on 25 January 2012 Ricciardone told a group of Ankara newspaper bureau chiefs:

> We think that historians need to grapple with this in an open and honest way so that you can come to a full and frank acknowledgment of what happened. We believe that you are beginning to do that. We like to see our friends get along and we hope that you will overcome this dispute. There needs to be a conversation. You need to get the historians together on both sides.[15]

Ricciardone is right. It is necessary to examine the question with an open mind and see both sides of the issue. The importance of research and study of the Armenian issue should be emphasized, and credible conferences should be organized to discuss the Armenian events of 1915 and bring the findings to the attention of the public. There is still much work to be done given the enormity and complexity of the question. An honest debate and constructive criticism will only serve to improve the quality of current and future output.

In the House of Lords Baroness Flather asked the British government on 16 June 2011 what their timetable was for recognizing the Armenian genocide. The Minister of State at the Foreign and Commonwealth Office, Lord Howell of Guildford, replied:

> The Turkish and Armenian people are trying their best through a protocol procedure to normalise their relations and establish the right nomenclature and attitudes between each other so that these two countries can live in peace with a common border and continue to work for their joint prosperity. Now that protocols have been initialed and now that other governments—the United States, France and other key countries—all take the same view as we do: this is the right way forward. Behind this is the other worry about Nagorno-Karabagh, and all that, which is being handled by the Minsk process of Russia, the United States and France. These two things together provide hope for the future and it would not be useful or constructive for us to take an issue and raise the heat of the matter by intervening in the way suggested by the noble Baroness.[16]

Lord Howell's arguments are sound and practical.

In answer to a written question on the "genocide denial in Turkish schoolbooks" by Mikael Gustafsson, vice chairman of the Confederal Group of the European United Left—Nordic Green Left, it was stated on 20 December 2011 by Commissioner for Enlargement and European Neighborhood Policy, Stefan Füle—on behalf of the EU Commission—that they encouraged Armenia and Turkey to remain committed to the process of normalization and called on both countries to ratify and implement the bilateral protocols without preconditions and within a reasonable time frame. The Commission believed that the full normalization of bilateral relations between Armenia and Turkey would be an important contribution to security, stability and cooperation in the Southern Caucasus. It would require vision, courage and dialogue to overcome the wounds of the past.[17]

Professor of Contemporary Islamic Studies in the Faculty of Oriental Studies at Oxford University, Tariq Ramadan, welcomed on 27 December 2011 the Turkish government's intention to set up a scientific research commission that would delve into history, and establish the facts. This, in Ramadan's opinion, is the only possible valid approach. Many people have saluted this initiative, and urged that the issue be faced openly and dealt with through scientific examination. The British scholar says he has arrived at his current position on the Armenian "genocide" in light of the knowledge acquired by the study of the question. But by no means did he rule out revising his judgment if new information or elements then unknown to him were to become available. An informed, prudent mind could deal with history in no other way, Ramadan pointed out. According to him,

> (T)he Gayssot Law [that incriminates any individual who denies the reality of a crime against humanity, the target being those who argue that the Jewish Holocaust never took place][18] and the current debate over the criminalisation of Armenian genocide denial are not only unhealthy; they are counterproductive. Instead of encouraging scientific research and discussion, positions are cast in concrete, with interpretations acquiring the weight of the legislation that protects them, rather than the facts that confirm them.

Ramadan believes there is every reason for concern and continues: "At the same time, the good will of the Turkish authorities is rejected and brushed aside. It is tempting to conclude that this polemic is being used to conceal other objectives. For ultimately, whatever one's position on the 'Armenian affair,' history cannot be codified and defined by law or political fiat."[19]

Ramadan makes it clear that the French decision to adopt such a law is "neither intelligent nor scientific." He goes on: "It represents, in the event, the exploitation of a historical question for unstated political aims (both domestic and international)" and then asks the pertinent question: " Can there be a single serious mind, a single competent historian, who could possibly accept that the past be regulated by the law, that research be penalised or criminalised?" And he aptly winds up his argument:

> Agree with the official Turkish position or not, it must be recognized that the just and proper position must remain the establishment of a scientific commission and the opening up of debate, rather than the imposition of one single valid (political) interpretation of history, all of which the new [French] government has undertaken.[20]

Robert Badinter, President of the French Constitutional Council from 1986 to 1995 and Senator for the Hauts-de-Seine in 1995–2011, wrote in the influential *Le Monde* on 15 January 2012 that it is true that the genocide of the Jews during the Second World War has been a subject of legislation in France, including in the Gayssot Law of 1990. But the genocide of the Jews committed by the Nazis was established and the perpetrators convicted at Nuremberg by the International Military Tribunal. French judges were present in that court, set up under the London Agreement of 8 August 1945 which was signed by France. The judgments handed down by that court have the authority of established law (*res judicata*) in France. Badinter indicated that there is nothing parallel to this in the Armenian case: no decision about it has been handed down by any court—national or international—whose authority would be recognized in France. He then asked two pertinent questions. Can French lawmakers possibly compensate for this absence of legal decisions having the force of law by decreeing that an Armenian genocide took place in 1915? Can the French Parliament appoint itself the court of world history and proclaim that the crime of genocide was committed by the rulers of the Ottoman Empire a century ago, although no French nationals were involved either as victims or as executioners? In answer, he replied to himself: the French Constitution has not assigned Parliament the authority to say what happened in history. "It is up to historians to do this, and to them alone." Badinter further remarked that at France's request UNESCO could appoint a commission of internationally known historians. This commission, which would have access to all the archives and be provided with all the relevant information, would prepare a White Paper on the nature and extent of the Armenian events of 1915.[21]

Badinter is not mistaken.

At an event with the United States State Department employees on 26 January 2012, Hillary Rodham Clinton was asked why the United States has not matched a move by French lawmakers to criminalize denial that the First World War era deaths of Armenians in the Ottoman Empire were genocide. Secretary of State Clinton said one of great strengths of the United States was they did not criminalize speech. In the United States, people can say nearly whatever they choose, and they do. Other countries, including close friends and allies like France, have different standards, and different histories, but the Americans were, she hoped, never going to go down the path of criminalizing speech. Clinton pointed out that the issue should be debated, but not settled by governments and it was best left for scholars. She remarked:

> I think it's fair to say that this has always been viewed, and I think properly so, as a matter of historical debate and conclusions rather than political. And I think that is the right posture for the United States Government to be in, because whatever the terrible event might be or how high emotions that it represents, to try to use government power to resolve historical issues, I think, opens a door that is a very dangerous one to go through. So the issue is a very emotional one; I recognize that and I have great sympathy for those who are just so incredibly passionate about it. But I think the free market of ideas, the academic community, the open architecture of communication that is even greater now than it was in the past, are the proper fora for this kind of engagement, and that's where I hope it is worked out. And eventually, people will have their own conclusions, which need to be respected, but we need to encourage anyone on any side of any contentious historical debate to get out into the marketplace of ideas. Muster your evidence, put forth your arguments, and be willing to engage, and that's what I think should happen on that too.[22]

Clinton's comments suggest that the subject is one worth exploring further. Two United States Congressmen, Adam Schiff and Robert Dold, described her characterization of the Armenian events of 1915 as a historical debate "much closer to that of the Turkish government than that of any other senior U.S. diplomat in recent memory."[23]

In Ottawa on 20 September 2012 after the unveiling ceremony of the monument dedicated to Colonel Atilla Altıkat, the military attaché of the Turkish Embassy assassinated by Armenian terrorists thirty years ago, the Turkish Minister of Foreign Affairs Ahmet Davutoğlu restated his government's position that it would like the establishment of a joint commission to discuss the historical facts surrounding the Armenian issue. " If Canada wants to contribute to the Turkish-Armenian reconciliation, the best way is to help in forming joint commissions, speaking with both sides about a fair and just memory and working together," said Davutoğlu. Canadian Minister of Foreign Affairs John Baird replied he appreciated a dialogue on the issue.[24]

Richard Outzen, a United States Army officer currently serving on faculty at the National Defense University in Washington DC, and a Middle East Foreign Area Officer who has served in diplomatic and operational assignments in Turkey, Israel, Afghanistan, and Iraq, most recently demonstrates that the possibility of a joint historical commission to review the documentary record of the period holds merit, and may ultimately replace the cycle of accusation and denial with a deeper understanding of how war poses a perpetual threat to civilian communities. Outzen further believes that such a cooperative effort might include the study of Muslim peoples slaughtered or expelled from the Caucasus and the Balkans by the Russians and their allies.[25]

ARMENIAN OBSTACLES

Under Armenia's constitution, international treaties signed by the government need to be endorsed by the Constitutional Court before they can be ratified by parliament and take effect. The two Turkish-Armenian protocols signed by the two countries on 10 October 2009 required parliamentary ratification.

On 17 November 2009, the Armenian government brought to its Constitutional Court "the Case on Determining the Issue of Conformity with the Constitution of the Republic of Armenia of the Obligations Stipulated by the Protocol on the Establishment of Diplomatic Relations between the Republic of Armenia and the Republic of Turkey and by the Protocol on the Development of Relations between the Republic of Armenia and the Republic of Turkey Signed in Zurich on 10 October 2009." Ankara opposed the move, stating it was an impediment to ratification.

The Armenian Youth Federation reported on 22 November 2009 that town hall meetings had begun throughout the western United States to inform Armenian communities of the current state of negotiations between Armenia and Turkey and the steps being taken to prevent the ratification of the agreements between the two countries. "Now that the protocols have been signed, everyone's main concern is which parliament is going to ratify it first," ARF-Western Region Central Committee member John Kossakian said, adding that Armenia is currently playing a waiting game with the document. "Instead of worrying about this, we should start working on our next step—to confront the Armenian government about the protocol issues." In his remarks Kossakian stressed that the anti-protocols campaign's latest initiative was to channel public sentiment against the protocols to pressure the Armenian parliament not to ratify the documents. Dissecting the actual provisions in the protocols, the ARF activist Dadayan discussed the legal implications of the documents and the burdens Armenia would be required to uphold if it is ratified. Through these protocols, Dadayan claimed, Turkey was seeking to legalize its current de facto border with Armenia. According to him, the current boundaries were illegal and based on the "illegitimate treaties of Moscow[26] and Kars, signed in the 1920s by the rogue Bolshevik and Kemalist regimes. If the protocols are ratified, Armenia will once and for all relinquish its rights to US President Woodrow Wilson's arbitral award of historic territories now under Turkish occupation."[27]

In arguing the unequal bargaining position Armenia had been placed in throughout the negotiations process, Dadayan recalled his encounter with Armenian President Serzh Sargsyan during his visit to Los Angeles in September 2009 to meet with Armenian community leaders. Dadayan said he had asked Sargsyan what international lawyers and experts of international law were consulted by the Armenian government about the legal implications of the protocols, which were drafted in English. "The president said he was not good in English nor was he a lawyer," Dadayan recalled, noting that "Sargsyan said he trusted his diplomats enough not to seek [other] professional advice."[28]

On 12 January 2010, the Constitutional Court upheld the protocols' conformity with the Constitution of the Republic of Armenia and a clause in the Declaration of Independence that stated, "The Republic of Armenia stands in support of the task of achieving international recognition of the 1915 genocide in Ottoman Turkey and Western Asia." The court's ruling indicated that the protocols "cannot be interpreted or applied" in a way that would contradict the provisions of the preamble of Armenia's constitution and the requirements of paragraph 11 of its Declaration of Independence.[29]

The ruling also stated that the implementation of the protocols did not imply Armenia's official recognition of the existing Turkish-Armenian border established by the Kars Treaty of 13 October 1921. By doing so, the court rejected one of the main premises of the protocols, namely "the mutual recognition of the existing borders between the two countries as defined by relevant treaties of international law." This was an unnecessary move which raised an issue that had been deliberately glossed over in the text of the protocols. The ruling introduced preconditions which undermined the spirit of the protocols.

The decision of Armenia's Constitutional Court was criticized in Turkey. "This decision contains preconditions and restrictive provisions that impair the objective and spirit of the Protocols," said Ahmet Davutoğlu, the Turkish Minister of Foreign Affairs. "This approach cannot be accepted on our part." It was a "very serious setback," Davutoğlu stated, "It was a political assessment influenced by the government to satisfy the Diaspora." Ankara noted that Article 11 of the Armenian Declaration of Independence refers to eastern Anatolia as western Armenia, thereby asserting that it is part of Armenia. Since the Armenian constitution recognizes "national aspirations engraved in the Declaration of Independence of Armenia," Ankara regarded the description of eastern Anatolia as western Armenia as the basis for territorial claims. Davutoğlu called on Clinton to relay concerns about the court's reference to Western Asia and its approach to the dialogue of historians. He reiterated that the commission of historians was important to Turkey. He questioned the commission's usefulness if the Armenian side had already predetermined the outcome.[30]

Armenia seemed to be trying to rewrite and set new conditions on the deals. All is not lost however. The protocols process is suspended, not dead, and there is a chance that it can be revived in the future.

Two American political scientists, Michael Gunter and Dirk Rochtus, drawing on Turkish sources, wisely concluded "[O]nce each side has to listen to the other's position instead of simply of 'preaching to the choir,' it is possible that some type of agreement will gradually emerge."[31] Gunter further suggests that "the two sides might be able to forego employing the g-word, in favor of the term *Büyük Felaket/Mets Yeghern* or Great Catastrophe." Then, through discussion and compromise, intermediate positions could be reached.[32]

POSSIBLE PROSPECTS FOR TURKISH-ARMENIAN COOPERATION

Armenians are now fully mobilized to organize worldwide activities commemorating the one-hundred-year anniversary of the Armenian "genocide" on 24 April 2015. However, trade can still play a helpful role by reducing tensions and creating positive momentum in Turkish-Armenian relations. Commercial contact involves mostly "suitcase trade" involving consumer goods transported from Turkey through Georgia to Armenia. But bigger business is possible. Armenia could sell surplus electricity to Turkey which needs energy to power its economic boom. Armenia could also tap into Turkey's fiber optic cable to meet its growing demand for Internet. Railway service between Kars and Gyumri (Gümrü) in Armenia could resume when Turkey opens its border gate. In anticipation, Armenia could begin conforming the country's Soviet-era railway gauge to Turkish and European standards. In addition, a Qualifying Industrial Zone (QIZ) could be established to catalyze joint enterprises between Turks and Armenians. A QIZ is an industrial park and a free-trade zone, linked to a free-trade agreement with the United States. Goods qualify when partners contribute raw material, labor, or manufacturing. Kazan, an area in Armenia on the Turkish border, would be a suitable destination for joint ventures in textile and piece goods manufacturing.[33]

The QIZ could proceed with steps to relax restrictions on the surface transport of commercial goods. Armenian trucks are allowed to use Turkey as a transit country, but cannot off-load on Turkish soil.

On 12 December 2013, the Turkish Minister of Foreign Affairs Ahmet Davutoğlu made Turkey's first high-level visit to Armenia in nearly five years, raising the prospect of a revival in peace efforts between the two countries which stalled in 2010.[34]

In his weekly parliamentary address to his party's legislators on 23 April 2014, Prime Minister Recep Tayyip Erdoğan expressed Turkey's willingness to "confront" the historical events, and again called upon Armenia and the Armenian diaspora to join this effort. He believed a process both parties were active participants would enable Turkey and Armenia to resolve many of the issues of conflict between them, and would allow them to move deeper into the twenty-first century while building a constructive relationship, as neighbors should.[35]

Speaking on 23 April 2014, the Turkish Prime Minister Recep Tayyip Erdoğan offered his condolences to the families of Armenians who lost their lives during the First World War, in Turkey's most conciliatory remarks yet over the highly contested episode. "The incidents of the First World War are our shared pain," Erdoğan said in an official statement that was translated into nine languages, including Eastern and Western Armenian. The speech was published widely in Turkish and world media. It was the first time that a Turkish leader had used such explicit language in relation to the deeply divisive affair.[36]

Erdoğan stated:

> Millions of people of all religions and ethnicities lost their lives in the First World War. Having experienced events which had inhumane consequences—such as relocation—during the First World War should not prevent Turks and Armenians from establishing compassionate and mutually humane attitudes toward one another. It is our hope and belief that the peoples of an ancient and unique geography, who share similar customs and manners, will be able to talk to each other about the past with maturity and to remember together their losses in a decent manner. And it is with this hope and belief that we wish that

> the Armenians who lost their lives in the context of the early twentieth century rest in peace, and we convey our condolences to their grandchildren.

Erdoğan also stressed that it was inadmissible for the events of 1915 to be used as an excuse today for hostility against Turkey. In his statement, he repeated Turkey's offer to establish a joint historical commission in which Turkish, Armenian, and international academics and researchers would study the events of 1915 together, an offer that has been declined up until now. He recalled that it was with this understanding that Turkey opened its archives to all researchers. Hundreds of thousands of documents in the Turkish repositories are now at the disposal of historians.

Archbishop Aram Ateşyan, the acting Armenian patriarch in İstanbul, remarked that Prime Minister Recep Tayyip Erdoğan's statement was "exciting and historic." "For the first time, we are hearing such a statement from a top Turkish official. This statement will make Turkish Armenians and Armenians around the world happy. This is a start of beautiful days and the start of a friendship bridge," he said. Rober Koptaş, editor of *Agos*, an Armenian and Turkish weekly newspaper published in Istanbul, was pleased with the new approach. He stressed that the speech was "the most positive and constructive statement that has ever come from a senior Turkish office."[37]

Orhan Dink, brother of the murdered Turkish-Armenian journalist Hrant Dink, welcomed the statement. "Today's message of condolence is a very important step," he said:

> If democracy is to be built in Turkey, this is one of the most basic bricks to do so. Both for Armenians and for me it is important that the Prime Minister of the Republic of Turkey makes such a statement. Some might say that it came late, but the important thing is that this first step was made. This step has to bring both societies toward normalization.[38]

The United States praised the Turkish move. "We welcome Prime Minister Erdoğan's historic public acknowledgment of the suffering that Armenians experienced in 1915. We believe this is a positive indication that there can be full, frank and just acknowledgments of the facts, which we hope will advance the cause of reconciliation between Turks and Armenians," State Department spokeswoman Jen Psaki told a regular news briefing. The EU hailed the condolences as a positive step. Stefan Füle, the EU Commissioner for Enlargement and European Neighborhood Policy, said that "reconciliation is a key EU value" and expressed hope that candidate Turkey would follow up with actions.[39]

But Prime Minister Recep Tayyip Erdoğan's words were dismissed as "cold-hearted and cynical" by Aram Hamparian, the executive director of the ANCA.[40] This is unfair. Erdoğan's comments were an important step in reconciliation between Turkey and Armenia, the beginnings of a dialogue about an eventful period in history.

Despite differing interpretations on what the statement actually meant both in Turkey and abroad, Ankara did something unprecedented and clearly a courageous move to tackle one of the most painful and delicate issues for Turks and Armenians together.[41]

NOTES

1. Gerry Rankin, "Turkey-Armenia Talks Cause for Celebration," Community Commentary, Glendale News Press, 13 October 2009.
2. Matthew Lee, "Turkey, Armenia Sign Historic Peace Accord: Agreement Restores Diplomacy, Pays Way to Reopen Border," *The Washington Times*, 11 October 2009, p. A6.
3. "Armenian Scholar Supports Turkey Panel on Mass Killings," Radio Free Europe/Radio Liberty, 9 September 2009.
4. "Reconciling History," Editorial, *The Los Angeles Times*, 13 October 2009, p. A20.
5. Dyer, "Was a Massacre Genocide? The Armenian Diaspora Won't Take No for an Answer," p. A11 and idem, "Armenia: The End of the Debate?" p. 6.
6. Lord Brett's remarks in House of Lords 1121 Column WA200, 15 January 2010.
7. Hans Wilhelm Longva, "The Concept of Genocide in International Law," Conference on Turkish-Armenian Relationship, 1 February 2010, p. 5.
8. Desmond Butler, "Obama Silent Ahead of Vote on Armenian Genocide," The Associated Press, 27 February 2010.
9. Sarah Ludford, "US Congress Panel 'Armenian Genocide' Vote Wrong," 8 March 2010.
10. Congressional Record, House of Representatives, Proceedings and Debates of the 111th Congress 2d Session, Report 111-622 Together With Additional Views [To Accompany House Resolution 252], Affirmation of the United States Record on the Armenian Genocide Resolution, 22 September 2010, pp. 8 and 10.
11. Mark Meirowitz, "U.S.-Turkey Relations Are on the Line," *The Hill*, p. 1.
12. Michael Hancock, Frozen Conflicts and Europe's Security, A/WEU/POL (2010) 6, 5 May 2010.
13. The text of the question and answer can be found in http://www.parlament.ch/d/suche/seiten/ges.
14. Sefa Kaplan, "ABD Tarihçiler Komisyonunu Desteklesin" (Let the United States Support the Joint Commission of Historians), *Hürriyet*, 19 April 2011, p. 19; "US Congress Commemorates the Armenian Genocide," Center for Armenian Remembrance, 18 April 2011, p. 1.
15. "US Envoy: Turkey Must Deal With Ghosts of the Past," *Hürriyet Daily News*, 27 January 2012, p. 1.
16. Lord Howell's remarks in House of Lords Column 874, 16 June 2011.
17. European Commission Reply E-010180/2011, 20 December 2011.
18. The French law outlawing Holocaust denial is named after Jean-Claude Gayssot, the Communist deputy who introduced the bill. Many critics opposed legislating *vérité d'état* (state or official truth), and a strong right-wing contingent in the Senate rejected it three times. Eventually the National Assembly passed the bill a fourth time, and this broke the deadlock. Promulgated by President François Mitterand, the Gayssot bill became law on 13 July 1990.
19. Tariq Ramadan, "French Politics Over Armenian 'Genocide'," Opinion, 27 December 011, gulfnews.com.
20. Ibid.
21. Robert Badinter, "Le Parlement n'est pas un tribunal," *Le Monde*, 15 January 2012, p. 3.
22. Desmond Butler, "Clinton Sidesteps Dispute Over French Genocide Law," Associated Press, 27 January 2012.

23. "Schiff-Dold Letter Presses Clinton to Disavow Offensive Comment on Armenian Genocide," Press Release of the ANCA, 6 February 2012, p. 1; "Ermeni Diasporasını Kızdırdı" (She Angered the Armenian Diaspora), *Akşam*, 31 January 2012, p. 15.

24. Ottawa Unveils Monument to Slain Turkish Diplomat, as Armenians Recall Genocide, The Canadian Press, 20 September 2012. http://www.ctvnews.ca/canada/ottawa-unveils-monument-to-slain-turkish-diplomats-as-armenians-recall-genocide-1.965300

25. Richard Outzen, "Between Counterinsurgency and Genocide," Book Reviews, 18 September 2014, http://warontherocks.com

26. Text of the Moscow Treaty of 16 March 1921 signed between Turkey and the Soviet Union can be found in *Türkiye Dış Politikasında 50 Yıl Kurtuluş Savaşımız (1919–1922)*, pp. 113–121. The English translation is in *British and Foreign State Papers*, Vol. 118, pp. 990–996. The north-east frontier of Turkey is fixed as follows: A line which begins at the village of Sarp, situated on the coast of the Black Sea, goes over the Khedismta mountain, then by the line of watershed of the Şavşat and Kani mountains, after which it follows the northern border of the districts of Ardahan and Kars, then the thalweg of the Rivers Arpaçay and Aras to the mount of the Lower Karasu. A detailed description of the frontier and connected matters is given in Annex I (A) and (B) and on the attached map signed by both contracting parties. The treaty came into force after the instruments of ratification were exchanged at Kars on 13 September 1921.

27. "Town Halls Raise Awareness on Next Steps Against Protocols," *Asbarez*, 23 November 2009, p. 1.

28. Ibid.

29. Phillips, Diplomatic History, p. 67.

30. Ibid., pp. 68–69.

31. Michael Gunter and Dirk Rochtus, "Special Report: The Turkish-Armenian Rapprochement," *Middle East Critique*, Vol. 19, No. 2 (Summer 2010), pp. 170–171.

32. Gunter, *Armenian History and the Question of Genocide*, p. 136.

33. David Phillips, Turkey and Armenia at Loggerheads, The Huffington Post, 26 March 2013, http://www.huffingtonpost.com/david-l-phillips/turkey-and-armenia-at-logb2957700.html. This and the following paragraph mainly draw on this source.

34. Anatolian News Agency, 13 December 2013.

35. Anatolian News Agency, 23 April 2014.

36. Anatolian News Agency, 23 April 2014; Jonny Hogg, Reuters, 23 April 2014. This and the subsequent paragraphs are based on these sources. Full text of the Turkish Prime Minister Recep Tayyip Erdoğan's Message on the Armenian Events of 1915 is in Appendix 8.

37. Anatolian News Agency, 23 April 2014.

38. Ibid.

39. Anatolian News Agency, 24 April 2014.

40. ANCA Statement, 23 April 2014.

41. See, among many, Laure Marchand, "Ankara présente ses condoléances aux Arméniens," *Le Figaro*, 24 April 2014, pp. 1 and 11; Guillaume Goubert, "La Turquie et la mémoire," Editorial, *La Croix*, 24 April 2014, p. 1; Agnès Rotivel, "La Turquie d'Erdogan fait un pas en direction des Arméniens," ibid., 24 April 2014, p. 7; Ava Djamshidi, "Les condoléances de la Turquie," *Le Parisien*, 24 April 2014, p. 7; Françoise Germain-Robin, "Erdogan et ses condoléances," *L'Humanité*, 24 April 2014, p. 19; "Les condoléances d'Erdogan aux Arméniens," *Libération*, 24 April 2014, p. 9; "Des condoléances aux petits-fils des Arméniens tués en 1915," *20 Minutes*, 24 April 2014, p. 6; Nicolas Camus, "Génocide: le premier pas de la Turquie," *Metro News*, 24 April 2014, pp. 1 and 3; "Condoléances Turques," *Direct Matin*, 24 April 2014, p. 18; "Ankara Fait Un Geste Pour Les Arméniens," *Les Echos*, 24 April 2014, p. 12.

Conclusion

Dialogue between Turkish and Armenian interests is needed. Reasonable discussion can overcome many emotions and lead the way toward eventual rapprochement between the two countries and their peoples. Such a rapprochement will, in turn, pave the way for greater stability in the Middle East and Caucasia, improving not only Turkish-Armenian relations, but Azerbaijani-Armenian relations as well.

Turks and Armenians should explore and understand their common past together through a joint commission and collecting all relevant documents, from whatever source, and analyzing these using accepted methods. Such an effort is the fairest and, indeed, the only means for assessing the past, which will pave the way for reconciliation between the two nations, in lieu of politically charged legislative or executive declarations by third parties. Many welcomed the Turkish Prime Minister Recep Tayyip Erdoğan's call of 10 April 2005 for a truly objective, independent and scholarly evaluation of history. The Turkish government supports an international commission of experts with access to all relevant archives to make an authoritative characterization of the treatment of Ottoman Armenians in the name of historical truth and forward-looking reconciliation.

The Turkish President, Abdullah Gül, took the initiative and went to a soccer match in Armenia. That brought about a meeting between the governments of Turkey and Armenia to try to create movement on the subject. Turkey took the high ground, letting the world know that Turks welcome honest inquiry into their history. Turkey's proposal aimed to narrow the gap between the two sides by allowing historians and experts to work together and, more importantly, reach conclusions based on their research in all relevant archives.

President Gül's visit was the first time a Turkish leader had set foot in Armenia. It signaled a thaw in relations between the two countries.

On 10 October 2009 in Zurich, Turkish and Armenian Ministers of Foreign Affairs signed two protocols that would move their countries closer to normalization of relations. The protocols made no mention of genocide. This historically unprecedented agreement, between the two neighboring states, called for a historical commission to investigate the events of 1915. That was a constructive step.

The accord was hotly debated by the Armenian people worldwide. Most Armenians were critical of the planned creation of a Turkish-Armenian panel of historians that would probe the events of 1915. This was, according to them, a thoroughly discredited idea; there was no dispute among scholars that the Armenians were the subject of genocide during the waning years of the Ottoman Empire and an historical commission was another effort to obfuscate the truth. The clause outlining mutual recognition of the existing border between the two countries, as defined by the relevant treaties of international law and its implication for the question of demanding restitution for the Armenian losses, was also a matter of contention.

The traditional political parties—the ARF, the Social Democratic Hunchakian Party, and the Ramkavars—opposed the initiative, while the AAA and the AGBU issued conditional endorsements. The protocols' opponents organized a series of public protests and public meetings to denounce the deal as compromising Armenian interests.

The Turkish and Armenian governments were expected to submit the instruments to their respective parliaments for ratification. Moves in that direction were stalled after the Armenian Constitutional Court upheld the legality of the protocols of cooperation. The judgment of the court complicated matters because its ruling referred to an article of the Armenian constitution that relates to genocide and the country's borders.

Writing scholarly history should not be about one's own experiences and eyewitness accounts, it is in the systematic examination of surviving written sources of the past. This is a crucial matter and to seek the full truth, Turkey opened its archives for research many years ago. Oceans of documentary resources which appear to be unique in every historical sense poured from once-secret repositories. Fresh material is coming out to better interpret the past. Not only does each year and each month bring new materials and information, but each week and each day. These collections are fully available to scholars. The vast holdings are made easy to access by the public. Photocopying is easy and inexpensive. New finding aids are being added to the BOA on a continuing basis and new material is added to the ATASE daily. The Ottoman legacy is generating fascinating research across the social sciences and humanities.

The BOA is an integral part of Ottoman history and it is important for what it represents, what it contains, and what it suggests. It documents not only the actions of the Sublime Porte, but also justifications and deliberations surrounding these actions. It is the lifeblood for those who write about the Ottoman past. The researcher finds his efforts amply rewarded, as witnessed by the numerous studies in Ottoman history currently in progress by local scholars, for whom the BOA is almost a second home. With each passing year the flow of Turkish books, articles, and dissertations on the Armenian question increases at a dizzying pace. Many Turkish scholars have turned their attention to the BOA and the ATASE and discovered mountains of unexamined files. They have made use of these original source-materials, giving them the ability to challenge conventional wisdom with newly-exposed historical evidence and not just ideologically pleasing paradigms and critiques.

The NL in Ankara is an important source of manuscript as well as published materials. One large factor contributing to its growth is the Turkish Copyright Law which requires that a copy of every book or publication be deposited gratis with the NL. Since the 1970s historians of the Middle East have increasingly used Muslim court records deposited in the NL. These documents are the most important source for the socioeconomic history of Ottoman cities, and also greatly contribute to our understanding of the life of common people at the time. They offer glimpses of the daily endeavors of the individuals who came to the courts, not only for litigation or as defendants in criminal cases but also to notarize important legal transactions. The Muslim judge had a definite administrative function, and this is reflected in their records. Aside from their judicial duties, it was the task of the Muslim judges to supervise, certify and register various administrative actions and orders; in addition they had had important positions in the various financial departments of the central government.

In the past dozen years or more, a younger generation of Turkish historians working on the Ottoman Empire has emerged that is as remarkable for its imaginative and innovative qualities as for its exceptional quality. The names which readily spring to mind include Gökhan Çetinsaya, Behçet Yeşilbursa, Metin Hülagü, Azmi Özcan, Tufan Buzpınar, Feridun Ata, Erhan Afyoncu and Hakan Erdem. It is an exciting time to research and write the history of the Ottoman world. Great quantities of Ottoman records—undoubtedly relevant for the historian—as well as for such related disciplines as Ottoman studies, sociology, and anthropology, remain to be evaluated and used.

Remarkably, the world has also shown much interest in Ottoman archives. Foreign researchers have found the BOA to be an important resource to complement the information available in archival records in their own countries. The repositories of the Ottoman Empire hold collections of great significance for nearly all aspects of Ottoman history and for many topics of European and world history. Destruction of the archives by fire or during the First World War was less extensive than has been apparently thought. In addition, several Balkan and Middle Eastern countries have turned over to Turkish authorities for special collections relevant to Ottoman history.

Each year more than a thousand investigators from outside Turkey work in the BOA, the largest proportion of whom come from the United States, Britain, France, Germany, Russia, Israel, and several Arab countries. Working in İstanbul has always been a great pleasure for foreign scholars, thanks in large part to the kindness and hospitality of the officials in charge of the archives there. They are unanimous in praising the efficiency, courtesy, and general helpfulness of the archival staff. Researchers are respected as scholars who have taken the time and trouble to master the complex language and scripts utilized in the Ottoman administration. Further, they are welcomed as friends who share the deep attachment of the archivists to the Ottoman past.

It is to be hoped, therefore, that the body of archival material now being unearthed in İstanbul, if rigorously subjected to the canons of historical criticism and used in conjunction with other qualitative material, may produce the work of genuine historical research into every aspect of the history of Turkish-Armenian relations.

Much remains to be done by governments and institutions that retain some portion of the shared recollection of the events of hundred years ago. Statesmen and politicians make history, and scholars write it. For this process to work scholars must be given unfettered access to the written records of the statesmen and politicians of the past.

There are files and collections still to be found and identified; there are files and archives to which access must be made more responsive to the needs of researchers, and there are files and collections that must be declassified and exposed to the light of scholarly scrutiny. Such material may provide guidance for the diplomat and policy maker to enrich his understanding of the past. It can serve as a vehicle to bring Turks and Armenians to an understanding of their common heritage.

One has been much taken with new discoveries from the Russian archives. For quite some time, the closely kept secrets in Czarist and Soviet files remained hidden and all efforts to research such records were turned away with spurious claims that such documents did not even exist.

The collapse of the Soviet Union in December 1991 opened (and partially reclosed) many Russian archives to international researchers. Since those early days, matters have improved. Archives have been opened on a more regular basis. Although Russian archivists are striving to put into effect a thirty-year rule for declassification, it is not automatic. Local and western historians, finally able to immerse themselves in primary sources, are producing invaluable works describing the non-Russian periphery of the former Soviet state. Russian foreign policy and military strategy during the First World War and in its aftermath is likely to be greatly redrawn on the basis of new material beginning to become available. The newly declassified documents allow us to add to or revise our understanding of certain aspects of the Armenian question. Turkish scholars have to travel to the archives in Moscow and St. Petersburg in order to uncover, study, translate, and photocopy the relevant materials.

Records on the intelligence operations of the First World War belligerents are slowly being declassified, but there is still a long way to go. This is especially true for the intelligence, counterintelligence, and code-breaking activities of the British. As always with intelligence sources, one must wonder what has been left out. Access to the records of the EMSIB will help to clarify the still-grey areas of British operations of the period. The officials of the NA should surely microfilm that large portion of records they are still refusing to declassify because, by the time they do declassify them in later decades, the records themselves may have disintegrated. Every step toward further openings should be welcomed by people who are interested in the First World War that shook the world and its inhabitants on an unprecedented scale.

The massive number of archive volume from the First World War—both those now available and those either still closed or until quite recently inaccessible—guarantees that there will be new perspectives and interpretations. There will be no lack of issues to probe and prior interpretations to review. The First World War will justifiably continue to excite the interest of both historians and the public.

While Armenian historians are examining Ottoman records, Turkish and other interested historians should also be looking at the Armenian archives in order that a more balanced picture of the period can be achieved. All this will make it possible for eligible scholars to begin unraveling the tangled threads of the Anatolian Armenians during the closing decades of the Ottoman Empire and to examine more intensely the larger question of Turkish and Armenian relations throughout the 623-year history of the Ottoman state. Such an effort will be well worth while.

Appendix 1

CRIMINAL CONVICTION FOR DENIAL THAT THE ATROCITIES PERPETRATED AGAINST THE ARMENIAN PEOPLE IN 1915 AND YEARS AFTER CONSTITUTED GENOCIDE WAS UNJUSTIFIED (PRESS RELEASE ISSUED BY THE REGISTRAR OF THE EUROPEAN COURT OF HUMAN RIGHTS. ECHR 370 (2013), 17 DECEMBER 2013)

In today's Chamber judgment in the case of Perinçek v. Switzerland (application no. 27510/08), which is not final[1], the European Court of Human Rights held, by a majority, that there had been a violation of Article 10 (freedom of expression) of the European Convention on Human Rights.

The case concerned the criminal conviction of Mr. Perinçek for publicly challenging the existence of the Armenian genocide.

The Court found that Mr. Perinçek, who during various conferences in Switzerland, had described the Armenian genocide as an "international lie," had not committed an abuse of his rights within the meaning of Article 17 of the Convention.

The Court underlined that the free exercise of the right to openly discuss questions of a sensitive and controversial nature was one of the fundamental aspects of freedom of expression and distinguished a tolerant and pluralistic democratic society from a totalitarian or dictatorial regime.

The Court also pointed out that it was not called upon to rule on the legal characterisation of the Armenian genocide. The existence of a "genocide," which was a precisely defined legal concept, was not easy to prove. The Court doubted that there could be a general consensus as to events such as those at issue, given that historical research was by definition open to discussion and a matter of debate, without necessarily giving rise to final conclusions or to the assertion of objective and absolute truths.

Lastly, the Court observed that those States which had officially recognised the Armenian genocide had not found it necessary to enact laws imposing criminal sanctions on individuals questioning the official view, being mindful that one of the main goals of freedom of expression was to protect minority views capable of contributing to a debate on questions of general interest which were not fully settled.

PRINCIPAL FACTS

The applicant, Doğu Perinçek, is a Turkish national who was born in 1942 and lives in Ankara (Turkey). Being a doctor of laws and the Chairman of the Turkish Workers' Party, Mr. Perinçek participated in various conferences in Switzerland in May, July, and September 2005, during which he publicly denied that the Ottoman Empire had perpetrated the crime of genocide against the Armenian people in 1915 and the following years. He described the idea of an Armenian genocide as an "international lie."

The association "Switzerland-Armenia" filed a criminal complaint against him on 15 July 2005. On 9 March 2007 the Lausanne Police Court found Mr. Perinçek guilty of racial discrimination within the meaning of the Swiss Criminal Code, finding that his motives were of a racist tendency and did not contribute to the historical debate.

Mr. Perinçek lodged an appeal that was dismissed by the Criminal Cassation Division of the Vaud Cantonal Court. In that court's view, the Armenian genocide, like the Jewish genocide, was a proven historical fact, recognised by the Swiss legislature on the date of the adoption of Article 261bis of the Criminal Code. The courts did not therefore need to refer to the work of historians in order to accept its existence. The Cassation Division emphasised that Mr. Perinçek had only denied the characterisation as genocide without calling into question the existence of the massacres and deportations of Armenians.

The Federal Court dismissed a further appeal by Mr. Perinçek in a judgment of 12 December 2007.

COMPLAINTS, PROCEDURE AND COMPOSITION OF THE COURT

Relying on Article 10 (freedom of expression), Mr. Perinçek complained that the Swiss courts had breached his freedom of expression. He argued, in particular, that Article 261bis, paragraph 4, of the Swiss Criminal Code was not sufficiently foreseeable in its effect, that his conviction had not been justified by the pursuit of a legitimate aim and that the alleged breach of his freedom of expression had not been "necessary in a democratic society".

The application was lodged with the European Court of Human Rights on 10 June 2008. The Turkish Government submitted written comments as a third party.

Judgment was given by a Chamber of seven judges, composed as follows:
Guido Raimondi (Italy), President,
Peer Lorenzen (Denmark),
Dragoljub Popović (Serbia),
András Sajó (Hungary),
Nebojša Vučinić (Montenegro),
Paulo Pinto de Albuquerque (Portugal),
Helen Keller (Switzerland),
And also Stanley Naismith, Section Registrar.

DECISION OF THE COURT

Article 17

The Court, in first examining whether Mr. Perinçek's comments were to be excluded from the protection of freedom of expression on the basis of Article 17 (prohibition of abuse of rights), reiterated that ideas which offended, shocked or disturbed were also protected by Article 10. The Court found it necessary to point out that Mr. Perinçek had never questioned the massacres and deportations perpetrated during the years in question but had denied the characterisation of those events as "genocide".

The limit beyond which comments may engage Article 17 lay in the question whether the aim of the speech was to incite hatred or violence. The rejection of the legal characterisation as "genocide" of the 1915 events was not such as to incite hatred against the Armenian people. Mr. Perinçek had never in fact been prosecuted or convicted for inciting hatred. Nor had he expressed contempt for the victims of the events. The Court therefore found that Mr. Perinçek had not abused his right to openly discuss such questions, however sensitive and controversial they might be, and had not used his right to freedom of expression for ends which were contrary to the text and spirit of the Convention.

ARTICLE 10

The Court took the view that the term "genocide" as used in the relevant Article of the Swiss Criminal Code was likely to raise doubts as to the precision required by Article 10/2 of the Convention. The Court nevertheless agreed with the Federal Court that Mr. Perinçek could not have been unaware that by describing the Armenian genocide as an "international lie", he was exposing himself on Swiss territory to a criminal sanction "prescribed by law."

The Court found that the aim of the measure in issue was to protect the rights of others, namely the honour of the relatives of victims of the atrocities perpetrated by the Ottoman Empire against the Armenian people from 1915 onwards. However, it regarded as insufficiently substantiated the Government's argument that Mr. Perinçek's comments posed a serious risk to public order.

The Court pointed out that it was not called upon to address either the veracity of the massacres and deportations perpetrated against the Armenian people by the Ottoman Empire from 1915 onwards, or the appropriateness of legally characterising those acts as "genocide", within the meaning of the relevant Article of the Criminal Code. The Court had to weigh up, on the other hand, the requirements of protecting the rights of third parties, namely the honour of the relatives of the Armenian victims, and on the other, Mr. Perinçek's freedom of expression.

The question whether the events of 1915 and thereafter could be characterised as "genocide" was of great interest to the general public. The Court took the view that Mr. Perinçek had engaged in speech of a historical,legal and political nature which was part of a heated debate. On account of the public interest of his comments, the Court found that the authorities' margin of appreciation was limited.

The essential ground for Mr. Perinçek's conviction by the Swiss courts was the apparent existence of a general consensus, especially in the academic community, concerning the legal characterisation of the events in question. However, the Federal Court itself admitted that there was no unanimity in the community as a whole concerning the legal characterisation in question. According to Mr. Perinçek and the Turkish Government, a third-party intervener in the case, it would be very difficult to identify a general consensus. The Court shared that opinion, pointing out that there were differing views among the Swiss political organs themselves. It appeared, moreover, that only about twenty States out of the 190 in the world had officially recognised the Armenian genocide. Such recognition had not necessarily come from the governments of those States—as was the case in Switzerland—but from Parliament or one of its chambers.

Agreeing with Mr. Perinçek, the Court took the view that the notion of "genocide" was a precisely defined legal concept. According to the case-law of the International Court of Justice and the International Criminal Tribunal for Rwanda, for the crime of genocide to be made out, the acts must have been perpetrated with intent to destroy not only certain members of a particular group but all or part of the group itself. Genocide was a very narrow legal concept that was, moreover, difficult to substantiate. The Court was not convinced that the general consensus to which the courts referred in convicting Mr. Perinçek could relate to such very specific points of law.

The Court thus doubted that there could be a general consensus as to events such as those in issue here, given that historical research was by definition open to discussion and a matter of debate, without necessarily giving rise to final conclusions or to the assertion of objective and absolute truths.

In this connection, the Court clearly distinguished the present case from those concerning the negation of the crimes of the Holocaust. In those cases, the applicants had denied the historical facts even though they were sometimes very concrete, such as the existence of the gas chambers. They had denied the crimes perpetrated by the Nazi regime for which there had been a clear legal basis. Lastly, the acts that they had called into question had been found by an international court to be clearly established.

The Court took the view that Switzerland had failed to show how there was a social need in that country to punish an individual for racial discrimination on the basis of declarations challenging the legal characterisation as "genocide" of acts perpetrated on the territory of the former Ottoman Empire in 1915 and the following years.

Two developments also had to be taken into account. Firstly, the Spanish Constitutional Court, in November 2007, had found unconstitutional the offence of negation and had taken the view that the mere negation of a crime of genocide did not constitute direct incitement to violence. Secondly, in February 2012, the French Constitutional Council had declared unconstitutional a law which made it a criminal offence to deny the existence of the genocides recognised by the law, finding it to be incompatible with freedom of expression and freedom of research. In the Court's view, the decision of the French Constitutional Council showed that there was in principle no contradiction between the official recognition of certain events as genocide and the conclusion that it would be unconstitutional to impose criminal sanctions on persons who questioned the official view.

Lastly, the Court pointed out that the United Nations Human Rights Committee had expressed its conviction[2] that "[l]aws that penalize[d] the expression of opinions about historical facts [were] incompatible with the obligations that the Covenant [on Civil and Political Rights] impose[d] on States parties…" and that the "Covenant [did] not permit general prohibition of expressions of an erroneous opinion or an incorrect interpretation of past events".

In conclusion, the Court doubted that Mr. Perinçek's conviction had been dictated by a "pressing social need". The Court pointed out that it had to ensure that the sanction did not constitute a kind of censorship which would lead people to refrain from expressing criticism. In a debate of general interest, such a sanction might dissuade contributions to the public discussion of questions which were of interest for the life of the community.

The Court found that the grounds given by the national authorities in order to justify Mr. Perinçek's conviction were insufficient. The domestic authorities had therefore overstepped the narrow margin of appreciation in this case in respect of a matter of debate of undeniable public interest.

There had accordingly been a violation of Article 10.

JUST SATISFACTION (ARTICLE 41)

The Court held that the finding of a violation of Article 10 constituted in itself sufficient just satisfaction for any non-pecuniary damage sustained by Mr. Perinçek.

SEPARATE OPINIONS

Judges Sajó and Raimondi expressed a joint concurring opinion and Judges Vučinić and Pinto de Albuquerque expressed a joint partly dissenting opinion. These opinions are annexed to the judgment.

NOTES

1. Under Articles 43 and 44 of the Convention, this Chamber judgment is not final. During the three-month period following its delivery, any party may request that the case be referred to the Grand Chamber of the Court. If such a request is made, a panel of five judges considers whether the case deserves further examination. In that event, the Grand Chamber will hear the case and deliver a final judgment. If the referral request is refused, the Chamber judgment will become final on that day. Once a judgment becomes final, it is transmitted to the Committee of Ministers of the Council of Europe for supervision of its execution. Further information about the execution process can be found here: www.coe.int/t/dghl/monitoring/execution.

2. General comment No. 34, given in 2011, on freedom of opinion and expression under Article 19 of the International Covenant on Civil and Political Rights.

Appendix 2

THE TURKISH PRIME MINISTER RECEP TAYYİP ERDOĞAN'S OFFICIAL LETTER ADDRESSED TO THE ARMENIAN PRESIDENT ROBERT KOCHARIAN OF 10 APRIL 2005 (ANATOLIAN NEWS AGENCY, 10 APRIL 2005)

His Excellency Robert Kocharian
President
Republic of Armenia
Yerevan

Dear Mr. President,

The Turkish and Armenian peoples not only shared a common history and geography in a sensitive region of the world, but also lived together over a long period of time. However, it is not a secret that we have diverging interpretations of events that took place during a particular period of our common history.

These differences that have in the past left behind traces of painful memories for our nations continue to hamper the improvement of friendly relations between our two counries today.

I believe that, as leaders of our countries, our primary duty is to leave to our future generations a peaceful and friendly environment in which tolerance and mutual respect shall prevail.

These views are also shared by the leader of our main opposition party, Mr. Deniz Baykal, the Chairman of the Republican People's Party (CHP). Within this framework, we are extending an invitation to your country to establish a joint group consisting of historians and other experts from our two countries to study the developments and events of 1915 not only in the archives of Turkey and Armenia but also in the archives of all relevant third countries and to share their findings with the international community.

I believe that such an iniative would shed light on a disputed period of history and also constitute a step towards contributing to the normalization of relations between our countries.

I hope that our proposal, which aims to create a friendly and more peaceful climate to be passed on to future generations, will meet with your consent. If we receive a favorable response from your side to our proposal of forming such a group, we will be ready to discuss the details of this proposal with your country.

Sincerely,
Recep Tayyip Erdoğan

Appendix 3

ARMENIAN PRESIDENT ROBERT KOCHARIAN'S
OFFICIAL RESPONSE OF 25 APRIL 2005
TO THE LETTER OF THE TURKISH PRIME MINISTER
RECEP TAYYİP ERDOĞAN
(ANATOLIAN NEWS AGENCY, 25 APRIL 2005)

H.E. Recep Tayyip Erdoğan
Prime Minister
Republic of Turkey
Ankara

Dear Prime Minister,

I'm in receipt of your letter. Indeed, as two neighbors, we both must work to find ways to live together in harmony. That is why, from the first day, we have extended our hand to you to establish relations, open the border, and thus start a dialogue between the two countries and two peoples.

There are neighboring countries, particularly on the European continent, who have had a difficult past, about which they differ. However, that has not stopped them from having open borders, normal relations, diplomatic ties, representatives in each other's capitals, even as they continue to discuss that which divides them.

Your suggestion to address the past cannot be effecive if it deflects from addressing the present and future. In order to engage in a useful dialogue, we need to create the appropriate and conducive political environment. It is the responsibility of governments to develop bilateral relations and we do not have the right to delegate that responsibility to historians. That is why we have proposed and propose again that, without pre-conditions, we establish normal relations between our two countries.

In that context, an intergovernmental commission can meet to discuss any and all outstanding issues between our two nations, with the aim of resolving them and coming to an understanding.

Sincerely,
Robert Kocharian

Appendix 4

PROTOCOL ON THE ESTABLISHMENT OF DIPLOMATIC RELATIONS BETWEEN THE REPUBLIC OF TURKEY AND THE REPUBLIC OF ARMENIA (ANATOLIAN NEWS AGENCY, 10 OCTOBER 2009)

The Republic of Turkey and the Republic of Armenia,

Desiring to establish good neighborly relations and to develop bilateral cooperation in the political, economic, cultural and other fields for the benefit of their peoples, as envisaged in the Protocol on Development of Relations signed on the same day,

Referring to their obligations under the Charter of the United Nations, the Helsinki Final Act, the Charter of Paris for a New Europe,

Reconfirming their commitment, in their bilateral and international relations, to respect and ensure respect for the principles of equality, sovereignty, non-intervention in internal affairs of other states, territorial integrity and inviolability of frontiers,

Bearing in mind the importance of the creation and maintenance of an atmosphere of trust and confidence between the two countries that will contribute to the strengthening of peace, security, and stability of the whole region, as well as being determined to refrain from the threat or the use of force, to promote the peaceful settlement of disputes, and to protect human rights and fundamental freedoms,

Confirming the mutual recognition of the existing border between the two countries as defined by the relevant treaties of law,

Emphasizing their decision to open the common border,

Reiterating their commitment to refrain from pursuing any policy incompatible with the spirit of good neighborly relations,

Condemning all forms of terrorism, violence and extremism irrespective of their cause, pledging to refrain from encouraging and tolerating such acts and to cooperate in combating against them,

Affirming their willingness to chart a new pattern and course for their relations on the basis of common interests, goodwill and in pursuit of peace, mutual understanding and harmony,

Agree to establish diplomatic relations as of the date of the entry into force of this Protocol in accordance with the Vienna Convention on Diplomatic Relations of 1961 and to exchange Diplomatic Missions,

This Protocol and the Protocol on Development of Relations between the Republic of Turkey and the Republic of Armenia shall enter into force on the same day, i.e. on the first day of the first month following the exchange of instruments of ratification.

Signed in Zurich on October 10, 2009 in Turkish, Armenian and English authentic copies in duplicate. In case of divergence of interpretation, the English text shall prevail.

For the Republic of Turkey
Ahmet Davutoğlu
Foreign Minister of the Republic of Turkey

For the Republic of Armenia
Edward Nalbandian
Foreign Minister of the Republic of Armenia

Appendix 5

PROTOCOL ON DEVELOPMENT OF RELATIONS BETWEEN THE REPUBLIC OF TURKEY AND THE REPUBLIC OF ARMENIA (ANATOLIAN NEWS AGENCY, 10 OCTOBER 2009)

The Republic of Turkey and the Republic of Armenia,

Guided by the Protocol on the Establishment of Diplomatic Relations between the Republic of Turkey and the Republic of Armenia signed on the same day,

Considering the perspectives of developing their bilateral relations, based on confidence and respect to their mutual interests,

Determining to develop and enhance their bilateral relations, in the political, economic, energy, transport, scientific, technical, cultural issues and other fields, based on common interests of both countries,

Supporting the promotion of cooperation between the two countries in the international and regional organizations, especially within the framework of the UN, the OSCE, the Council of Europe, the Euro-Atlantic Partnership Council and the BSEC (Black Sea Economic Cooperation),

Taking into account the common purpose of both States to cooperate for enhancing regional stability and security for ensuring the democratic and sustainable development of the region,

Reiterating their commitment to the peaceful settlement of regional and international disputes and conflicts on the basis of the norms and principles of international law,

Reaffirming their readiness to actively support the actions of the international community in addressing common security threats to the region and world security and stability, such as terrorism, transnational organized crimes, illicit trafficking of drugs and arms,

1. Agree to open the common border within 2 months after the entry into force of this Protocol,

2. Agree to conduct regular political consultations between the Ministries of Foreign Affairs of the two countries;

implement a dialogue on the historical dimension with the aim to restore mutual confidence between the two nations, including an impartial scientific examination of the historical records and archives to define existing problems and formulate recommendations;

make the best possible use of existing transport, communications and energy infrastructure and networks between the two countries, and to undertake measures in this regard;

develop the bilateral legal framework in order to foster cooperation between the two countries;

cooperate in the fields of science and education by encouraging relations between the appropriate institutions as well as promoting the exchange of specialists and students, and act with the aim of preserving the cultural heritage of both sides and launching common cultural projects;

establish consular cooperation in accordance with the Vienna Convention on Consular Relations of 1963 in order to provide necessary assistance and protection to the citizens of the two countries;

take concrete measures in order to develop trade, tourism and economic cooperation between the two countries;

engage in a dialogue and reinforce their cooperation on environmental issues.

3. Agree on the establishment of an intergovernmental bilateral commission which shall comprise separate sub-commissions for the prompt implementation of the commitments mentioned in operational paragraph 2 above in this Protocol. To prepare the working modalities of the intergovernmental commission and its sub-commissions, a working group headed by the two Ministers of Foreign Affairs shall be created 2 months after the day following the entry into force of this Protocol. Within 3 months after the entry into force of this Protocol, these modalities shall be approved at ministerial level. The intergovernmental commission shall meet for the first time immediately after the adoption of the said modalities. The sub-commissions shall start their work at the latest 1 month thereafter and they shall work continuously until the completion of their mandates. Where appropriate, international experts shall take part in the sub-commissions.

The timetable and elements agreed by both sides for the implementation of this Protocol are mentioned in the annexed document, which is an integral part of this Protocol.

This Protocol and the Protocol on the Establishment of Diplomatic Relations between the Republic of Turkey and the Republic of Armenia shall enter into force on the same day, i.e. on the first day of the first month following the exchange of instruments of ratification.

Signed in Zurich on October 10, 2009 in Turkish, Armenian and English authentic copies in duplicate. In case of divergence of interpretation, the English text shall prevail.

For the Republic of Turkey
Ahmet Davutoğlu
Foreign Minister of the Republic of Turkey

For the Republic of Armenia
Edward Nalbandian
Foreign Minister of the Republic of Armenia

Appendix 6

THE STATEMENT THAT WAS TO BE MADE BY THE TURKISH MINISTER OF FOREIGN AFFAIRS AHMET DAVUTOĞLU AFTER THE SIGNING CEREMONY OF THE TURKISH-ARMENIAN PROTOCOLS OF 10 OCTOBER 2009 (ANATOLIAN NEWS AGENCY, 10 OCTOBER 2009)

Madame Federal Counselor,
Distinguished Colleagues,
Ladies and Gentlemen,

Today we are here as Turkey and Armenia to take an important step in embarking upon a new road. This road is long. This road is fraught with difficulties. However, it is worth travelling. This journey can only be made hand in hand with our partners present here, as well as all the peoples of the Caucasus.

I consider myself to be fortunate enough to see that a vision, a courageous step that has taken a considerable time to develop, has finally reached maturity. Indeed, this is a historic moment that we need to cherish and be proud of.

A few years ago there were those who didn't believe that we could ever reach this stage. We have proven them wrong.Today we celebrate an important stage in the process of normalizing relations between Turkey and Armenia.

The initiative launched in the Autumn of 2007 that has made this ceremony possible, has brought two neighboring countries closer together.

In this historic juncture, I would like to make the following call upon the Turkish and Armenian nations across the world and the international community:

- we don't want to live with frozen conflicts that affect the stability of our neighborhood.
- we don't want unresolved issues and animosities.
- we want to resolve our bilateral problems and to achieve harmony among all nations in our region.
- we want to help establish a new order that is beneficial for all.
- we want to achieve a new perspective for the Caucasus that entails comprehensive normalization.
- we had proposed the establishment of the Caucasus Stability and Cooperation Platform for this reason. This was also the motivation for our efforts in the Middle East and the Balkans.
- we want prosperity in our region. Our neighbors' prosperity is our prosperity.
- we all have responsibilities to achieve comprehensive peace, including those present here today.
- we all know that achieving peace is not easy. Only the visionary and courageous can take such steps under difficult circumstances. Turkey and Armenia have taken this step.

Dear Friends,

Our host, Switzerland, competently assumed a very important and constructive role in this process. I would like to express through the Head of the Swiss Federal Department of Foreign Affairs, Her Excellency Madame Micheline Calmy-Rey, my sincere gratitude to Switzerland for this valuable contribution and her hospitality.

I would also like to thank those guests who are present at this ceremony; our dear colleagues, Hillary, Sergey; Bernard, Samuel and Javier.

Ladies and Gentlemen,

This is not only a historic moment for the future of the relations between Turkey and Armenia, but also between the Turkish and Armenian peoples. The signatures we have placed on the Protocols today represent a first step towards the effective normalization of our bilateral relations. We genuinely believe that this process will be crowned with success.

The normalization of relations between the two countries and peoples constitute an exemplary achievement of a new civilizational policy approach, in line with the requirements and expectations of the 21st century.

The success of the normalization of our relations, no doubt, will depend on the continuation of the courage and determined political will displayed by the parties today. Turkey is ready to build with her neighbor, Armenia, a common vision for the future.

We expect that this joint initiative which seeks to cultivate compromise and good-neighborly relations will foster other compromises in our region. This is the method to shape the present and prepare the future of our common region.

Distinguished Colleagues,

The documents that we have just signed create important ground for the Turkish and Armenian peoples to rekindle their friendship, to be able to offer coming generations the spirit to live and work together towards building a common and prosperous future.

These Protocols provide us opportunities that will serve the better interests of both Turkish and Armenian peoples. We look forward to working together with Armenia in order to make the most of these opportunities.

Dear Colleagues and Distinguished Guests,

Turkish and Armenian peoples have a different perception of the events of a very tragic period of common history. We should not leave to our future generations a legacy of prejudice and vengeance.

The Protocol on Development of Relations also addresses this issue.

We are confident that the Sub-Commission foreseen in this Protocol will scientifically examine the painful episode of our common history and shed light on the truth.

This is the only way for these two great and dignified nations to leave behind the conflict of their collective memories and jointly reach an understanding on historical facts as well as a just memory.

It is an honor to sign these Protocols on behalf of the Republic of Turkey. I hope they will pave the way for a wide normalization and comprehensive peace in the region.

Ladies and Gentlemen,

This is the day for peace.

This is the day for courage.

This is the day for wisdom.

And I truly believe that everybody in this hall shares this vision.

Thank you.

Appendix 7

ATTENTION MEMBERS OF THE U.S. HOUSE OF REPRESENTATIVES (*THE WASHINGTON POST* AND *THE NEW YORK TIMES*, 19 MAY 1985)

The undersigned American academicians who specialize in Turkish Ottoman and Middle Eastern studies are concerned that the current language embodied in House Joint Resolution 192 is misleading and/or inaccurate in several respects.

Specifically, while fully supporting the concept of a "National Day of Remembrance of Man's Inhumanity to Man," we respectfully take exception to that portion of the text which singles out for special recognition:

"… the one and one half million people of Armenian ancestry who were victims of genocide perpetrated in Turkey between 1915 and 1923 …"

Our reservations focus on the use of the words "Turkey" and "genocide" and may be summarized as follows:

From the fourteenth century until 1922, the area currently known as Turkey, or more correctly, the Republic of Turkey, was part of the territory encompassing the multi-national, multi-religious state known as the Ottoman Empire. It is wrong to equate the Ottoman Empire with the Republic of Turkey in the same way that it is wrong to equate the Hapsburg Empire with the Republic of Austria. The Ottoman Empire, which was brought to an end in 1922, by the successful conclusion of the Turkish Revolution which established the present day Republic of Turkey in 1923, incorporated lands and peoples which today account for more than twenty-five distinct countries in Southeastern Europe, North Africa, and the Middle East, only one of which is the Republic of Turkey. The Republic of Turkey bears no responsibility for any events which occurred in Ottoman times, yet by naming "Turkey" in the Resolution, its authors have implicitly labeled it as guilty of the "genocide" it charges transpired between 1915 and 1923;

As for the charge of "genocide," no signatory of this statement wishes to minimize the scope of Armenian suffering. We are likewise cognizant that it cannot be viewed as separate from the suffering experienced by the Muslim inhabitants of the region. The weight of evidence so far uncovered points in the direction of serious inter-communal warfare (perpetrated by Muslim and Christian irrregular forces), complicated by disease, famine, suffering and massacres in Anatolia and adjoining areas during the First World War. Indeed, throughout the years in question, the region was the scene of more or less continuous warfare, not unlike the tragedy which has gone on in Lebanon for the past decade. The resulting death toll among both Muslim and Christian communities of the region was immense. But much more remains to be discovered before historians will be able to sort out precisely responsibility between warring and innocent, and to identify the causes for the events which resulted in the death or removal of large numbers of the eastern Anatolian population, Christian and Muslim alike.

Statesmen and politicians make history, and scholars write it. For this process to work scholars must be given access to the written records of the statesmen and politicians of the past. To date, the relevant archives in the Soviet Union, Syria, Bulgaria and Turkey all remain, for the most part, closed to dispassionate historians. Until they become available the history of the Ottoman Empire in the period encompassed by H. J. Res. 192 (1915-1923) cannot be adequately known.

We believe that the proper position for the United States Congress to take on this and related issues, is to encourage full and open access to all historical archives, and not to make charges on historical events before they are fully understood. Such charges as those contained in H. J. Res. 192 would inevitably reflect unjustly upon the people of Turkey, and perhaps set back irreparably progress historians are just now beginning to achieve in understanding these tragic events.

As the above comments illustrate, the history of the Ottoman-Armenians is much debated among scholars, many of whom do not agree with the historical assumptions embodied in the wording of H. J. Res. 192. By passing the resolution, Congress will be attempting to determine by legislation which side of a historical question is correct. Such a resolution, based on historically questionable assumptions, can only damage the cause of honest historical enquiry, and damage the credibility of the American legislative process.

Signatories to the Statement on House Joint Resolution 192 Addressed to the Members of the U.S. House of Representatives:

Rifaat Abou-el-Haj, professor of history, California State University at Long Beach.

Sarah Moment Atis, associate professor of Turkish language and literature, University of Wisconsin at Madison.

Karl Barbir, associate professor of history, Siena College (New York).

Ilhan Basgoz, Director of the Turkish Studies Program at the Department of Uralic and Altaic Studies, Indiana University.

Daniel G. Bates, professor of anthropology, Hunter College, City University of New York.

Ulku Bates, professor of art history, Hunter College, City College of New York.

Gustav Bayerle, professor of Uralic and Altaic Studies, Indiana University.

Andras G. E. Bodrogligetti, professor of Turkic and Iranian Languages, University of California at Los Angeles.

Kathleen Burrill, associate professor of Turkish studies, Columbia University.

Timothy Childs, professorial lecturer, SAIS, Johns Hopkins University.

Shafiga Daulet, associate professor of political science, University of Connecticut.

Roderic Davison, professor of history, George Washington University, Washington, DC.

Walter Denny, professor of art history and Near Eastern studies, University of Massachusetts.

Dr. Alan Duben, anthropologist, researcher, New York City.

Ellen Ervin, research assistant professor of Turkish, New York University.

Caesar Farah, professor of Islamic and Middle Eastern history, University of Minnesota.

Carter Findley, associate professor of history, the Ohio State University.

Michael Finefrock, professor of history, College of Charleston.

Alan Fisher, professor of history, Michigan State University.

Cornell Fleischer, assistant professor of history, Washington University (Missouri).

Peter Golden, professor of history, Rutgers University, Newark.

Tom Goodrich, professor of history, Indiana University of Pennsylvania.

Andrew Gould, Ph. D. in Ottoman history, Flagstaff, Arizona.

William Griswold, professor of history, Colorado State University.

Tibor Halasi-Kun, professor emeritus of Turkish studies, Columbia University.

William Hickman, associate professor of Turkish, University of California, Berkeley.

J. C. Hurewitz, professor of government emeritus, former director of the Middle East Institute (1971-1984), Columbia University.

John Hymes, professor of history, Glenville State College, West Virginia.

Halil Inalcik, university professor of Ottoman history and member of the American Academy of Arts & Sciences, University of Chicago.

Ralph Jaeckel, visiting assistant professor of Turkish, University of California at Los Angeles.

Ronald Jennings, associate professor of history and Asian studies, University of Illinois.

James Kelly, associate professor of Turkish, University of Utah.

Kerim Key, adjunct professor, Southeastern University, Washington, DC.

Metin Kunt, professor of Ottoman history, New York City.

Frederick Latimer, associate professor of history, retired, University of Utah.

Avigdor Levy, professor of history, Brandeis University.

Bernard Lewis, Cleveland E. Dodge Professor of Near Eastern History, Princeton University.

Dr. Heath W. Lowry, Institute of Turkish Studies, Inc., Washington, DC.

Justin McCarthy, associate professor of history, University of Louisville.

Jon Mandaville, professor of the history of the Middle East, Portland State University (Oregon).

Michael Meeker, professor of anthropology, University of California at San Diego.

Rhoads Murphy, assistant professor of Middle Eastern languages and cultures and history, Columbia University.

Thomas Naff, professor of history and director, Middle East Research Institute, University of Pennsylvania.

Pierre Oberling, professor of history, Hunter College of the City University of New York.

William Ochsenwald, associate professor of history, Virginia Polytechnic Institute.

Robert Olson, associate professor of history, University of Kentucky.

William Peachy, assistant professor of the Judaic and Near Eastern languages and literatures, the Ohio State University.

Donald Quataert, associate professor of history, University of Houston.

Howard Reed, professor of history, University of Connecticut.

Dankwart Rustow, distinguished university professor of political science, City University Graduate School, New York.

Ezel Kural Shaw, associate professor of history, California State University, Northridge.

Stanford Shaw, professor of history, University of California at Los Angeles.

Elaine Smith, Ph. D. in Turkish history, retired Foreign Service Officer, Washington, DC.

Grace M. Smith, visiting lecturer in Turkish, University of California at Berkeley.

John Masson Smith, Jr., professor of history, University of California at Berkeley.

Dr. Svat Soucek, Turcologist, New York City.

Robert Staab, assistant director of the Middle East Center, University of Utah.

June Starr, associate professor of anthropology, SUNY Stoneybrook.

James Stewart-Robinson, professor of Turkish studies, University of Michigan.

Dr. Philip Stoddard, executive director, Middle East Institute, Washington, DC.

Frank Tachau, professor of political science, University of Illinois at Chicago.

Metin Tamkoc, professor of international law and relations, Texas Tech University.

David Thomas, associate professor of history, Rhode Island College.

Margaret L. Venzke, assistant professor of history, Dickinson College (Pennsylvania).

Warren S. Walker, Horn Professor of English and Director of the Archive of Turkish Oral Narrative, Texas Tech University.

Donald Webster, professor of Turkish history, retired.

Walter Weiker, professor of political science, Rutgers University.

John Woods, associate professor of Middle Eastern history, University of Chicago.

Madeline Zilfi, associate professor of history, University of Maryland.

Appendix 8

TURKISH PRIME MINISTER RECEP TAYYİP ERDOĞAN'S MESSAGE ON THE ARMENIAN EVENTS OF 1915 ON 23 APRIL 2014 (ANATOLIAN NEWS AGENCY, 23 APRIL 2014)

The 24th of April carries a particular significance for our Armenian citizens and for all Armenians around the world, and provides a valuable opportunity to share opinions freely on a historical matter.

It is indisputable that the last years of the Ottoman Empire were a difficult period, full of suffering for Turkish, Kurdish, Arab, Armenian and millions of other Ottoman citizens, regardless of their religion or ethnic origin. Any conscientious, fair and humanistic approach to these issues requires an understanding of all the sufferings endured in this period, without discriminating as to religion or ethnicity.

Certainly, neither constructing hierarchies of pain nor comparing and contrasting suffering carries any meaning for those who experienced this pain themselves. As a Turkish proverb goes, "Fire burns the place where it falls." It is a duty of humanity to acknowledge that Armenians remember the suffering experienced in that period, just like every other citizen of the Ottoman Empire.

In Turkey, expressing different opinions and thoughts freely on the events of 1915 is the requirement of a pluralistic perspective as well as of a culture of democracy and modernity.

Some may perceive this climate of freedom in Turkey as an opportunity to express accusatory, offensive and even provocative assertions and allegations.

Even so, if this will enable us to better understand historical issues with their legal aspects and to transform resentment to friendship again, it is natural to approach different discourses with empathy and tolerance and expect a similar attitude from all sides.

The Republic of Turkey will continue to approach every idea with dignity in line with the universal values of law. Nevertheless, using the events of 1915 as an excuse for hostility against Turkey and turning this issue into a matter of political conflict is inadmissible.

The incidents of the First World War are our shared pain. To evaluate this painful period of history through a perspective of just memory is a humane and scholarly responsibility.

Millions of people of all religions and ethnicities lost their lives in the First World War. Having experienced events which had inhumane consequences—such as relocation—during the First World War, should not prevent Turks and Armenians from establishing compassion and mutually humane attitudes towards one another. In today's world, deriving enmity from history and creating new antagonisms are neither acceptable nor useful for building a common future.

The spirit of the age necessitates dialogue despite differences, understanding by heeding others, evaluating means for compromise, denouncing hatred, and praising respect and tolerance.

With this understanding, we, as the Republic of Turkey, have called for the establishment of a joint historical commission in order to study the events of 1915 in a scholarly manner. This call remains valid. Scholarly research to be carried out by Turkish, Armenian and international historians would play a significant role in shedding light on the events of 1915 and an accurate understanding of history.

It is with this understanding that we have opened our archives to all researchers. Today, hundreds of thousands of documents in our archives are at the service of historians.

Looking to the future with confidence, Turkey has always supported scholarly and comprehensive studies for an accurate understanding of history. The people of Anatolia, who lived together for centuries regardless of their different ethnic and religious origins, have established common values in every field from art to diplomacy, from state administration to commerce.

Today they continue to have the same ability to create a new future.

It is our hope and belief that the peoples of an ancient and unique geography, who share similar customs and manners will be able to talk to each other about the past with maturity and remember together their losses in a decent manner. And it is with this hope and belief that we wish that the Armenians who lost their lives in the context of the early twentieth century rest in peace, and we convey our condolences to their great grandchildren.

Regardless of their ethnic or religious origins, we pay tribute, with compassion and respect, to all Ottoman citizens who lost their lives in the same period and under similar conditions.

Sources

I. UNPUBLISHED PRIMARY SOURCES

Foreign Office Papers (FO), National Archives, Kew, London
Prime Minister's Office Ottoman Archive (BOA), Kağıthane, İstanbul
Turkish General Staff Military History and Strategic Studies Directorate Archive (ATASE), Ankara
Turkish Historical Society Archive, Ankara
Turkish Ministry of Foreign Affairs Archive, Karakusunlar, Ankara
United States National Archives, College Park, Maryland

II. PUBLISHED PRIMARY SOURCES

Official

Britain

Atherton, Louise, *Top Secret: An Interim Guide to Recent Releases of Intelligence Records at the Public Record Office*, London: Public Record Office Publications, 1993.
Beckett, Ian, *The First World War: The Essential Guide to Sources in the United Kingdom National Archives*, Kew, Richmond/Surrey: National Archives Public Record Office, 2002.
British and Foreign State Papers.
Guide to the Contents of the Public Record Office, Vol. 2: *State Papers and Departmental Records*, London: Her Majesty's Stationery Office, 1963.
House of Commons Hansard.
House of Lords Hansard.
Twigge, Stephen, Edward Hampshire and Graham Macklin, *British Intelligence: Secrets, Spies and Sources*, Kew, Richmond/Surrey: The National Archives, 2008.

India

Index to the Foreign and Political Department Records, Delhi: National Archives of India.

Turkey

Akbay, Cemal, *Birinci Dünya Harbinde Türk Harbi* (Turkish War in the First World War), 2 Vols., Ankara: Genelkurmay Basımevi, 1991.

Aren, Tülin, *Arşiv Problemleri ve Arşivcilik* (Problems of Archives and Archival Administration), Ankara: Başbakanlık Basımevi, 1976.

Arşiv Belgeleriyle Ermeni Faaliyetleri 1914–1918 (Armenian Activities Through Archival Documents 1914–1918), 8 Vols., Ankara: Genelkurmay Basımevi, 2005–2008.

Belen, Fahri, *Birinci Dünya Harbinde Türk Harbi 1914–1918 Yılı Hareketleri* (Turkish War in the First World War: Movements of the Years 1914–1918), 5 Vols., Ankara: Genelkurmay Basımevi, 1965–1967.

Binark, İsmet, ed., *Armenians in Ottoman Documents, 1915–1920*, Ankara: Başbakanlık Basımevi, 1995.

———, *Arşiv ve Arşivcilik Bilgileri* (Archives and Information on Archival Management), Ankara: Başbakanlık Basımevi, 1980.

———, *Cumhuriyet Döneminde Arşiv Hizmetlerinin Geliştirilmesi Konusunda Yapılmış Çalışmalar ve Cumhuriyet Arşivi* (Activities Relating to the Development of Archival Services in the Republican Period and the Republican Archive), Ankara: Başbakanlık Basımevi, 1991.

———, *Türk Arşivlerinin Kısa Tarihçesi ve Devlet Arşivleri Genel Müdürlüğünün Faaliyetleri* (A Brief History of the Turkish Archives and the Activities of the Directorate General of State Archives), Ankara: Başbakanlık Basımevi, 1994.

Birinci Dünya Harbinde Türk Harbi Kafkas Cephesi Üçüncü Ordu Harekatı (Turkish War in the First World War: Caucasian Front Operations of the Third Army), 2 Vols., Ankara: Genelkurmay Basımevi, 1993.

Çakmak, Fevzi, *Birinci Dünya Savaşında Doğu Cephesi* (Eastern Front in the First World War), Ankara: Genelkurmay Basımevi, 2nd ed., 2005.

Genç et al., Yusuf İhsan, *Başbakanlık Osmanlı Arşivi Rehberi* (Guide to the Prime Minister's Office Ottoman Archive), Ankara: Başbakanlık Basımevi, 1992.

Gürsoy et al., Şakir, *Başbakanlık Devlet Arşivleri Genel Müdürlüğü Cumhuriyet Arşivi Daire Başkanlığı Rehberi* (Guide to the Prime Minister's Office Directorate General of State Archives Department of the Republican Archive), Ankara: Başbakanlık Basımevi, 2nd expanded ed., 1996.

Karacakaya et al., Recep, *Osmanlı Belgelerinde Ermeni-Amerikan İlişkileri, 1839–1919* (Armenian-American Relations in Ottoman Documents, 1839–1919), Vols. 1–2, Ankara: Başbakanlık Basımevi, 2007.

———, *Osmanlı Belgelerinde Ermeni-Fransız İlişkileri, 1879–1922* (Armenian-French Relations in Ottoman Documents, 1879–1922), Vols. 1–3, Ankara: Başbakanlık Basımevi, 2002.

———, *Osmanlı Belgelerinde Ermeni-İngiliz İlişkileri, 1845–1922* (Armenian-British Relations in Ottoman Documents, 1845–1922), Vols. 1–4, Ankara: Başbakanlık Basımevi, 2004 and 2006.

———, *Osmanlı Belgelerinde Ermeni-Rus İlişkileri, 1841–1921* (Armenian-Russian Relations in Ottoman Documents, 1841–1921), Vols. 1–3, Ankara: Başbakanlık Basımevi, 2006.

Karaer, İbrahim, Rahim Erişti and Ahmet Ceylan, eds., *Dünden Bugüne Başbakanlık 1920-2004* (The Prime Minister's Office from Yesterday to the Present 1920–2004), Ankara: Başbakanlık Basımevi, 2004.

Küçük et al., Mustafa, *Başbakanlık Osmanlı Arşivi Katalogları Rehberi* (Guide to the Catalogs of the Prime Minister's Office Ottoman Archive), Ankara: Başbakanlık Basımevi, 1995.

Özkul, İsa, *Türk Arşivleri Bugünü ve Geleceği* (Turkish Archives Its Present and Future), Ankara: Başbakanlık Basımevi, 2000.

Öztürk, Said, *Osmanlı Belgelerinde Siyakat Yazısı* (Siyakat Script in Ottoman Documents), Ankara: Başbakanlık Basımevi, 1994.

Pehlivanlı, Hamit, *Genelkurmay Askeri Tarih ve Stratejik Etüt Başkanlığı Süreli Yayınları Makaleler Dizini I* (Periodical Publications of the Turkish General Staff Directorate of Military History and Strategic Studies Article Series I), Ankara: Genelkurmay Basımevi, 1992.

———, *Genelkurmay Askeri Tarih ve Stratejik Etüt Başkanlığı Süreli Yayınları Makaleler Dizini II* (Periodical Publications of the Turkish General Staff Directorate of Military History and Strategic Studies Article Series II), Ankara: Genelkurmay Basımevi, 2000.

Sakin, Orhan, *Makedonya'daki Osmanlı Evrakı* (Ottoman Documents in Macedonia), Ankara: Başbakanlık Basımevi, 1996.

Sertoğlu, Midhat, *Muhteva Bakımından Başvekalet Arşivi* (Contents of the Prime Minister's Office Archive), Ankara: Türk Tarih Kurumu Basımevi, 1955.

Tetik, Ahmet, "Dünden Bugüne Genelkurmay ATASE Arşivi" (Turkish General Staff Military History and Strategic Studies Directorate Archive From Yesterday to Present), in *International Symposium on Turkish Archives 17–19 November 2005 (Presentations and Discussions)*, Ankara: Başbakanlık Basımevi, 2006.

Toker, Hülya and Nurcan Aslan, eds., *Birinci Dünya Savaşına Katılan Alay ve Daha Üst Kademedeki Komutanların Biyografileri* (Biographies of the Regiment and More Senior Level Commanders Who Participated in the First World War), 3 Vols., Ankara: Genelkurmay Basımevi, 2009.

Türk Parlamento Tarihi Cumhuriyet Senatosu Üyelerinin Özgeçmişleri (History of the Turkish Parliament: Curricula Vitae of the Members of the Republican Senate), 2 Vols., Ankara: Türkiye Büyük Millet Meclisi Vakfı Yayınları, 1998.

Türkiye Cumhuriyeti Dışişleri Bakanlığı Arşivlerimiz Hakkında Bilgi Aralık 2011 (Republic of Turkey Ministry of Foreign Affairs Information on Our Archives December 2011), Ankara: Dışişleri Bakanlığı Matbaası, 2011.

Türkiye Cumhuriyeti Genelkurmay ATASE ve Denetleme Başkanlığı Yayın Kataloğu (Publication Catalog of the Turkish General Staff Directorate of Military History and Strategic Studies and Directorate of Inspection), Ankara: Genelkurmay Basımevi, 2005.

Türkiye Dış Politikasında 50 Yıl Kurtuluş Savaşımız (1919–1922) (Fifty Years in the Foreign Policy of Turkey: Our War of Liberation [1919–1922]), Ankara: Dışişleri Bakanlığı Matbaası, 1973.

United States

Congressional Record-House of Representatives, Proceedings and Debates.

Congressional Record-Senate, Proceedings and Debates.

Private (Memoirs, Correspondence, Statements, Contemporary Studies)

Bidwell, Robin, ed., *The Arab Bulletin Bulletin of the Arab Bureau in Cairo, 1916–1919*, Vol.1: 1916, London: Archive Editions, 1986.

Bourne, Kenneth and David Cameron Watt, "General Introduction," in Kenneth Bourne and David Cameron Watt, eds., British Documents on Foreign Affairs: Reports and Papers From the Foreign Office Confidential Print, Part I: From the Mid-Nineteenth Century to the First World War, Series B: The Near and Middle East, 1856–1914, Vol. 1: The Ottoman Empire and the Balkans, 1856–1875, Frederick, MD: University Publications of America, 1984.

Elgood, Percival George, *Egypt and the Army*, London: Oxford University Press, 1924.

Gates, Caleb Frank, *Not To Me Only*, Princeton, NJ: Princeton University Press, 1940.

Girici, Abdülgani, *1920 Adana Ermeni Mezalimi Hatıraları* (Recollections of 1920 Adana Armenian Atrocities), Ankara: Türk Tarih Kurumu, 2011.

Mackenzie, Compton, *Greek Memories*, Ann Arbor, MI: University Publications of America, 1987, orig. London: Cassel, 1932.

Mayakon, İsmail Müştak, *Yıldız'da Neler Gördüm* (What I Saw in Yıldız), İstanbul: Sertel Matbaası, 1940.

Pasdermadjian, Garekin, *Why Armenia Should Be Free Armenia's Role in the Present War*, Boston, MA: Hairenik Publishing Company, 1918.

Rice, Condoleeza, *No Higher Honor: A Memoir of My Years in Washington*, New York: Crown Publishing Group, 2011.

Weldon, Lewen Francis Barrington, *"Hard Lying" Eastern Mediterranean 1914–1919*, London: Herbert Jenkins Limited, 1925.
Woolley, Leonard, *As I Seem to Remember*, London: George Allen and Unwin Ltd, 1962.
Yeghiayan, Zaven Der, trans. Ared Misirliyan, *My Patriarchal Memoirs*, Barrington, RI: Mayreni Publishing, 2002.

III. NEWSPAPERS

English: *Arab News* (Riyadh), *Arab Times* (Riyadh), *Armenian Mirror Spectator* (Watertown, Massachusetts), *Asbarez* (Fresno, California), *Chicago Sun Times*, *Chicago Tribune*, *Financial Times* (London), *Haaretz* (Tel Aviv), *Houston Chronicle*, *Hürriyet Daily News* (İstanbul), *International Herald Tribune* (Paris), *Los Angeles Times*, *Pittsburg Post-Gazette*, *The Armenian Observer* (Hollywood, California), *The Armenian Reporter* (Burbank, California), *The Chicago Sunday Tribune*, *The Globe and Mail* (Toronto), *The Guardian* (London), *The Hill* (Washington), *The Independent* (London), *The Jerusalem Post*, *The New York Times*, *The Times* (London), *The Wall Street Journal* (New York), *The Wall Street Journal Europe* (London), *The Washington Post*, *The Washington Times*.
French: *L'Humanité* (Paris), *La Croix* (Paris), *Le Figaro* (Paris), *Le Monde* (Paris), *Le Parisien*, *Le Quotidien de Paris*, *Le Vif/L'Express* (Brussels), *Les Echos* (Paris), *Direct Matin* (Paris), *Libération* (Paris), *Méridional* (Marseilles), *Metro News* (Paris), *20 Minutes* (Paris).
German: *Neue Züricher Zeitung*, *Rheinische Post* (Düsseldorf), *Westdeutsche Zeitung* (Düsseldorf).
Turkish: *Akşam* (İstanbul), *Cumhuriyet* (İstanbul), *Güneş* (İstanbul), *Hürriyet* (İstanbul), *Milliyet* (İstanbul), *Tercüman* (İstanbul), *Türkiye* (İstanbul), *Vatan* (İstanbul), *Zaman* (İstanbul).

IV. SECONDARY SOURCES

Books

Abu-Husayn, Abdul-Rahim, *The View from Istanbul: Lebanon and the Druze Emirate in the Ottoman Chancery Documents, 1546–1711*, London and New York: I. B. Tauris, 2004.
Afyoncu, Erhan, *Tanzimat Öncesi Osmanlı Tarihi Araştırma Rehberi* (Research Guide to Pre-Tanzimat Ottoman History), İstanbul: Yeditepe Yayınevi, 2007.
Akarlı, Engin Deniz, *The Long Peace: Ottoman Lebanon, 1861–1920*, Berkeley and Los Angeles, CA: University of California Press, 1993.
Akçam, Taner, *'Ermeni Meselesi Hallolunmuştur': Osmanlı Belgelerine Göre Savaş Yıllarında Ermenilere Yönelik Politikalar* ('The Armenian Problem Is Solved': The Policies Towards Armenians During the War Years According to Ottoman Documents), İstanbul: İletişim Yayınları, 2008.
———, *The Young Turks' Crime Against Humanity: The Armenian Genocide and Ethnic Cleansing in the Ottoman Empire*, Princeton, NJ: Princeton University Press, 2012.
Akgündüz, Ahmed, *Osmanlı Devletinde Gayrimüslimlerin Yönetimi* (The Governance of the Non-Muslims in the Ottoman State), İstanbul: Timaş Yayınları, 2008.
———, *Şer'iyye Sicilleri: Mahiyeti, Toplu Kataloğu ve Seçme Hükümler* (Muslim Court Records, Its Comprehensive Catalog and Selected Rulings), 3 Vols., İstanbul: Türk Dünyası Araştırmaları Vakfı, 1988.
Aksakal, Mustafa, *The Ottoman Road to War in 1914: The Ottoman Empire and the First World War*, Cambridge: Cambridge University Press, 2008.
Aktaş, Necati, "Osmanlı Dönemi Arşivciliğimiz ve Tasnif Çalışmaları" (Our Ottoman Period Archival Administration and Declassification Activities), in Alâaddin Aköz, Bayram Ürekli and Ruhi Özcan, eds., *Uluslararası Kuruluşunun 700. Yıl Dönümünde Bütün Yönleriyle Osmanlı Devleti Kongresi, Konya 7–9 Nisan 1999. Bildiriler* (International Congress on the

Ottoman Empire with All Its Aspects on the 700th Anniversary of Its Founding, Konya 7–9 April 1999. Communications), Konya: Selçuk Üniversitesi Basımevi, 2000.

Akyıldız, Ali, "Hazine-i Evrakın Kurulması ve İlk Tasnif Usulleri (1846–1856)" (The Establishment of the Treasury of Documentation and the First Declassification Methods [1846–1856]), in Mustafa Çetin Varlık, İnci Enginün, Mücteba İlgürel, İsmail Erünsal, Zikri Altun and Mustafa Berkem, eds., *Prof. Dr. Hakkı Dursun Yıldız'a Armağan* (Dedication to Prof. Dr. Hakkı Dursun Yıldız), İstanbul: Marmara Üniversitesi Fen-Edebiyat Fakültesi Yayınları, 1995.

Akyol, Taha, "İlber Ortaylı Tarihçiliği" (The İlber Ortaylı Historianship), in Taha Akyol and İlber Ortaylı, *Osmanlı Mirası* (The Ottoman Heritage), İstanbul: Timaş Yayınları, 2010.

———, *Osmanlı Mirasından Cumhuriyet Türkiye'sine İlber Ortaylı İle Konuşmalar* (From the Ottoman Heritage to the Republican Turkey: Conversations With İlber Ortaylı), İstanbul: Ufuk Kitapları, 2002.

Al-Sudairi, Abdulaziz, *A Vision of the Middle East: An Intellectual Biography of Albert Hourani*, London: I. B. Tauris, 1999.

Altındağ, Ülkü, *Topkapı Sarayı Müzesi Osmanlı Saray Arşivi Kataloğu (Hükümler-Beratlar)* (Ottoman Palace Archives Catalog of the Topkapı Palace Museum [Rulings-Berats]), 2 Vols., Ankara: Türk Tarih Kurumu Basımevi, 1988.

Andrew, Christopher, *Secret Service The Making of the British Intelligence Community*, New York: Viking Penguin, 1986.

Ar, Fikret, *Arşivlerin Organizasyonu Hakkında Araştırma Raporu* (Research Report on the Organization of Archives), Ankara: Türkiye ve Orta Doğu Amme İdaresi Enstitüsü Yayınları, 1971.

Armenian Allegations: Myth and Reality. A Handbook of Facts and Documents, Washington, DC: The Assembly of Turkish American Associations, 1987.

Ata, Feridun, *İşgal İstanbul'unda Tehcir Yargılamaları* (Trials for Relocations in Occupied İstanbul), Ankara: Türk Tarih Kurumu Basımevi, 2005.

———, *Süleymaniyeli Nemrut Mustafa Paşa (Bir İşbirlikçinin Portresi)* (Nemrut Mustafa Pasha of Süleymaniye: The Portrait of a Collaborator), Konya: Palet Yayınları, reprinted, 2010.

Ataman, Bekir Kemal, *Arşivcilik Terimleri Sözlüğü* (Dictionary of Archival Administration Terms), İstanbul: Librairie Péra, 1995.

Aydemir, Şevket Süreyya, *Makedonya'dan Ortaasya'ya Enver Paşa* (From Macedonia to Central Asia: Enver Pasha), 3 Vols., İstanbul: Remzi Kitabevi, 2nd ed., 1995.

Aykut, Nezihi, İdris Bostan, Feridun Emecen, Yusuf Halaçoğlu, Mehmet İpşirli, İsmet Miroğlu, Abdülkadir Özcan and İlhan Şahin, eds., *Mühimme Defteri 90* (Important Affairs Register 90), İstanbul: Türk Dünyası Araştırmaları Vakfı, 1993.

Badem, Candan, *Çarlık Rusyası Döneminde Kars Vilayeti* (The Province of Kars under the Tsarist Russian Rule), İstanbul: Birzamanlar Yayıncılık, 2010.

Baer, Marc David, *The Dönme: Jewish Converts, Muslim Revolutionaries, and Secular Turks*, Stanford, CA: Stanford University Press, 2010.

Bakar, Bülent, *Ermeni Tehciri* (Armenian Relocations), Ankara: Atatürk Araştırma Merkezi, 2009.

Balta, Evangelia, "Ottoman Archives in Greece," in *Balkanlar ve İtalya'da Şehir ve Manastır Arşivlerindeki Türkçe Belgeler Semineri (16–17 Kasım 2000)* (Seminar on Turkish Documents in the Archives of Balkan Countries and Italian Cities and Monastries [16-17 November 2000]), Ankara: Türk Tarih Kurumu Basımevi, 2003.

Baltacı, Cahid, "Şer'iyye Sicillerinin Tarihsel ve Kültürel Önemi" (Historical and Cultural Importance of the Muslim Court Records), in *Osmanlı Arşivleri ve Osmanlı Araştırmaları Sempozyumu 17 Mayıs 1985* (Symposium on Ottoman Archives and Ottoman Studies 17 May 1985), İstanbul: Türk-Arap İlişkileri İncelemeleri Vakfı, 1985.

Banerji, Arup, *Writing History in the Soviet Union: Making the Past Work*, New Delhi: Social Science Press, 2008.

Baron, Salo, *A Social and Religious History of the Jews*, Vol.18, New York: Columbia University Press, 2nd rev. ed., 1983.

Baron, Samuel and Cathy Frierson, eds., *Adventures in Russian Historical Research: Reminiscences of American Scholars from the Cold War to the Present*, New York: M. E. Sharpe, 2003.

Bayramol, Eray, *Rus Kaynaklarında Ermeni Sorunu* (The Armenian Question in Russian Sources), İstanbul: Bilge Kültür Sanat Yayın, 2013.

Bevan, Amanda, *Tracing Your Ancestors in the National Archives*, Kew, Richmond: The National Archives, 7th ed., 2006.

Beyoğlu, Süleyman, "Ermeni Tehcirine Dair Araştırmalara Toplu Bir Bakış" (An Overview of Studies on Armenian Relocations), in Şenol Kantarcı, Kamer Kasım, İbrahim Kaya and Sedat Laçiner, eds., *Ermeni Araştırmaları I. Türkiye Kongresi Bildirileri* (Communications Presented to the First Turkish Congress on Armenian Studies), Ankara: Avrasya Stratejik Araştırmalar Enstitüsü Yayınları, 2003.

Bildirici, Faruk, "Fransız ve Türk Arşivlerinin Karşılaştırılmalı Denemesi: Tarih ve Teşkilat" (A Comparative Trial of French and Turkish Archives: History and Organization), in Hamza Kandur, ed., *Arşivcilik Konferansları I* (Conferences on Archival Administration I), İstanbul: Librairie Péra, 1995.

Binder, Leonard, ed., *The Study of the Middle East: Research and Scholarship in the Humanities and the Social Sciences*, New York: John Wiley and Sons, Inc., 1976.

Birinci, Ali, *Tarihin Hududunda Hatırat Kitapları, Matbuat Yasakları ve Arşiv Meseleleri* (Reminiscences Books, Press Prohibitions and Archival Questions in the Boundary of History), İstanbul: Dergah Yayınları, 2012.

Bobroff, Ronald Park, *Roads to Glory: Late Imperial Russia and the Turkish Straits*, London: I. B. Tauris, 2006.

Broadbent, Harvey, *Gallipoli: The Fatal Shore*, Camberwell, Victoria: Penguin Books, 2009.

Brown, Carl, *International Politics and the Middle East: Old Rules, Dangerous Game*, Princeton, NJ: Princeton University Press, 1984.

Budaybek, Gülsüm, "Osmanlı Askeri Arşivleri" (Ottoman Military Archives), in *Osmanlı Arşivleri ve Osmanlı Araştırmaları Sempozyumu 17 Mayıs 1985*.

Butler, L. J. and Anthony Gorst, eds., *Modern British History: A Guide to Study and Research*, London and New York: I. B. Tauris Publishers, 1997.

Büyüklimanlı et al., Gönül, *Geçmişten Geleceğe Köprü: Milli Kütüphane* (A Bridge from the Past to the Future: The National Library), Ankara: Milli Kütüphane Yayınları, 2011.

Calvocoressi, Peter, Guy Wint and John Pritchard, The Penguin History of the Second World War, London: Penguin Books, 1989.

Canbakal, Hülya, *Society and Politics in an Ottoman Town: 'Ayntab in the 17th Century*, Leiden: E. J. Brill, 2007.

Casale, Giancarlo, *The Ottoman Age of Exploration*, New York: Oxford University Press, 2010.

Çanlı, Mehmet, "Cumhuriyet Arşivi Tasnif Çalışmalarına Bir Bakış" (A Glance at the Declassification Activities of the Republican Archive),in Rahim Erişti, Hacı Osman Yıldırım, Vahdettin Atik and Yusuf Yay, eds., *Birinci Milli Arşiv Şurası (Tebliğler-Tartışmalar) 20–21 Nisan 1998* (First National Archives Congress [Communications-Discussions] 20–21 April 1998), Ankara: Başbakanlık Basımevi, 1998.

Çaykara, Emine, ed., *Tarihçilerin Kutbu Halil İnalcık Kitabı* (Pole of the Historians: The Halil İnalcık Book), İstanbul: Türkiye İş Bankası Kültür Yayınları, 2005.

Çetin, Attila, *Başbakanlık Arşivi Kılavuzu* (Guide to the Prime Minister's Office Archive), İstanbul: Enderun Kitabevi, 1979.

Çiçek, Kemal, *Ermenilerin Zorunlu Göçü, 1915–1917* (Relocation of Armenians, 1915-1917), Ankara: Türk Tarih Kurumu Basımevi, 2005.

Çiçek, Talha, *War and State Formation in Syria: Cemal Pasha's Governorate During World War I, 1914–1917*, London: Routledge, 2014.

Çoker, Fahri, *Türk Tarih Kurumu: Kuruluş Amacı ve Çalışmaları* (Turkish Historical Society: Purpose of Its Foundation and Activities), Ankara: Türk Tarih Kurumu Basımevi, 1983.

Dadrian, Vahakn, The History of the *Armenian Genocide: Ethnic Conflict from the Balkans to Anatolia to the Caucasus*, Providence, RI: Berghahn Books, 1995.

———, "Ottoman Archives and Denial of the Armenian Genocide," in Richard Hovannisian, ed., *The Armenian Genocide: History, Politics, Ethics*, New York: St. Martin's Press, 1992.
Dadrian, Vahakn and Taner Akçam, *Judgment at Istanbul: The Armenian Genocide Trials*, New York and Oxford: Berghahn Books, 2011.
Darendeliler, Adnan and İhsan Dede, *Arşivin Bugünkü Durumu Hukuk ve İlim Açısından Arşiv İdaresi* (The Current Condition of the Turkish Archives: Archival Administration from a Legal and Scholarly Point of View), Ankara: Gürsoy Basımevi, 1968.
Davies, R. W., *Soviet History in the Yeltsin Era*, New York: St. Martin's Press, 1997.
Davison, Roderic, *Essays in Ottoman and Turkish History, 1774–1923: The Impact of the West*, Austin, TX: University of Texas Press, 1990.
———, "European Archives as a Source for Later Ottoman History," in Kathleen Brown, ed., *Report on Current Research 1958: Survey of Current Research on the Middle East*, Washington, D.C.: The Middle East Institute, 1958.
Demirel, Muammer, *British Documents on Armenians (1896–1918)*, Ankara: Yeni Türkiye Yayınları, 2002.
Deringil, Selim, *The Ottomans, the Turks, and World Power*, Istanbul: The Isis Press, 2000.
Elker, Selahattin, "Mustafa Reşit Paşa ve Türk Arşivciliği" (Mustafa Reşit Pasha and Turkish Archival Administration), in IV. Türk Tarih *Kongresi, Ankara 10–14 Kasım 1948. Kongreye Sunulan Tebliğler* (Fourth Turkish Historical Congress, Ankara Communications Presented to the Congress), Ankara: Türk Tarih Kurumu Basımevi, 1952.
Erdem, Selim Efe, ed., *İstanbul'un Yaşayan Efsanesi Semavi Eyice Kitabı* (The Living Legend of İstanbul: The Semavi Eyice Book), İstanbul: Timaş Yayınları, 2014.
Ergeç, Özer, "Halil İnalcık'ın Türkiye'nin Sosyal ve Ekonomik Tarihçiliğindeki Yeri" (The Place of Halil İnalcık in the Social and Economic Historianship of Turkey), in Mehmet Öz, ed., *Cumhuriyet Döneminde Türkiye'de Tarihçilik ve Tarih Yayıncılığı Sempozyumu Bildiriler Ankara, 18–20 Mart 2010* (Symposium on Historianship and Historical Publications in Republican Turkey Communications Ankara, 18-20 March 2010), Ankara: Türk Tarih Kurumu Basımevi, 2011.
Ergene, Boğaç, *Local Court, Provincial Society and Justice in the Ottoman Empire: Legal Practice and Dispute Resolution in Çankırı and Kastamonu*, Leiden: E. J. Brill, 2002.
Erickson, Edward, *Defeat in Detail: The Ottoman Army in the Balkans, 1912–1913*, Westport, CT: Praeger, 2003.
———, *Ordered to Die: A History of the Ottoman Army in the First World War*, Westport, CT: Greenwood Press, 2001.
———, *Ottoman Army Effectiveness in World War I: A Comparative Study*, London and New York: Routledge, 2007.
———, *Ottomans and Armenians: A Study in Counterinsurgency*, New York: Palgrave Macmillan, 2013.
Erişti, Rahim, "Cumhuriyet Arşivi Daire Başkanlığının Kuruluşu ve Çalışmaları" (Establishment and the Activities of the Republican Archive), in Erişti, Yıldırım, Atik and Yay, *Birinci Milli Arşiv Şurası (Tebliğler-Tartışmalar) 20–21 Nisan 1998.*
Erten, Hayri, *Konya Şer'iyye Sicilleri Işığında Ailenin Sosyo-Ekonomik ve Kültürel Yapısı (XVIII. Yüzyıl İlk Yarısı)* (Socio-Economic and Cultural Structure of the Family in the Light of the Konya Muslim Court Records [First Half of the Eighteenth Century]), Ankara: Türkiye Cumhuriyeti Kültür Bakanlığı, 2001.
Faroqhi, Suraiya, *Approaching Ottoman History: An Introduction to the Sources*, Cambridge: Cambridge University Press, 1999.
Fekete, Lajos, *Die Siyaqat-Schrift in der Türkischen Finanzverwaltung*, Budapest: Akadémiai Kiadó, 1955.
———, *Einführung in die osmanisch-türkische Diplomatik der türkischen Botmäþigkeit zu Ungarn*, Budapest: Royal Hungarian State Archive, 1926.
Figes, Orlando, *Crimea: The Last Crusade*, London: Allen Lane, 2010.
Fleischer, Cornell, *Bureaucrat and Intellectual in the Ottoman Empire: The Historian Mustafa Ali (1541–1600)*, Princeton, NJ: Princeton University Press, 1986.
Florence, Ronald, *T.E. Lawrence, Aaron Aaronsohn, and the Seeds of the Arab-Israeli Conflict*, New York: Viking Penguin, 2007.

Ford, Roger, *Eden to Armageddon: World War I in the Middle East*, New York: Pegasus Books, 2010.

Foster, Janet and Julia Sheppard, *British Archives: A Guide to Archive Resources in the United Kingdom*, London: Macmillan, 1995.

Galili, Ziva, "Archives and Historical Writing," in Francis Blouin, Jr. and William Rosenberg, eds., *Archives, Documentation and Institutions of Social Memory*, Ann Arbor, MI: University of Michigan Press, 2006.

Gallagher, Nancy, ed., *Approaches to the History of the Middle East: Interviews with Leading Middle East Historians*, Reading: Ithaca Press, 1994.

Gawrych, George, *The Crescent and the Eagle: Ottoman Rule, Islam and the Albanians, 1874–1913*, London and New York: I. B. Tauris, 2006.

Gedikli, Fethi, "Şer'iyye Sicillerinin Hukuk Tarihi Açısından Önemi ve Sicillere Dayalı Araştırmalar" (Importance of the Muslim Court Records As Regards the History of Law and Studies Based on Muslim Court Records) in Ali Akyıldız, Tufan Buzpınar and Mustafa Sinanoğlu, eds., *Dünden Bugüne Osmanlı Araştırmaları Tespitler-Problemler-Teklifler Sempozyum* (Ottoman Studies From Yesterday to the Present Diagnoses-Problems-Proposals Symposium), İstanbul: İsam Yayınları, 2007.

Gedikli, Yusuf, *Enver Paşa: Nutukları, Makaleleri, Bazı Beyannameleri ve Mektupları* (Enver Pasha: His Speeches, Articles, Some Declarations and Letters), İstanbul: Ufuk Ötesi Yayınları, 2005.

Gerlach, Christian, *Extremely Violent Societies: Mass Violence in the Twentieth-Century World*, New York: Cambridge University Press, 2010.

Gingeras, Ryan, *Sorrowful Shores Violence, Ethnicity, and the End of the Ottoman Empire, 1912–1913*, Oxford and New York: Oxford University Press, 2009.

Glantz, David and Jonathan House, *When Titans Clashed: How the Red Army Stopped Hitler*, Lawrence, KS: University Press of Kansas, 1995.

Goffman, Daniel, *Britons in the Ottoman Empire 1642–1660*, Seattle and London: University of Washington Press, 1998.

———, *The Ottoman Empire and Early Modern Europe*, Cambridge: Cambridge University Press, 2002.

Goldstone, Patricia, *Aaronsohn's Maps: The Untold Story of the Man Who Might Have Created Peace in the Middle East*, Orlando, FL: Harcourt, Inc., 2007.

Gökbilgin, Tayyib, *Osmanlı Paleografya ve Diplomatik İlmi* (Ottoman Paleography and Diplomatics), İstanbul: Enderun Kitabevi, reprinted, 1992.

Görgülü, Aybars, Alexander Iskandaryan and Sergey Minasyan, *Assessing the Rapprochement Process*, İstanbul: Caucasus Institute, 2010.

Grainger, John, *The Battle for Syria 1918–1920*, Woodbridge, Suffolk: The Boydell, 2013.

Grimsted, Patricia Kennedy, ed., *Archives of Russia: A Directory and Bibliographic Guide to Holdings in Moscow and St. Petersburg*, New York and London: M.E. Sharpe, 2000.

———, *Handbook for Archival Research in the USSR*, Washington DC: Kennan Institute for Advanced Russian Studies, 1989.

Gunter, Michael, *Armenian History and the Question of Genocide*, New York: Palgrave Macmillan, 2011.

Gust, Wolfgang, ed., *The Armenian Genocide Evidence from the German Foreign Office Archives, 1915–1916*, New York and Oxford: Berghahn Book, 2014.

Güçlü, Yücel, *Armenians and the Allies in Cilicia 1914–1923*, Salt Lake City, UT: University of Utah Press, 2010.

———, *The Holocaust and the Armenian Case in Comparative Perspective*, Lanham, MD: University Press of America, 2012.

Günday, Dündar, *Arşiv Belgelerinde Siyakat Yazısı Özellikleri ve Divan Rakamları* (Characteristics of the Siyakat Script and Divan Numbers in Archival Documents), Ankara: Türk Tarih Kurumu Basımevi, 1974.

Halaçoğlu, Yusuf, *Ermeni Tehciri* (Armenian Relocations), İstanbul: Babıali Kültür Yayıncılığı, 2005.

———, "Osmanlı Devletinde Arşivcilik" (Archival Administration in the Ottoman State), in *XIII. Türk Tarih Kongresi , Ankara 4–8 Ekim 1999. Kongreye Sunulan Bildiriler* (Thirteenth

Turkish Historical Congress, Ankara 4–8 October 1999. Communications Presented to the Congress), Vol. 2, Ankara: Türk Tarih Kurumu Basımevi, 2002.

———, *Sürgünden Soykırıma: Ermeni İddiaları* (From Exile to Genocide: Armenian Claims), İstanbul: Babıali Kültür Yayıncılığı, 2006.

———, *Tarih Gelecektir* (History Is The Future), İstanbul: Babıali Kültür Yayıncılığı, reprinted, 2011.

Hanioğlu, Şükrü, *Atatürk: An Intellectual Biography*, Princeton, NJ: Princeton University Press, 2011.

———, *Kendi Mektuplarında Enver Paşa* (Enver Pasha in His Own Letters), İstanbul: Der Yayınları, 1989.

Hasanlı, Cemil, *Stalin and the Turkish Crisis of the Cold War, 1945–1953*, Lanham, MD: Lexington Books, 2011.

———, *Tarafsızlıktan Soğuk Savaşa Doğru Türk-Sovyet İlişkileri 1939–1953* (From the Neutrality Toward the Cold War: Turkish-Soviet Relations 1939–1953), Ankara: Bilgi Yayınevi, 2011.

Haskan, Nermi and Çelik Gülersoy, *Hükümet Kapısı Bab-ı Ali Kuruluşundan Cumhuriyete Kadar* (Gate of Government Sublime Porte: From Its Foundation to the Republic), İstanbul: Çelik Gülersoy Vakfı, 2000.

Heyd, Uriel, *Ottoman Documents on Palestine 1552–1615: A Study of the Firman According the Mühimme Defteri*, London: Oxford University Press, 1960.

Heydarov, Tale, ed., *The Armenian Question in the Caucasus: Russian Archive Documents and Publications*, 3 Vols., Reading: Ithaca Press, 2011.

Holquist, Peter, *Making War, Forging Revolution: Russia's Continuum of Crisis, 1914–1921*, Cambridge, MA: Harvard University Press, 2002.

Hovannisian, Richard, *The Republic of Armenia: From Versailles to London, 1919–1920*, 3 Vols., Berkeley and Los Angeles, CA: University of California Press, 1971–1982.

Hunter, Gregory, *Developing and Maintaining Practical Archives*, New York and London: Neal-Schuman Publishers, 1997.

Hurewitz, J. C., *Diplomacy in the Near and Middle East A Documentary Record: 1535–1914*, Vol. 1, Princeton, NJ: D. Van Nostrand Company, Inc., 1956.

Isom-Verhaaren, Christine, *Allies with the Infidel: The Ottoman and French Alliance in the Sixteenth Century*, London and New York: I. B. Tauris, 2011.

İğdemir, Uluğ, *Cumhuriyetin 50. Yılında Türk Tarih Kurumu* (Turkish Historical Society in the Fiftieth Anniversary of the Founding of the Republic), Ankara: Türk Tarih Kurumu Basımevi, 1973.

———, *Yılların İçinden Makaleler, Anılar, İncelemeler* (Inside the Years: Articles, Recollections, Studies), Ankara: Türk Tarih Kurumu Basımevi, 1976.

İnal, İbnülemin Mahmud Kemal, *Osmanlı Devrinde Son Sadrazamlar (The Last Grand Viziers in the Ottoman Era)*, İstanbul: Maarif Matbaası, 1940–1944.

İnalcık, Halil, "Ottoman Archival Materials on *Millets*," in Benjamin Braude and Bernard Lewis, eds., *Christians and Jews in the Ottoman Empire: The Functioning of a Plural Society*, Vol. 1: *The Central Lands*, New York and London: Holmes and Meier Publishers, 1982.

———, "The Shaykh's Story Told by Himself," in Thomas Naff, ed. and comp., *Paths to the Middle East: Ten Scholars Look Back,* Albany, New York: State University of New York Press, 1993.

———, "Son Yıllarda Türkiye'de Kaynak Çalışmaları" (Recent Source Studies in Turkey), in *Communications Presented to the IXth International Congress of Economic and Social History of Turkey, Dubrovnik 20–23 August 2002*, Ankara: Atatürk Supreme Council for Culture, Language and History Publications of the Turkish Historical Society, 2005.

İnalcık, Halil and Bülent Arı, "Klasik Dönem Osmanlı Tarihçiliği" (Classical Period Ottoman Historianship), in Vahdet Engin and Ahmet Şimşek, eds., *Türkiye'de Tarihyazımı* (Historiography in Turkey), İstanbul: Yeditepe Yayınevi, 2011.

İnan, Arı, ed., *Enver Paşa'nın Özel Mektupları* (Enver Pasha's Private Letters), Ankara: İmge Kitapevi, 1997.

İrtem, Süleyman Kani, *Sultan Abdülhamid ve Yıldız Kamarillası* (Sultan Abdülhamid and the Yıldız Camaraderie), İstanbul: Temel Yayınları, 2003.

Jaeschke, Gotthard, trans. Cemal Köprülü, *Kurtuluş Savaşı İle İlgili İngiliz Belgeleri* (British Documents on the War of Liberation), Ankara: Türk Tarih Kurumu Basımevi, reprinted, 1991.

Jeffrey, Keith, *MI6 The History of the Secret Intelligence Service 1919–1949*, London: Bloomsbury, 2010.

Jennings, Jr., Ronald Carlton, The Judicial Registers ('Şer'i Mahkeme Sicilleri') of Kayseri (1550–1630) as a Source for Ottoman History, Doctoral Dissertation, University of California at Los Angeles, 1972.

———, *Studies on Ottoman Social History in the Sixteenth and Seventeenth Centuries Women, Zimmis and Sharia Courts in Kayseri, Cyprus and Trabzon*, İstanbul: The Isis Press, 1999.

Jwaideh, Albertine, "Aspects of Land Tenure and Social Change in Lower Iraq During Late Ottoman Times," in Tarif Khalidi, ed., *Land Tenure and Social Transformation in the Middle East*, Beirut: American University of Beirut Press, 1984.

———, "Midhat Pasha and the Land System of Lower Iraq," in Albert Hourani, ed., *St. Anthony's Papers: Middle Eastern Affairs*, No. 3, London: Chatto and Windus, 1963.

———, "The Saniya Lands of Sultan Abdülhamid II in Iraq," in George Makdisi, ed., *Arabic and Islamic Studies in Honor of H.A.R. Gibb*, Leiden: Brill, 1965.

Kapıcı, Özhan and İbrahim Köremezli, "Osmanlı Askeri Tarihçiliğinin Eksik Aynası: Rusya Federasyonu Arşivleri" (The Imperfect Mirror of the Ottoman Military Historianship: Archives of the Russian Federation), in Cevat Şayin and Gültekin Yıldız, eds., *Osmanlı Askeri Tarihini Araştırmak: Yeni Kaynaklar Yeni Yaklaşımlar* (Researching Ottoman Military History: New Sources New Approaches), İstanbul: Yurt Yayınları, 2012.

Karpat, Kemal, "Introduction: Turks Remember Their Ottoman Ancestors," in Kemal Karpat, ed., *Ottoman Past and Today's Turkey*, Leiden: E. J. Brill, 2000.

Kayoko, Hayashi and Mahir Aydın, eds., *The Ottoman State and Societies in Change: A Study of the Nineteenth Century Temettuat Registers*, London, New York and Bahrain: Kegan Paul Limited, 2004.

Kedourie, Elie, "Minorities," in *Chatham House Version and Other Middle-Eastern Studies*, London: Weidenfeld and Nicolson, 1970.

Kévorkian, Raymond, *The Armenian Genocide: A Complete History*, London and New York: I. B. Tauris, 2011.

Koç, Yunus, "Türk Tarih Kurumu ve Türk Tarihçiliğindeki Yeri" (Turkish Historical Society and Its Place in Turkish Historianship), in Öz, *Cumhuriyet Döneminde Türkiye'de Tarihçilik ve Tarih Yayıncılığı Sempozyumu Bildiriler Ankara, 18–20 Mart 2010.*

Kortepeter, Carl Max, *Ottoman Imperialism During the Reformation: Europe and the Caucasus*, London: University of London Press Ltd, 1973.

Kurt, Yılmaz, "Tapu Tahrir Defterleri ve Bunların Yayınlanması Hakkında" (On Land Deed Registers and Their Publication), in Erişti, Yıldırım, Atik and Yay, *Birinci Milli Arşiv Şurası (Tebliğler-Tartışmalar) 20–21 Nisan 1998.*

Kurt, Yılmaz and Mehmed Ceyhan, *Osmanlı Paleografyası ve Osmanlı Diplomatikası* (Ottoman Paleography and Diplomatics), Ankara: Akçağ Yayınları, 2012.

Kütükoğlu, Mübahat, "Mühimme Defterlerindeki Muamele Kayıdları Üzerine" (On the Transaction Notes in the Important Affairs Register), in *Tarih Boyunca Paleografya ve Diplomatik Semineri 30 Nisan–2 Mayıs 1986 Bildiriler* (Seminar on Paleography and Diplomatics 30 April–2 May 1986 Communications), İstanbul: Edebiyat Fakültesi Basımevi, 1988.

———, *Osmanlı Belgelerinin Dili (Diplomatik)* (Language of the Ottoman Documents [Diplomatics]), İstanbul: Kubbealtı Neşriyatı, 1994.

Lemkin, Raphael, *Axis Rule in Occupied Europe: Laws of Occupation, Analysis of Government, Proposals for Redress*, Washington, D.C.: Carnegie Endowment for World Peace, 1944.

Lewis, Bernard, *From Babel to Dragomans: Interpreting the Middle East*, Oxford and New York: Oxford University Press, 2004.

———, *Notes and Documents from the Turkish Archives: A Contribution to the History of the Jews in the Ottoman Empire*, Jerusalem: The Israel Oriental Society, 1952.

———, *Notes on a Century: Reflections of a Middle East Historian*, London: Weidenfeld and Nicolson, 2012.
Lewy, Guenter, *The Armenian Massacres in Ottoman Turkey: A Disputed Genocide*, Salt Lake City, UT: University of Utah Press, 2005.
———, *Outlawing Genocide Denial: Dilemmas of Official Historical Truth*, Salt Lake City, UT: University of Utah Press, 2014.
Litvin, Alter, trans. and ed., John Keep, *Writing History in Twentieth-Century Russia: A View from Within*, London and Basingstoke: Palgrave Macmillan, 2001.
Litvin, Alter and John Keep, *Stalinism: Russian and Western Views at the Turn of the Millenium*, London and New York: Routledge, 2005.
Lohr, Eric, *Nationalizing the Russian Empire: The Campaign against Enemy Aliens during World War I*, Cambridge, MA: Harvard University Press, 2003.
Lowry, Heath, "The State of the Field: A Retrospective Overview and Assessment of Ottoman Studies in the United States of America and Canada," in *XIII. Türk Tarih Kongresi, Ankara 4–8 Ekim 1999. Kongreye Sunulan Bildiriler.*
Mandaville, Jon, "The Jerusalem Shari'a Court Records: A Supplement and Complement to the Central Ottoman Archives," in Moshe Maoz, ed., *Studies on Palestine During the Ottoman Period*, Jerusalem: The Magnes Press, the Hebrew University and Yad Izhak Ben-Zvi, 1975.
Marcus, Abraham, *The Middle East on the Eve of Modernity: Aleppo in the Eighteenth Century*, New York: Columbia University Press, 1989.
Martin, Terry, *The Affirmative Action Empire: Nations and Nationalism in the Soviet Union, 1923–1939*, Ithaca, New York: Cornell University Press, 2001.
Masters, Bruce, *Christians and Jews in the Ottoman Arab World: The Roots of Sectarianism*, Cambridge: Cambridge University Press, 2001.
Mazza, Roberto, *Jerusalem: From the Ottomans to the British*, London and New York: Tauris Academic Studies, 2009.
McCarthy, Justin, *Conference on the Reality of the Armenian Question*, Ankara: Türkiye Büyük Millet Meclisi Basımevi, 2005.
McCarthy, Justin, Esat Arslan, Cemalettin Taşkıran, and Ömer Turan, *The Armenian Rebellion at Van*, Salt Lake City, UT: University of Utah Press, 2006.
McMeekin, Sean, *The Russian Origins of the First World War*, Cambridge, MA and London: Belknap Press of Harvard University Press, 2011.
Mennecke, Martin, "The Crime of Genocide and International Law," in Barbara Boender and Wichert ten Have, eds., *The Holocaust and Other Genocides: An Introduction*, Amsterdam: Amsterdam University Press, 2012.
Mikhail, Alan, *Nature and Empire in Ottoman Egypt: An Environmental History*, New York: Cambridge University Press, 2011.
Miner, Steven Merritt, *Stalin's Holy War: Religion, Nationalism, and Alliance Politics,* Chapel Hill, NC and London: University of North Carolina Press, 2003.
Moran, Christopher and Christopher Murphy, eds., *Intelligence Studies in Britain and the US: Historiography Since 1945*, Edinburgh: Edinburgh University Press, 2013.
Moumdjian, Garabet, "From Millet-i Sadıka to Millet-i Asiya," in Hakan Yavuz with Peter Sluglett, eds., *War and Diplomacy: The Russo-Turkish War of 1877–1878*, Salt Lake City, UT: University of Utah Press, 2011.
Naff, Thomas, ed. and comp., *Paths to the Middle East: Ten Scholars Look Back*, Albany, New York: State University of New York Press, 1993.
Naimark, Norman, *The Russians in Germany*, Cambridge, MA and London: The Belknap Press of Harvard University Press, 1995.
Ocak, Ahmet Yaşar, "Usta Tarihçiler Nasıl Çalışıyorlar?" (How Do Master Historians Work?), in Ahmet Şimşek, ed., *Tarih Nasıl Yazılır? Tarihyazımı İçin Çağdaş Bir Metodoloji* (How Is History Written? A Modern Methodology for Historiography), İstanbul: Tarihçi Kitabevi, 2011.
Olney, R. J., *Manuscript Sources for British History: Their Nature, Location and Use*, London: University of London, Institute of Historical Research, 1995.

XI. Türk Tarih Kongresi, Ankara 5–9 Eylül 1990. Kongreye Sunulan Bildiriler (Eleventh Turkish Historical Congress, Ankara 5–9 September 1990. Communications Presented to the Congress), Vol. 5, Ankara: Türk Tarih Kurumu Basımevi, 1994.
Orel, Şinasi and Süreyya Yuca, *The Talat Pasha Telegrammes: Historical Fact or Armenian Fiction?* Nicosia: Rustem, 1986.
Ortaylı, İlber, "Cumhuriyet Devri Tarihyazıcılığının Umumi Görünümü" (The General View of the Republican Period Historiography), in Zeynep Tarım Ertuğ, ed., *Prof. Dr. Mübahat Kütükoğlu'na Armağan* (Dedication to Prof. Dr. Mübahat Kütükoğlu), İstanbul: İstanbul Üniversitesi Edebiyat Fakültesi Yayınları, 2006.
———, *Defterimden Portreler Tarihten ve Günümüzden* (Portraits From My Notebook: From History and Our Day), İstanbul: Timaş Yayıncılık, 2011.
———, *Kırk Ambar Sohbetleri* (Forty Store Conversations), Ankara: Aşina Kitaplar, 2006.
———, *Osmanlı Barışı* (Pax Ottomana), İstanbul: Timaş Yayınları, 2007.
———, *Osmanlıyı Yeniden Keşfetmek* (Rediscovering the Ottoman), İstanbul: Timaş Yayınları, 2006.
———, "Rusya Arşivleri ve Osmanlı Tarihi" (Archives of Russia and Ottoman History), in *Tarih Boyunca Türk Tarihinin Kaynakları Semineri, 6–7 Haziran 1996 Bildiriler* (Seminar on Sources of Turkish History Throughout History, 6–7 June 1996 Communications), İstanbul: Edebiyat Fakültesi Basımevi, 1997.
———, *Son İmparatorluk Osmanlı* (The Last Empire Ottoman), İstanbul: Timaş Yayınları, 2006.
———, *Tarih Yazıcılık Üzerine* (On Historiography), Ankara: Cedit Neşriyat, 2009.
———, *Türkiye'nin Yakın Tarihi* (The Recent History of Turkey), İstanbul: Timaş Yayınları, 2010.
Osmanlı Arşivleri ve Osmanlı Araştırmaları Sempozyumu 17 Mayıs 1985 (Symposium on Ottoman Archives and Ottoman Studies 17 May 1985), İstanbul: Türk-Arap İlişkileri İncelemeleri Vakfı, 1985.
Öğün, Tuncay, *Kafkas Cephesinin Birinci Dünya Savaşındaki Lojistik Desteği* (Logistical Support of the Caucasian Front in the First World War), Ankara: Atatürk Araştırma Merkezi, 1999.
Ökte, Ertuğrul Zekai, *Osmanlı Arşivi, Yıldız Tasnifi, Ermeni Meselesi* (Ottoman Archives, Yıldız Collection, The Armenian Question), 3 Vols., İstanbul: Tarihi Araştırmalar ve Dokümantasyon Merkezleri Kurma ve Geliştirme Vakfı, 1989.
Öz, Tahsin, "Yıldız Maruzat Dairesi Arşivi" (Yıldız Petition Registers), in *IV. Türk Tarih Kongresi Ankara, 10–14 Kasım. Kongreye Sunulan Tebliğler.*
Özçelik, İsmail, *Tarih Araştırmalarında Yöntem ve Teknikler* (Method and Techniques in Historical Studies), Ankara: Gündüz Eğitim ve Yayıncılık, 2001.
Özdemir, Hikmet, *Ermeni İddiaları Karşısında Türkiye'nin Birikimi* (Accumulation of Turkey Regarding the Armenian Allegations), Ankara: Türkiye Büyük Millet Meclisi Kültür, Sanat ve Yayın Kurulu Yayınları, 2008.
———, Şaban Kardaş, trans., *The Ottoman Army 1914–1918: Disease and Death on the Battlefield*, Salt Lake City, UT: University of Utah Press, 2008.
———, *Turgut Özal: Biyografi* (Turgut Özal: Biography), İstanbul: Doğan Kitapçılık, 2014.
Özel, Oktay, "Bir Tarih Okuma ve Yazma Pratiği Olarak Türkiye'de Osmanlı Tarihçiliği" (Ottoman Historianship in Turkey as a Practice of Historical Reading and Writing) in Oktay Özel, ed., *Dün Sancısı Türkiye'de Geçmiş Algısı ve Akademik Tarihçilik* (Pain of Yesterday: Perception of the Past and the Academic Historianship in Turkey), İstanbul: Tarih Vakfı Yayınları, reprinted, 2012.
Özgen, Yüksel, "Belleten Dergisinin Türk Tarihçiliğindeki Yeri" (The Place of Belleten Journal in Turkish Historianship), in Öz, *Cumhuriyet Döneminde Türkiye'de Tarihçilik ve Tarih Yayıncılığı Sempozyumu Bildiriler Ankara, 18–20 Mart 2010.*
Özgökmen, Ali, Konya Şer'iyye Sicilleri Işığındaki Müslim-Gayrımüslim Münasebetleri (Muslim-Non-Muslim Relations in the Light of the Konya Muslim Court Records), Selçuk University, Doctoral Dissertation, 1996, Konya.
Özkul, İsa, "Osmanlı Arşivlerinin Osmanlı Coğrafyası ve Dünya Tarih Araştırmaları Bakımından Önemi" (Importance of the Ottoman Archives Regarding the Ottoman Geogra-

phy and World Historical Studies), in Aköz, Ürekli and Özcan, *Uluslararası Kuruluşunun 700. Yıl Dönümünde Bütün Yönleriyle Osmanlı Devleti Kongresi,*
Özsoy, Osman, *Özal'ın Misyonu* (The Mission of Özal), İstanbul: Türday Yayınları, 1998.
Öztuna, Yılmaz, "Türk Tarihçiliği ve İlber Ortaylı" (Turkish Historianship and İlber Ortaylı), in Ahmet Nezihi Turan, ed., *Gezgin ve Bilgin İlber Ortaylı'yı Tanımak* (To Know the Traveler and Scholar İlber Ortaylı), İstanbul: Paradigma Yayıncılık, 2009.
Özvar, Erol, ed., *Türk Tarihçiliğinde Dört Sima: Halil İnalcık, Halil Sahillioğlu, Mehmet Genç, İlber Ortaylı* (Four Faces in Turkish Historianship: Halil İnalcık, Halil Sahillioğlu, Mehmet Genç, İlber Ortaylı), İstanbul: Timaş Yayınları, 2013.
Peirce, Leslie, *Morality Tales: Law and Gender in the Ottoman Court of Aintab*, University of California Press, 2003.
Perinçek, Mehmet, *Ermeni Devlet Adamı B. A. Borian'ın Gözüyle Türk-Ermeni Çatışması* (Turkish-Armenian Conflict Through the Eye of the Armenian Statesman B. A. Borian), İstanbul: Kaynak Yayınları, 2006.
———, *Rus Devlet Arşivlerinden 100 Belgede Ermeni Meselesi* (Armenian Question in 100 Documents from the Russian State Archives), İstanbul: Doğan Kitapçılık, 2007.
———, *Rus Kafkas Ordusu Kurmay Başkanı Tuğgeneral L. M. Bolhovitinov 11 Aralık 1915 Tarihli Resmi Ermeni Raporu* (Chief of Staff of the Russian Caucasian Army Brigadier General L. M. Bolhovitinov: Official Armenian Report of 11 December 1915), İstanbul: Doğan Kitapçılık, 2009.
———, "Sovyet Arşivleri Türkiye'nin Tezlerini Doğruluyor" (The Soviet Archives Corroborate the Theses of Turkey), in Kantarcı, Kasım, Kaya and Laçiner, *Ermeni Araştırmaları I. Türkiye Kongresi Bildirileri.*
Popkin, Jeremy, *History, Historians and Autobiography*, Chicago and London: University of Chicago Press, 2005.
Power, Samantha, *"A Problem From Hell" America and the Age of Genocide*, New York: Harper Perennial, 2007.
Pryce-Jones, David, *The War That Never Was: The Fall of the Soviet Empire 1985–1991*, London: Phoenix Giant, 1996.
Quataert, Donald, "Ottoman History Writing at a Crossroads," in Donald Quataert and Sabri Sayarı, eds., *Turkish Studies in the United States*, Bloomington, IN: Indiana University Ottoman and Modern Turkish Studies Publications, 2003.
Reychman, Jan and Ananiasz Zajaczkowski, trans. Andrew Ehrenkreutz, *Handbook of Ottoman-Turkish Diplomatics*, Mouton: J. J. Augustin, rev. and expanded, 1968.
Reynolds, Michael, *Shattering Empires: The Clash and Collapse of the Ottoman and Russian Empires 1908–1918*, New York: Cambridge University Press, 2011.
Safi, Polat, The Ottoman Special Organization—*Teşkilat-ı Mahsusa*: An Inquiry Into Its Operational and Administrative Characteristics, Doctoral Dissertation, Bilkent University, 2012.
Sakwa, Richard, *Gorbachev and His Reforms*, Englewood Cliffs, NJ: Prentice Hall, Inc., 1991.
Satia, Priya, *Spies in Arabia: The Great War and the Cultural Foundations of Britain's Covert Empire in the Middle East*, New York: Oxford University Press, 2008.
Schellenberg, T.R. , *Modern Archives: Principles and Techniques*, Chicago: University of Chicago Press, reprinted, 1968.
Sertçelik, Seyit, *The Emergence of the Armenian Question 1678–1914*, Ankara: Council of Culture, Art and Publications of the Grand National Assembly of Turkey, 2010.
Shaw, Stanford, "Archival Sources on the Ottoman Empire I," in *International Symposium on Turkish Archives 17–19 November 2005 (Presentations and Discussions).*
———, "Cairo's Archives and the History of Ottoman Egypt," *Report on Current Research on the Middle East, 1956*, Washington, DC : The Middle East Institute, 1956.
———, *From Empire to Republic: The Turkish War of National Liberation, 1918–1923 A Documentary Study*, 5 Vols., Ankara: Türk Tarih Kurumu Basımevi, 2000–2001.
———, "Ottoman and Turkish Studies in the United States," in Kemal Karpat, ed., *The Ottoman State and Its Place in World History*, Leiden: E. J. Brill, 1974.
———, *The Ottoman Empire in World War I*, 2 Vols., Ankara: Türk Tarih Kurumu Basımevi, 2006–2008.
———, *Studies in Ottoman and Turkish History*, İstanbul: The Isis Press, 2000.

———, "Turkish Source Material for Egyptian History," in P.M. Holt, ed., *Political and Social Change in Modern Egypt*, London: Oxford University Press, 1968.

Shaw, Stanford and Ezel Kural Shaw, *History of the Ottoman Empire and Modern Turkey*, Vol. 2: *Reform, Revolution, and Republic: The Rise of Modern Turkey 1808–1975*, Cambridge: Cambridge University Press, 2nd ed., 1977.

Sheffy, Yigal, *British Military Intelligence in the Palestine Campaign 1914–1918*, London: Frank Cass, 1998.

Shields, Sarah, *Fezzes in the River: Identity Politics and European Diplomacy in the Middle East on the Eve of World War II*, New York: Oxford University Press, 2011.

Singer, Amy, *Palestinian Peasants and Ottoman Officials: Rural Administration Around Sixteenth-Century Jerusalem*, Cambridge and New York: Cambridge University Press, 1994.

Smith, Abby, "Russian History: Is It in the Archives?" in Blouin, Jr. and Rosenberg, *Archives, Documentation and Institutions of Social Memory*.

Sonyel, Salahi, *Displacement of the Armenians and Documents*, Ankara: Baylan Matbaası, 1978.

Spahr, Walter Earl and Rinehart John Swenson, *Methods and Status of Scientific Research With Particular Application to the Social Sciences*, New York and London: Harper and Brothers Publishers, 1930.

Suny, Ronald Grigor, "Writing Genocide: The Fate of the Ottoman Armenians," in Ronald Grigor Suny, Fatma Müge Göçek, and Norman Naimark, eds., *A Question of Genocide:* Armenians *and Turks at the End of the Ottoman Empire*, New York: Oxford University Press, 2011.

Suny, Ronald Grigor and Terry Martin, eds., *A State of Nations: Empire and Nation-making in the Age of Lenin and Stalin*, Oxford: Oxford University Press, 2001.

Tamdoğan-Abel, Işık, Les Modalités de l'Urbanité dans une Ville Ottomane: Les Habitants d'Adana au XVIIIème Siècle d'après les Registres des Cadıs, Ecole des Hautes Etudes en Sciences Sociales, Doctoral Dissertation, 1998, Paris.

Tams, Christian, Lars Berster and Björn Schiffbauer, *Convention on the Prevention and Punishment of the Crime of Genocide: A Commentary*, München: Verlag C. H. Beck oHG, 2014.

Tarım Ertuğ, Zeynep, "Prof. Dr. Mübahat Kütükoğlu Hayatı ve Eserleri" (Prof. Dr. Mübahat Kütükoğlu Her Life and Works), in Ertuğ, *Prof. Dr. Mübahat Kütükoğlu'na Armağan*.

Taş, Kenan Ziya, "Arşiv Malzemesi Olarak Şer'iyye Sicilleri ve Taşra Üniversitelerinde Tarih Araştırmaları" (Muslim Court Records as Archival Materials and Historical Studies in Provincial Universities), in Erişti, Yıldırım, Atik and Yay, *Birinci Milli Arşiv Şurası (Tebliğler-Tartışmalar) 20–21 Nisan 1998*.

Ternon, Yves, *Enquêtes sur la négation d'un génocide*, Paris: Parenthèses, 1989.

Tetik, Ahmet, *Teşkilat-ı Mahsusa (Umur-ı Şarkıyye Dairesi) Tarihi Cilt I: 1914–1916* (History of the Special Organization [Department of Eastern Affairs], İstanbul: Türkiye İş Bankası Kültür Yayınları, 2014.

Thomassian, Levon, *Summer '42 A Study of German-Armenian Relations During the Second World War*, Atglen, PA: Schiffer Publishing Ltd., 2012.

Travers, Tim, *Gallipoli 1915*, Stroud, Gloustershire: Tempus Publishing, 2001.

Tülüveli, Güçlü, "Mikrotarihçilik ve Kaynak Kullanımı Problemi: Kadı Sicilleri Örneği" (Microhistorianship and the Problem of Source Use: Example of Muslim Court Records), in Zeynel Abidin Kızılyaprak, ed., *Tarih Yazımında Yeni Yaklaşımlar: Küreselleşme ve Yerelleşme Üçüncü Uluslararası Tarih Kongresi* (New Approaches in Historiography: Globalization and Localization Third International History Congress), İstanbul: Türkiye Ekonomik ve Toplumsal Tarih Vakfı Yayınları, 2000.

Türk Tarih Kurumu Yayınları Kataloğu 2011 (Publications Catalog of the Turkish Historical Society 2011), Ankara: Türk Tarih Kurumu Basımevi, 2011.

Türkiye Cumhuriyeti Dışişleri Bakanlığı Arşivlerimiz Hakkında Bilgi Aralık 2011 (Republic of Turkey Ministry of Foreign Affairs Information on Our Archives December 2011), Ankara: Dışişleri Bakanlığı Matbaası, 2011.

Uysal, Nilgün, ed., *Zaman Kaybolmaz İlber Ortaylı Kitabı* (Time Is Not Lost: The İlber Ortaylı Book), İstanbul: Türkiye İş Bankası Kültür Yayınları, 2006.

Vass, Elöd, "The Ottoman Documents in the Archives of Hungary From the XVIth to the XVIIth Century," in Jean-Louis Bacqué-Grammont and Emeri van Donzel, eds., *Comité International D'Etudes Pré-Ottomanes et Ottomanes VIth Symposium Cambridge, 1rst–4th July 1984*, Istanbul, Paris and Leiden: The Divit Press, 1987.
Verdeja, Ernesto, "Genocide: Debating Definitions," in Adam Lupel and Ernesto Verdeja, eds., *Responding to Genocide: The Politics of International Action*, Boulder and London: Lynne Rienner Publishers, 2013.
Verrier, Anthony, ed., *Agents of Empire: Anglo-Zionist Intelligence Operations 1915–1919 Brigadier Walter Gribbon, Aaron Aaronsohn and the NILI Ring*, London: Brassey's Ltd, 1995.
Weems, Samuel, *Armenia Secrets of a "Christian" Terrorist State*, Dallas, TX: St. John Press, 2002.
Weinberg, Gerhard, *A World at Arms*, New York: Cambridge University Press, 2nd ed., 2005.
———, *Germany, Hitler, and World War II: Essays in Modern German and World History*, New York: Cambridge University Press, 1995.
Weitz, Eric, "Germany and the Ottoman Borderlands," in Omer Bartov and Eric Weitz, eds., *Shatterzone of Empires: Coexistence and Violence in the German, Habsburg, Russian, and Ottoman Borderlands*, Bloomington and Indianapolis, IN: Indiana University Press, 2013.
Westrate, Bruce, *The Arab Bureau: The British Policy in the Middle East, 1916–1920*, University Park, PA: Penn State University Press, 1992.
White, Stephen, *After Gorbachev*, New York: Cambridge University Press, 1993.
Yalçın, Semih, *Türkiye Cumhuriyeti Tarihinin Kaynakları* (Sources on the History of the Turkish Republic), Ankara: Berikan Yayınları, 2003.
Yamauchi, Masayuki, *Hoşnut Olmamış Adam Enver Paşa: Türkiye'den Türkistan'a* (Discontented Man Enver Pasha: From Turkey to Turkestan), İstanbul: Bağlam, 1995.
Yediyıldız, Bahaeddin, "Türkiye'de Osmanlı Araştırmaları II-Cumhuriyet Dönemi Türkiye'sinde Osmanlı Tarihi Araştırmaları" (Ottoman Studies in Turkey II-Studies on Ottoman History in the Republican Period Turkey) in *XIII. Türk Tarih Kongresi Ankara, 4–8 Ekim 1999 Kongreye Sunulan Bildiriler*.
Yıldız, Gültekin, "Bütüncül, Karşılaştırmalı ve Felsefi Bir Askeri Tarihe Doğru: Türkiye'de Askeri Tarih Araştırması ve Öğretiminin Geleceği Üzerine (Toward a Total, Comparative and Philosophical Military History: On the Future of the Research and Teaching of Military History in Turkey), in Şayin and Yıldız, *Osmanlı Askeri Tarihini Araştırmak*.
Yüceer, Nasır, "Genelkurmay Askeri Tarih ve Stratejik Etüt (ATASE) Başkanlığı Arşivi (Tasnif, Bakım-Onarım, Yararlanmaya Sunma, Kopyalama)" (Turkish General Staff Directorate of Military History and Strategic Studies Archive [Declassification, Maintenance-Reparation, Presenting for Utilization, Duplication]), in *Birinci Milli Arşiv Şurası (Tebliğler-Tartışmalar) 20–21 Nisan 1998*.
Zilfi, Madeline, *The Politics of Piety*, Minneapolis, MN: Bibliotheca Islamica, 1988.

Articles

Afyoncu, Erhan, "Türkiye'de Tahrir Defterlerine Dayalı Olarak Hazırlanmış Çalışmalar Hakkında Bazı Görüşler" (Some Reflections on the Studies Based Upon Tax Registers in Turkey), *Türkiye Araştırmaları Literatür Dergisi*, No.1 (2003).
Akçam, Taner, "Deportation and Massacres in the Cipher Telegrams of the Interior Ministry in the Prime Ministerial Archive (Başbakanlık Arşivi)," *Genocide Studies and Prevention*, Vol. 1, No. 3 (December 2006).
Akgündüz, Ahmed, "Shari'ah Courts and Shari'ah Records: The Application of Islamic Law in the Ottoman State," *Islamic Law and Society*, Vol. 16 (2009).
Aksakal, Mustafa, "Why Did the Ottomans Enter a European War in 1914? New Sources, New Views," *The Journal of Ottoman Studies*, No. 36 (2010).
Aldrich, Richard, "Policing the Past: Official History, Secrecy and British Intelligence since 1945," *English Historical Review*, Vol. CXIX, No. 483 (September 2004).
"An Interview with Halil İnalcık by the Editor," *The Turkish Studies Association Bulletin*, Vol. 17, No. 2 (Fall 1993).

Anderson, Margaret Lavinia, Michael Reynolds, Hans-Lukas Kieser, Peter Balakian, A. Dirk Moses and Taner Akçam, "Taner Akçam, The Young Turks' Crime Against Humanity: The Armenian Genocide and Ethnic Cleansing in the Ottoman Empire (Princeton, NJ: Princeton University Press, 2012)," *Journal of Genocide Research*, Vol. 15, No. 4 (December 2013).

Arıkan, Zeki, "Tahrir Defterlerinde Geçen Deyimler" (Expressions Used in the Tax Registers), *Osmanlı Araştırmaları*, No. 16 (1996).

Baer, Marc David, Ussama Makdisi, and Andrew Shryock, "Tolerance and Conversion in the Ottoman Empire: A Conversation," *Comparative Studies in Society and History*, Vol. 51, No .4 (October 2009).

Bahar, Hasan, "Osmanlı Tahrir Defterleri Çalışmalarındaki Gelişmeler Üzerine Gözlemler" (Observations on Developments Regarding the Studies About the Ottoman Tax Registers), *Osmanlı Araştırmaları*, No. 16 (1996).

Bayerle, G., "Ottoman Records in the Hungarian Archives," *Archivum Ottomanicum*, Vol. 4 (1972).

Beyhan, Mehmet Ali, "Zengin Bir Kültür Kaynağımız Olarak Osmanlı Arşivleri" (Ottoman Archives as One of Our Rich Cultural Sources), *Milli Kültür*, No. 68 (January 1990).

"1972 Yılı Çalışma Raporu" (Annual Report of the Board of Governors of the Turkish Historical Society for 1972), *Belleten*, Vol. 37, No. 147 (July 1973).

Bliwise, Robert, "The Strange Case of Yektan Turkyılmaz An International Incident," *Duke Magazine*, Vol. 91, No. 6 (November–December 2005).

"Bones to Pick," *The Economist*, Vol. 393, No. 8652 (10–16 October 2009).

Brummett, Palmira, "Mühimme 959: A Source for Ottoman Central Government Interaction with the Eastern Beys," *The Turkish Studies Association Bulletin*, Vol. 10, No. 1 (March 1986).

Coşgel, Metin, "Ottoman Tax Registers (Tahrir Defterleri)," *Historical Methods*, Vol. 37, No. 2 (Spring 2004).

Çetin, Atilla, "Arşiv Terimleri ve Deyimleri" (Archival Terms and Expressions), *Vakıflar Dergisi*, No. 12 (1978).

———, "Osmanlı Devleti Arşivinin Kuruluşu ve Tasnif Çalışmaları" (Founding of the Ottoman State Archive and Declassification Activities), *Türk Dünyası Araştırmaları Dergisi*, Vol. 14, No. 21 (December 1982).

———, "Türkiye'de Önemli Arşivler ve Özellikleri" (The Important Archives in Turkey and Their Features), *Türk Dünyası Araştırmaları Dergisi*, Vol. 1, No. 5 (April 1980).

———, "Yabancı Ülkelerde Bulunan Osmanlı Arşiv Malzemeleri, Yayınları ve Önemi" (Ottoman Archival Materials and Publications Abroad and Their Importance), *Türk Dünyası Araştırmaları Dergisi*, Vol. 2, No. 7 (August 1980).

Çiçek, Kemal, "Osmanlı Tahrir Defterlerinin Kullanımında Görülen Bazı Problemler ve Metod Arayışları" (Some Problems and Quests for Method Seen in the Use of Ottoman Tax Registers), *Türk Dünyası Araştırmaları Dergisi*, No. 97 (1995).

Çuluk, Sinan, "Heath Lowry İle Tarih Metodu, Arşiv Çalışmaları ve Türkiye Macerası Üzerine Mülakat" (Interview With Heath Lowry on the Historical Method, Archival Studies and His Experiences in Turkey), *Arşiv Dünyası*, No. 5 (January 2005).

———, "Prof. Dr. Suraiya Faroqhi İle Mülakat" (Interview With Prof. Dr. Suraiya Faroqhi), *Arşiv Dünyası*, No. 7 (January 2006).

———, "Yaşayan En Eski Arşivcimiz: Turgut Işıksal" (Our Oldest Living Archivist: Turgut Işıksal), *Arşiv Dünyası*, No. 11 (July 2008).

Dadrian, Vahakn, "The Documents of the World War I Armenian Massacres in the Proceedings of the Turkish Military Tribunal," *International Journal of Middle East Studies*, Vol. 23, No. 4 (November 1991).

Daniels, Robert, "The Soviet Union in Post-Soviet Perspective," *The Journal of Modern History*, Vol. 74, No. 2 (June 2002).

Davison, Roderic, "Review of Atilla Çetin's Başbakanlık Arşivi Kılavuzu," *The Turkish Studies Association Bulletin*, Vol. 4, No. 2 (September 1980).

Demirel, Fatmagül, "İngiliz Devlet Arşivinde Kısa Bir Gezinti" (A Short Walk in the British National Archives), *Arşiv Dünyası*, No. 8 (June 2006).

Duru, Yaşar, "Atilla Çetin'in Başbakanlık Arşivi Kılavuzu" (Atilla Çetin's Başbakanlık Arşivi Kılavuzu), *Türk Dünyası Araştırmaları Dergisi*, Vol. 1, No. 5 (April 1980).
Epstein, Mark, "Review of Atilla Çetin's Başbakanlık Arşivi Kılavuzu," *Middle East Studies Association Bulletin*, Vol. 14, No. 1 (July 1980).
Erickson, Edward, "The Turkish Official Military Histories of the First World War: A Bibliographic Essay," *Middle Eastern Studies*, Vol. 38, No. 3 (July 2003).
Faroqhi, Suraiya, "Taxation and Urban Activities in Sixteenth-Century Anatolia," *International Journal of Turkish Studies*, Vol. 1 (1979–1980).
Fisher, Alan, "Research Access in Turkey," *The Turkish Studies Association Bulletin*, Vol. 14, No.2 (September 1990).
Garthoff, Raymond, "Some Observations on Using the Soviet Archives," *Diplomatic History*, Vol. 21, No. 2 (Spring 1997).
Gauin, Maxime, "Aram Andonian's Memoirs of Naim Bey and the Contemporary Attempts to Defend Their 'Authencity'," *Review of Armenian Studies*, No. 23 (2011).
Gedikli, Fethi, "Osmanlı Hukuk Tarihi Kaynağı Olarak Şer'iyye Sicilleri" (Muslim Court Records as Source of Ottoman History of Law), *Türkiye Araştırmaları Literatür Dergisi*, Vol. 3, No. 5 (2005).
"German Guilt for Armenian Blood," *The Literary Digest*, Vol. 55, No. 17 (27 October 1917).
Grimsted, Patricia Kennedy, "Increasing Reference Access to Post-1991 Russian Archives," *Slavic Review*, Vol. 56, No. 4 (Winter 1997).
———, "Russian Archives in Transition: Caught Between Political Crossfire and Economic Crisis," *American Archivist*, Vol. 56 (Fall 1993).
Griswold, William, "The National Archives in Turkey," *The Muslim World*, Vol. 64, No. 1 (January 1974).
Gunter, Michael and Dirk Rochtus, "Special Report: The Turkish-Armenian Rapprochement," *Middle East Critique*, Vol. 19, No. 2 (Summer 2010).
Güçlü, Yücel, "Current Political Implications of the Armenian Question," *Journal of South Asian and Middle Eastern Studies*, Vol. 31, No. 4 (Summer 2008).
———, "Review of Michael Reynolds's *Shattering Empires: The Clash and Collapse of the Ottoman and Russian Empires 1908–1918*," *Middle East Quarterly*, Vol. 19, No. 3 (Summer 2012).
———, "Will Untapped Ottoman Archives Reshape the Armenian Debate?" *Middle East Quarterly*, Vol. 16, No. 2 (Spring 2009).
Güler, Ali, "Osmanlı Devletinde Gayrımüslimlerin Din-İbadet, Eğitim-Öğretim Hürriyetleri ve Bu Bakımdan Kilise Defterlerinin Kaynak Olarak Önemi" (The Religion-Worship, Education-Instruction Liberties of Non-Muslims in the Ottoman State and the Importance of Church Registers as Sources in This Regard), *Ankara Üniversitesi Osmanlı Tarihi Araştırma ve Uygulama Merkezi Dergisi*, No. 9 (1998).
Güzel, Hasan Celal, "Devlet Arşivlerinde Yeniden Yapılanmanın Yirminci Yılı 1987–2007" (The Twentieth Year of the Restructuring of the State Archives 1987–2007), *Arşiv Dünyası*, No. 9 (January 2007).
Hanioğlu, Şükrü, "Review of Sarah Shields's *Fezzes in the River: Identity Politics and European Diplomacy in the Middle East on the Eve of World War II*," *The American Historical Review*, Vol. 117, No. 5 (December 2012).
Harris, George, "Communications," *The Middle East Journal*, Vol. 51, No. 2 (Spring 1997).
Haslam, Jonathan, "Russian Archival Revelations and Our Understanding of Cold War," *Diplomatic History*, Vol. 21, No. 2 (Spring 1997).
Hourani, Albert, "How Should We Write the History of the Middle East?" *International Journal of Middle East Studies*, Vol. 23, No. 2 (May 1991).
———, "Review of Carter Findley's *Bureaucratic Reform in the Ottoman Empire*," *The Journal of Modern History*, Vol. 54, No. 1 (March 1982).
Hovannisian, Richard and Shaw, Stanford and Ezel Kural Shaw, "Forum: The Armenian Question: The Critic's View: Beyond Revisionism and the Author's Respond," *International Journal of Middle East Studies*, Vol. 9, No. 3 (August 1978).
Howard, Harry, "Preliminary Materials for a Survey of the Libraries and Archives of Istanbul," *Journal of the American Oriental Society*, Vol. 59, No. 2 (June 1939).

Işıksal, Turgut, "Arşivlerimizin Durumu ve Problemleri" (The Condition of Our Archives and Their Problems), *Türk Kültürü*, Vol. 10, No. 119 (September 1972).
İğdemir, Uluğ, "Belleten Yirmibeş Yaşında" (Belleten at Its Twenty-fifth Year), *Belleten*, Vol. 25, No.100 (January 1961).
İnalcık, Halil, "Osmanlı Tarihi Hakkında Mühim Bir Kaynak" (An Important Source on Ottoman History), *Ankara Üniversitesi Dil, Tarih-Coğrafya Fakültesi Dergisi*, Vol. 1, No. 2 (1942).
Jennings, Jr., Ronald Carlton, "Women in Early 17th Century Ottoman Judicial Records: The Shari'a Court of Anatolian Kaiseri," *Journal of the Economic and Social History of the Orient*, Vol. 18 (1975).
Kaiser, Hilmar, "Regional Resistance to Central Government Policies: Ahmed Djemal Pasha, the Governors of Aleppo, and Armenian Deportees in the Spring and Summer of 1915," *Journal of Genocide Research*, Vol. 12, No. 3–4 (September–December 2010).
Karpat, Kemal, "An Update on Turkish Archives," *Middle East Studies Association Bulletin*, Vol. 23, No. 2 (December 1989).
Kavas, Ahmet, "Fransız Arşivleri" (French Archives), *Arşiv Dünyası*, No. 4 (August–September 2004).
Kéchichian, Joseph, "The Turkish-Armenian Protocols: Perceptions in the Diaspora," *Journal of the Society for Armenian Studies*, Vol. 19, No. 1 (June 2010).
Küçük, Mustafa, "Türkiye'yi Geçmişten Geleceğe Taşıyan Güç: Başbakanlık Osmanlı Arşivi" (The Force That Carries Turkey from the Past to the Future: The Prime Minister's Office Ottoman Archive), *Arşiv Dünyası*, No. 4 (August–September 2004).
Lemercier-Quelquejay, Chantal, "Les Bibliothèques et les archives de Turquie en tant que sources de documents sur l'histoire de Russie," *Cahiers du Monde russe et soviétique*, Vol. 5, No. 1 (janvier–mars 1964).
———, "Une source inédite pour l'histoire de la Russie au XVIe siècle: Les registres des "Mühimme Defterleri" des Archives du Baş-vekâlet," *Cahiers du Monde russe et soviétique*, Vol. 8, No. 2 (avril-juin 1967).
Lemkin, Raphael, "Genocide as a Crime under International Law," *The American Journal of International Law*, Vol. 41, No. 1(January 1947).
Lewis, Bernard, "Other People's History," *The American Scholar*, Summer 1990.
———, "Ottoman Archives: A Source for European History," *Archives*, Vol. 4, No. 24 (Michaelmas 1960).
———, "The Ottoman Archives as a Source for the History of the Arab Lands," *Journal of the Royal Asiatic Society*, Nos. 3–4 (October 1951).
———, "Studies in the Ottoman Archives—I," *Bulletin of the School of Oriental and African Studies*, Vol. 16 (1954).
Lobba, Paolo, "A European Halt to Laws Against Genocide Denial?" *European Criminal Law Review*, Vol. 4, No. 1 (2014).
Lowry, Heath, "The Reorganization of the Ottoman Archives," *The Turkish Studies Association Bulletin*, Vol. 13, No. 2 (Fall 1989).
Masters, Bruce, "The Sultan's Entrepreneurs: The *Avrupa Tüccarıs* and the *Hayriye Tüccarıs* in Syria," *International Journal of Middle East Studies*, Vol. 24, No.4.
Matossian, Bedross Der, "The Genocide Archives of the Armenian Patriarchate of Jerusalem," *The Armenian Review*, Vol. 52, No. 3–4 (Fall–Winter 2011).
Meyer, James, "For the Russianist in Istanbul and the Ottomanist in Russia: A Guide to the Archives of Eurasia," *Ab Imperio*, Vol. 4 (2008).
Moumdjian, Garabet, "Tracing Ottoman Documents: A Letter Delivered 95 Years Late," *Journal of the Society for Armenian Studies*, Vol. 18, No. 2 (December 2009).
Mouradian, Khatchig, "Pamboukian Talks about ARF Archives," *The Armenian Weekly*, 29 April 2009.
Ortaylı, İlber, "Başbakanlık Arşivinin 1995 Yılı Yayınları Üzerine: Verimli Bir Yılın Değerlendirilmesi" (On the Publications of the Prime Minister's Office Archive in 1995: Assessment of a Productive Year), *Türkiye Günlüğü*, No.38.

———, "Osmanlı Kadısı (Tarihi Temeli ve Yargı Görevi) (Ottoman Kadi [Its Historical Basis and Judicial Duty]), *Ankara Üniversitesi Siyasal Bilgiler Fakültesi Dergisi*, Vol. 30, No.1–4 (1977).
Özel, Oktay, "Arşiv Meselemiz" (Our Archive Question), *Toplumsal Tarih*, No. 217 (January 2012).
———, "Ermeni Meselesi Tarihçisini Arıyor" (The Armenian Question Is Looking For Its Historian), *Kebikeç*, No.19 (2005).
Özel, Oktay and Gökhan Çetinsaya, "Türkiye'de Osmanlı Tarihçiliğinin Son Çeyrek Yüzyılı: Bir Bilanço Denemesi" (The Last Quarter Century of Ottoman Historianship in Turkey: A Trial Balance Sheet), *Toplum ve Bilim*, No. 91 (2001–2002).
Peirce, Leslie, "The Milli Kütüphane in Ankara," *The Turkish Studies Association Bulletin*, Vol. 18, No. 2 (Fall 1994).
"PM Erdoğan Attends Turkish Diaspora Meeting in Baku," *Briefing*, 12 March 2007.
Pollock, Sean, "Historians and Their Sources: Discourses of Empire and Islam in Eurasian Archives," *Ab Imperio*, Vol. 4 (2008).
Popplewell, Richard, "British Intelligence in Mesopotamia 1914–1916," *Intelligence and National Security*, Vol. 5, No. 2 (April 1990).
Quataert, Donald, "The Massacres of Ottoman Armenians and the Writing of Ottoman History," *The Journal of Interdisciplinary History*, Vol. 37, No. 2 (Autumn 2006).
———, "Recent Writings in Late Ottoman History," *International Journal of Middle East Studies*, Vol. 35, No. 1 (February 2003).
"Russian History; The Battle for the Moscow Archives; With the End of Communism in Russia, Long-secret State Archives Were Thrown Open. Or Were They?" *The Economist*, Vol. 338, No. 7955 (2 March 1996).
Safi, Polat, "History in the Trench: The Ottoman Special Organization—*Teşkilat-ı Mahsusa* Literature," *Middle Eastern Studies*, Vol. 48, No. 1 (January 2012).
Salati, Marco, "The Prayer and the Bread: A Document on the Mevlevi Order from the Qadi Court Registers of Aleppo (1154–1741)," *Eurasian Studies*, Vol. 10 (2012).
Salt, Jeremy, "The Armenian 'Relocation': The Case for 'Military Necessity'," *Review of Armenian Studies*, No. 29 (2014).
———, "The Narrative Gap in Ottoman Armenian History," *Middle Eastern Studies*, Vol. 39, No. 1 (January 2003).
Sarınay, Yusuf, "Arap Ülkelerinin Tarihi Kaynakları Bakımından Türk Arşivlerinin Önemi" (The Importance of the Turkish Archives As Regards the Historical Sources of the Arab Countries), *Belleten*, Vol. 74, No. 4 (December 2010).
———, "The Relocation (Tehcir) of Armenians and the Trials of 1915–1916," *Middle East Critique*, Vol. 20, No. 3 (Fall 2011).
———, "Türk Arşivleri ve Ermeni Meselesi" (Turkish Archives and the Armenian Question), *Belleten*, Vol. 70, No. 257 (April 2006).
Schabas, William, "Genocide and the International Court of Justice: Finally, a Duty to Prevent the Crime of Crimes," *Genocide Studies and Prevention*, Vol. 2, No. 2 (August 2007).
Seibert, William, Wanda Williams, and Nancy Schuster, "1 Archives Drive Personnel Records Are Consolidated at New Location in St. Louis," *Prologue*, Vol. 43, No. 3 (Fall 2011).
Seligmann, Mathew, " 'A Barometer for National Confidence': A British Assessment of the Role of Insecurity in the Formulation of German Military Policy before the First World War," *English Historical Review*, Vol. CXVII, No. 471 (April 2002).
Seng, Yvonne, "The Şer'iyye Sicilleri of the Istanbul Müftülüğü as a Source for the Study of Everyday Life," *The Turkish Studies Association Bulletin*, Vol. 15, No. 2 (September 1991).
Shaw, Stanford, "Archival Sources for Ottoman History: The Archives of Turkey," *Journal of the American Oriental Society*, Vol. 80, No. 1 (January–March 1960).
———, "The Archives of Turkey: An Evaluation," *Wiener Zeitschrift für die Kunde des Morgenlandes*, No. 69 (1977).
———, "New Research Opportunities in the Ottoman Archives of Istanbul," *Belleten*, Vol. 58, No. 222 (August 1994).
———, "To the Editor," Communications, *The American Historical Review*, Vol. 90, No. 4 (October 1985).

———, "The Yıldız Palace Archives of Abdülhamid II," *Archivum Ottomanicum*, Vol. 3 (1971).

Sheffy, Yigal, "British Intelligence and the Middle East, 1900–1918: How Much Do We Know?" *Intelligence and National Security*, Vol. 17, No. 2 (Spring 2002).

———, "Chemical Warfare and the Palestine Campaign, 1916–1918," *The Journal of Military History*, Vol. 73, No. 3 (July 2009).

Shirinian, Razmig, "Reflections on the Turkish-Armenian Protocols," *Journal of the Society for Armenian Studies*, Vol. 19, No. 1 (June 2010).

Shougarian, Rouben, "Armenian-Turkish Diplomacy: Track I Failures and Track II Prospects," *The Armenian Review*, Vol. 54, No. 1–2 (Spring–Summer 2013).

Singer, Amy, "Tapu Tahrir Defterleri ve Kadı Sicilleri: A Happy Marriage of Sources," *Tarih*, Vol. 1 (1990).

Sonyel, Salahi, " Armenian 'Massacres'; The 'Great Lie' Re-Visited; A Good Yarn That the British Weaved," *Impact International*, Vol. 20:10 (25 May–7 June 1990).

Steiner, Zara, "The Soviet Commissariat of Foreign Affairs and the Czechoslovakian Crisis in 1938: New Materials from the Soviet Archives," *The Historical Journal*, Vol. 42, No. 3 (September 1999).

Şakiroğlu, Mahmut, "Başbakanlık Arşivi Kılavuzu" (Guide to the Prime Minister's Office Archive), *Belleten*, Vol. 46, No. 181 (January 1982).

———, "La bibliothèque nationale d'Ankara," *Turcica*, Vol. 20 (1998).

Şaşmaz, Eftal, "Rusya Devlet Askeri Arşivi" (Russian State Military Archive), *Kebikeç*, No.17 (2004).

———, "Rusya Federasyonu Arşivi" (State Archive of the Russian Federation), *Kebikeç*, No.16 (2003).

Toprak, Zafer, "Stanford Shaw İle Mülakat" (Interview With Stanford Shaw), *Tarih ve Toplum*, Vol. 13, No. 76 (April 1990).

Travers, Tim, "Liman von Sanders, the Capture of Lieutenant Palmer, and Ottoman Anticipation of the Allied Landings at Gallipoli on 25 April 1915," *The Journal of Military History*, Vol. 65, No. 4 (October 2001).

"Turkey and Armenia: When History Hurts," *The Economist*, Vol. 376, No.8438.

Türkay, Cevdet, "Osmanlı İmparatorluğunda Arşiv" (Archive in the Ottoman Empire), *Belgelerle Türk Tarih Dergisi*, Vol. 2, No. 7 (1968).

Uğur, Yunus, "Mahkeme Kayıtları (Şer'iyye Sicilleri): Literatür Değerlendirmesi ve Bibliyografya" (Muslim Court Records: Assessment of Literature and Bibliography), *Türkiye Araştırmaları Literatür Dergisi*, Vol. 1, No. 1 (2003).

Uzunçarşılı, İsmail Hakkı, "Şer'i Mahkeme Sicilleri" (Muslim Court Records), *Ülkü Halkevleri Mecmuası*, Vol. 5, No. 29 (1935).

Ünal, Mehmet Ali, "Tahrir Defterlerindeki Bilgilerin Güvenilirliği" (Reliability of the Data in the Tax Registers), *Süleyman Demirel Üniversitesi Sosyal Bilimler Dergisi*, No. 1 (1995).

Walton, Calder, Reviews of Christopher Murphy's *Security and Special Operations: SOE and MI5 during the Second World War* and R. A. Ratcliff's *Delusions of Intelligence: Enigma, Ultra, and the End of Secure Ciphers*, *English Historical Review*, Vol. CXXIV, No. 506 (February 2009).

Weinberg, Gerhard, "The End of Ranke's History? Reflections on the Fate of History in the Twentieth Century," *Syracuse Scholar*, Vol. 9, No. 1 (1988).

Westad, Odd Arne, "The Foreign Policy Archives of Russia: New Regulations on Declassification and Access," *Society for the History of American Foreign Policy Newsletter*, Vol. 23 (June 1992).

———, "Secrets of the Second World War: The Russian Archives and the Reinterpretation of Cold War History," *Diplomatic History*, Vol. 21, No. 2 (Spring 1997).

Yazıcı, Nesimi, "Başbakanlık Osmanlı Arşivi Rehberi" (Guide to the Prime Minister's Office Ottoman Archive), *Belleten*, Vol. 57, No. 220 (December 1993).

Yazıcıoğlu, Ayşe, "Cemal Kafadar İle Mülakat" (Interview With Cemal Kafadar), *Toplumsal Tarih*, No. 219 (March 2012).

Ze'evi, Dror, "The Use of Ottoman Shar'ia Court as a Source for Middle Eastern Social History: A Reappraisal," *Islamic Law and Society*, Vol. 5, No. 1 (1998).

Zens, Robert, "Turkish Historiography in the United States," *Türkiye Araştırmaları Literatür Dergisi*, Vol. 8, No. 15 (2010).

Index

About the Author

Yücel Güçlü is a historian. His previous publications include *The Question of the Sanjak of Alexandretta: A Study in Turkish-French-Syrian Relations*, Ankara: Turkish Historical Society, 2001; *Eminence Grise of the Turkish Foreign Service: Numan Menemencioğlu*, Ankara: Ministry of Foreign Affairs of Turkey, 2002; *The Life and Career of a Turkish Diplomat: Cevat Açıkalın*, Ankara: Ministry of Foreign Affairs of Turkey, 2002; *The Turcomans and Kirkuk*, Philadelphia, PA: Xlibris Corporation, 2007; *Armenians and the Allies in Cilicia 1914-1923*, Salt Lake City, UT: University of Utah Press, 2010; *The Holocaust and the Armenian Case in Comparative Perspective*, Lanham, MD: University Press of America, 2012; *Zeki Kuneralp and the Turkish Foreign Service*, New Castle upon Tyne: Cambridge Publishers, 2015, and numerous articles on Turkish diplomatic history which appeared in the United States, Canada, Britain, Italy, and Turkey. He is the winner of the Afet İnan Historical Studies Prize in 1996. He is currently engaged in research on the Armenian events of Adana in 1909 and Cemal Paşa.